Acts

Published by
Spiritbuilding Publishing
15591 N. State Rd. 9
Summitville, IN 46070

Printed in the United States of America

ACTS

By Chad Sychtysz

ISBN 978-0-9990684-0-3

Spiritual "equipment" for the contest of life

Spiritbuilding
Publishing

Dedication

This work is fondly dedicated to Larissa (my "favorite daughter") and Logan (my "favorite son"), cherished souls with whom my life has been greatly blessed and for whom my prayers are unceasingly offered.

Table of Contents

Acknowledgements

Given a work of this nature, I cannot help but feel humbly indebted to the many biblical scholars and commentators who have paved the way for me—men for whom I have deep respect, and to whom I do not deserve to be compared. Even what I might consider to be "my own words" are really the distilled thoughts of the many thousands of pages of learned writings that I have internalized in my more than 30-year journey as a Christian.

Carl "Mac" McMurray, the personification of Spiritbuilding Publishing, has done more for my writing career (if it can be called that) than any other single person. He has, once again, extended himself for my sake, and has believed in me more than most. I deeply appreciate the great investment he has made on my behalf.

Several key people have helped to polish and refine what began as a "rough" manuscript. Jamey Hinds (whom I fondly refer to as "the layout guy") has, once again, given my work a clean and professional look. Curtis and Patsy Cantwell volunteered many hours to the painstaking job of editing. This includes everything from correcting grammar to double-checking biblical citations. My longtime friend and literary antagonist, Paul Mitchell, provided critical analysis of much of the manuscript (as well as plenty of good-hearted banter); his contributions to this work have been very valuable. Many thanks, too, go out to my congregation (my "Kent family") for providing feedback and encouragement on earlier versions of this work. And I gladly acknowledge my wife, Honey, for her unending support and patience.

Most of all, I thank God—literally and often—for blessing me with such a great privilege as what I have been given to prepare this material. My prayer is that it will make some contribution, however small, to the great heritage that we call Christ's church.

Introduction

The Book of Acts is easily one of the most significant works of Scripture. Besides serving as a natural bridge between the gospels and epistles, Acts provides a conclusion to Christ's earthly ministry as well as the implementation of His teachings for the newly-formed church that bears His name. The advent of the so-called Church Age also ushered in the close of the Jewish Age, bringing to an end 1,500 years of law, festal rites, priesthood, and sacrifice.

Acts is also a significant work of secular history. Luke is most certainly its author/narrator, and he was a historical writer of the highest caliber. "Ramsay dares to call Luke, all things considered, the greatest of all historians, even above Thucydides."[1] Luke pays great attention to political, historical, and geographical details. He lists over one hundred personal names, many of which are described as belonging to a particular city, province, or region. He also lists over one hundred place names. "And last, with many nautical, climatic, and geographical terms Luke has given a reliable account of Paul's voyage to Rome (27—28)."[2] Sir William Ramsay says:

> ... The historical work of the highest order [is one] in which a writer commands excellent means of knowledge either through personal acquaintance or through access to original authorities, and brings to the treatment of his subject genius, literary skill, and sympathetic historical insight into human character and the movement of events. Such an author seizes the critical events, concentrates the reader's attention on them by giving them fuller treatment, touches more lightly and briefly on the less important events, omits entirely a mass of unimportant details, and makes his work an artistic and idealised picture of the progressive tendency of the period.[3]

---

1 A. T. Robertson, *Word Pictures in the New Testament* (Grand Rapids: Baker Book House, no date), xii.

2 Simon J. Kistemaker, *Acts* (Grand Rapids: Baker Book House, 1990), 7.

3 William Ramsay, *St. Paul the Traveller and the Roman Citizen* (Grand Rapids: Baker Book House, 1965), 2-3.

Acts serves as the literary and historical hub for most of the New Testament (NT). Most of the NT epistles were written during the period covered by Acts; some of the writers themselves, such as Paul and James, are here first introduced. Many of the recipients of the NT letters are also introduced: Timothy; Titus; Christians from Galatia, Corinth, and Rome; the Thessalonians; and the churches of Asia (particularly Ephesus, where Paul spent nearly three years). Without such critical information, we would be wondering what link these people and places had to the proclamation of the gospel, and (thus) why it would be relevant to study them.

To appreciate what we have in the Book of Acts, try to imagine our knowledge and comprehension of the NT *without* it. For example, we would not know:

❑ What happened to Jesus' disciples after receiving the "great commission."
❑ How the remaining apostles dealt with Judas' suicide.
❑ What the promise of the power of the Holy Spirit was.
❑ How the gospel was originally preached (or received).
❑ The conversion process (or method) by which a person is made a Christian.
❑ Who Paul was, or why he was authorized to write epistles to the churches.
❑ Why Paul was arrested and imprisoned (as mentioned in his epistles).
❑ Any firsthand information about the condition of the early church.
❑ How the church handled internal problems.
❑ How the church handled external persecution.
❑ God's response to Judaism, in light of the gospel of Christ.
❑ How the Old Testament scriptures were used in preaching the gospel.
❑ How and why Gentiles were permitted in the church.
❑ How the early church supported itself financially.
❑ How the gospel spread beyond Judea and into Asia Minor, then into Europe.
❑ What effect Christianity had on the heathen world.

❑ The (early) Roman disposition toward Christianity.
❑ The Jewish position against Christianity.
❑ The faith, determination, and devotion of the many men and
    women who serve as examples and martyrs for all successive
    generations of believers.

Theological and Historical Perspectives

God's schedule always works according to two major criteria: the
sequence of certain events and the fulfillment of certain *conditions*.
"Sequence" refers to the serial or chronological order of things (as
in, "But first He must suffer many things and be rejected by this
generation"—Luke 17:25). "Conditions" refers to God letting a
situation run its course or reach a known objective (as when Christ was
manifested to the world "at the proper time"—Titus 1:3). In Acts, both
of these criteria are addressed, though the scope of God's work exceeds
what was actually recorded.

Christ had promised to build His church upon the fact that He was
both the Christ (i.e., Messiah) *and* the Son of God (Matthew 16:16-18,
John 20:31). These truths were irrefutably proved through Christ's own
resurrection from the dead, which served as the crowning achievement
of Christ's earthly ministry *and* the foundation for the entire gospel
(Acts 17:30-31, 1 Corinthians 15:3-4). Since His resurrection did occur
exactly as He promised, then all else that He declared is also true. By
the same power and authority with which He raised Himself from the
dead, so He flawlessly fulfilled the entire Law and Prophets, as He
promised (Matthew 5:17, Luke 24:44). Everything carried out by Christ
was "given at the proper time" (1 Timothy 2:5-6; see also Romans 5:6),
and in "the fullness of the time" (Galatians 4:4). Thus, the sequence of
events that led to the establishment of the church *and* the conditions
that had to be met for that establishment were fulfilled in Christ and by
Christ's authority (as delegated to His apostles).

The spiritual church of God rests upon Christ's position and authority
as the King over all of creation (1 Corinthians 15:27-28, Ephesians
1:22-23). It could not be established unless or until Christ ascended

to the throne of God for this very purpose. His death, burial, and resurrection were necessary for His ascension to the right hand of God as both King of kings *and* eternal High Priest of those redeemed by His blood (Acts 2:33, Hebrews 8:1-2). The "kingdom of God"—Christ's rule over God's kingdom for the purpose of salvation to men—was established as soon as He received that kingdom from His Father. (This is predicted in Daniel 7:9-10, 13, and shown to be fulfilled in Revelation 5:1-9.) R. C. H. Lenski provides an excellent overview of God's kingdom:

> It is the kingdom of the heavens because heavenly powers make it and also give it heavenly character; the kingdom of God (Christ) because he is over and in it everywhere, at once its source and its control. This rule or kingdom goes back to the beginning and extends to eternity. When we look at the power and the omnipotence, it rules the whole universe; when we look at grace, it embraces the whole church; when we contemplate the glory, we see heaven and all its inhabitants. The kingdom and rule of grace fills the whole Testament from Adam onward; it is the rule of grace through the Messianic promise. A new era began when the promise was fulfilled in Christ, the era of the New Testament which extends to the end of time.[4]

While His kingship was secured even before His literal ascension (Matthew 28:18), nonetheless Christ had to ascend into heaven *first* and take His rightful place upon His Father's throne before His church could be established. With His authority legitimately and permanently secured, Christ could then do what He had promised: add souls to His church and simultaneously send the Holy Spirit to those who had been so added.[5] Acts provides the realization and historical record of these promises. The invitation is offered to the Jews first, then the Gentiles (cf. Romans 1:16). Jim McGuiggan rightly observes: "Since the book

---

4   R. C. H. Lenski, *Acts of the Apostles* (Peabody, MA: Hendrickson Publishers, 1998), 25.

5   Jesus *personally* promised the Holy Spirit to His disciples (John 14:16-19, 15:26-27, and 16:12-15), but *practically* to all who become Christians (Acts 5:32). He (the Spirit) is the church's "Comforter" or "Helper," and carries out the work of Christ on earth in ways both known and unknown to us.

of Acts proclaims the existence of the kingdom the Gospels looked forward to, we should expect Acts to show the kingdom to be peculiarly related to the Jews. And that's what we find. The proof is plentiful."[6]

The *timing* of Christ's presentation of His gospel to the world is remarkable and ingenious, as we should expect from an intelligent and all-powerful God. The world into which the gospel was first taught and distributed was much more advanced and commercialized than we might first imagine. Although relatively primitive and crude by today's standards, the civilization of the first century (AD) was modernized and mobilized like the ancient world had never seen before—and like the world would never see again for over a thousand years. Nonetheless, this world was still predicated upon the ancient foundations of the Greek Empire, which the Romans adopted and then improved upon as they saw fit. While the Greeks were very self-centered and ethnocentric in their thinking and politics, the Romans were much more practical and adaptable. They took remnants from numerous vanquished people and assimilated them into their own, so as to create a great melting pot of ideas and cultures—and religions—that assumedly would serve the best interest of the Empire as a whole. (Ironically, this assimilation actually led to its downfall, as predicted in the prophecy of Nebuchadnezzar's dream; see Daniel 2:40-43.)

Consider the Roman infrastructure that provided the successful transmission of the gospel to a diverse and expansive Empire without any modern communications:

❑ The *Pax Romana* ("Roman Peace"), made possible through Octavian (Augustus) Caesar's capable administration (31 BC—AD 14), provided for the greatest economic and political stability in the history of the Empire. "Under this ruler one of the world's most efficient organizations was perfected with a resulting era of peace, security and progress that has seldom been equaled. Unconsciously

---

6   Jim McGuiggan, *The Reign of God* (Fort Worth, TX: Star Bible Publications, 1992), 69.

Rome was preparing the way for the gospel of Christ. It would be difficult to overestimate this contribution."[7]

❑ *Koine* ("common") Greek was nearly universal throughout the Empire, allowing people to communicate through this language even though they often maintained their native tongue. *Koine* Greek is very precise and descriptive; appropriately, it is the language of the original text of the entire NT. We can only imagine how difficult it would have been (as modern missionaries can attest) to spread the gospel awkwardly and inefficiently through an interpreter rather than to speak directly to the people in a universal language.

❑ The Roman road system was the best, most extensive, and widely-used travel system the world had ever seen. (Some of these roads were so well-laid that they are still in use today.) This provided for expanded trade, mobility, and access; the Roman military kept the more popular thoroughfares (*vias*) free from robbers and bandits that often interfered with travel (see 2 Corinthians 11:26); inns and horse exchanges were available along some routes. Arches (which the Romans perfected with the keystone) were used for bridges, spanning rivers and ravines in ways that the ancients had never before enjoyed. (Some of these spans have also survived to this day.)

❑ The Roman army is what literally subjugated the Mediterranean world. Garrisons were everywhere; Roman soldiers kept the peace in every province and demanded the respect of the Roman government. It is remarkable how many references are made to soldiers, centurions, the Roman army, and the Roman government (that controlled this army) throughout the New Testament and especially Acts. It is the Roman army that literally saved Paul on several occasions from the hands of both Jewish and Gentile opponents. Also, seafaring was safer than ever from piracy, since the Roman navy regularly patrolled the Mediterranean Sea to keep trade routes open.

❑ Rome enjoyed a single economy and a universal coinage system, which meant that people could do business with other countries within the Empire without monetary loss through currency exchange or unbalanced trade practices. (Jews in Jerusalem,

7   H. I. Hester, *The Heart of the New Testament* (Liberty, MO: The Quality Press, Inc., 1963), 44.

however, demanded that all Temple donations be converted to *their* coinage—for a transaction fee—which is one reason why moneychangers were present at the Temple during feast days; see John 2:12-16.)

❑ Jews had been dispersed throughout the Empire through previous centuries of deportation, exile, commercial ventures, and other reasons. This seeding of God's people among Gentile nations provided an excellent opportunity for the pagan world to hear the gospel from those many Jews who heard it, understood it (in light of the Law and the prophets of old), and obeyed it. These would become the "first fruits" (cf. James 1:18) of the church harvest, so to speak, from which an untold number of Gentile believers would follow.

Thus, the gospel was introduced into a world that had unknowingly been prepared (by God) for centuries to receive it. Not only was the *world* (logistically and politically) ready to receive it, but *individual people* were ready as well. We see this in the great responses that Peter and Paul received when they preached the gospel to both Jewish and Gentile audiences. Such reception was proportionately greater than perhaps at any other time in all of human history. We cannot be deterred by the great *rejection* they also received; this is typical of man's response to God's kindness.

The gospel of Christ was not limited to any one group or status of people. Men and women of all strata of society heard and obeyed it, from Jewish priests to Gentile soldiers to Hellenist widows. In fact, the early church was comprised of a large percentage of slaves, just as slaves also comprised a healthy percentage of the Empire's entire social structure. "Slaves" covers a broad sweep of social positions, from those assigned to hard labor to those who served as professionals (household managers, copyists, secretaries, paralegals, doctors, etc.). Estimates of the number of slaves in the Roman Empire range from about 20 to 50 percent of the entire population.

Slavery was an entrenched institution which few questioned and apparently none was willing to challenge. The extent of it was amazing. To occupy a place of respectability a family must have a minimum of ten slaves. Prominent families considered two hundred slaves an adequate supply, though some lords owned thousands of them. Slave markets were common sights on the streets of Rome.

The lot of slaves in the empire was extremely hard. In legal language they were called, not *personae* (human beings), but *res* (things). They were bought and sold for profit. They were mated like cattle and their offspring were sold as "the increase of the herd." Treatment of them usually was extremely cruel. Runaway slaves were branded with the letter F (fugitive) on the forehead.[8]

Not all slaves were treated badly or inhumanely. In any case, such people were literally owned by a master, regardless of how much "freedom" they may have enjoyed in whatever occupation they held. For this reason, the spiritual freedom that was offered through the gospel of Christ had a particular attraction for slaves. Slavery was often a hopeless and dead-end life; the gospel provided a purpose *to* life, and the realistic hope of a happy afterlife. We cannot underestimate the effect that this new message of light, purpose, and hope would have provided for those who were trapped in a social system from which they might never escape.

Theme and Purpose

Every NT book or epistle was written for one or more specific purposes. Acts does not necessarily have one singular purpose (to the exclusion of all others) but has a manifold purpose that directly supports Christ and His gospel. The scholar F. F. Bruce writes:

When we examine the way in which Luke develops his narrative, we can hardly fail to be struck by his apologetic emphasis, especially in the second volume [chapters 13—28].

---

8   Hester, *The Heart of the New Testament*, 47-48.

He is concerned to defend Christianity against the charges which were popularly brought against it in the second half of the first century. We must recognize that in the eyes of those who set some store by law and order in the Roman Empire Christianity started off with a serious handicap. Its Founder had admittedly been condemned to death by a Roman governor on a charge of sedition. And the movement which He inaugurated seemed to be attended by tumult and disorder wherever it spread, both in the Roman provinces and in Rome itself. Luke sets himself to reduce this handicap, or rather to remove it altogether.[9]

This is an excellent synopsis of the situation, yet does not provide specific details of its apologetic tone. (Formally, an "apology" is an argued defense of something; in this context, it has nothing to do with saying "I'm sorry" for anything.) However, it is conspicuous that, on every turn, Luke provides historical proof that the authorities who called for Christ's crucifixion were themselves corrupt and disobedient to the very Law they claimed to cherish. Likewise, Roman authorities appear at first to be uninterested in Christianity (see 18:14-17), completely ignorant of it, or unconvinced by it—largely because of their own political agendas. In other words, point by point Luke unfolds the truth about "what happened" surrounding the crucifixion of Jesus. Not only does he show Jesus to be innocent of any crime, but the apostles themselves are undeserving of legal prosecution. Furthermore, he demonstrates (through the preaching, miracles, and virtuous conduct of its genuine representatives) that the church truly "is of God," as Gamaliel had ominously proposed was possible (Acts 5:38-39).

Besides providing a defense for the gospel of Christ as a legitimate (versus illegal) religion in the Roman world, another major theme of Acts is the salvation offered through that gospel. This salvation is wholly dependent upon Jesus' divine nature, the historical reality of His ministry (from His baptism by John the Baptist to His death, burial, resurrection, and ascension into heaven), and the credibility of

---

9   F. F. Bruce, *The Book of the Acts* (Grand Rapids: Eerdmans Publishing Co., 1964), 20; bracketed words are mine.

eyewitnesses to these things (1:8). Thus, the authenticity of the gospel message depends upon the biblical facts (of prophecy) and the historical events necessary to substantiate it. "Luke was 'both a reliable historian and a good theologian. ... We believe that the validity of his theology stands or falls with the reliability of the history on which it is based."[10] For this reason, Luke pays considerable attention to those speeches (sermons) and accounts which underscore the reality and universality of salvation through Christ. Samples of this include:

- ❏ "And it shall be that everyone who calls upon the name of the LORD will be saved" (2:21). "And there is salvation in no one else; for there is no other name under heaven that has been given among men by which we must be saved" (4:12).
- ❏ "Therefore let it be known to you, brethren, that through Him forgiveness of sins is proclaimed to you, and through Him [Christ] everyone who believes is freed from all things, from which you could not be freed through the Law of Moses" (13:38-39).
- ❏ "...I [Christ] am sending you [Paul] to open their eyes so that they may turn from darkness to light and from the dominion of Satan to God, that they may receive forgiveness of sins and an inheritance among those who have been sanctified by faith in Me" (26:17b-18).

Critical to this gospel and its proclamation of salvation is the resurrection of Jesus Christ. The power that Christ possesses to save souls is dependent upon the historical reality of His bodily resurrection, which itself is dependent (as a proclaimed message) upon the evidence and eyewitnesses supporting this event. If Jesus was not raised from the dead, then His authority to establish His church is nothing but a grandiose idea. As Paul said, "But if there is no resurrection of the dead, not even Christ has been raised; and if Christ has not been raised, then our preaching is vain, your faith also is vain. Moreover we are even found to be false witnesses of God, because we testified against God that He raised Christ, whom He did not raise, if in fact the dead

---

10   Howard Marshall, quoted in John Stott, *The Spirit, the Church, and the World* (Downers Grove, IL: InterVarsity Press, 1990), 30.

are not raised" (1 Corinthians 15:13-15). It is no surprise, then, that Luke makes certain—by inspiration of the Holy Spirit[11]—to include the testimony of Jesus' resurrection throughout Acts, such as in the following passages:

- ❑ "But God raised Him up again, putting an end to the agony of death, since it was impossible for Him to be held in its power" (2:24).
- ❑ "… [David] looked ahead and spoke of the resurrection of the Christ, that He was neither abandoned to Hades, nor did His flesh suffer decay" (2:31).
- ❑ "This Jesus God raised up again, to which we are all witnesses" (2:32).
- ❑ "For you [Jews] first, God raised up His Servant and sent Him to bless you by turning every one of you from your wicked ways" (3:26).
- ❑ "And with great power the apostles were giving testimony to the resurrection of the Lord Jesus, and abundant grace was upon them all" (4:33).
- ❑ "The God of our fathers raised up Jesus, whom you had put to death by hanging Him on a cross" (5:30).
- ❑ "God raised Him up on the third day and granted that He become visible…" (10:40).
- ❑ "But God raised Him from the dead …" (13:30).
- ❑ "… He [God] has fixed a day in which He will judge the world in righteousness through a Man whom He has appointed, having furnished proof to all men by raising Him from the dead" (17:31).

---

11   It goes beyond this commentary to address properly the subject of divine "inspiration." Traditionally, and as influenced by English translations of 2 Timothy 3:16, "inspiration" [from *theopneustos*, lit., "God-breathed"] is thought to mean that God gave His endorsement or approval to men's writings, thus making it "Scripture." Biblically, however (as evidenced in John 1:14, "And the Word became flesh"), Scripture is not merely endorsed by God but comes *from* Him. Scripture *is* Scripture because God Himself is the Source of its content and message. If God needed someone to write down the history of the early church as *He* desired for it to be recorded, then He (in essence) *breathed* into the heart of a man like Luke to do this. Thus, men wrote down what God put into their heart to say, and yet He allowed them to maintain their own style, personality, and (as it suited God's purpose) word choices in their writings.

❏ "… [T]hat the Christ was to suffer, and that by reason of His resurrection from the dead He would be the first to proclaim light both to the Jewish people and to the Gentiles" (26:23).

The resurrection of Christ is the greatest miracle of His ministry. It manifests a mastery of power and authority over the physical realm as well as the spiritual realm. It is the core of Paul's preaching— among the things of "first importance" in the preaching of the gospel (1 Corinthians 15:1-4).

Besides providing a testimony of Christ's resurrection, there are a number of other reasons for which Acts was written:

❏ As Luke's well-researched compilation of Jesus' ministry for "most excellent" Theophilus (Luke 1:1-4, Acts 1:1).
❏ To provide a brief historical overview of the church to all generations to follow. Since the logical faith of Christianity is based upon knowledge and evidence, there must be an authentic and credible source *of* this. Luke—by inspiration and the providence of the Holy Spirit—sought to provide this source.[12] This does not mean that Luke set out to write a book of history, *per se*; it means that Acts is undoubtedly historical in nature, and that Luke was fully aware of this.
❏ To provide a brief account of Peter's inclusion of both Jews and Gentiles into Christ's church—to fulfill his role regarding the "keys of the kingdom of heaven" (cf. Matthew 16:13-19) *and* support the legitimacy of universal salvation.

---

12   There is *no good reason* to question the historical reality of Luke's writing. While some scholars think that Luke sought to preserve a theological perspective *regardless* of historical facts, this remains the opinions (or "tends") of such scholars and serves an agenda that either questions or rejects altogether the factual basis of Acts (Dennis Gaertner, *The College Press NIV Commentary: Acts* [Joplin, MO: College Press Publishing Co., 1993], 23-24). If Luke's history is beside the point, as some assume, then what does this say about the *real* and *factual* circumstances that the apostles and early church faced? And what does this say about the present-day church: are we to operate in a purely theological mindset, regardless of and without being affected by our own historical reality? This study rejects such views, simply because they: do not make sense; stand in opposition to the actual record; are without critical basis; do not contribute to one's understanding of Acts, but instead rob it of its contextual and practical value.

❑ To provide a bold apologetic for the church, and thus to establish legal and biblical justification for its existence (to counter Jews' claims of heresy or apostasy). "Christianity and not Judaism is the true fulfillment of the revelation given through Moses and the prophets"[13]; see Acts 24:14-15.

❑ To provide a legal defense for Paul; to show that he did not violate the Law of Moses or the laws of Rome; and to prove that Christianity cannot be considered an illegal or illegitimate religion (to be discussed in more detail later).

❑ To show the illegitimate response of Jews who opposed the gospel—i.e., to expose their methods and reasoning as similar to that which Christ Himself confronted and condemned. In Acts, the Jews are condemned (by Peter) for their part in the murder of Messiah; later they are condemned (by Paul) for being stumbling blocks to themselves and the Gentiles (compare, for example, Matthew 23:13 and Acts 13:44-52). It was the Jewish authorities, and not the Christians themselves, that created the confusion, disturbances, and riots in cities in which the gospel was preached.

❑ To demonstrate, both directly and indirectly, the gospel's superiority over paganism, superstition, sorcery, and demonism (through the ministry of Paul and others).

❑ To record the success of the church despite all odds against it. (Acts records the church's success against Jewish persecution; Revelation [prophetically] records the church's success against secular persecution.)

❑ To answer definitively, "What must I do to be saved?" (cf. Acts 16:30-33).

❑ To prove that the so-called "great commission" was indeed fulfilled (compare Matthew 28:19 and Colossians 1:23).

❑ To prove that this commission was impossible without divine intervention. Likewise, all present-day evangelism does not rest upon mere human effort but necessarily requires divine intervention—not in the form of visible miracles, but through providence and the unseen ministry of the Holy Spirit.

---

13   Ibid., 24.

Despite Acts' classification of as a book *of* history, its main focus is not *on* history. It is not merely "the acts of the apostles," since all twelve apostles are only mentioned once (1:13), and only the highlights of a few of them are recorded. In fact, several people included in the account are not even of the twelve apostles (Barnabas, Stephen, Philip, Silas, Apollos, etc.).[14] If anything, it would be better referred to as "the acts of Peter and Paul." Acts is not merely a chronicle of the beginning of the church either, since much is omitted and there are years of faithful brethren's work about which the narrative is silent. Those details and events that *are* recorded, however, necessarily drive the main purpose for the book. In some respect, "Acts is a book of conversions," since "practically the whole of it revolves around a series of conversions and attempted conversions."[15] Even so, there is a great deal of material in Acts that has nothing directly to do with specific conversions. Some Bible students believe that Acts was written as a kind of legal deposition to exonerate Paul from any actual criminal guilt with the Roman Empire. While this theme does have considerable merit, one would be hard-pressed to prove that Luke wrote the entire narrative with this in mind. "The problem with this suggestion is that Luke includes so much material [in Luke *and* Acts] that has nothing to do with Paul's defense.

---

14 "'Apostle' has two uses in the New Testament. The first is a generic one which refers to one (who is) sent' to fulfill a certain work or mission. The word (*apostolos*) implies both conveyance (of something) and representation (of someone). Thus, an apostle is generally one who conveys a message provided by the one whom he also represents. We can see this generic usage in such passages as Luke 11:49, John 13:16 ("one...sent"), Acts 14:14, 2 Corinthians 8:23 ("messengers"), and Philippians 2:25 ("messenger"). The other sense in the New Testament is that of an office, for which one is 'called' and 'set apart' (Romans 1:1). This does not describe only what certain men did (in conveying and representing), but also the authority which such men possessed. These men collectively are known as 'the' apostles, designating a specific group of hand-picked ambassadors (Matthew 10:2-4). When Judas abandoned this calling, he was replaced by another whom the Lord Himself also selected (Acts 1:23-26). ...The original twelve apostles were personally selected by Christ out of all the many disciples who followed Him (Luke 6:13-16). After this, only Matthias and Paul were added to this unique and distinguished group. Matthias was added to complete the 'twelve' just prior to their unveiling of the gospel of Christ to the Jews. Paul was added as an ideal ambassador to the Gentiles (Acts 9:15-16, Romans 15:15-16). These men all had the same *authority*, even though one could well argue that both Peter and Paul had certain *responsibilities* that differed from the others. Nonetheless, 'the signs of a true apostle' must be confirmed 'by signs and wonders and miracles' (2 Corinthians 12:12)" (Chad Sychtysz, *The Holy Spirit of God* [Summitville, IN: Spiritbuilding Publishing, 2010], 132-133).

15   James Coffman, *Commentary on Acts* (Austin, TX: Firm Foundation, 1976), 3.

Why would he include the birth, ministry, death, and resurrection of the Lord? Why would he focus on the Apostle Peter in the early chapters of Acts? Acts would be very tedious reading if the main purpose were a defense of Paul."[16]

Acts can be divided into four sections, each roughly equal in length:

- ❑ 1:1—7:60, the church in Jerusalem.
- ❑ 8:1—14:28, the response to the gospel in Samaria, among "God-fearing" men, and Gentiles; the church in Antioch becomes a base for missionary journeys.
- ❑ 15:1—21:17, the Jerusalem council places Jews and Gentiles on equal footing within the church; Paul's journeys into the Gentile world bring this egalitarian message to both groups.
- ❑ 21:18—28:31, Paul's arrest and imprisonment, and the legal battles and delays involved in these.

Practically-speaking, Acts really revolves around two characters—not so much Peter and Paul, but far more so Christ and the Holy Spirit. Christ is the central theme and purpose for the book; without Him, there would be no apostles, no church, and nothing to write about. The Holy Spirit provides the authority, navigation, and inspiration for the apostles and early Christians to fulfill their moral responsibilities to Christ as His servants. Without the Spirit's work, the church would be a lifeless, directionless, and uninspired group of people trying desperately to find their *own* "Way." Without Christ *and* the Spirit, there would be no atoning sacrifice, no sanctification of the human soul, no "gifts" of God, no miracles, no salvation, and no hope. It seems most appropriate, then, to recognize the preeminence of Christ and the critical role of the Holy Spirit in everything related to the establishment, development, and success of Christ's church.

---

16 Gaertner, 21; bracketed words are mine. For what it is worth, I agree with this observation: there is simply too much in Acts (especially) that is irrelevant to substantiate *merely* a legal defense for Paul. It is worth noting, too, that there is other material that may be *missing* as well if one were to pursue that conclusion, especially more background information about Paul, his connections with the party of the Pharisees (and possibly the Hellenistic Freedmen?), and other details that would bolster this position.

Christ is the Founder of His church, as He Himself declared (Matthew 16:18). Having been given "all authority" in heaven and on earth (Matthew 28:18), Christ was made the head and preeminent figure of this holy sanctuary of all believers (Ephesians 1:19-23, Colossians 1:15-20). It is Christ who chose His own apostles, provided them with His gospel, empowered them to produce miracles sufficient to confirm this gospel, sent them on their missions, and delivered them from their predicaments (as suited His purpose).

> Once He took His rightful place in the heavens, Jesus sent the Holy Spirit into His church, to give life to it. Just as our own body is dead without our spirit to give it life (James 2:26), so Christ's "body" (church) must be filled with the Spirit of God. Otherwise, the church would have existed, but only as a lifeless construction. God "breathed into [Adam's] nostrils the breath of life; and man became a living being" (Genesis 2:7); likewise, Christ breathed the Holy Spirit into His church, and it became a living, God-breathing organism. When we are baptized into Christ's body (church), we are not brought into a lifeless, empty chamber, like a church building or a mere holding pen. Rather, we are made a part of an *animate body* that pulses with the blood of Christ and breathes with the Spirit of God. Each soul that is brought into this body is made a functional member of it (Romans 12:4-5); together with Christ and the Spirit, this living body serves as a living temple of God (Ephesians 2:19-22; 1 Peter 2:4-5).[17]

Even so, Acts chronicles the efforts of specific *people* as they strive to implement Christ's commission and follow the Holy Spirit's bidding. Unquestionably, then, Peter and Paul dominate the immediate attention of the reader of Acts, even though they are both merely servants of a purpose far greater than the span of their individual ministries. Furthermore, the student of Acts cannot help but notice the parallels between the ministries of Peter (chapters 1—12) and Paul (chapters 13—28):

---

17   Sychtysz, *The Holy Spirit of God*, 106.

Peter's Ministry	Paul's Ministry
Healing of a lame man (in Jerusalem; 3:1-8)	Healing of a lame man (in Lystra; 14:8-10)
People healed through Peter's shadow (5:15)	People healed by Paul's clothing articles (19:11-12)
Peter confronts a (former) sorcerer (8:18-21)	Paul confronts a sorcerer (13:8-10)
Tabitha is raised from the dead (9:36-40)	Eutychus is raised from the dead (20:9-12)
Cornelius tried to worship Peter (10:25)	Pagans tried to worship Paul (14:11-13)
In Peter's vision of the sheet being lowered, the instruction to "arise, kill, and eat" is given three times (10:9-16)	Paul's vision of his meeting with Christ is recorded three times (9:3-6, 22:6-10, and 26:12-15)
Peter faced the Sanhedrin, but was spared by a Pharisee (Gamaliel) (5:34)	Paul faced the Sanhedrin, but was spared by the Pharisees (23:6-7)
Peter was beaten (5:40)	Paul was beaten (16:22-23, et al)
Peter was arrested and imprisoned (12:3-4)	Paul was imprisoned (16:24, 24:27)
Peter was miraculously released from prison (5:19)	Paul was miraculously released from prison (16:26)

"The early church noted this parallel, and carried it on. They said that both died in Rome on the same day. [But] just because a certain parallel outline seems to be followed as the lives of Peter and Paul are presented is not reason to doubt the truthfulness of Luke. ... It cannot be said that such a practice of comparison falsified the story for either character being compared. Neither can it be said that the Acts record is falsified."[18]

While the principal characters in Acts are indeed Christ and the Holy Spirit, we see both Personages working through the apostles, and then

18   Gareth L. Reese, *A Critical and Exegetical Commentary on the Book of Acts* (Joplin, MO: College Press, 1976), xxxii.

through other dedicated men and women as well. All of this is intended
to bring about the Father's will, that all men would hear the message of
His salvation (Isaiah 49:6). Stott sums it up well: "Nevertheless, if the
title 'the Acts of the Apostles' over-emphasizes the human element, 'the
Acts of the Holy Spirit' over-emphasizes the divine, since it overlooks
the apostles as the chief characters through whom the Spirit worked. ...
The most accurate (though cumbersome) title, then, which does justice
to Luke's own statement in verses 1 and 2 [of chapter one] would be
something like 'The Continuing Words and Deeds of Jesus by his Spirit
through his Apostles.'"[19]

Author and Dates

The authorship of Acts is almost unanimously attributed to Luke,
the "beloved physician" (Colossians 4:14).[20] Luke no doubt had
unparalleled access to numerous primary sources and witnesses,
including the apostles themselves, and to certain legal records. His
historical and geographical accuracy have been vindicated time and
again through comparisons to the political and social conventions of
his day and through modern archaeology. His travels with Paul (the
conspicuous "we" sections of Acts 16, 20, 21, 27, and 28) gave him
first-person perspectives of exactly what it meant to be a missionary
preacher in the first century. Later Christian apologists (Irenaeus,
Clement of Alexandria, Tertullian, and Eusebius, all of whom were
of the first few centuries AD) confirm that Luke is most certainly the
author of Acts.[21] It is clear, too, that whoever wrote the Gospel of Luke

---

19   Stott, *The Spirit, the Church, and the World*, 33-34; bracketed words are mine.

20   "He was Paul's medical adviser, and doubtless prolonged his life and rescued him
from many a serious illness" (A. T. Robertson, "Luke, the Evangelist," *International
Standard Bible Encyclopedia* [electronic edition], database © 2004, WORDsearch
Corp.). While this may be true in a general sense, it does not contradict whatever
divine protection and healing God provided to Paul, as what is implied in Acts 14:19-
20. William Ramsey has suggested that Luke and Titus are actually blood brothers,
and that the "we" section (beginning in Acts 20:5) actually includes both men. Other
commentators have found this to be a reasonable explanation as well (see footnote on
20:4).

21   H. Leo Boles, *A Commentary on Acts of the Apostles* (Nashville: Gospel Advocate
Co., 1976), 11-12; Kistemaker, 20-21; and especially Reese, *Commentary on the Book
of Acts*, xxiv – xxv.

also wrote Acts, since the prologue in both works (Luke 1:1-4 and Acts 1:1-2) and the overlapping of events (Luke 24:50-53 and Acts 1:9-11) indicates that these are two volumes of one great compilation.

Luke was a Gentile, and thus he saw the world (and the gospel) in a perspective different than that of the original Jewish believers. His handling of difficult subjects—namely, the Jewish reaction to the gospel, and then the Jewish Christians' reaction to the inclusion of the Gentiles into the church—is balanced and objective, proving him to be a competent and well-trained rhetorician.[22] He not only recorded the substance of what was said (in speeches, sermons, and conversations) but he also maintained the linguistic nuances of those who did the speaking. Luke's own writing style, use of the Greek language, and particular attention to detail are nothing short of exceptional, as also demonstrated in his gospel account.[23] His accounts are not only

---

22   Rhetoric is the art of speech designed to influence people to a particular manner of thinking, change in beliefs, or change in policy. A well-spoken rhetorician "is a person of power, and the ancient world gave recognition to both the great general and the great rhetor. ... Rhetoric was, to the ancients, *power*, whether for good or ill. In the Graeco-Roman world, *speaking* was central to success. ... A failure to appreciate the ancient 'power' or 'art' of rhetoric and the centrality of oratory in the culture in which early Christianity grew up would be disastrous for the student of the New Testament" (Conrad Gempf, "Public Speaking and Published Accounts," *The Book of Acts in Its First Century Setting*, vol. 1 [Grand Rapids: Eerdman's Publishing Co., 1993], 260, 262).

23   "Acts was known to the early church in two Greek texts, the 'Alexandrian,' especially in the great fourth- and fifth-century codices (Sinaiticus, Vaticanus and Alexandrinus) and the 'Western,' especially in the fifth- or sixth-century Codex Bezae (which is kept in the Cambridge University Library), although its existence has been traced back at least to the second century. The latter differs from the former as being in size longer (about 1,500 more words), in style smoother, and in content more colorful" (Stott, *The Spirit, the Church, and the World*, 36, fn. 49). *ISBE* clarifies: "[The Codex Bezae] is the early known manuscript which Theodore Beza obtained in 1562 from the monastery of Irenaeus at Lyons and which he gave in 1581 to the University of Cambridge, where it now is. It is a Greek-Latin text, the Greek holding the chief place on the left-hand page, measuring 8 x 10 in., and dates probably from the end of the 5th century. Both Greek and Latin are written in large uncials and divided into short clauses, corresponding line for line. The hands of no less than nine correctors have been traced, and the critical questions arising from the character of the readings are among the most interesting in the whole range of Biblical criticism and are still unsettled. It contains only the Gospels and Acts with a fragment of 3 John" (Charles F. Sitterly, "Texts and Manuscripts of the New Testament," *ISBE* [electronic edition]; bracketed words are mine). Given the questionable authenticity of the Codex Bezae (Western text), this study will use specific information from that text only as a commentary to the

remarkable but are also invaluable social, political, and historical portals into the life and times of the first century AD. "It is ... well worth our while to notice, as a mere matter of Christian evidence, how accurately St. Luke writes concerning the political characteristics of the cities and provinces which he mentions. He takes notice in the most artless and incidental manner of minute details which a fraudulent composer would judiciously avoid, and which in the mythical result of mere oral tradition would surely be loose and inexact."[24]

It is widely believed that Acts was written in Rome in the early AD 60s, during Paul's Roman imprisonment but before the Jewish Revolts (66-70). The best date seems to be circa 62, which precedes the burning of Rome (64) for which Paul and other Christian leaders were blamed, arrested, and (for Paul, tradition tells us) executed. The conspicuous absence of the burning of Rome and siege of Jerusalem, both of which would have directly impacted Paul's ministry, necessarily imply a date of writing prior to these major events. Nonetheless, some assume otherwise: "Many scholars fix the date [of writing] between AD 70—80. The reasons often given for this date have to do with the subject matter of Luke's Gospel, especially Luke 21:5-38. In these verses Jesus speaks of the destruction of Jerusalem. His description is so vivid that many scholars believe Luke must have recorded it after the event had occurred in AD 70."[25] This is not sound scholarship, however, as it assumes more than it proves. It also calls into question the authenticity of Luke's gospel, since he attributes these words to Jesus—they are not his own summary of "what happened." And *this* calls into question Jesus' ability to prophecy future events with great accuracy (as in Matthew 16:21), as we would expect of a Divine Being. With such logic, too, we might as well regard *all* detailed prophecies (especially those in the Old Testament) as after-the-fact accounts rather than what they *are*—prophecies of the future. (It is this same liberal revisionist attitude that refuses to accept Daniel as the author of the book by his name, for example, because his historical prophecies are "too

---

more credible Alexandrian text, and not as a primary source.

24   W. J. Conybeare and J. S. Howson, *The Life and Epistles of St. Paul* (Grand Rapids: Eerdmans Publishing Co., 1964), 259.

25   Gaertner, *Acts*, 15; bracketed words are mine.

accurate.") If we apply this to Isaiah's account of Jesus' death (in Isaiah 53), for example, we may as well conclude that Isaiah (or God Himself) could *not* have given such accurate details of events 700 years in the future, so then the book of Isaiah must have been *after* Jesus' death and not *before* it! This study summarily rejects all such theories that refuse to accept the genuineness of divine prophecy and divine inspiration of the NT writers.

Also conspicuous is the absence of the outcome and details of Paul's release from Roman prison. Acts ends with: "And he [Paul] stayed two full years in his own rented quarters and was welcoming all who came to him, preaching the kingdom of God and teaching concerning the Lord Jesus Christ with all openness, unhindered" (28:30-31). Church history is fairly consistent concerning the end of Paul's life: he was released from this imprisonment, continued in further missionary journeys, was re-arrested and brought to trial before Emperor Nero (allegedly for being responsible for the fires that burned part of the city of Rome, even though Nero himself was suspected of this), and executed in (or soon after) AD 64. Another proposal by some scholars is that Luke merely *avoided* Paul's martyrdom "in order to preserve his focus on the victorious progress of the church."[26] This would allow for a date of writing between AD 70 – 80. Given such logic, we wonder what is to be done with Revelation, for example, in which *many* Christians face martyrdom, and the church appears at one point to be defeated (Revelation 11:3-13)? This seems far more damaging to the physical church than does the martyrdom of one apostle. (And what do we do with James, another apostle whose martyrdom is actually *recorded* in Acts [12:1-2]?)

Such theories are purely speculative in nature, and (again) create more questions than they answer. Practically-speaking, it is far more natural to maintain that Luke did not record Paul's release from prison, later re-imprisonment, or execution because these things had not yet happened. (It is for this same reason that the Hebrews writer does not mention the destruction of Jerusalem, but speaks of things that are "still standing" [9:8]: he definitely writes prior to the *fall* of such "things"

---

26 Gaertner, *Acts*, 16.

[the temple], thus prior to AD 70.) Given this, the following is offered as a reasonable timeline for the period of Acts (AD 30-62):

Date	Events
AD 30	Christ is crucified (in the spring); the church begins 50 days later on Pentecost.
34-35	Saul (Paul) is converted. He spends some time in Damascus, escapes to Jerusalem, spends three years in Arabia, returns to Damascus, then is sent to Tarsus (in Cilicia) and remains there for several years (Acts 9:20-30, Galatians 1:17—2:1, 2 Corinthians 11:32-33).
40-42	Barnabas finds Saul in Tarsus and brings him to Antioch (Acts 11:22-26); while in this city, Saul is called into the ministry of an apostle (13:1-3).
45-48	First missionary journey, led by Saul (Paul) and Barnabas (Acts 13—14).
51	Council in Jerusalem (Acts 15).
51-54	Second missionary journey, led by Paul and Silas (Acts 15—18).
54-58	Third missionary journey, led by Paul himself (Acts 18—20).
58	Paul is arrested in Jerusalem (Acts 21).
58-60	Paul spends two years in the custody of Roman governors, Felix and Festus (Acts 22—26).
60-62	Having appealed to Caesar, Paul is sent to Rome, where he spends two years in fairly comfortable custody (Acts 27—28) awaiting his trial before Caesar Nero.

It is believed that Paul was released from Roman imprisonment in 62 or 63, having been exonerated of any crime. He then continued in his apostolic ministry, possibly visiting Spain as he had hoped (Romans 15:22-29). After (and as a scapegoat for) the burning of Rome in 64, Paul was re-arrested by Roman authorities, tried, and executed. (See notes at the end of this study for more detail.)

The Jewish Situation

Something needs to be said about the Jewish world in which the gospel was first preached. The Jews despised Roman rule, but could not do much of anything to remove it, once it was established. (Ironically, it was the Jews' invitation for the Roman general Pompey into their country [in 63 BC] to settle a rivalry between two high-priestly families that led to Roman occupation in the first place.) Nonetheless, they resisted, as best as they could, assimilation into the Greco-Roman culture. The Jews actually enjoyed unprecedented and unparalleled favored status from the Romans; to Rome, Judea was a "special case," an emotionally-charged powder keg that had to be treated carefully and diplomatically. Thus, Judea was given self-governing status (autonomy); Jewish men were not conscripted into the Roman army; Jews were exempt from certain Roman taxes; etc. In return, Jewish aristocrats—and especially the Sadducees (see below)—supported Rome politically, even though many of them still despised the "uncircumcised heathen" presence in their country. Unfortunately, Rome did not always provide Judea with competent leadership that understood the volatile Jewish situation. This indiscretion heavily contributed to the Jewish Revolts in AD 66-70, and ultimately fueled the siege against and destruction of Jerusalem in AD 70.

The Jewish political-religious establishment was divided into four main parties, all of which represented a very small percentage of the people but (collectively) exercised substantial religious, political, social, and economic influence over Judea.

❑ **Sadducees:** These were often the wealthiest of the Jews, and the most politically-active. They controlled the Jewish court (a.k.a. the Council or Sanhedrin) through the office of the high priest. They did not believe in the afterlife, angels, spirits, or resurrection (see Matthew 22:23-33, Acts 23:6-8); notably, they denounced any teaching on Jesus' resurrection (Acts 4:1-2), and may have believed that the soul dies with the body.[27] Jesus' popularity threatened

---

27 See Josephus (*Josephus: Complete Works*, trans. Wm. Whiston [Grand Rapids: Kregel Publications, 1978]), "Antiquities," 18.1.4; "Wars of the Jews," 2.8.14. But

their own local authority; more specifically, He threatened Judea's relationship with Rome (so they presumed; see John 11:47-50). These men had little tolerance for the apostles.

❑ **Pharisees:** These men were the closest to "the multitudes," the general God-fearing populace; however, they always kept a conspicuous distance between themselves and "the people."[28] Often wealthy and heavily involved with the temple, Pharisees adhered strictly to the entire Law *and* Prophets, whereas Sadducees only observed the Law (i.e., the Pentateuch or Torah). They regarded their long-held rabbinical "traditions" which had been handed down for generations as sacred; these traditions were often viewed on par with the Law of Moses as binding requirements (Matthew 15:1-9). Pharisees typically viewed Jesus as a defiant blasphemer of the Law. F. F. Bruce adds:

> In the first century A.D. they were about five or six thousand strong, organized in "brotherhoods" (*haburoth*). They had great religious influence with the people, the more so as most of the scribes, the public expositors of the law, belonged to their party. Their two chief schools in NT times were those of Hillel and Shammai, two leading rabbis who flourished in the later part of Herod [the Great]'s reign. After the

---

Alfred Edersheim disagrees: "[Josephus's conclusions] may be dismissed as among those inference which theological controversialists are too fond of imputing to their opponents. ...We may therefore credit Josephus with merely reporting the common inference of his party. But it is otherwise in regard to their denial of the resurrection of the dead" (*The Life and Times of Jesus the Messiah* [Peabody, MA: Hendrickson Publishers, 1993], 219; bracketed words are mine). In other words, we know for certain that they did not believe in a bodily resurrection from the dead; what they thought of the final disposition of the soul is difficult to determine conclusively.

28   The Pharisees prided themselves on their learning and rabbinic education, as taught in the Jewish academies. "The result of attendance at one of these schools for a prolonged period of time was absorption of an incredible amount of memorized data, critical acumen, and a faculty for biblical argumentation. With these proficiencies, however, there often came an attitude of condescension and patronizing hate for the common man. 'This people who knoweth not the law are cursed' (John 7:49) is indicative." Furthermore, these men believed that those not schooled in their academies "had no right to do Biblical exegesis and so could not possibly be good or pious. Their inquiry, 'By what power, or in what name, have ye done this?' is tantamount to asking, 'What academy did you attend and who was the headmaster?'" (Daniel H. King, *At the Feet of the Master: Studies in the Background, Content and Methods of Jesus' Teaching* [Bowling Green, KY: Guardian of Truth Foundation, 1997], 55).

fall of Jerusalem and the temple in A.D. 70 it was the Pharisaic party, and more particularly the school of Hillel, that proved best able to survive the collapse of the old temple-constitution and preserve the continuity of national life.[29]

❑ **Zealots:** This radical group of nationalists loathed Roman domination of Judea with a vehement passion, and conducted terrorist attacks against Roman sympathizers. Eventually they incited the great Jewish Revolt (AD 66-70) that spelled irrevocable doom for Jerusalem and whatever remained of the nation of Israel. Their absolutist position—either full independence of Judea or full-scale military revolt, even to the point of self-martyrdom—made the relationship between Rome and Judea (and Jews in general) difficult, tense, and irreconcilable.[30]

❑ **Essenes:** Though not directly mentioned in Scripture, these people nonetheless had a powerful religious impact upon Jewish society. Monastic, ascetic, separatist, and radical in their beliefs, the Essenes accused the religious sects of Jerusalem of being corrupt and religiously impure. They accused the high priests, often who were appointed by Roman proconsuls, of not being of pure lineage; thus, the Essenes had little to do with the temple. They voluntarily chose stringent diets and difficult lifestyles; their views were extremist, communal, and often misogynistic (i.e., contemptuous of women). Paul alluded to some of their ascetic practices in Colossians 2:20-23, but certainly did not support them.

The Herodian dynasty of Judean kings corresponds with the life of Christ and the early church. The Herods were not actually of Jewish

---

29 Bruce, *The Book of Acts*, 123, fn 42; bracketed words are mine.

30 In the listing of the apostles is "Simon the Zealot" (Matthew 10:4, Mark 3:18, Luke 6:15, and Acts 1:13). ("Cananaean," as found in some versions, is the Aramaic word for "Zealot." The KJV word "Canaanite" is incorrect, and "Zelotes" is a poor translation at best.) It is possible that Simon originally associated with these radicals—though not as an assassin—and maintained his staunch anti-Roman position during his apostolic ministry. Or, it is possible that Simon abandoned his party affiliation when he became an apostle, but was called "the Zealot" simply to differentiate him from the other apostle named Simon (Peter). Regardless, whatever conjecture we come up with cannot contradict Simon's *foremost* allegiance which was to Christ, not to the national liberation of Judea.

descent, but for political reasons befriended the Jews (or at least pretended to) and supported their religion, and even claimed to have converted to it.[31] They built many buildings (most notably, the great temple in Jerusalem) and contributed a great deal of money to Jewish causes. Yet, regardless of such outward gestures, most Jews hated the Herods—and the feeling was mutual. For reference purposes, these kings are as follows:

❑ **Herod the Great** (reigned 37 – 4 BC). Mentioned in Matthew 2:1-19 and Luke 1:5, this Herod was responsible for the slaughter of the children near the time of Christ's birth. Paranoid, power-hungry, and ruthless, he had his own family members murdered for fear that they would usurp his throne. Upon his death, his kingdom was divided among his three sons: Archelaus, Antipas, and Philip.[32]

❑ **Herod Archelaus** (ruled 4 BC – AD 6) became ethnarch of Judea, Samaria, and Idumea (Matthew 2:22) according to the terms of his father's will. However, he was such an inept ruler that the Jews petitioned Rome to remove him. As a result of this action, Archelaus was deposed, and his "kingdom" was turned over to Roman prefects and procurators. This is the reason why Pontius Pilate (and other Roman governors before and after him) ruled over Judea during the time of Christ instead of a Herodian king.

❑ **Herod Antipas** (ruled 4 BC – AD 39). This king ruled over the districts of Galilee and Perea; he built the city of Tiberius and ruled from there when it was completed (in AD 23). He is the one who had John the Baptist executed (Matthew 14:3-12,

---

31   Herod was actually descended from the Idumeans, the lingering vestige of the ancient Edomites. Thus, the age-old antagonism between Edom and Israel was revived through Herod's kingship over the Jews.

32   "[T]he son of a king did not automatically become king of his father's domain on his death; he was more likely to be assigned to another area by the Romans, according to their need. If unsatisfactory, he was apt to find himself summarily removed, 'pensioned off,' like Herod Archelaus and Antipater, to retirement in some pleasant spot on the other side of the Roman world.... If satisfactory, he might be 'promoted' to somewhere more important or more sensitive, and might indeed well end up as a king of somewhere, though if it turned out to be his father's kingdom this was more a matter of luck than anything else. This is not kingship by anybody's definition; this is civil service" (Robyn Tracey, "Syria," *The Book of Acts in Its First Century Setting*, vol. 2, 248-249).

Mark 6:17-29, and Luke 3:19-20). John had spoken out boldly against Herod since he had married the (divorced) wife of his brother Philip. Herod also tried to scare Jesus away (Luke 13:31-33), but Jesus referred to him as a "fox"—a relatively weak creature that uses cunning to achieve its objectives.[33] Later, Jesus stood trial before Herod Antipas at the time of His death (Luke 23:6-12).

- **Herod Agrippa I** (ruled AD 41 – 44). This Herod acquired the territory of Antipas by befriending the new Caesar Claudius (after Caligula's death) in his ascension to Emperor. To win the favor of the Jews, he had (the apostle) James executed, and imprisoned Peter, intending to have him executed as well. This plan, of course, failed miserably (Acts 12:1-19). Agrippa died unexpectedly in Caesarea Palestina, being "eaten by worms" (Acts 12:20-23). Because his son, Agrippa II, was only 17 years old at the time of his death, his territories were given over to appointed procurators until AD 50.

- **Herod Agrippa II** (ruled AD 50 – 100) lived—incestuously, it is generally believed—with his sister Bernice (whose husband, king of Chalice, died in 48). Agrippa oversaw the Jerusalem temple operations, including the appointment of its high priests, and was the religious liaison between Judea and Rome. He is the Agrippa before whom Paul testified in Acts 26. His death in AD 100 marked the end of the Herodian dynasty.

Outline and Chapter Titles

The outline for Acts closely follows its chapter breaks. This makes for a rather easy-to-remember outline format (below). In chapters 1-12, Peter is a principal character; ministry to the Jews is the main focus; and Jerusalem is the central location of the events described. In chapters 13-28, Paul is the principal character; ministry to the Gentiles is the main

---

33   Actually, either Herod tried to scare Jesus away or the Pharisees tried to scare Jesus *with* alleged threats from Herod. The first scenario seems more natural, however. Herod was "haunted" with guilt over his unjustified execution of John the Baptist (see Mark 6:14-29), and thought that Jesus was a resurrection of John (see Matthew 14:1-2). Even so, his solution to this problem may have been to get rid of Jesus as well.

focus; and numerous cities are involved (though Antioch of Syria serves
as a kind of base camp for Paul's missionary journeys).

∼ Chapter 1 ∼
Christ's Ascension; Choosing an Apostle

Christ's Ascension (1:1-11)

Introduction to the book (1:1)
"Theophilus" ("lover of God") may be a benefactor and/or person of high civil rank (due to the use of "most excellent," which may indicate nobility).[34] This is Luke's second volume of historical record that he has written for this man, his gospel account ("Luke") being the first (see Luke 1:1-4). The beginning of Acts dovetails nicely with the close of Luke's gospel, which is intentional.[35] The actual question of "Why did Luke write these things for Theophilus in the first place?" may be best answered by John rather than Luke: "… these have been written so that you may believe that Jesus is the Christ, the Son of God; and that believing you may have life in His name" (John 20:31). John's words actually serve as a thesis statement for the four gospel accounts *and* Acts, since this is the ultimate reason for all such inspired writings.

Jesus' final instructions to His disciples (1:2-5)
Jesus gives His final words of instruction to His disciples "of the things concerning the kingdom of God" (1:2-3). Just as it was by the Holy Spirit that Jesus performed miracles (Matthew 12:28, Luke 4:14), so it was by Him [the Spirit] that Jesus gave instructions to His disciples. In

---

34 "The word [that is translated "most excellent"—CMS] appears only three other times in the New Testament, and each time is given to men of high *office*. The title was often used to denote a member of the Roman equestrian order. It is therefore probable that Theophilus was some distinguished Roman or Greek, who had been converted to Christianity," and possibly a nobleman of Antioch (Reese, *The Book of Acts*, 1).

35 "The usage of contemporary Emperors and the incidence of the title in inscriptions and the papyri confirm that 'most excellent' people were people of very considerable rank and position. Theophilus, then, is the cover name for a highly placed figure in Roman circles. Acts' abrupt ending is explained if 'Theophilus' knew the sequel to Paul's years of arrest. 'Theophilus' had heard of Paul's trial and execution: perhaps he had attended both. He wished to know the truth of a faith which had interested him but now lay under this recent cloud. Acts and the third Gospel are the first, and greatest, of Christian apologies to be addressed to highly placed pagans" (Robin Lane Fox, *Pagans and Christians* [New York: HarperCollins Publishers, 1986], 430).

other words, whatever Jesus did (as miracles) or said (as instruction) is completely united with His Father's Holy Spirit, as He [Jesus] had said (see John 17:20-23). The legitimacy of His actual human appearance to His eleven disciples is confirmed by "many convincing proofs" [Greek, *tekmerion*, lit., irrefutable signs or arguments].[36] These "convincing proofs" are specific miracles that Jesus has performed in their midst (as in Luke 24:31, 36, and John 21:5-6). A miracle is not just a rare or unusual *natural* event, but is completely *supernatural* in its effect, timing, and/or method. Its explanation is not merely unknown to this world (but could be discovered), but it has no natural or human explanation. Miracles are not permanent alterations to natural laws, but they temporarily interrupt or override them altogether. This interruption is for the purpose of confirming that its accompanying message is indeed not of this world—it is from God (see Luke 4:36, Mark 16:20, John 5:36, Hebrews 2:3-4, et al).[37] Thus, Jesus did not perform magic tricks for His disciples (through sleight-of-hand or elaboration manipulations), but genuine, supernatural, and irrefutable *signs* designed to convince them that what they heard (His words) was indeed *true* and what they saw (His resurrected body) was indeed *real*.

Paul later says that over 500 disciples literally saw Christ in His resurrected body (1 Corinthians 15:3-8). Certainly Christ could have appeared to *all* the Jews—including those who conspired to have Him executed—and proved to them *personally* that He had risen from the dead. One has to wonder, of course, if even this would have been convincing (given His own words in Luke 16:30-31). Even when He was *alive*, Jesus proved irrefutably that He was the Christ, and most of the Jews refused to believe in Him. The phrase "whom He had chosen" is significant in what it means as well as what it does not mean. Positively, it means that He has personally commissioned only certain men to be His designated spokesmen; negatively, it means that there were many other people who would be chosen for *salvation* (see

36   James Strong, *Strong's Greek and Hebrew Dictionary* (electronic edition in QuickVerse10 © 2009), #G5039.

37   I strongly recommend reading chapter 10 ("Miracles and the Holy Spirit") in my book, *The Holy Spirit of God: A Biblical Perspective*, for a practical overview of what miracles and signs really are in the context of the New Testament; go to www. spiritbuilding.com.

2 Thessalonians 2:13, for example) but not chosen to be His *apostles*. The word "chosen" requires context to define those who are being chosen (as well as the reason for their having been chosen).

Regardless, it is clear that Christ wanted His resurrection to be conveyed through a different route: eyewitness accounts; the inspired proclamation of His gospel; visible and public miracles; and (ultimately) the written record of all of these things. The reason for this has not been fully disclosed to us, but God has often chosen to reveal Himself through men and miracles rather than a personal showing.[38] The unconverted world needs to be convinced by relevant and credible evidence, not a personal visit from Christ; believers are to "...walk by faith, not by sight" (2 Corinthians 5:7). The gospel of Christ is a believable and intelligent message—one that is timeless, universal, unique, and unchanging. As Paul previously says, "[M]y message and my preaching were not in persuasive words of wisdom, but in demonstration of the Spirit and of power, so that your faith would not rest on the wisdom of men, but on the power of God" (1 Corinthians 2:4-5). Thus, long after the apostles have died, visible miracles have ceased, and history has marched on, the powerful verdict of Christ's resurrection remains as powerful and convincing as it was in the first century. God most certainly has "furnished proof to all men" for all time that His Son was raised from the dead (cf. Acts 17:31).

"Forty days" (1:3) is a recurring period of time in Scripture, "forty" almost always designating a time of trial, probation, and/or transition. Some familiar "forty" (days or years) references include: the days of rain during the Flood (Genesis 7:12); the days Moses twice remained on Mt. Sinai (Exodus 24:18 and 34:28); the days the Hebrew spies spent in Canaan (Numbers 13:25); the years Israel spent in the wilderness (Numbers 14:34); the days Goliath reproached Israel (1 Samuel 17:16); the days Elijah remained in the wilderness (1 Kings 19:8); the days Jonah preached to Nineveh (Jonah 3:4); and the days Jesus spent fasting

---

38   Obviously, this is a general statement, not an absolute one. Certainly Christ *has* shown Himself (post-resurrection) to a number of people; otherwise, there would be no witnesses *of* His resurrection. He did reveal Himself to Saul (Paul), but out of necessity and not as a routine course of action. Christ does what He does, reveals Himself to whomever He chooses, and interrupts His normal policy (if that is the right word) in whatever cases He deems it appropriate to do so.

in the wilderness (Matthew 4:2). Forty (10 x 4) seems to be the fullness (symbolized by the number 10) of a transition or period of endurance in an earthly context (symbolized by the number 4). In the present case, Jesus appeared in bodily form to His disciples over a forty-day period which symbolized not only a great transition (the interlude between His earthly ministry and His heavenly reign), but also the disciples-turned-apostles' time of learning, preparation, and wonder.

"The kingdom of God" in the NT context refers to the rule and realm of Christ after He is appointed as King over His Father's kingdom (Acts 2:33, Ephesians 1:19-21, Hebrews 8:1, 1 Peter 3:22, et al). This is related to but not interchangeable with Christ's church, the sacred body of believers who are baptized into Christ.[39] *All of Creation* is under Christ's rule as King, but only *obedient believers* are in His church. Christ's church could not exist until His authority and position as King was actually and wholly secured. The establishment of the church is possible only because "…all authority has been given to Me [Christ] in heaven and on earth" (Matthew 28:18). Entering into the kingdom of God (by way of being added to Christ's church; see Acts 2:47) means to surrender to the King Himself, agree to His terms and conditions of salvation, live according to the kingdom's heavenly perspective (see Matthew 5:3-12), and ultimately receive an eternal citizenship in that kingdom (2 Peter 1:10-11).

With regard to the promise (1:4-5), it is important to pay attention to whom Christ is speaking in this section. This instruction is directed *not* to a general group of disciples; it is specifically to "the apostles whom He had chosen" (recall 1:2), men who are later identified by name (see 1:13). Christ tells these men (in essence) that the proof of His ascension to His Father's throne will be proven through a supernatural impartation of authority upon them—a "power." The giving of this

---

39 "To say the kingdom is 'spiritual' is correct. But if by saying this we mean it is confined to religious goings on within the Christian, we are badly off the mark. **Christ is King over more than the hearts of Christians!** His sovereignty is not to be cramped within buildings with stained glass windows. To make the point that God aims to reign within every heart is biblical. To say he rules nowhere and nothing else is false! (It is easier to fall into this error when we narrow the 'kingdom of God' down until it is coextensive with 'the Church.' These two are not to be regarded as identical" (McGuiggan, *The Reign of God*, 65).

power is characterized as a type of "baptism," not of water but "with the Holy Spirit." In this sense, the apostles will be fully immersed in the Spirit as they (and others) had been immersed in the water of John's baptism (John 15:26-27, Matthew 3:1-12). Thus, they shall "receive power" from the Holy Spirit—power to perform miracles, as a confirmation of the gospel message that they will preach (Mark 16:20, Hebrews 2:3-4). John Calvin says, "This passage is not about baptism, but about the difference between Jesus and John."[40] Actually, it *is* about baptism, in that this is what Jesus said. However, it is *also* about the vast difference between the authority He possesses as the Son of God (and what great things He *does* by that authority) and the ministry of John the Baptist as a prophet of God (and what limited things he did in *that* ministry). John used his baptism to prepare the Jews to receive their Messiah; Jesus will use His baptism to build His church and sanctify it with the power of God's Spirit. These two baptisms need each other but are for considerably different purposes.

While it is true that those Jews who obey Christ's gospel will receive the Holy Spirit with reference to salvation (Matthew 3:11, Acts 2:38, 5:32, et al), it is *not* true that all of these Jews will receive the "power" of which Christ speaks here. It is only the (soon to be) twelve apostles themselves who actually receive this power. *Power* here refers to the authority not only to perform miracles but also to transmit that privilege to others upon whom the apostles lay their hands. No one else will have this power unless the apostles transmit it to them through this method. The fact that believing Jews *as a distinct group of people* have been immersed in the Holy Spirit will be manifested through these miracles.[41]

---

40   John Calvin, *Acts* (Wheaton, IL: Crossway Books, 1995), 15.

41   The two "groups" that will be invited into the church will be Jews (first) and Gentiles (second), as per the order prescribed by God (Romans 1:16). The assimilation of the two groups—thus making irrelevant any further distinction *of* them—is explained in Ephesians 2:11-18. Only representatives from each group need *literally* to manifest the miracles of the Holy Spirit without any human intervention in order for the entire group to be deemed acceptable to receive the gospel. Thus, the apostles serve as the Jewish representatives, while Cornelius and company serve as the Gentile representatives (Acts 10). For a much more detailed study on this, I recommend my book, *The Holy Spirit of God*; go to www.spiritbuilding.com.

The question of the restoration of Israel (1:6-8)

The eleven apostles then ask Christ about the restoration of Israel (1:6). This "restoration" (or, regeneration) concept is rooted in the prophecies concerning the reign of Messiah. It involved the reunification of "Israel" (the northern tribes) and "Judah" (the southern tribes) that were divided from each other in the days of King Rehoboam (compare 1 Kings 12 and Ezekiel 37:15-28). "The form of their question indicates that they expected a political reign. 'Restore' suggests a return to the national independence enjoyed under former kings."[42] It is clear that, despite His teaching on the subject of the kingdom of God, the apostles still did not entirely grasp what Jesus meant by it. Their long-held belief—one deeply embedded in the religious teaching of the Jews for centuries—was that Messiah would usher in an age of unprecedented glory, greatness, and prosperity for a unified Israel (see Isaiah 60, for example). They believed that all this would be fulfilled *literally* upon the earth (Luke 19:11, John 6:15, et al), even though Jesus was speaking of a *spiritual* kingdom (John 18:36-37).

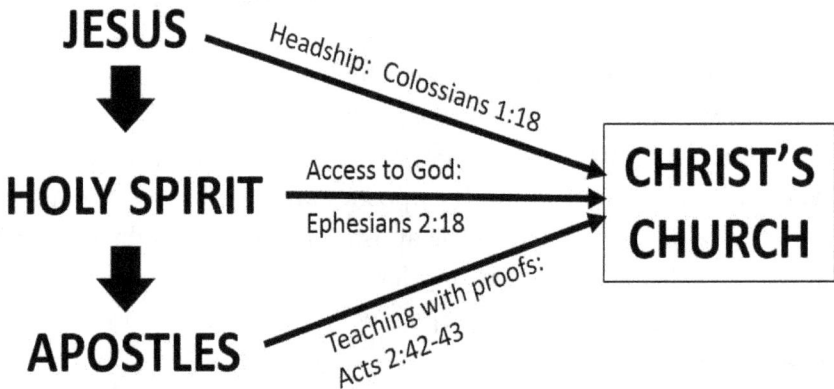

Instead of explaining Himself further, however, Jesus defers the question for now, knowing that things will be made clear soon enough (1:7-8; see Acts 3:19-21). In fact, Jesus does not deny the restoration of Israel but only addresses the question concerning the *timing* of it.[43]

---

42   Gaertner, *Acts*, 55.

43   "It is curious how eager people have always been to fix definite dates about the second coming of Christ as the apostles were about the political Messianic kingdom

This does not mean, however, that these men's understanding of this restoration was accurate. "Times or epochs" are under God's control, not men's; it is not necessary that believers know *how* or *when* God will unveil His plans, only that they believe in His power and His promises. This is as true for us today as it was for the apostles (see 1 Thessalonians 5:1). It is not necessary that we know all the details of God's existence and activity in order to believe that He most certainly does exist and is active. He has provided sufficient evidence for our faith (Hebrews 11:6); He has not provided the answers to all of our questions. The only way for God to give us *full* understanding of His ways would be to tell us *everything* He knows—a proposition which is neither possible nor necessary. Thus, "It is not for you to know." This has not stopped many men and women throughout the last two millennia from *presuming* to know God's "times and epochs," especially with regard to Christ's Second Coming, but they have done so in defiance of what is written, not faithful response to it. "You shall be My witnesses..." (1:8)—"witness" (a testifier to the facts; a first-hand observer; a primary source record of such observation) is from the root word *martus*, the Greek word from which our English word "martyr" is derived. Jesus did not go away without leaving behind credible witnesses to perpetuate His teachings and defend the truth of what really happened.

"But *you* will receive power when the Holy Spirit has come upon *you*" (1:8, emphasis added)—again, a direct reference to the apostles, not a general reference to all Jewish believers.[44] It is true that *Christ's church* will be "baptized" (immersed) in the Holy Spirit; it is *not* true that every person *in* His church will receive "power," or even the miraculous evidence of that baptism. Put another way: it is true that *all* those who become Christians will receive the gracious intercession (or "gift") of the Holy Spirit; it is *not* true that all Christians will receive His *power*

---

which they were expecting" (Robertson, *Word Pictures*, 10).

44   "It has been pointed out that the geographical terms of v. 8 provide a sort of 'Index of Contents' for Acts. 'Ye shall be my witnesses' might be regarded as the theme of the book; 'in Jerusalem' covers the first seven chapters; 'in all Judea and Samaria' Chs. 8:1 to 11:18; and the remainder of the book deals with the progress of the gospel outside the frontiers of the Holy Land until at least it reaches Rome" (Bruce, *The Book of the Acts*, 39).

to perform miracles. These two things are not interchangeable and serve related but different purposes.

Christ's ascension into heaven (1:9-11)

In Luke 19:12ff, Jesus gave a parable about a "nobleman" who "went to a distant country to receive a kingdom for himself, and then return." This foretold Jesus' ascension into heaven to receive the heavenly kingdom and sit down at the right hand of His Father. Thus, at the end of His conversation with the apostles (in 1:4-8), "He was lifted up while they were looking on" (1:9). There was no whirlwind or chariot of fire, as in the case of Elijah (2 Kings 2:11), but there are at least eleven witnesses to this incredible event. Jesus rises from the earth until He is obscured from their sight by a cloud, no doubt symbolic of God's presence (as in Luke 9:34, during Jesus' transfiguration).[45] Just as at Christ's tomb (Luke 24:1-7), two angels—for there is little doubt that these "two men in white clothing" *are* angels—appear in order to validate what these men had seen (1:10). "In white clothing" is a common distinction of heavenly messengers (Matthew 28:2-3, Mark 16:5, John 20:12, Luke 24:4, Revelation 19:14, et al). "Why do you stand looking...?" (1:11) is not a question for seeking information, but draws attention to the non-productive nature of the apostles' actions. It is as if to say, "There is no point in continuing to look toward where He went, for He will return in due time." He is not gone forever, but He is gone for now; His physical absence, however, does not mean that He leaves them "orphans," as He told them earlier. And, He *has* to go in order to send the "Helper," the Holy Spirit (see John 14:16-20).

The angels' testimony that He "will come in just the same way as you have watched Him go" does not mean He will return to "[dwell] among us" again (cf. John 1:14), but that He will be personally

---

45   This may be "the Shekinah-cloud, the pavilion of the manifested presence of God with his people, called 'the excellent' or 'manifest glory' by Peter (2 Pet. 1:17)" (Robert Jamieson, Andrew R. Fausset, and David Brown [hereafter cited as JFB], *New Commentary on the Whole Bible: New Testament Volume*, electronic edition [© 1990 Tyndale House Publishers; © 2012 WORDsearch Corp.], on Luke 9:34). This cloud of glory also filled the tabernacle upon its ordination (Exodus 40:34-38) and the Solomonic temple during *its* ordination (1 Kings 8:10-11). Yet, the ordinariness of the text (in Acts 1:9) suggests that this may be simply an ordinary cloud that serves no other purpose than to provide a point of transition in this event.

manifested to men again. The interpretive question here is: to *which* manifestation are the angels referring? In the Luke 19:12ff parable (cited earlier), the "nobleman" returns among the very people who rejected him, and he rewards his servants who remained faithful to him, but executed those who rejected his kingship. The context there is specifically *Jewish* in nature, that is, it is a pointed condemnation of Israel for its national rejection of Jesus as her King. In *this* context, however, there is no reference to a divine judgment of Israel or any allusion to the destruction of Jerusalem in particular; the "come again" reference lacks a specific objective or point of reference. There are actually three different contexts in the NT in which Jesus will "come":

- ❑ **In judgment against Jerusalem** (Israel) for the Jews' rejection of their Messiah (Matthew 24:29-31). This "coming" is symbolic in nature, since He did not literally or physically appear, but it was clear that the destruction of Jerusalem is initiated and carried out by *Him* (the "Son of Man") as a divine vengeance against God's covenant-bound people who nonetheless would not believe in His Son, despite all the evidence He provided them (Matthew 11:20-24, Luke 19:41-44, et al). This "coming" puts an end to God's relationship with the physical nation of Israel.
- ❑ **In judgment against the four-nation Gentile empire** (i.e., Babylon, Medo-Persia, Greece, and Rome; see Daniel 2:32-45, 7:1-7) for its persecution of Christ's church. This particular judgment is the dominant subject of Revelation (see Revelation 1:7). This "coming" is also symbolic in nature, since we have no evidence that Jesus literally or physically appeared, but it will be clear that the Empire's destruction is an act of divine vengeance and a vindication of many Christian martyrs. Thus, the *Jews* (those who "pierced" Him) "saw" Him, and so did the *Gentiles* (the "tribes of the earth") when He fulfilled all the prophecies of that Empire's destruction.[46] This "coming" puts an end to the four-nation Gentile empire that waged

---

46   Jesus' "I am coming quickly" references in the letters to the seven churches of Asia are part of this same "coming" in judgment against the Empire. Jesus tells the impenitent Christians, in essence, "If you are not going to identify with Me but live instead like the ungodly Empire, then you will be judged along *with* the Empire." This is also what the "mark of the beast" is all about—not a literal imprint upon the flesh, but an imprint of loyalty of the heart that is manifested in a specific kind of behavior.

war against God's people throughout history, from the Babylonian Empire to the Roman Empire (the prophetic "Babylon"—Revelation 16:17-21).

❏ **In judgment against the world** (2 Thessalonians 1:6-9, 2 Peter 3:7-13, and Revelation 21:1). This "coming" is *not* symbolic but literal: Jesus will *literally* and *personally* make an appearance (1 Thessalonians 4:13-18). This "coming" puts an end to the physical system which has been thoroughly corrupted by men, ushering in a "new heavens and a new earth"—i.e., a completely *new* dwelling place for God's people in His very presence. This is the only "coming" that is consistent with the manner in which He left: He literally and personally rose *to* the clouds, and He will literally and personally return *in* the clouds in order to receive His church from the earth prior to its destruction. For this reason, it seems clear that the angels who said that He will come again spoke of His *final* coming (for salvation *and* judgment) rather than a judgment that is limited to a specific group of people and a limited period in human history.

For now, Christ allows people to believe in Him because of the gospel record; in due time, however, He will show Himself for the purpose of calling an end to all such opportunity and to bring to Himself those who *did* believe in Him. The gospel record is clear about Christ's Second Coming: the surety of it as well as the suddenness of it ("like a thief in the night"—1 Thessalonians 5:2).

Christ's appearance will be "from heaven," since this is where He is right now (Colossians 3:1-2). He will be accompanied by a heavenly host of angels; He will be revealed as the Commander of this great army (as depicted symbolically in Revelation 19:11-16). His appearance will also be "in flaming fire," since fire (as an element of either purification or destruction) often accompanies divine judgment (Daniel 7:9-10, Hebrews 10:27, 12:29, and 2 Peter 3:7). He "... will appear a second time for salvation ... to those who eagerly await Him" (Hebrews 9:28), but He will be "dealing out retribution [vengeance]" to those who stand opposed to Him (2 Thessalonians 1:8).[47]

Modern ideas (which are actually continuations of ancient, pre-Christian ideas) that Christ will reign upon the earth for a thousand years in Jerusalem sometime in the future are baseless and unbiblical. There is nothing in Scripture stating that He will set foot upon this earth again, or that this will even be necessary. His work in the flesh is done; "It is finished" (John 19:30). His ascension from the earth into the sky and out of earthly view ends His physical presence upon the earth forever; we will "know Him in this way no longer" (cf. 2 Corinthians 5:16).[48]

Jesus' ascension (1:9-11) occurs at Olivet [Mount of Olives, or Olive Grove] near Bethany, less than two miles from Jerusalem. This event marks the critical transition between His earthly ministry and His heavenly rule.[49] The apostles are not only witnesses of Christ's ministry,

---

47   Cited from my *1 & 2 Thessalonians Study Workbook* (Summitville, IN: Spiritbuilding Publishing, 2014), 49. I strongly recommend reading this material for a further investigation into the subject of the Second Coming.

48   On this section, Stott makes an insightful proposition: "Looking back, I think we may say that the apostles committed two opposite errors, which both had to be corrected. First, they were hoping for political power (the restoration of the kingdom to Israel). Secondly, they were gazing up into the sky (preoccupied with the heavenly Jesus). Both were false fantasies. The first is the error of the politicist, who dreams of establishing Utopia on earth. The second is the error of the pietist, who dreams only of heavenly bliss. The first vision is too earthy [*sic*], and the second too heavenly. Is it fanciful to see a parallel here between Luke's Gospel and the Acts? Just as at the beginning of the Gospel Jesus in the Judean desert turned away from false ends and means, so at the beginning of the Acts the apostles before Pentecost had to turn away from both a false activism and a false pietism. And in their place, as the remedy for them, there was (and is) witness to Jesus in the power of the Spirit, with all that this implies of earthly responsibility and heavenly enabling" (*The Spirit, the Church and the World*, 51).

49   Some commentators have discounted the literalness of the ascension (as Stott cites in *The Spirit, the Church, and the World*, 47). Their arguments include: Luke is the only writer who mentions it; Luke does not mention the 40 days in his gospel; the ascension is an unnecessary account, being the exact same event as Jesus' resurrection; and it is without precedent. These are unconvincing arguments. Luke mentions a number of things (in his gospel) that no one else mentions; are we to disbelieve the reality of these, too? Perhaps Luke did not mention the 40 days in his gospel because he knew he would mention it in the second volume of his investigation—a far superior idea than to suggest

death, and resurrection, but also of His ascension (Luke 24:50-53). This is significant, since it answers the anticipated question, "What happened to Jesus *after* He was resurrected—where is He now?" "Therefore, let us learn that we must not seek Christ, either in heaven or upon earth, except by faith. Also, we must not long to have him with us physically in this world. Those who cling to either of these wishes will often go further away from him."[50]

Choosing an Apostle (1:12-26)

The eleven apostles ("they") return to Jerusalem from the direction of Bethany by way of Olivet (1:12).[51] "A Sabbath day's journey" marks the distance between Olivet and Jerusalem, not Bethany and Jerusalem.[52] "Returning from the Mount of Olives was an uphill climb on a winding road with some spectacular views of Jerusalem to

---

he *forgot* or merely *invented* it. Making Jesus' resurrection synonymous with His ascension is pure fiction: the two events are not compatible in any way (except for the "raised" part), much less one and the same. The resurrection occurred without human witnesses; the ascension occurred in front of the eleven apostles. Finally, "miracles do not need precedents to validate them" (ibid.). When scholars and commentators arbitrarily decide when Luke (or any other inspired author) is being literal or just making stuff up, this only discredits those who make such accusations, not the inspired authors themselves. We simply have no good reason to take Luke's words at face value.

50   Calvin, *Acts*, 19.

51   In my understanding, "they" most certainly does refer to the eleven apostles, yet this phrasing does not prevent the possibility for others to have witnessed Jesus' actual ascension. Luke is focusing on the apostles because of their special and exclusive role in what comes next (in chapter 2); his intention is not to exclude others who may have been only secondarily or even passively involved.

52   "A 'Sabbath day's journey' was a distance of about 2000 cubits, or about 3/5 of a mile. According to Jewish thinking in the first century, this was as far as one might travel on the Sabbath. To travel further would be to violate the prohibition about working on the Sabbath. No such distance limitation was fixed by the laws of Moses. Jewish religious teachers had fixed the distance. Hence it was a tradition, not a law" (Reese, 17). "This special command had been made by the Rabbis [as] the basis of a general rule fixing the distance which might be lawfully traversed on the Sabbath at '2000 cubits' (about six furlongs), the space kept between the ark and the people in the wilderness (Josh. 3:4), the distance to which the suburbs of a Levitical city extended (Numb. 35:5), and the traditional distance which separated the tabernacle from the furthest part of the camp" (Thomas E. Page, *The Acts of the Apostles* [London: MacMillan and Co. Ltd., 1911], 77; bracketed word is mine).

the west and the Dead Sea to the east."[53] This passage provides the final listing of Christ's hand-picked disciples, less Judas Iscariot (1:13), which is consistent with previous listings of these men in the gospels (Matthew 10:2-4, Mark 3:16-19, and Luke 6:13-16). From this point forward, this specific group of men is called "the apostles" (1:2).[54] These men gather together in an "upper room," possibly a meeting hall of some kind provided by a (wealthy) benefactor, along with some 120 other believers.[55] "Women" are specifically mentioned, since they had played a significant role in the support of Jesus' ministry (see Luke 8:1-3, for example). This is the final reference to Mary, the mother of Jesus (except by implication—Galatians 4:4).[56] "His brothers" refers to the physical half-brothers of Christ (Mark 6:3), who, though once antagonistic to His ministry (John 7:3-5), are now convinced of His divinity. Likely, His bodily resurrection was the crucial element in their change of heart.[57] We take note of this group's unity ("one mind"; see 1 Corinthians 1:10, Philippians 1:27, and 2:2) and devotion to prayer, both hallmarks of genuine believers (Acts 6:4, Romans 12:12, and Colossians 4:2).

---

53   Gaertner, *Acts*, 60.

54   "Disciple" means student or pupil; "apostle" literally means "one sent." Thus, these eleven men are no longer in a learning mode as before, but now they are to take what they have learned and proclaim it to others. They are sent by Christ into the world with a message, and they will exercise miracles to confirm the authenticity and power of that message (2 Corinthians 12:12, Hebrews 2:3-4).

55   Some believe this was the same "upper room" in which Jesus ate His last meal with His disciples (Luke 22:12), in which case it would be a privately-owned room as opposed to one of the meeting rooms in the Temple area; yet, we have no way of ascertaining this connection. "The traditional location of the 'upper room' [in 1:13] is in the Mount Zion region in the southwestern part of the old city of Jerusalem. A case has been made that this site was venerated continuously from the first century and that it may have originally belonged to a wealthy disciple in Jerusalem" (Paul Barnett, *Jesus and the Rise of Early Christianity* [Downers Grove, IL: InterVarsity Press, 1999], 196).

56   "A delicate touch by Luke that shows Mary with her crown of glory at last. She had come out of the shadow of death with the song in her heart and with the realization of the angel's promise [Luke 1:28-36] and the prophecy of Simeon [Luke 2:25-35]. It was a blessed time for Mary" (Robertson, *Word Pictures*, 14; bracketed citations are mine).

57   One of these brothers (James) will figure prominently in the Jerusalem church later on (chapter 15). It is firmly believed that James is also the author of the Epistle of James, while Jude—another brother of Jesus—is the author of the Epistle of Jude.

Peter, both moved by the Holy Spirit and himself having an increasingly clearer understanding of the things about which Jesus had taught the apostles, stood before the group of believers, "about one hundred and twenty persons" (1:15). (While some commentators have tried to assign a symbolic interpretation to this number—especially as a multiple of 12—Luke instead refers to a rough estimate, not a specific head count.)   Peter's primary objective at this time is to appoint an apostle to replace Judas Iscariot. The Scripture to which Peter alludes (1:16) is Psalm 69:25 and 109:8, which he will quote shortly (in 1:20). Judas had "received his share in this ministry," yet forfeited the privilege of serving as Christ's apostle (1:17 and 25). "Judas had been chosen to the place by Jesus, but he was disqualified by his wickedness and went to his own place, and now another must be chosen by the authority of God to take his place."[58]   In other words, a man with a corrupted heart such as what Judas exhibited turns *away* from whatever he could have received from God and *toward* an awful destiny of his own choosing. God did not make Judas a betrayer; Judas chose this for himself. On the other hand, God prophesied that there would *be* a betrayer, and that that person would become a "son of perdition" (John 13:18, 17:12). There is a difference between God "foreknowing" something and His forcing a person against his own will to do it.

While Peter only alludes to Judas' demise, Luke adds a parenthetical side note to fill in the details for Theophilus (1:18-19). This supplements what has already been said elsewhere (Matthew 27:1-10). The graphic depiction of Judas' death and his split-open corpse actually underscores the especially awful nature of his crime as the betrayer of his Lord for a mere thirty pieces of silver. This money, in a twist of irony—and another fulfillment of Scripture (see Jeremiah 19:1-11 and Zechariah 11:12-13)—was returned to the chief priests and elders and used to purchase an empty field in which he was buried.[59]   This

---

58   Boles, *A Commentary on Acts*, 30-31.

59   "The hypocritical priests could not use the money in the treasury of the temple, so they bought a potter's field in which to bury the poor (since some could not afford to bury their own dead) or the strangers (pilgrims who came to Jerusalem, died there, and no one could identify them). In reality, then, Judas purchased the field because the priests used his money. Apparently the field was purchased after the death of Judas; and when it was given closer inspection, they found Judas' body. Why was the field

"potter's field" or "field of blood" was located on the southern slope of the Valley of Hinnom (a.k.a. Topheth), the ancient site of cultic sacrifices near Jerusalem. King Ahaz and Manasseh both used this location for such sacrifices (2 Chronicles 28:1-3, 33:6). This site was later rendered unusable for such rituals during Josiah's reforms (2 Kings 23:10; see Jeremiah 7:32, 19:6).

Judas' particular vacancy must be filled before the apostles (as a group) receive power from the Holy Spirit (recall 1:8). Thus, "it is necessary" *before the public invitation into Christ's church is offered to the Jews* to restore the number of apostles to twelve (1:21). Just as there are twelve tribes of Israel, so there must be twelve apostles representing Israel. ("Twelve" regularly symbolizes a God-ordained religious organization in Scripture.) This symbolic number applies only to the ministry to the Jews (Matthew 19:28), not to the Gentiles.[60] Furthermore, Peter quotes Scripture (Psalm 69:25, 109:8) as justification for this action, which becomes the first business of the apostles.

Peter, who has already been recognized as the natural leader and spokesman for the eleven apostles, officiates over the selection of Judas' replacement. He asks for nominees to be "put forward" from the crowd of "about one hundred and twenty persons"; such candidates must fulfill specific criteria (1:21-22).[61] The fact that these nominees

---

so cheap? It was a worthless piece of real estate. It was a potter's field; a potter was a person who made pottery out of clay, so all the good earth was gone from this field, and it was therefore worthless" (Reese, *The Book of Acts*, 25).

60   This is why not *all* of the apostles were succeeded upon their deaths. Once the gospel was offered to the Jews, the need for the twelve witnesses (representatives) was no longer necessary; their ministry had been fulfilled. Paul—while technically a thirteenth apostle—was not part of this initial proclamation of the gospel to the Jews, but served as an apostle to the Gentiles instead (Romans 11:13, 15:16, Galatians 2:8, et al). Just as the gospel was offered "to the Jew first" (Romans 1:16) and *then* to Gentiles, so the twelve apostles to the Jews were chosen first, and *then* an apostle to the Gentiles.

61   "Who did the putting forward? Is it to be supposed that the 120 disciples... did this? There is no evidence whatever that such a group had been disciples from the beginning of John's baptism; and thus it is not reasonable to suppose that anyone participated in the selection of Justus and Matthias except the apostles. Furthermore, there is a strong inference in this passage that only two qualified men could be found, other than the apostles themselves. It appears that those two were equally qualified, hence the decision through casting lots" (Coffman, *Commentary on Acts*, 28-29).

must have accompanied Jesus "all the time" of His earthly ministry is significant. It proves that the original twelve apostles were not the only ones who accompanied Him, heard His teaching, and saw His miracles—and especially His resurrected body. His total ministry lasted a period of three and a half years. Thus, whoever is "put forward" has not only been an eyewitness of Jesus' earthly ministry but has also made some significant personal sacrifices in order to do so. An eyewitness can have an equal (i.e., another eyewitness), but not a successor. Once the eyewitnesses have died, they cannot be replaced or succeeded by "new" eyewitnesses.

From "the baptism of John until the day that He was taken up from us" (1:22) must not be pressed literally, as though every candidate had to be witnesses both of these events and also have spent every single day with Jesus in-between. (We cannot even ascertain that every one of the original twelve apostles were witnesses of Jesus' baptism by John.) Instead, these two events provide the bookends of Jesus' specific ministry in His role as Messiah. Jesus' baptism by John the Baptist marked the beginning point of His earthly ministry; His ascension marked its final event. On the other hand, Peter does later say of Jesus' crucifixion, His resurrected body, and His exaltation to heaven that "we"—the original eleven *and* the one chosen to replace Judas—"are witnesses of these things" (Acts 5:32; compare with Luke 24:48).

Two men are nominated: Joseph (a.k.a. Barsabbas or Justus) and Matthias (1:23). This is our first—and last—introduction to these two men. Calling upon God to make the actual decision (see Proverbs 16:33), the apostles cast lots and "the lot fell to Matthias" (1:24-26).[62] All of the other apostles had been personally chosen by Christ (Mark 3:13-19); Saul also will be chosen personally by Him (Acts 9:15-16); thus, it is necessary that Christ do the choosing for Judas' replacement as well. For reasons not known to us—possibly not even to the eleven

---

62   Casting lots—similar to throwing dice, drawing straws, or drawing names—has biblical precedent: choosing of the scapegoat on the Day of Atonement (Leviticus 16:8); division of the land of Canaan (Numbers 26:55); determination of guilt (Joshua 7:14); and selection of Israel's first king (1 Samuel 10:20-21). However, once the church was blessed with the miraculous knowledge imparted by the Holy Spirit, the use of lots (or similar "chance" methods) was no longer necessary.

apostles themselves—He chose one man (Matthias) over the other (Joseph). This is not a rejection of Joseph's character, since it was an honor for him even to be nominated. Yet, God knew that Matthias would be the better man for the job. "And he was added to the eleven apostles" provides the specific context not only for what is being *done* (restoring the group of *twelve* apostles), but also what will follow (i.e., identifying those who will be the recipients of the power manifested by the Holy Spirit). According to church tradition, Matthias will later preach and then suffer martyrdom in Ethiopia.

∽ Chapter 2 ∽
Peter's First Sermon; Conversions to Christ

Peter's First Sermon (2:1-37)

The Day of Pentecost (2:1-4)

"Pentecost" [lit., "fiftieth"], a.k.a. Feast of Weeks, served as the Jewish celebration of the end of the spring harvests according to the Law (Exodus 34:22, Leviticus 23:15-21). We should not miss its appropriateness here: just as Pentecost signified a celebration of the wheat harvest (and thus involved the presentation of the "first fruits" of that harvest), so we see the celebration of the "first fruits" of Christ's ministry or harvest. (The first generation of converts is referred to as the "first fruits" of the church in Romans 8:23, James 1:18, and Revelation 14:4.) The dating of Pentecost was reckoned yearly by counting fifty days after the Sabbath immediately following Passover; thus it always fell on the first day of the week (our Sunday).

"They" who are gathered together (2:1) refers to the apostles, because:

❑ The grammatical antecedent of this pronoun is "the eleven [apostles]" to which Matthias is added (1:26). If we had no such antecedent, then we could guess at who was being mentioned; as it is, however, we have a specific designation of people. It is impossible—grammatically and logically—to reference the "one hundred and twenty persons" (from 1:15) when we have a much more recent reference than this.[63]

---

63 Simon Kistemaker, despite his credentials, draws a less-than-scholarly conclusion concerning the word "all" in 2:1 and 2:4. "The last verse of the preceding chapter (1:26) mentions the apostles; in the second chapter, not the 120 but Peter and the Eleven occupy center stage (v. 14); and at the conclusion of Peter's sermon, the crowd addresses the apostles and not the 120 (v. 37). Conversely, we cannot limit the adjective *all* to the twelve apostles when the context of the preceding chapter stresses basic Christian harmony. Therefore, we interpret the adjective to include all the believers mentioned in the preceding chapter" (*Acts*, 76). In other words, despite all grammatical and contextual evidence, "basic Christian harmony" decides his point. (Never mind that the implications of this conclusion are far-reaching and important.) Then, he uses this conclusion to draw *another* conclusion in 2:4: "We should not limit the adjective *all* as applying only to the apostles, for Peter in his sermon shows that Joel's prophecy has been fulfilled: 'Your sons and daughters will prophesy'" (ibid., 77). Yet Joel also talks about "young men" seeing visions, "old men" dreaming dreams, and

❑ Jesus only promised the power of the Holy Spirit to the apostles (1:1-5). While the Jews *as a group* will be invited into Christ's church, not all Jews will be given power and authority within this church. This belongs to and remains with the apostles alone. Jesus spoke directly to these apostles earlier when He said, "<u>You</u> are witnesses of these things. And behold, I am sending forth the promise of My Father upon <u>you</u>; but <u>you</u> are to stay in the city until <u>you</u> are clothed with power from on high" (Luke 24:48-49, emphasis added).

❑ When Peter says (in 2:32) that "we all are witnesses," he means this specifically, not generically: *we apostles*—those to whom were given the charge by Jesus Himself—are now His witnesses! (See also Acts 5:32 and 1 John 1:1-4.) There is no evidence that the entire group of 120 people witnessed Christ's resurrection and ascension, yet this is an absolute requirement of the twelve apostles. There is also no responsibility entrusted to the entire 120 to "witness" the resurrected and ascended Christ in the same manner as that which was entrusted to the twelve apostles.

❑ We have no record of anyone *but* the apostles being given this power. It is true that others (later) will be able to perform miracles, but only after the apostles have conferred this power upon them through the laying on of their hands. (The only necessary exception is that of Cornelius, when the Holy Spirit acted apart from the apostles; see comments on Acts 10.) In the early days of the church, no one but the apostles alone are performing any kind of miracles (2:43).

❑ Peter will take his stand "with the eleven," who are all "Galileans" (2:7, 14, 37). This confirms what was stated earlier concerning which specific group is under discussion.[64]

"bondslaves" prophesying, but none of this is taken into account. If it is only the twelve apostles displaying this miraculous power, then there is no need to wonder whether or not the women of the "upper room" crowd also display it: they do not. In due time, *all* the different strata of people will exercise spiritual gifts, but at *this* time it is crucial that only the twelve apostles do so.

64   H. Leo Boles draws this same conclusion in his commentary (*A Commentary on Acts*, 33).

The Holy Spirit—apart from any human bidding—manifests His power with reference to two non-tangible elements: wind and fire (2:2-4). The *sound* of wind attracts observers to the apostles; the *sight* of fire [lit., the fire-like appearance] indicates a supernatural manifestation.[65] The *source* of both the wind and fire—even though there is no actual wind or fire—has no natural explanation and cannot be humanly produced. The speaking in tongues [Greek: *glossolalia*] also has no human or earthly explanation. Clearly, "the Spirit was giving them utterance," indicating that this is a supernatural sign from God. What happens to these men is the visible *manifestation* of the baptism with the Holy Spirit: this baptism is for the *benefit* of all Jewish believers, but the public display of this baptism is carried out through the twelve representatives of Israel—the apostles.

The manner in which the Spirit has demonstrated His presence with the apostles—a rushing wind sound, tongues "as of" fire, and a number of languages—indicates the *intangible nature* of the kingdom of God (which "is not of this world"—John 18:36). Formerly, God's people were identified with a physical temple in a specific city (Jerusalem), a select hereditary priesthood separated from all other covenant believers, flesh-and-blood sacrifices, and other tangible features of their religion. From this point forward, however, everything begins to shift toward a *spiritual* kingdom that will not be defined by these same things. Jesus predicted this in John 4:23-24: "But an hour is coming, and now is, when the true worshipers will worship the Father in spirit and truth; for such people the Father seeks to be His worshipers. God is spirit, and those who worship Him must worship in spirit and truth." (See this shift also implied in Hebrews 9:1-12.) The intangibility of the Spirit's *miracles* also says something about the work and nature of the Spirit *Himself* (as implied in John 3:6-8).

> There is also something remarkable in how the Holy Spirit is nearly always defined with an indefinite shape. Just as a liquid does not have any particular shape of its own, so the Spirit cannot be described in a physical form. Just as a liquid is able

---

65   A "fire" that does not consume calls to mind the burning bush that Moses saw; see Exodus 3:1-3.

to adapt to the shape of whatever vessel into which it is put, so the Spirit is able to adapt to any person of any age, size, status, color, ethnicity, or nationality. Just as a liquid can be applied (or daubed upon) any person, so the Spirit can be universally "applied" to any person. The Spirit's fluid, pliable, and completely versatile "application" to the human soul is perfectly conducive for His sanctifying work. In a similar thought, a person's physical or social circumstances are of no difficulty for the Spirit, and He has already proved His mastery over the human context (as illustrated in Acts 2:4-11, with regard to language, for example). In other words, no human or earthly obstacles can prevent the Spirit from carrying out the will of God in those who belong to Him—except for one: human unbelief.[66]

Christians today are most certainly "filled with the Spirit"—we cannot *be* Christians otherwise—but this indwelling is not accompanied by visible or audible miracles, nor is this necessary. Several passages in the NT talk about the Spirit's indwelling with no reference to miracles (see, for example, Romans 8:9, 1 Corinthians 6:19-20, 2 Corinthians 13:14, Ephesians 5:18, and 1 John 4:13). The events being described during the inception of Christ's church are necessary in order to provide validation and authenticity to what will be available to *all* faithful believers—the active presence of the Holy Spirit in their lives, as well as in the entire body (church) of Christ. But we have no reason to expect that these events will be (or need to be) reproduced for every believer or generation of believers. The miracles carried out *through* the twelve apostles are exclusive *to* those men; we should not expect to have them carried out through us today. God did then what was necessary to substantiate His gospel; now that it has been finally substantiated ("once for all"—Jude 3), there is no need to continue proving it over and over.[67]

---

66 Sychtysz, *The Holy Spirit of God*, 33-34.

67 "Pentecost was the inauguration of the new era of the Spirit. Although his coming was a unique and unrepeatable historical event, all the people of God can now always and everywhere benefit from his ministry. Although he equipped the apostles to be the primary witnesses, he also equips us to be secondary witnesses. Although the inspiration of the Spirit was given to the apostles alone, the fullness of the Spirit is for

The people's response to the apostles' speaking in tongues (2:4-13)
Jerusalem is filled with foreign-born Jews at this time because of
Pentecost, one of Israel's three significant yearly festal events.[68] Since
Pentecost follows less than two months after Passover, it is common for
families (that can afford it) to remain in Jerusalem for both festivals.
"Living in Jerusalem" (2:5) may be understood in this context, referring
to a temporary residence, not a permanent one. Or, it may be that
some of these people are *now* "living in Jerusalem" but were born
and raised in other nations. Regardless, they hear the apostles speak
fluently in known, recognizable languages that they [the apostles]
have never learned (2:6-8). That these men are "Galileans"—i.e., rural
citizens from the region of Galilee—adds to the intrigue of the miracle:
Galileans are not typically eloquent, and are regularly mocked for their
dialect and their butchering of Aramaic by Jewish purists (see Matthew
26:73). While it is often assumed that each apostle is speaking only
one foreign language apiece, the text does not require this. It is entirely
possible that they are speaking *several* different languages *each*, one
after the other. (Gareth Reese makes a good point by saying that the
miracle is performed upon the apostles, not those who hear them;
thus, it is not logical to say that the listeners *hear* their own language
regardless of what the apostles actually uttered.[69]) Regardless, it is
unnecessary to impose human explanations or earthly expectations
(such as comparing the number of nationalities listed with the number
of apostles speaking) upon a miraculous event.[70] If God can feed 5,000

---

us all" (Stott, *The Spirit, the Church, and the World*, 61).

68   "These pilgrims had to stay somewhere, and it appears that they stayed in
community centres built especially for them. Archaeologists have discovered several
buildings south of the Temple mount with a large number of rooms, ritual baths and
many cisterns. There was also a large inscription found that one Paris, a Jew from
Rhodes, had donated a pavement in the vicinity evidently for a community centre for
pilgrims" (David A. Fiensy, "The Composition of the Jerusalem Church," *The Book of
Acts in Its First Century Setting*, vol. 4, 233).

69   Reese, *The Book of Acts*, 52.

70   "It has been proposed by some that the loss of unity of language at Babel, as
recorded in the book of Genesis, is restored in the Gospel message. 'In Genesis 11, the
whole world was of one language. In their pride they proposed to build a tower that
would reach to heaven. God came down and confused their language so they could
not understand one another's speech. Sin ruined the unity of language. Babel brought
darkness, discord, and separation. Pentecost brought light, understanding, and unity'"
(ibid., 49). It might be more accurate to say that *God's truth* as revealed by the Holy

people with a few loaves of bread, then certainly He can provide (if necessary) 5,000 languages from a dozen men.

The list of nationalities (2:9-11) reveals the great diversity of Jews that have gathered in Jerusalem for Pentecost:

❑ Parthians, Medes, and Elamites—peoples who have lived near the confluence of the Euphrates and Tigris Rivers (modern-day Iran) since ancient times.

❑ Residents of Mesopotamia and Judea—"residents" because these people were likely not from these areas originally. "Mesopotamia" refers to the area north-northeast of Syria, extending to the Euphrates River. "Judea" likely indicates the farthest extent of the kingdom of Judah, south to the Egyptian border.

❑ Cappadocia, Pontus, Asia (Minor), Phrygia, and Pamphylia—all regions or Roman provinces of the Anatolian Peninsula (modern-day Turkey).

Two Related but Different Purposes for These Signs upon the Apostles:

ONE PURPOSE:	SECOND PURPOSE:
To demonstrate that the apostles have received power from the Holy Spirit: *Fulfillment* of what Jesus had promised them (from 1:8)	To demonstrate God's acceptance of Jews into His church: *Confirmation* of what Jesus already began in His ministry

❑ Egypt and...Cyrene—north and northeastern Africa. Alexandria, Egypt, has at this time the largest concentration of Jews in the world outside of Judea. Cyrene is the capital of Libya, an African nation on the southern coast of the Mediterranean Sea.

❑ Visitors from Rome, both Jews and proselytes—i.e., both ethnic Jews and those *non-*Jews who have converted to the Jewish religion (and have thus accepted circumcision and are bound to keep the Law of Moses). Rome, Italy, is of course the capital of the Roman Empire.

❑ Cretans—people from the island of Crete, located just south of Greece in the Mediterranean Sea.

❑ Arabs—this may be a loosely-defined group of desert-dwellers from the wilderness regions on the eastern side of the Sea of Galilee, Jordan River, and Dead Sea. More specifically, it could refer to

---

Spirit will serve as the universal "language" of the church.

the Nabateans, an Arab people whose capital is Petra in the place formerly known as Edom.

The dispersion of the Jews to foreign countries dates back to the time of Israel's exile to Assyria (721 BC) and Judah's exile to Babylon (586 BC), except for "proselytes" (2:10) who are non-Jewish converts to the Jewish religion.[71] This collection of Jews and proselytes is providential, of course, in that all of these people will eventually take back to their native countries what they have seen and heard regarding the gospel. The fact that the twelve apostles—all Jews—are recipients of the Spirit's power (with signs that the people can "see and hear"; see 2:33)— indicates God's acceptance of the Jews as a whole into His kingdom. In due time, the Spirit will manifest Himself through miraculous works upon other Jewish believers, in order to fulfill the prophecy of Joel (to be discussed shortly), but this will be initiated through the laying on of the apostles' hands.

Naturally, the great display of power prompts some to ask in wonder and amazement, "What does this mean?" (2:12). This is an appropriate response, similar to what is seen during Jesus' ministry (see Mark 1:27, 6:2, and Luke 4:36). God does not produce miracles for *no reason* or *without purpose*; the manifestation of miracles thus *means* something, and these people desire to know what it is. Others, however, mock with contempt (2:13); they say, in essence, "Pay these men no mind—they're just *drunk!*"

Peter confronts the gathering (2:14-21)

Peter, once again serving as a spokesman for the other apostles, responds to the charges of drunkenness (and mockery in general) (2:14-15).[72] The "third hour" indicates 9:00 a.m., which is far too early

---

71 Proselyting to the Jewish religion required a covenantal vow to obey the Law of Moses, observation of the various Jewish festivals, and circumcision. There is a difference in context (and the actual Greek words being used) between a "proselyte" and a "God-fearer" such as Cornelius (Acts 10:2). One refers to a person who has taken on the Jewish religion; the other refers to an uncircumcised man who respects that religion but has not become a follower of it (Paul Levertoff, "Proselytes in the New Testament," *ISBE* [electronic edition]).

72 Peter has been the main spokesman on at least three occasions previously:

in the day to even *begin* drinking.[73] (Furthermore, it is a violation
of Jewish law to have any intoxicating drink on a feast day.[74]) The
malicious accusation deserves little attention: drunken men cannot
speak fluently and eloquently of the "mighty deeds of God" in
languages they have never learned. With this baseless charge dispelled,
Peter launches into the substance of his speech (by inspiration of the
Spirit; cf. Luke 12:11-12, 21:12-15).

Peter uses a "this is that" formula (2:16-21): *this* which you hear is
that which was prophesied in Joel 2:28-32. In general, "last days"
indicates the final part or dispensation in a sequence of multiple time
periods (Hebrews 1:2). It also indicates that there will be no more
"days" or phases of time after this (since it is "last"). Specifically, it
has to do with God's revelation to man concerning his salvation. It
began with the first coming of Christ (in the flesh); it will end with the
second coming of Christ (in the clouds). Until this present event on
Pentecost, God's Spirit had only been poured out upon His prophets or
specially-selected people (such as a divinely-appointed king); with the
advent of the church age, however, His Spirit will now be given to "all
mankind"—i.e., believers of every nation but also to *all strata* of such
people (including women, slaves, etc.). "What Joel promised would
bring to pass a sentiment of Moses who exclaimed, 'I wish that all the
Lord's people were prophets and that the Lord would put his Spirit on
them.'"[75] "In those days" indicates that this action is not limited to a
specific "day" (i.e., Pentecost), but a time period; thus, the gradual

---

Matthew 16:13-16, John 6:66-69, and Acts 1:15-22. In the present scenario (in Acts 2:14ff), he exercises the responsibility imparted to him by Jesus as the holder of the "keys to the kingdom" (Matthew 16:19)—a reference not to unilateral power, but to his prominence in the initial proclamation of the gospel.

73   The ancient Jews reckoned daytime hours from 6:00 a.m. to 6:00 p.m.: the first hour was 6:00 a.m.; the second hour, 7:00 a.m.; and so on (see Matthew 20:1-6 for an actual implementation of this time system). Thus, "the third hour" to a Jew would be 9:00 a.m.

74   Reese, *The Book of Acts*, 57. Kistemaker notes: "The feast of Pentecost is the harvest festival of wheat and not of grapes. The grape harvest takes place at the conclusion of the summer. Therefore, the word *wine* refers not to new wine but to sweet wine from the harvest of the past year" (*Acts*, 86).

75   Gaertner, *Acts*, 74; his quote is taken from Numbers 11:29 (NIV).

application of the Spirit's power to various believers over time does not at all contradict the prophecy.

The initial manifestation of this "pouring out" of the Spirit is *accompanied* by miraculous wonders, but these wonders will not be required forever (2:17-18).[76] The purpose of the miracles is to confirm the authenticity of the message, not to become a permanent characteristic of the Spirit's work among men. Just as scaffolding is no longer needed once a building is completed, so the miracles among believers will no longer be needed once the gospel message has been fully revealed and recorded (1 Corinthians 13:9-10). The emphasis in the present passage (2:16ff) is on the *Spirit* being given to "all mankind," not the signs themselves. Miraculous signs are not the entirety of God's gifts to men, but prove the *divine source* of those gifts (Hebrews 2:3-4). On the other hand, the fact of these miracles also points to the fact of the Spirit's full support of the gospel message. If there are no miracles, then Peter's sermon is simply his opinion and not a divinely-revealed message. This statement is in the context of what is happening: men like Samuel, John the Baptist, etc., certainly did not need miracles to support their prophetic discourses. However, they spoke within an already-established context—i.e., the Law and the Prophets. Peter is speaking beyond this—saying something new (as a revealed message) that has never been said before. Just as Moses needed miracles to prove "his" law when he spoke it, so Peter needs miracles to prove this superseding "law" of the gospel.

"Wonders in the sky," "blood and fire," "the sun will be turned into darkness," etc., are all figurative Old Testament expressions of the "day of the Lord" (2:19-20). This "day"—a historical event or era, not an actual 24-hour period of time—refers to the *divine upheaval of an earthly (or physical) system or nation* (as in Isaiah 13:9-13 and 24:17-23). Some common features of "the day of the Lord" include:[77]

---

76   In my understanding: God "pours forth" His Spirit upon believers, beginning with the apostles, until the entire church is *immersed* in His [the Spirit's] life-giving presence; thus, every person who comes into Christ's church is also immersed in the power and life-giving power of God's Holy Spirit (John 6:63)—not to perform miracles, but for the purpose of sanctification (1 Peter 1:2) and fellowship (2 Corinthians 13:14).

77   This is adapted from my *1 & 2 Thessalonians Study Workbook*, 34-35.

❑ A "day" or time that God has fixed by His own authority.

❑ When these "days" will actually happen cannot be known precisely until they occur in history, but neither can men prevent, postpone, change, or avoid these "days" once they have been decreed against them.

❑ While people cannot always predict these days precisely, God nonetheless warns men that they are coming so that they can be prepared for them (through repentance and righteous living). Such warnings are invariably and divinely revealed through prophecy, but are also accompanied by signs or harbingers that ought to be taken seriously (as in Amos 4:6-12).

❑ They are divinely-appointed events imposed upon humankind because of sin—whether due to impenitence or as a means of atoning for sin. In this sense, they are always referred to as a "day" of *judgment*, although what serves as judgment to some will be salvation to others. (In God's judgment against ancient Israel, for example, He punished the entire nation for its infidelity to His covenant, yet in the very same process He purified that nation for its future participation in the salvation of the entire world.)

❑ They create a great upheaval, major transition, or termination of something—society, nation, religion, means of salvation (covenant), or realm of man in general.[78] In some context or another, this upheaval depicts a turning point (of some kind) after which the realm or people that are affected will *never be the same*.

❑ While "the day of the Lord" certainly has a negative aspect to it (as divine judgment against sin), its ultimate purpose is to advance God's will in heaven and on the earth. Dealing with sin (or, removing impenitent sinners from the realm of men) provides an opportunity for the living to turn to God for salvation rather than remain in their condemned state of being. Even in the *final* "day of the Lord," the destruction of the world provides for the eternal

---

78   In the case of a covenant between God and men for the purpose of salvation, we should not use the word "terminate" in the literal sense, because God *fulfills* His covenants rather than "terminates" them. Our covenant with God through Jesus Christ was not the result of a *terminated* covenant with Israel, but was the *fulfillment* of that covenant. Nonetheless, in the most general sense, the "day of the Lord" may render the effects of an existing covenant as no longer valid, thus conveying a sense that that covenant was "terminated."

union of Christ and His church in the hereafter. This brings about what God has always desired through the creation of man: "I will be their God, and they will be My people" (Ezekiel 37:27, et al).

The *judgment* that is implied here (in 2:19-20) is upon those Jews who reject Jesus as Messiah (see John 16:7-11), which will culminate in the destruction of Jerusalem (AD 70). The *change* is the cessation of the Jewish system (i.e., Law of Moses) and its supersession by the gospel of Christ (Ephesians 2:11-22, Hebrews 8:11-13). Thus, God (through Joel) predicted a time of great upheaval and disruption of the entire Jewish nation. This upheaval is for the purpose of bringing to an end that which has been fulfilled in Christ (i.e., the Law of Moses) and providing unprecedented access into the "holy place" (i.e., God's Presence; Hebrews 10:19-22). Both of these objectives—fulfillment of the Law *and* a once-for-all atonement that provided for such access to God— were accomplished through Christ's ministerial work on the cross. To say that this "day of the Lord" refers to Christ's coming at the end of the world is to ignore: the actual context of Joel's prophecy (which is *not* about the end of the world); the messianic kingdom as prophesied by the Old Testament prophets; the Jewish expectation of this kingdom; and Christ's fulfillment of this kingdom (and its subsequent judgment against those who rejected His rule, as depicted in Luke 19:11-27, for example).

Peter speaks (by inspiration) *in anticipation of* the complete fulfillment of Joel's prophecy. Jesus Himself spoke in anticipation of things yet to be fully manifested (see, for example, John 3:3-5, 4:23-24, and 7:37-39). We have not yet seen (in Acts) the Spirit "poured out" upon all people, regardless of gender, race, status, or any earthly distinction. Just as the gospel of Christ will take time to be unveiled in its entirety, so the full application of the Spirit's work will take time to be unveiled. So far, this "pouring out" is limited to the apostles for a very specific purpose; in a short while, other Jews will experience this "pouring out"; shortly after that, even Gentiles will be recipients of this. It is a mistake to assume that whatever Joel prophesied—and Peter's use of that prophecy to make his point—is completely and immediately fulfilled on the actual day of Pentecost.

"And it shall be that everyone who calls ... shall be saved" (2:21)—this necessarily anticipates a universal salvation (the revealed "mystery" of Ephesians 3:4-12). This salvation will no longer be predicated on a physical or legal association with Israel. Rather, it will be individually attained through the Holy Spirit, who is given only to those who obey the gospel of Christ—a point that will be disclosed at the conclusion of Peter's message (in 2:38). To "call" upon God's name is to choose to *identify* with the Lord by petitioning Him (through His gospel) for forgiveness and fellowship. The one who calls upon God for salvation must do so in whatever way God has prescribed, as is the case with any petitioning or worship of God (see John 4:23-24).

The substance of Peter's message (2:22-36)
Peter's speech (or sermon) to the Jews is of pivotal importance. It serves as the official *explanation* of what really happened to Christ as well as the official *invitation* into fellowship with God through His Son. It also provides concise yet profound appeals to different forms of authority in order to establish these conclusions. Speaking by inspiration of the Holy Spirit, Peter draws on:

- ❑ Old Testament prophecy (Joel 2:28-32, 2 Samuel 7:12-16, and Psalm 110:1).
- ❑ Words of David (from Psalm 16:8-11, 132:11, et al), whom the Jews highly revered.
- ❑ Historical facts (i.e., of Christ's existence, the miracles that He wrought, His crucifixion, etc.) which are publicly known and can be corroborated by numerous witnesses.
- ❑ Divine revelation—information that no man could know apart from it having been revealed to him by God.

Peter begins by challenging his audience, in essence, to try to *deny* the fact of Christ's miracles which He performed "in your midst" (2:22). While the Jews had tried to explain the power *behind* such miracles as belonging to Satan and not God—something which Christ soundly condemned as both illogical and blasphemous (Matthew 12:22-32)—they could not deny the miracles themselves (Luke 4:36, John 7:31, 11:47, et al). In fact, Jesus said that these "works" validate His testimony (John 5:36, 10:37-38, 14:11, et al): "If I cast out demons by the finger of God, then the kingdom of God has come upon you" (Luke 11:20). Since the Jews could not deny Jesus' miracles, no legitimate conclusion was possible except that God indeed was with Jesus, which meant that everything He said was true. The authenticity of these miracles continues to confirm Jesus' divine nature and authority even today.

Next, Peter explains the crucifixion of Christ in the context of God's omniscience: He (God) *knew exactly* what would happen if His Son was placed in the midst of Peter's generation (2:23). ("An evil and adulterous generation" [Matthew 16:4] is exactly the kind of people that will kill their own King out of fear, jealousy, and wickedness.) God predicted their actions just as He predicted (to Moses) the eventual apostasy of Israel (Deuteronomy 31:14-21). Jesus Himself had predicted what would happen to Him (Matthew 16:21 and 21:33-39). In other words, His crucifixion was no accident or coincidence; the rulers of the Jews did not force Christ's hand but played right into it, since He knew their hearts better than they did (John 2:24-25). Christ *allowed* Himself to be executed; He voluntarily *surrendered* His life for the sake of what His death would accomplish (John 10:18, Colossians 1:19-20). In fact, Christ actually forced *their* hand in choosing the time, place, and circumstances under which He would be killed.[79] Peter's point is this: even though Jesus was "attested by God," the Jews ultimately hated Him because He threatened their status and did not fulfill their expectations of Messiah.[80] God did not make the Jews kill

---

79 Notice the dual charges of guilt in Peter's statement: "*you* nailed [Christ] to a cross by the hands of *godless men*" (2:23, emphasis added). The Jews did not literally nail Christ to the cross; the Romans did. However, the Jews orchestrated and incited this action and were thus just as guilty as if they had crucified Him themselves. "Godless men" literally is translated from a Greek phrase meaning "men without law [of Moses]." The Jews, in essence, conscripted heathen men to carry out their bidding—a method they will continue to use in their persecution of the early church.

80 "The Jewish rulers were mortified, disgusted and outraged that one so poor and lowly would claim to be the Messiah. Their pride, ambition and selfishness simply could not accept Jesus as the fulfillment of an expectation they had so long cherished of some spectacular leader on a white horse who would overthrow the power of Rome and restore the defunct Solomonic empire" (Coffman, *Commentary on Acts*, 95).

His Son. At the same time, He knew full well that if He put His Son in the middle of the religious, social, and political vortex that existed at that time, it would result in His Son's crucifixion.

"But God raised Him up again" (2:24)—i.e., not even your bold attempts to silence or rid yourselves of Jesus could interfere with God's plan. Jesus predicted His resurrection—and the Jews certainly had heard Him—but they did not believe that this would actually happen. He defeated not only death, but also: the Jewish authorities (Colossians 2:15); all temptation to sin (Hebrews 4:15); Satan (who "had the power of death"—Hebrews 2:14); and "the world" (John 16:33). When Jesus rose from the dead, He also rose above all the human weakness, limitation, and corruption of those who succumb to death as a result of God's curse (Genesis 3:19, Romans 8:10). In doing so, He serves as our Redeemer *from* this curse, inasmuch as those who believe in Him will also rise from their physical death, never to die again (John 11:25-26, Romans 8:11, 1 Corinthians 15:40-49, et al).

Yet, not only was Jesus resurrected but His physical body was preserved by God so that it would not be affected by decomposition or deterioration.[81] David spoke of this event (2:25-28), but certainly he did not speak of himself since he *did* die, *was* buried, and *never rose* from that death. (The quote of David is from Psalm 16:8-11.) His tomb is not empty like Christ's. David's tomb is the only royal tomb inside of Jerusalem's city walls, and was once filled with much wealth. Later, it was plundered by Hyrcanus, then by Herod the Great.[82] (It will finally be destroyed by Emperor Hadrian in the early 2nd century.) The people hold David to be a prophet, and yet likely they remember Jesus' own challenge to them concerning His supremacy over David (Matthew 22:41-46), to which Peter also later alludes (2:34-35). Speaking *as* a prophet, David foretold "that God had sworn to him with an oath to seat one of his descendants on his throne" (2:30). This

---

81 This supernatural prevention against "decay" (i.e., natural decomposition of a physical body) bears upon our partaking *of* that body and blood in our observance of the Lord's Supper. We do not internalize the rotting flesh and spoiled blood of a *corpse*, but of a Living Savior. His body and blood impart *life*, not corruption and death, as He said (see John 6:48-58).

82 Josephus, "Wars of the Jews," 1.2.5, 3.15.3, and 16.7.1.

specifically refers to Psalm 89:3-4 and 132:11. This "oath" is a decision not based upon laws given to men but a divine promise that transcends what mortal men are capable of fulfilling (see Hebrews 6:13-18). Jesus was not made the King over God's kingdom simply because He was a "son" of David, but because He also was the Son of God (Romans 1:1-4). His kingship, then, is not only determined by human ancestry, but also by His being the "beloved Son" of God (Colossians 1:13). (It is also by a divine oath that Jesus is declared our High Priest; see Hebrews 7:17-22.)

There has been a longstanding controversy over the term "Hades" (2:27 and 2:31). In ages past, some have said that it refers to hell, the final destination of the soul (but see Revelation 20:14); some say it refers to the spiritual dual-compartment of the dead, one compartment being a place of torment, and the other, Paradise (almost entirely based upon a literal interpretation of Luke 16:19ff); some say it refers merely to the grave, the state of death itself (and not a literal "place"). This latter definition seems the most natural and logical, given what scant information we have in the New Testament of the afterlife.[83] Even less is the amount of human understanding or comprehension we have of a realm none of us has ever seen or experienced. Many people try to literalize (or, "three-dimensionalize," so to speak) the *spiritual* realm of the departed souls of men, and then try to force Lazarus, the rich man, the thief on the cross (Luke 23:43), and Jesus into such rigid scenarios.[84] Peter's words—based on a rather general term used

---

83   "*Sheol* [from the Psalm 16 citation] is here translated 'hades.' The word *sheol* is used in a wide sense: at death all men go into *sheol*, and around the word in this sense cluster all the dark, painful, dreadful things that we still associate with death, leaving this bright world, and entering the grave. Neither the Greek nor the English has a true equivalent for *sheol* in this sense; the Greek used its 'hades,' we use our 'grave.' It was the best that translation could do" (Lenski, *Acts of the Apostles*, 89; bracketed words are mine).

84   I simply cannot accept the fanciful idea that Jesus *went to hell* in order to experience it, to release souls from it, or for any other reason. The Scripture simply does not teach this; the thought must be forced into the text, as it does not come natural to it. If Jesus experienced anything like "hell," then it was on the cross, not in the spiritual world. There are many questions we all have concerning what happened to Jesus between the cross and His resurrection. Instead of inventing stories, however, we would do well simply to admit that we do not have solid answers for that time period. Suffice it to say: if we had needed to know this information—if it was crucial to our

by David—are not meant to provide an *explanation* of Hades, but simply a *reference* to it. Peter does not say, for example, "Jesus' soul went to the Paradise compartment of Hades"; rather, he simply says, in essence, "Jesus was not *left* in the realm of the dead, because He (as a Divine Being) is more powerful than death." Peter's emphasis is *not*, "Jesus' soul was resurrected from Hades," but, in essence, "His *body* was resurrected from *the dead*"—"the dead" being a practical understanding of Hades as it is used in this context.

"This Jesus God raised up again, to which we are all witnesses" (2:32)—no doubt Peter gestures to the other eleven apostles at this point, and possibly other disciples who are with him as well. In other words, there is sufficient and credible testimony to confirm that what Jesus *said* would happen actually *did* happen. Coffman has this to say:

> In the certification of so important an event as the resurrection to all times and conditions of men, Jesus trained and qualified a group of men fully equal to the task. They were outdoorsmen, unspoiled by any human sophistication, but still prepared in the most complete and perfect manner to witness and proclaim the resurrection. It is simply incredible that such men as the Twelve could have been led, either intentionally or otherwise, into believing the resurrection of Christ *unless it had indeed occurred*.[85]

"Therefore having been exalted to the right hand of God" (2:33)—this is an explanation of where Christ is *now* since His tomb is empty and His body is no longer on earth. (If the Jews had indeed stolen the body of Christ, this would have been the perfect time to expose Peter as a fraud. Meanwhile, the disciples had no access to the body, since His tomb had been put under tight security; see Matthew 27:62-66.) Being at the "right hand of God" implies power and authority second only *to* the Father Himself. The "throne" which Christ was given is not of this world, yet He was a legitimate heir to David's throne (Luke 1:31-33,

---

salvation—then God would have revealed it to us.

85   Coffman, *Commentary on Acts*, 52.

Romans 1:3-4). David's eternal kingdom is thus fulfilled in *heaven* and not upon the *earth,* as people had originally thought (compare 2 Samuel 7:12-13 and John 18:36).

❖ **Jesus the Man:** real, flesh-and-blood, historical person who was born according to prophecy

❖ **Lord (King) of God's heavenly kingdom:** a Divine Personage, since no mere human being is capable of ruling this

❖ **Christ (Messiah):** the Redeemer and Savior of prophecy, the One who fulfills God's promises to the Jews and brings salvation to the entire world

One and the same Person: the Lord Jesus Christ

Having confirmed Jesus' divinity through the miracles that He [Jesus] performed, God the Father exalted His Son to the most pre-eminent position in all of Creation (2:33; see Acts 5:31, Ephesians 1:19-23, Philippians 2:9-11, and Hebrews 8:1-2). The only way that Christ could receive "all authority in heaven and on earth" (Matthew 28:18) is to sit at the right hand of the Father Himself—the One who possesses all this authority in the first place. As the one is true, so is the other. Similarly, "The proof of Christ's having been exalted to God's right hand is seen in the Spirit's presence."[86] The presence of the Holy Spirit, as just demonstrated by the roar of wind, flames of fire, and speaking in tongues, proves that Peter's words are true and that God is with him, just as His Holy Spirit was with Christ. "For it was not David who ascended into heaven" (2:34)—i.e., David could never occupy the heavenly throne of God. David was a great king, but he was not the Son of God; he lacked the authority and moral supremacy to perform as a Divine Being. Peter alludes to the statement that Jesus Himself had put before the Jews shortly before His death (Matthew 22:42-46).

Peter has made an irrefutable defense of Christ and His testimony—a defense inspired by the Holy Spirit Himself (as Jesus had promised; see

---

86   McGuigan, *The Reign of God,* 75.

Matthew 10:16-20). He now states the plain and inescapable verdict: "God has made Him both Lord and Christ [Messiah]—this Jesus whom you crucified" (2:36). Think of the accusation: *you people just killed your own Messiah!* Or, just as awful: *you just killed the Son of the God whom you claim to revere and worship!* It was bad enough to kill a prophet of God, but to kill His own Son will certainly bring upon them a dreadful curse. Even so, Jesus had predicted all of this (Matthew 21:33-45).

If Jesus is not Lord, then we have no reason to obey Him; if He is not the Christ, then He is a false prophet, posing as one who only pretended to fulfill God's prophecies—and we have no reason to obey Him. If He was not a *real person*—if there really was no flesh-and-blood "Jesus" to begin with—then we have no reason to obey Him. The *fact* of Jesus being both Lord *and* Christ is absolutely essential to our salvation. Only because He is who He said He was—and proved it sufficiently with signs and miracles, culminating in His resurrection from the dead—do we have the hope of eternal life in His name. Just as we are baptized in His name, so we believe He will save our souls in the power and authority of that name. As Peter will later say, "There is salvation in no one else; for there is no other name under heaven that has been given among men by which we must be saved" (Acts 4:12). The *emphasis* in this passage (2:36) is on Jesus' authority as King (Lord); it simply does not address His simultaneous role as our Eternal High Priest. The Jews needed to know that Jesus' position exceeded even that of Moses, since they would not have obeyed Him otherwise. This is a point Peter will address directly in his second sermon (in chapter 3).

Peter's invitation for salvation (2:37-40)

Peter's words have a powerful and sobering impact on the minds of all those who hear them. There are literally thousands of listeners gathered before him—a "multitude" like what often assembled around Christ in His early ministry. These people are "pierced [lit., pricked, stung, or cut] to the heart" for one or more of the following reasons:

- ❏ Sorrow—for the loss of their Long-anticipated Messiah.
- ❏ Guilt—for having been exposed as the *murderers* of this Messiah.
- ❏ Fear—for God's wrath and vengeance for this murder.
- ❏ Finality—in that what was done could not be undone.

Those within the crowd who are overcome with sorrow and dread ask pleadingly, "Brethren, what shall we do?" (2:37). While some men had just mocked Peter for being drunk, now many are turning to him for help. "Denial on their part was impossible. The question they asked is a full admission of their guilt."[87] Peter's response (2:38) is clear and direct:

- ❏ "Repent": this requires a change (turning) of one's heart *and* behavior. God cannot show mercy and grace to anyone who refuses to *stop* doing what is sinful and *begin* doing what is right in His sight. Such repentance, in itself, is nothing different than what John the Baptist preached, although many of the Jewish rulers rejected John to be a genuine prophet of God (Matthew 3:1-12, Luke 7:26-30; see also Matthew 21:23-27).
- ❏ "Be baptized" [Greek, *baptizo*, lit., "immersed" or "whelmed (with something)"]:[88] Peter's audience is familiar with the rite of baptism. It had been practiced as a ritual cleansing among the Essenes, as a part of a Gentile's induction as a proselyte of the Jewish religion, and most recently as a response to John the Baptist's preaching. But this baptism has two unprecedented features: it is administered "in the name of Jesus Christ"; it is associated with the "gift of the Holy Spirit." Burial in water symbolizes one's death to his former life *and* his full immersion in his new vocation (Romans 6:3-7). Baptism is a divine requirement necessary for being clothed with Christ (Galatians 3:27), cleansing one's conscience (1 Peter 3:21), and calling upon the name of the Lord for salvation (Acts 22:16).[89]

---

87   Lenski, *Acts of the Apostles*, 104.

88   *Strong's* (electronic edition), #G907.

89   John MacArthur says (on 2:38): "Those who teach baptismal regeneration—the false teaching that baptism is necessary for salvation—see this verse as a primary proof text for their view" (*The MacArthur New Testament Commentary: Acts 1—12* (Chicago: Moody Press, 1994), 73. MacArthur mistakenly puts together two different

"Each of you" indicates a personal commitment to Jesus Christ; there is no possibility for baptism on behalf of someone else.

❑ "In ... Jesus Christ": Peter deliberately puts Jesus (the Man) together with Christ (the Messiah).[90] This is the first time this is spoken in Scripture (chronologically) after Jesus' own use of the compound name in John 17:3. "In the name" means *by the authority of*, necessarily implying an appropriate and permissible appeal *to* that authority (see Matthew 7:21-23, Matthew 28:19, and Acts 4:12).

❑ "For the forgiveness of your sins": If the Jews want God to forgive them, they must comply with Peter's instructions. What Peter is *really* saying (though it is not yet fully understood) is that they need to cease being Jews (in their allegiance to the Law of Moses) and become *Christians* instead.[91] If they refuse to repent and be baptized, they cannot be forgiven; they will remain guilty of murdering the Son of God (and all of their other sins).[92]

---

things: "baptismal regeneration" and the necessity of baptism for salvation. Baptismal regeneration *is* a false doctrine that teaches that baptism *by itself* is the means of salvation. "Baptism is pure gospel that conveys grace and salvation from God through Christ; it dare not be changed into a legal or legalistic requirement that is akin to the ceremonial requirement of Moses such as circumcision" (Lenski, *Acts of the Apostles*, 107). Yet, it is *not* a false doctrine to teach that baptism is necessary *for* salvation. The entire book of Acts supports this teaching, as does the rest of the NT. It is not "proof-texting" to teach exactly what a passage states. MacArthur's desperate defense of the "baptism is not necessary" position (73-75) fails entirely to handle the subject of baptism in becoming a Christian in a biblically contextual manner. Furthermore, there is not a single instance in the NT of anyone becoming a Christian or being referred to as being "saved" (from Acts forward) apart from being baptized into Christ. "The idea of an unbaptized Christian is simply not entertained in the NT" (Bruce, *The Book of the Acts*, 77). For further study on the subject of baptism, I recommend my book, *Being Born of God: The Role and Significance of Baptism in Becoming a Christian* (Summitville, IN: Spiritbuilding Publishing, 2014); go to www.spiritbuilding.com.

90   Proving that Jesus and Messiah are one and the same Person is a consistent practice used throughout Acts in any preaching to the Jews; see Acts 17:1-3 for an excellent summation of this. John will later say that to *deny* that Jesus is Messiah [Christ] is blasphemous and makes one an "antichrist" (1 John 2:22-23, 4:2-3, and 5:1).

91   For detail on the term "Christian," please see comments on Acts 11:26.

92   We cannot say, "Baptism *itself* forgives sins," because this is not biblical. It is God who forgives sins through one's appeal to the blood of Christ (Ephesians 1:7, Colossians 1:13-14, et al). However, it is also true that water baptism is a necessary act of faith in the *process* of that appeal (or, calling on His name), so that the result of baptism *as* an act of faith most certainly *is* forgiveness (1 Peter 3:21).

"Forgiveness" is a hallmark of the new covenant which Christ's blood inaugurated (Ephesians 1:7, Hebrews 8:12).[93] Peter is inviting these people *into* this new covenant relationship. Their appropriate demonstrations of faith constitute an acceptance of its terms and conditions. It is impossible, all attempts by denominational commentators aside, to separate "repentance" from "baptism" grammatically, contextually, or theologically. If the one (repentance) is necessary, then so is the other (baptism).[94] "Peter's response makes both of these actions equally necessary. ... Whatever Peter says about the forgiveness of sins follows from both imperatives."[95]

❑ "And you will receive ... the Holy Spirit": Whatever God gives to people that they cannot obtain by any human effort or merit is a "gift"—an unearned, undeserved blessing bestowed with a distinct objective in mind. His saving grace includes any and all gifts of God for the purpose of salvation (Ephesians 2:8-9). In the present case, the "gift" is the sanctification of one's soul *by* the Spirit, which is impossible to separate from the indwelling of the Spirit Himself (see Romans 8:9, 1 Corinthians 6:11, and 1 Peter 1:2). There is a difference between "gifts" [plural] of the Spirit (as in 1 Corinthians 12:1-7) and "the gift" [singular] of the Spirit. In the context of salvation, this "gift" is given to *all* believers, not just some (Acts

---

93   "Repentance, baptism, and faith are theologically related. When the believer who repents is baptized he makes a commitment of faith. He accepts Jesus Christ as his Lord and Savior and knows that through Christ's blood his sins are forgiven. Indeed Peter instructs the people that baptism must be 'in the name of Jesus Christ for the forgiveness of your sins.' Forgiveness of sins takes place only through Christ in consequence of his death and resurrection (see Rom. 6:1-4)" (Kistemaker, *Acts*, 105).

94   The argument put forward by "faith only" proponents that "for" (from the Greek *eis*) in "for the forgiveness of sins" actually means "because of" is a desperate attempt to avoid the necessity of baptism in conversion. "...Many lexicons do not even give a 'causal use of *eis*' (because out of 1,773 occurrences of *eis* in the New Testament, only 4 might mean 'because'), and those that do, admit that such a translation is at best controversial" (Reese, *Book of Acts*, 77). "Faith only" believers claim that one must only *believe* in Christ to be forgiven of Him (often citing John 3:16). Yet *repentance* is far more than mere believing, and involves a work of human faith that is no different in kind than baptism. Both acts of faith are required in order to receive that which is promised: forgiveness of sins. Forgiveness is most certainly conditional, and the Holy Spirit here declares what (at least) two of those conditions are: repentance *and* baptism. One cannot "believe" in Christ while failing to do what God says is necessary in order to demonstrate that belief.

95   Gaertner, *Acts*, 80-81.

5:32); the Spirit is given *regardless* of any (later) ability to perform miracles.[96] The Spirit thus "testifies with our spirit that we are children of God" (Romans 8:16-17)—not *instead* of our spirit, or *despite* our spirit, but *with* our spirit. There must be agreement, then, between what the Spirit commands and what the believer actually does; both parties testify to this.

Being baptized "in the name of Jesus Christ" is *not* the same as being "baptized with the Holy Spirit" (Matthew 3:11, Mark 1:8, Luke 3:16, John 1:33, Acts 1:5). Baptism with the Holy Spirit is something *Christ* does, not the believer; baptism in water is something the *believer* does, not Christ. We must not confuse or interchange the two actions. Water baptism is commanded here, not Holy Spirit baptism. The following table helps to clarify the difference between: what is accomplished through baptism in water; receiving the Holy Spirit in becoming a Christian; and receiving the Holy Spirit (i.e., His power) for the purpose of performing miracles.

	Baptism in water	Receiving the Holy Spirit for salvation	Receiving the Holy Spirit for the ability to perform miracles
What is the purpose for this action?	Necessary act of obedient faith for becoming a Christian	Necessary act of God for becoming a Christian	Confirmation that the message (being preached) is truly from God

---

96   The imparting of this gift—in *the context of receiving forgiveness and salvation*—has nothing specifically to do with the ability to perform miracles. To "receive" the Holy Spirit in *this* context means to gain access to God through His Spirit (Ephesians 2:18). Later—and in a *different* context—to "receive" the Holy Spirit refers to the power to perform miracles (as in Acts 8:14-17 and 19:6). This latter context does require that a person first be made a Christian—we have no evidence of the apostles conferring the ability to perform miracles upon anyone who is not yet a Christian—but the two contexts must be understood separately. It is when people blend them that they arrive at erroneous conclusions (such as, becoming a Christian automatically grants you the power to perform miracles).

	Baptism in water	Receiving the Holy Spirit for salvation	Receiving the Holy Spirit for the ability to perform miracles
Who participates in this action?	The believer in God who is becoming a Christian	All those who are redeemed by Christ: His entire church	Only those whom the Holy Spirit chooses and those upon whom the apostles lay their hands to impart this action
Who performs this action?	A Christian (in helping a believer become a Christian)	The Holy Spirit, by the authority of Christ	The Holy Spirit, whether by His own decision or through the agency of the apostles
What is the result of this action?	When accompanied by any other necessary acts of faith, one becomes a Christian and is forgiven of his sins	The newly-formed Christian receives access to the Father through the Spirit for all spiritual blessings	The believer is able to perform miracles, with no specific reference to salvation
How often will this action be performed (historically)?	As often as people respond in obedience to Christ's gospel— i.e., perpetually	Only twice: once for the Jews (as a group; Acts 2) and once for the Gentiles (as a group; Acts 10)	Only until Christ's gospel has been fully revealed or the apostles are alive to impart this through the laying on of their hands

Regarding the question of whether the apostles and the 120 in the "upper room" were also baptized into Christ:

It is true that we do not have a specific account of these peoples' baptisms; it is not true that this proves anything by itself. We cannot prove anything for certain based upon silence alone.

What we do know, however, is what Peter—one of the apostles in that upper room—preached just a short time later: "Repent, and each of you be baptized in the name of Jesus Christ for the forgiveness of your sins…" (Acts 2:38). It is illogical to assume that Peter would command the Jews to do this, yet excluded himself and others. It was also Peter who wrote by inspiration, "Baptism now saves you" (1 Peter 3:21). Even though he was an apostle, Peter was not exempt from the process of salvation required of everyone else. Likewise, there is no record of Apollos being baptized into Christ (Acts 18:24-28), and yet both Peter [Cephas] and this man went about baptizing others (1 Corinthians 1:11-13). This latter action would be contradictory to these men's teaching, if indeed they were not baptized themselves.[97]

Likewise, those who had been baptized by (or according to) John the Baptist must now be baptized into Christ (see 19:3-5, for example). John's baptism and *this* baptism are not interchangeable; they are not for exactly the same reasons; they do not accomplish the same things. Being baptized by John did not make anyone a Christian; being baptized in the name of Christ did not make anyone a disciple of John. No one, having been baptized by John, entered into the Lord's church, since this church did not exist until Christ ascended to the right hand of the Father. It is with His authority as *King* that He was able to become the builder of His *church*; one necessarily follows the other. In reality, John's baptism *prepared* (or, was intended to prepare) these Jews for baptism into Christ (Matthew 3:1-3, Luke 1:13-17, et al). This is not a "re-baptism," as some have called it, but a different baptism altogether. ("Re-baptism" indicates the repeat of the exact same action for the exact same outcome, as in a re-marriage or re-enlistment. While both baptisms are indeed immersions in water, the purposes and outcomes are entirely different.)

The "promise" (2:39) alludes to the substance of Joel's prophecy, summed up in 2:21: "everyone who calls on the name of the Lord will be saved." Thus, God promised long ago that there would be a

97   Sychtysz, *Being Born of God*, 238-239.

time when *any* person could be saved through a singular and universal means and enjoy the indwelling of His Spirit. "For you and your children" (2:39) does *not* mean that literal children are being invited into the kingdom; this is unnecessary (see Matthew 18:1-4) and we see zero evidence of this here or later in Acts. It *does* mean that not only are those present being invited, but the invitation is extended to future generations as well. More so, *whoever* God calls to Himself through His gospel will be invited into this new covenant. This anticipates the admission of the Gentiles [non-Jews] into Christ's church, as Jesus Himself foretold (John 10:16). Peter speaks "many other words" to the people, indicating that we are getting the highlights from this sermon, not the entire delivery (2:40).[98] If we wonder sometimes how these people could have made a lifelong commitment to Christ based on what little Peter has said so far, we should remember that he actually spoke much more than this. "Perverse [crooked] generation" refers to the prevailing mindset of the Jews that resists God by rejecting His Son.[99] It is the same phrase that Jesus used in anticipation of such rejection (Matthew 17:17).

What is being offered to the Jews at this time is what is offered to every believer thereafter. God invites the believer through the preaching of His gospel to enter into fellowship with Him (2 Thessalonians 2:13-14). No one can come to the Father who is not called by Him in the first place (John 6:44). The believer responds to this invitation through his

---

98   Some commentators have been very critical of Luke, who was not present during the delivery of Peter's sermon, of taking the liberty of *inventing* what Peter might have said. This baseless charge is dismissed in light of the facts: Luke is an inspired writer; he no doubt learned of Peter's words from eyewitness accounts, even from Peter himself, in his investigation into the matter (Luke 1:1-4); accusations against Luke must be proven by evidence, otherwise they are mere opinions and nothing more; and the Holy Spirit would not allow something as important as the first proclamation of the gospel of Christ to be corrupted by the creative invention of any historian. I refer the reader to John Stott's much more elaborate response in his commentary, *The Spirit, the Church, and the World* (69-72).

99   "Perverse" is from the Greek *skolios*, from which "scoliosis," a deformed curvature of the spine, is derived. It refers to anything that is morally crooked or lacking in moral reasoning, as used in Philippians 2:15 ("crooked") and 1 Peter 2:18 ("unreasonable"). Essentially, Peter is telling his audience, "This present generation has abandoned the covenant of God and thus stands in divine condemnation—do not be swept away with it!"

obedience to the terms and conditions set forth in that gospel. Thus, God initiates the call, and the believer responds obediently to it; God offers divine grace, yet this grace is predicated upon one's genuine faith in Him. Christ is the reason *why* God can offer fellowship to the sinner and the sinner can enter into that fellowship with God. The Holy Spirit is necessarily involved in the entire process of this conversion. Christ provides a blood offering to atone for sins; the Spirit provides sanctification to make access to the Father possible; the Father owns salvation and gives this gift to whoever obeys His Son's gospel.

Three thousand people are added to Christ's church (2:41-47)
Three thousand people respond to God's calling; thus, three thousand people are baptized (2:41).[100] "That day" indicates a specific time period: not a week later, not a month later, not at some convenient time in the future, but *that day* in which Peter gave the instruction. These new converts continue in practices that will become common expressions of fellowship enjoyed by Christians everywhere. Devotion to these practices helps to ensure the health, endurance, and success of all believers, both individually and collectively. Four specific activities are mentioned:

❑ **Apostolic teaching**—teaching which originates from Christ's handpicked spokesmen. These men provide a direct link to divine authority, which is necessary for the instruction, direction, and mission of Christ's church. Just as the Hebrew prophets spoke the word of God to Israel, so the apostles' teaching provides the "commandment of the Lord" for His church (2 Peter 3:1-2). In fact, they are eager to hear and receive the apostles' instructions and to obey what they taught by the authority of Jesus Christ.

❑ **Fellowship with God's people.** The church is the spiritual *family* of all those who have been purchased by the blood of Christ; it is a

---

100   There is no need to explain the logistics of *how* this was accomplished. All alleged "problems" with this—there was not enough water; the apostles could not have baptized so many on their own; so many people would not have responded so quickly; etc.—can be met with reasonable explanation. But, in the end, we must simply accept the statement (that 3,000 people were baptized as a direct result of Peter's speech) at face value. Incidentally, there is a conspicuous connection between 3,000 people being saved at the unveiling of this new gospel and the 3,000 men who were killed at the unveiling of God's law for Israel during the golden calf incident; see Exodus 32:25-28.

holy *community* of "fellow heirs and fellow members of the body [of Christ], and fellow partakers of the promise in Christ Jesus through the gospel" (Ephesians 3:6). For this reason, Christians are admonished not to "forsake" their assembling together (Hebrews 10:25), but are expected to honor the brotherhood of believers with their mutual participation, edification, and collective worship of God.

☐ **Breaking of bread**—in this context, this refers to a *specific* "breaking of bread," not a common or ordinary one (as in 2:46).[101] In the context of collective worship, the only thing that this can possibly refer to is the Lord's Supper. This memorial is a primary reason *for* their coming together in the first place (see 1 Corinthians 11:17-26, where the same practice is mentioned but is being mishandled). This "bread" is meant as a sharing *of* the body of Christ (1 Corinthians 10:16), but is also to be shared *among* His body of believers.

☐ **Prayer**—the believer's lifeline to God for all communication, petitions, appeals for forgiveness, and thanksgiving. The church is told repeatedly to be "devoted to prayer" (Acts 1:14, Romans 12:12, Ephesians 6:18, and Colossians 4:2). Prayer is not for God's sake, since He already knows what we need (Matthew 6:8), but for *our* sakes, so we will learn to depend upon Him rather than ourselves or other people.

Meanwhile, the apostles continue to demonstrate the authenticity of their message by performing miracles in the presence of believers and unbelievers alike (2:43). Notice that the *apostles* perform these signs, not the "one hundred and twenty" of the upper room (1:15). Until the apostles lay their hands upon anyone, no one else performs miracles but these twelve men. Also, the task of teaching and addressing such a huge number of new converts is enormous; it may be *here* that the rest of the "one hundred and twenty" provide some assistance. On the other hand, we should not assume that the *entire* brotherhood is meeting at

---

101   "Breaking of bread" in the context of 2:42 indicates the Lord's Supper, as in Acts 20:7. There is a definite article used twice in the Greek text, rendering it "<u>the</u> breaking of <u>the</u> bread." This is immediately contrasted with "breaking bread" in 2:46, a euphemism for the sharing of common meals (like "doing lunch" today).

the same time and same place every day. The indication here is that of regular and purposeful fellowship, not limited to a weekly assembly. These people still have families, jobs, and other responsibilities; however, they manifest their devotion to the church by these collective actions. Likely, the Jerusalem temple may be the only venue capable of accommodating large gatherings; nonetheless, gatherings of the saints are happening on a much smaller scale as well ("house to house").

"Those who had believed" (2:44-45)—i.e., who had become Christians—begin providing for those in need among their own group, as we will see again in 4:32-35. "All things in common" does not at all indicate an obligated extraction of money from the believers, nor a forceful confiscation of private property. The monies collected are distributed based on *need*, not for the purpose of *equality* (i.e., in order to give every believer an equal share). Such benevolence is not given to the general public but is exclusive to the church itself. "[A]nd breaking bread from house to house, they were taking their meals together with gladness and sincerity of heart" (2:46)—to share a meal together (in the first-century culture) symbolizes an endorsement of one's beliefs or an acceptance of one's fellowship. (We also have examples of the opposite of this in 1 Corinthians 5:11 and 2 John 10-11.) "[H]aving favor with all the people" (2:47) indicates a widespread acceptance among the general populace due to the good behavior of these Christian men and women.[102] This will change in due time, however—not because this behavior will change, but because the Jewish leadership will drive a wedge between the general public and this newly founded church. "The new believing community was, in fact, the faithful remnant of the old Israel and at the same time the nucleus of the new Israel, the Christian church."[103]

---

102   Pliny the Younger, governor of Bithynia in the early 2nd century, wrote concerning Christians: "They assemble on a fixed day before daybreak, and sing responsively a hymn to Christ, as a god, at which time they bind themselves by means of an oath not to enter into any wickedness, or to commit thefts, robberies, or adulteries, or to falsify their work, or to repudiate trusts committed to them. When these things are ended, it is their custom to depart, and on coming together again, to take food, men and women together, yet innocently" (quoted in Hester, *The Heart of the New Testament*, 71-72). This provides a secular perspective into the noble character of early Christian assemblies.

103   Bruce, *The Book of the Acts*, 79.

"And the Lord was adding ... those who were being saved" (2:47) indicates that, because the church belongs to Christ, He alone has the authority to "add" to it. Such additions are made only when people submit to the terms and conditions of what He requires of them: specifically, repentance and baptism; generally, whatever else is required by Christ (such as in Matthew 16:24 and Romans 10:9-10) but is not mentioned here. While Christians baptize believers, they cannot add these people to Christ's church; this is the Lord's business, not ours. (Likewise, we can remove impenitent Christians from our assemblies, but we cannot remove them from Christ's church—that also is His business, not ours.) We should also recognize a clear distinction between our adding someone to our *congregation* and Christ adding souls to *His church*. These are not the same thing; these practices are done for different reasons and reach different conclusions.

∽ Chapter 3 ∽
Healing of the Lame Man; Peter's Second Sermon

Healing of the Lame Man (3:1-10)

It is not known how much time has passed between Pentecost and this account (3:1). Likely, it may have been weeks or even months. The "hour of prayer" refers to one of the Jewish times for prayer that correspond with the daily sacrifices (9:00 a.m. and 3:00 p.m.). The "ninth hour" is reckoned from a 6:00 a.m. beginning point; thus, it means 3:00 p.m.[104] It is not at all unusual—or improper—for Jewish Christians to continue the Jewish habit of going to the temple at the usual times of prayer. Notice that anyone going to the temple goes "up" to it, even though it is not the highest elevation in the city. This connotation implies a certain ethical and spiritual quality to the temple, suggesting that simply by being there one is closer to God.[105]

On the way to the temple is a lame man who has never walked, though he is over 40 years old (3:2; see 4:22). He is, by any natural standard, incurably crippled. Friends carry him to a certain place where there will be a great amount of foot traffic, since he makes his living by collecting alms from the people. The Herodian temple courtyard has nine massive gates, all 45 feet high except for one, which is 75 feet high. It is possible that this highest gate is the "Beautiful" Gate, also known as the Nicanor Gate (named after the wealthy Alexandrian Jew who donated it), which is decorated with gold, silver, and Corinthian bronze.[106] The temple area itself is massive (490 x 325 yards) and surrounded by an equally massive stone wall that towers over the Kidron Valley just outside the city. Blocks of limestone weighing up to several hundred tons apiece serve as its foundation, so finely engineered and positioned that a piece of paper cannot pass between them.[107]

---

104   See comments on 2:15.

105   Adapted from Lenski, *Acts of the Apostles*, 124.

106   Coffman, *Commentary on Acts*, 67. See also Josephus, "Wars," 5.5.2.

107   Paul Mitchell, "Acts of the Apostles and New Testament History" (unpublished; cited 2001), 3.2.

Peter and John may well have been good friends from their youth; they also worked together in the fishing industry (Luke 5:10). They also were two of the three closest associates of Jesus, James being the third (Mark 5:37, 9:2, 13:3, 14:33, et al). It is not at all unusual to see them paired together as we do in this account. It is possible that Peter and John have seen (and helped?) this lame man before. However, there is no indication that they purposely approach this man in order to heal him; they are on their way to the temple for other reasons. Rather, it is the lame man himself who attracts the attention of Peter and John in his begging for alms (3:3).

Instead of money, Peter offers him something far better: the opportunity to *walk* (3:4-6). "In the name of Jesus Christ" (3:6) means by His *authority*, which Peter will explain later (in 3:12-16). "Nazarene" refers to the town in which Jesus grew up (Nazareth), with which the people have long associated Him.[108] It is clear that the lame man does not understand what is being offered to him; Peter has to grab his hand and pull him to his feet (3:7). Instantly, however, the man is able to walk.[109] What Peter gives to this man is more than what earthly or man-made wealth could ever purchase: the ability to be *made whole*, to function as a normal, healthy human being.[110] Furthermore, the lame man not only leaps up on his own two feet, but he is immediately able to walk

---

108   We should remember that Jesus did not have a very good reception in His own hometown after He had begun His ministry (see Mark 6:1-6); at one point, the people there tried to stone Him to death (Luke 4:24-30). Also, because of the low status of Nazareth in comparison to the purist culture of Jerusalem, "Nazarene" was used by some as a term of derision and ridicule (see John 1:46). Here, however, Peter uses it intentionally to show that a Man (Christ) with the power to heal congenital paralysis is hardly one who lacks power or credentials. Just as with the "word of the cross" (cf. 1 Corinthians 1:18), Christ makes that which is otherwise shameful into a badge of honor.

109   Literally (in the Greek), Peter says to the man, "Be walking!"—a present imperative indicating continuous action (Lenski, *Acts of the Apostles*, 128). In other words, this man will not only walk for the present time, but will "be walking" from this point forward. He is instantly, completely, and permanently healed of his lameness.

110   According to the Law, a lame man could not serve as a priest (Leviticus 21:18); by extension, a man who was not *physically whole* (or, intact) could not participate in the holy assemblies of Israel. Thus, this miracle demonstrates more than just Christ's power to heal; it symbolizes that no physical defect can prevent a person from entering into God's covenant of salvation (see Micah 4:6). This will be especially evident in the conversion of the Ethiopian eunuch in chapter 8.

around without exercise (3:8).[111] The crowd's reaction to the miracle of the healing of the lame man is "wonder" and "amazement" (3:9-10). For *decades* they have seen this man lying helplessly, begging for alms—yet with a single command he is healed and leaping for joy!

Peter's Second Sermon (3:11-26)

Peter's accusation against the Jews (3:11-16)

The news of the lame man's healing electrifies the city, and people throng to the epicenter of attention: Peter, John, and the healed man himself (3:11). No doubt the man's own enthusiasm helps to fan the people's astonishment. The crowd is dumbfounded over what has occurred and seeks an explanation. This situation provides another ideal opportunity for Peter to proclaim the message of Christ. The "portico of Solomon" refers to a 60-foot-wide covered porch or colonnade on the eastern side of the Temple in Jerusalem, the roof of which was supported by a number of impressive pillars (John 10:23, Acts 5:12).

Peter first dismisses any of his *own* power or authority as the source of this man's healing (3:12). He immediately defers to Jesus Christ as the power behind the miracle. Notice how Peter links together "the God of Abraham, Isaac and Jacob"—a covenant-name expression—and "His servant Jesus" (3:13). Thus, Jesus' power to heal is from *the same God* that the Israelites have worshiped for centuries; God is therefore in full *support* of Jesus.[112] This fact only heightens the criminality of the Jews:

---

111   "The first word [leap] is a present middle participle. He was leaping up and down repeatedly. This would be the natural expression resulting from his joy at being healed. The verb 'walk' is in the imperfect tense. He continued to walk around, just as he had been commanded to do" (Reese, *Book of Acts*, 155; bracketed word is mine). As a side note: one trade secret of every magician is to have full control over the environment in which he performs his magic tricks. (We see this even today with regard to the so-called "miracle workers" and "faith healers.") What is impressive here, as in all other bona fide miracles, is that there is no manipulation of the environment, no pulling the lame man aside to mask any sleight-of-hand, and no need for a number of stage hands to help pull off the stunt. A miracle is not a trick, magic act, or dramatic performance. It is a genuine display of supernatural power that cannot be naturally explained or humanly duplicated.

112   Remember that Jesus was crucified as an alleged blasphemer of God (Matthew 26:65-66). Also, by deferring to Jesus' power as being that which healed the lame man,

they not only killed an innocent Man, but they killed a genuine *Servant of God* (3:14-15). Even worse, they killed "the Holy and Righteous One"—not *a* holy one, but *the* Holy One—a direct allusion to a Divine Being (Isaiah 43:15, Psalm 16:10, and John 6:69). The major points of the first part of Peter's message (3:12-18) include:

❑ This (lame) man was healed with supernatural power. No one is denying this or can deny it.

❑ This power came from Jesus, who, like Abraham, Isaac, and Jacob, is a servant of God. Yet, Jesus has already shown supremacy over any of these men, including His pre-existence of them (John 8:56-58).

❑ Jesus Christ is the One for whose death the Jewish *leaders* collaborated and to which the *people* consented.

❑ He is God's Holy One—but the Jews treated Him with dishonor and contempt, just as Jesus had accused them of earlier (John 8:49).

❑ He is the Prince [lit., Author] of life—but the Jews traded His life for a murderer (Barabbas) instead (Mark 15:7-15).

❑ God raised Him from the dead—because God's divine will *cannot be altered* by human intervention, and divine life is more powerful than death itself (implied).

❑ (Reprise:) The power these people have witnessed is from this Jesus, who has legitimate authority to perform such extraordinary miracles.

The use of "servant" (in 3:13) naturally recalls to the Jewish mind the so-called "Servant songs" of Isaiah 40 – 66, in which it is prophesied that the Servant of God will be highly exalted as a Great Redeemer of Israel (see Isaiah 42:1-4 and 52:13-15, for example). And "the faith which {comes} through Him ..." (3:16)—i.e., Peter and John's connection to this miracle is through their faith *in* Jesus Christ. The miracle could not have been performed otherwise. Thus, it is not

---

Peter necessarily implies that He is very much *alive* and able to exert this power. If God is *presently* the God of Abraham, Isaac, and Jacob—meaning, these men are still alive to God (Matthew 22:31-32)—then Jesus is also alive to God and no longer dead.

the lame man's faith that led to his healing, but the apostles' faith in Christ.[113]

A second invitation for salvation (3:17-26)

"I know that you acted in ignorance ..." (3:17)—this is not a concession, nor an exoneration of the crime; it is simply a statement of fact (see 1 Corinthians 2:6-8). Christ suffered in accordance with the prophecies concerning Him, yet this does not absolve the guilt of those who *made* Him suffer. The Law of Moses did not excuse an Israelite's ignorance of that Law when it was clear that he should have known better (see Leviticus 5:17-19). Even the heathen's ignorance of God was "without excuse" since he had sufficient evidence in the physical world to know of His existence and power (Romans 1:18-20). Calvin rightly notes, "Peter was saying that they acted through blind zeal rather than deliberate wickedness."[114] Yet Boles clarifies, "Their ignorance did not justify their crime, nor excuse them; but it was grounds for calling on them to repent."[115] In fact, there is never a need to speak of repentance except in the case of actual guilt. In the present case, such guilt will not be resolved until those responsible for His execution respond properly to the terms and conditions of God's salvation.

Peter gives an abbreviated course of action ("repent and return" —3:19), but the full instruction cannot be different than what he had earlier stated through the inspiration of the Spirit (recall 2:38). In other words, such conversion cannot exclude calling on His name, baptism,

---

113   We should add here: this formerly-lame man was indeed healed of his lameness, but in order for his *sins* to be forgiven, he will have to do whatever any other person who hears and believes in the gospel of Christ must do: he must believe that Jesus Christ is both Lord and Savior; he must repent of his sins; he must be baptized into Christ; and he must live thereafter as the Lord's disciple. We must not assume that people are made Christians simply because they are the recipients of miraculous action. Personal obedience to Christ is not negated or rendered unnecessary in *any* case, including those cases involving miracles. This point bears also upon the situation with Cornelius and company in chapter 10.

114   Calvin, *Acts*, 55.

115   Boles, *A Commentary on Acts*, 58.

or any other demonstration of faith and piety that is required for forgiveness of sins.[116] Their "return" is not to the Law, nor to God's covenant with Israel that served as the basis for that Law, but to God Himself (Luke 1:16). The only way *now* to "return" (or, be reconciled) to God is through obedience to His Son (John 14:6). "Wiped away" (3:21) is synonymous for forgiveness of sins, as in Acts 2:38. "The expression 'to wipe away' (or, 'to blot out') is taken from the practice of creditors charging their debtors, and when the debt is paid, the record is cancelled or blotted out, removed from the record. The word used here refers to the practice of writing such records on tablets covered with wax, and then by inverting the stylus, or instrument of writing, smoothing the wax again with the blunt end, thus removing every trace of the writing."[117] This calls to mind the promise God makes to those who call upon Him: "I will remember their sins no more" (Hebrews 8:12). The phrases, "times of refreshing" from the Lord, and "that He may send Jesus, the Christ [Messiah] appointed for you" (3:19b-20) refer to being at peace with God after having been reconciled to Him through His Son. God will not *literally* send Jesus to anyone, for He has already done this for the entire world (John 3:16), but His Son does become an Advocate to those who seek His intercession between them and the Father (1 John 2:1-2). The sending of Jesus in this manner necessitates forgiveness of sins, and vice versa.

The implications of 3:20-21 may be easily misunderstood. Jesus said that He would come again (Matthew 24:29-31), but *that* coming is in the context of judgment against Israel (in AD 70) for unfaithfulness toward its covenant with God. In the context of Peter's message, however, the "sending" of Jesus indicates the personal intercession of Christ, not a national "coming" (in judgment) and certainly not the end of the world (as some have assumed). Thus, the coming of "the Christ

---

116   This logic works both ways: in cases where only *believing* and *baptism* are mentioned (such as in Acts 8:12-13), this cannot exclude the need for *repentance* and *sincerity*. The only legitimate and responsible way to determine what must be done to become a Christian is to examine *all* the passages having to do with this process rather than just those verses that conform to one's preferred conclusion. There is no single passage in the NT that tells *everything* required of a person in order to become Christian.

117   Reese, *Book of Acts*, 165.

[Messiah] appointed for you" is a blessed event *for those who believe in Him*, accompanied with "times of refreshing" from the bondage of sin and their condemnation from God. Specifically, this coming of the Messiah is a fulfillment of the Old Testament prophecies that linked Him with the spiritual—not physical—restoration of Israel (compare Ezekiel 37:15-28 and Matthew 19:27-30, for example). This restoration is fulfilled in the establishment of Christ's church, the spiritual "Israel of God" (cf. Galatians 6:16) and the "heavenly Jerusalem" (cf. Hebrews 12:22).[118]

Moses predicted that a greater prophet than himself would arise from amongst the Israelites. He also warned that the failure to "give heed" to Him would warrant a divine curse (3:22-23; see Deuteronomy 18:15, 19).[119] Unless these Jews repent of their sins—and especially the proud defiance and wicked intentions that led to their having crucified their Messiah—God will destroy them. The Old Testament prophets' warnings of this kind of destruction (which came against unfaithful Israel and Judah) ought to be sufficient to convince them of what is coming.

The Jews virtually worshiped both Moses and his Law, yet Peter declares here that everything Moses wrote has been fulfilled in Jesus

---

118   Bruce (and others) thinks that this "restoration" is eschatological in nature, that is, it has to do with the end of time. Thus, he says that this requires a "renovation of all nature," meaning (I think) a complete restoration of the physical earth to an Eden-like condition (*The Book of the Acts*, 91, fn 36). This forces us to believe that there will *be* a physical restoration of the earth, or that this will even be necessary. Furthermore, this kind of far-reaching conclusion simply cannot be supported by Peter's words, nor can it have any connection to the points that he is making to the Jews.

119   The phrase "God will raise up for you a prophet" (in Deuteronomy 18:15) certainly has a double meaning. Not only did God *appoint* this new "prophet," but the prophecy itself conspicuously anticipates the fact that God *literally* raised (up) Jesus from the dead. While Moses died and was buried, and "no one knows his burial place to this day" (Deuteronomy 34:6), Jesus was *raised* from His burial place and we know *exactly* where He is today (recall 2:33). Thus, Moses was a *servant* of God, but Jesus is the *Son* of God (see Hebrews 3:1-6); Moses deferred to Jesus' authority, yet Jesus never deferred to Moses' authority except to say that "...he wrote of Me" (John 5:46); and Moses is dead, but Jesus is very much alive. By all accounts, Jesus is clearly the Prophet of whom Moses spoke; Peter only confirms for us what we already know by connecting the dots in Scripture. Despite this, many of the Jews did not listen to God's appointed Prophet—the risen Jesus—which is exactly what Jesus Himself predicted (in essence) in Luke 16:31.

Christ (3:24; see John 5:43-47). The "covenant" Peter mentions (3:25)
is actually that which God made with Abraham, *not* with Israel. The
Jews had failed to keep *their* covenant with God, but Abraham was
faithful to *his*.[120] God Himself was (is) still faithful to Abraham,
since everyone who comes to Christ becomes a recipient of blessings
promised through that covenant. God sent Christ to the Jews for this
reason, to fulfill this ancient promise; however, the Jews (and everyone
thereafter) must respond properly to Him (Christ) in order to inherit
such blessings (Galatians 3:6-9, 26-29). "Sons of the prophets" is an
honorable designation, but only if such "sons" demonstrate faithfulness
to the Father as the prophets did. "Families" does not mean that God is
saving whole families at a time, but that *no* "family"—i.e., national or
ethnic group of people—will be denied the opportunity to enter into a
covenant relationship with God through Jesus Christ. ("Family" in this
context is used in the same way "house" is used in 2:36, as a distinct,
identifiable group of many people, not a singular household.)

"For you first, God raised up His Servant and sent Him to bless you
by turning every one of you from your wicked ways" (3:26)—"for you
[Jews] *first*," but not *only* you (as in Romans 1:16). The fact that "all
the families ... shall be blessed" (cited from Genesis 12:3) indicates
that this covenant of salvation through Christ will not be limited to the
Jews but will be open to all men in due time. But the actual entrance
into the kingdom is conditioned upon repentance, just as Jesus foretold
(Luke 24:44-47). No one can enjoy fellowship with God who refuses to
abandon his "wicked ways." "Christ does not do away with the sins of
the faithful so that they are free to sin; he makes them new people."[121]

---

120   Moses told the Israelites that, while God's covenant with Israel was in response
to Abraham's covenant, they were actually two different covenants (see Deuteronomy
5:1-3). Even so, Christ fulfilled *both* covenants: He is the "seed" promised to Abraham
(compare Genesis 22:18 and Galatians 3:16); and He has satisfied everything required
by the law *of* the Israelite covenant (the Law of Moses).

121   Calvin, *Acts*, 59.

∽ Chapter 4 ∽
Peter and John's Arrest

The effect of the gospel in Jerusalem (4:1-4)
Peter's sermons have a powerful effect on the people of Jerusalem.
Literally *thousands* of Jews are turning to Christ—which means
thousands are turning *away* from the control of the priestly class, and
Judaism in particular. Every convert to Christ also symbolizes another
witness *against* the criminality of the Jewish rulers' treatment of Him.
This creates an unavoidable tension between the Jewish Council and
the church that will reverberate throughout the rest of Acts. Everett
Harrison rightly notes: "One of the main purposes of Acts is to show
that the Jews who rejected and crucified Jesus continued their rebellion
against God by rejecting the gospel of the resurrected and ascended
Jesus proclaimed by the apostles."[122]

The Sadducees are relatively small in number, but they wield great
power over the Jewish Council; the "chief priests" are Sadducees.[123]
Since the Sadducees do not believe in resurrection, Peter's preaching of
a resurrected Christ is particularly offensive and antagonistic to them.
Just as they sought to silence Jesus, so they now attempt to silence these
apostles. Underlying this, however, is another significant point: the
Sadducees' power (and wealth) is directly tied to their support of Rome
and its imperial oversight of Judea. Any disruption among the people
jeopardizes that already-fragile relationship (as alluded to in John
11:47-48).

> Luke makes it plain that both waves of persecution were
> initiated by the Sadducees (4:1 and 5:17). They were the
> ruling class of wealthy aristocrats. Politically, they ingratiated
> themselves with the Romans, and followed a policy of
> collaboration, so that they feared the subversive implications
> of the apostles' teaching. Theologically, they believed that
> the Messianic age had begun in the Maccabean period [post-
> Babylonian exile, ca. 167 BC]; so they were not looking for

---

122   Quoted in Coffman, *Commentary on Acts*, 82.

123   Bruce, *The Book of the Acts*, 97; also see "Introduction" in this commentary.

> a Messiah... They thus saw the apostles as both agitators and heretics, both disturbers of the peace and enemies of the truth.[124]

Thus, the Sadducees' concern is not merely theological; it is also (if not largely) political, and most certainly economical, and is complicated by their own conflicts of interest.

While Peter and John are in the middle of teaching new converts, a group of priests and Sadducees have them arrested (4:1-3). "The captain of the temple guard" belongs to one of the families of the chief priests and ranks just below the high priest in authority. The "temple guard" is a hand-picked body of Levites whose job it is to maintain law and order in the Temple courts.[125] This arrest happens somewhere between 6:00 p.m. and 9:00 p.m., which means several hours have passed since the healing of the lame man, assuming the two events occurred on the same day. The priests and Sadducees waste no time in convening the Council on the following day to render judgment against these men. Nonetheless, the preaching of the gospel continues without these two apostles, and "many of those who had heard the message believed; and the number of the men came to be about five thousand" (4:4). (This appears to be an aggregate number which includes the original three thousand believers from Acts 2:41.) This shows that the success and propagation of the gospel is aided by but not wholly dependent upon the firsthand involvement of Peter and John. "The Sadducees could arrest the apostles," Stott observes, "but not the gospel."[126] As time went on, the apostles will die out, but the church will carry on with its earthly task without them—but not without the record of their witness or the authority of their teaching.

Peter and John stand trial before the Council (4:5-12)
In the first century, the Council (a.k.a. Sanhedrin, lit. "[the] head seat")

---

124   Stott, *The Spirit, the Church, and the World*, 95; bracketed words are mine.

125   Bruce, *The Book of the Acts*, 95, fn. 4; see also 1 Chronicles 9:11, 2 Chronicles 31:13, and Nehemiah 11:11, where the "leader of the house of God" is the same position as "the captain of the temple guard."

126   Stott, *The Spirit, the Church, and the World*, 96.

consisted of seventy (some say seventy-two) men—elders, scribes, and priests.[127] It is thought to be modeled after the seventy elders who were appointed to help Moses in judging cases for the Israelites (see Numbers 11:16-17). This group serves as a sort of Supreme Court for all Jewish legal, ethical, and religious matters. These men have the right to sentence a man to capital punishment, but they require Roman permission to carry it out (see John 18:31-32). Council members are often Pharisees and Sadducees, and are overseen by the high priest, who in the present text is Caiaphas (served AD 18-36). Annas, his father-in-law, is himself a former high priest (served AD 7-15); five of his sons become high priests for some period of time. The other men mentioned (John and Alexander) are unknown to us for certain. High priests are, at this time, imposed and deposed at the decision of Roman governors; the tenure of a high priest can be long or short, the transitions often abrupt and undignified. Often the candidates for office pay the Roman officials handsomely for an appointment.

The charge against Peter and John is implied rather than stated (4:7). Instead of specifying a particular crime, the Jewish leaders indirectly accuse them of speaking without proper authority. (Anyone speaking about Jewish Law without the approval of the Council is, in their eyes, speaking without authority, since they recognize themselves as "the" authority. This same stratagem was used against Jesus [Matthew 21:23] but failed miserably.) It is characteristic of the Council to be vague and ambiguous, hoping that their defenders—in this case, Peter and John— will unwittingly incriminate themselves with their own testimony. "It appears the authorities are highly disturbed and making tactical mistakes in their state of mind. The first mistake a lawyer should never make is, 'Never ask a question you don't already know the answer to!' It could be added, 'Don't ask a question in court when you don't want

---

127   "The whole history of post-exilic Judaism circles round the high priests, and the priestly aristocracy always played the leading part in the Sanhedrin. But the more the Pharisees grew in importance, the more were they represented in the Sanhedrin. ... In the time of Christ, the Sanhedrin was formally led by the Saducean high priests, but practically ruled by the Pharisees" (Paul Levertoff, "Sanhedrin," *ISBE* [electronic edition]; see also Josephus, "Antiquities," 18.1.4). The Sanhedrin ceased to exist in AD 70 upon the destruction of Jerusalem.

the answer to be made known!' They are about to get an answer they didn't want brought up!"[128]

Jesus promised that His disciples would be brought to trial, but He also promised that they would not be left alone (Matthew 10:17-20):

> But beware of men, for they will hand you over to the courts and scourge you in their synagogues; and you will even be brought before governors and kings for My sake, as a testimony to them and to the Gentiles. But when they hand you over, do not worry about how or what you are to say; for it will be given you in that hour what you are to say. For it is not you who speak, but it is the Spirit of your Father who speaks in you.

Seizing the initiative—and capitalizing on their failure to be specific—Peter thus turns the tables on his accusers (4:8-12). First, he questions their problem with having a sick man made *well*—as if this was a crime at all. Second, he accuses *them* of being the murderers of an innocent Man, whose identity cannot be mistaken: "Jesus Christ the Nazarene, whom you crucified...." Not just "Jesus the Nazarene," but Jesus *the Man* who is also *the Messiah of prophecy* whom they call *the Nazarene*. This is as if to say, "Think about it: I *healed* a sick man, but you *killed* an innocent man, yet you are putting *me* on trial! This is completely *wrong* on all accounts." While the Jewish leaders had crucified Jesus in order to silence Him, "God raised [Him] from the dead." The necessary implication is: if God is with this Man (whom He raised), then He cannot be with those who murdered Him.[129] Lenski rightly observes:

> Peter says this to men like Annas and Caiaphas here in the midst of their Sanhedrin following. The whole Sanhedrin had tried to hush up the resurrection of Jesus, Matt. 28:11-15. Here it faced them with even stronger evidence than that which the Roman guard brought from the tomb. No dead Jesus could work a miracle such as this; the risen and glorified Jesus alone could

---

128   Mitchell, "Acts," 4.2.

129   This is, in essence, the same argument that Jesus has already made; see John 8:37-49 and 16:1-3.

do that. So Jesus had healed when he was alive; lo, so he had healed now after this Sanhedrin had crucified him![130]

"He is the stone which was rejected ..." (4:11)—i.e., they had themselves unwittingly fulfilled the very prophecy spoken against them, which further vindicates Christ's innocence (Psalm 118:22; see Matthew 21:42, 1 Peter 2:7). A "cornerstone" refers to the first-laid and most important foundation stone of a structure that determines its levelness, orientation, and stability.[131] Clearly, the structure implied in this statement is Christ's church. Just as the foundation of the temple in Jerusalem was set in place with a cornerstone, so Christ's spiritual temple—His church—is established by the power and authority He possesses as the Son of God (see Matthew 26:59-64, John 2:18-22, and Ephesians 2:19-22).

Peter then makes a pivotal and exclusive statement: "And there is salvation in no one else; for there is no other name under heaven that has been given among men by which we must be saved" (4:12). "Salvation" [Greek, *soteria*] literally means "deliverance" or "a rescuing." The *connection* to the lame man is his deliverance from his lameness; the *context* clearly implies a spiritual "salvation," that is, the deliverance of one's soul from divine condemnation. "In no one else" is an emphatic negative statement: there is no other route to salvation apart from submitting to Christ's authority. There is no other *Savior*, and there is no other *way* to the Father (John 14:6). Being "saved" necessarily implies that we were previously (and otherwise remain) *lost*—"dead" in our sins (Ephesians 2:1) and "excluded from the life of God" (Ephesians 4:18). It also means that we stand in *divine condemnation*, and will thus receive the "wrath of God" unless and until we are saved. If there was no such condemnation, then there

---

130   Lenski, *Acts of the Apostles*, 163.

131   "While all the passages [in which "cornerstone" is found] indicate the stone at the corner, there appear to be two conceptions: (a) the foundation-stone upon which the structure rested (Job 38:6; Isaiah 28:16; Jeremiah 51:26); or (b) the topmost or capstone, which linked the last tier together (Psalm 118:22; Zechariah 4:7); in both cases it is an important or key-stone, and figurative of the Messiah, who is 'the First and the Last'" (Edward Mack, "Cornerstone," *ISBE* [electronic edition]; bracketed words are mine).

would be no need for forgiveness. Likewise, "salvation" is the state of being saved *from* something—in this case, God's divine wrath—and not just a religious state of mind. "But God demonstrates His own love toward us, in that while we were yet sinners, Christ died for us. Much more then, having now been justified by His blood, we shall be saved from the wrath of God through Him" (Romans 5:8-9). All this to say: whenever we talk about being "saved," we should remember what it is we are being saved *from*, and the awful price that Christ paid to save us.

The Council's response to Peter's defense (4:13-22)

Peter's defense is possibly only summarized by Luke; he likely said much more than what is recorded here.[132] The career scribes, theologians, and religious politicians are stunned by having Galilean fishermen take them to task in their own areas of expertise. "Uneducated and untrained" (4:13) indicates that Peter and John have not been schooled in the rabbinical teachings or academies; the same was said of Jesus (John 7:15). Yet the wisdom, clarity, and boldness of these fishermen-turned-evangelists is impressive; the Jewish rulers are "amazed" with their poise and eloquence. They also begin to associate Peter and John with Jesus—despite Peter's earlier denials (John 18:25-27).

The impact of Peter's words rattles these men to their core (4:14-17). As when Jesus had confounded them before, "they had nothing to say in reply" (Mark 3:4, Luke 14:5-6).

---

132   The goal of Luke's narrative, as with any use of genuine rhetoric, is not to write verbatim what a speaker said (because this is virtually impossible without a recording device), but to focus instead upon the content and arguments that the speaker puts forth. "Just as a writer was expected to represent faithfully the strategies, tactics and results of a battle, but not necessarily all the fine movements of each combatant, so a writer was expected to represent faithfully the strategies, tactics and results of a speech, without necessarily recording the exact words used on the day" (Gempf, "Ancient Literary Setting," 264). This does not take away from the *authenticity* of a speech or our focus on specific words used by the recorder/historian. Luke chooses words carefully and precisely to document what happened and what was said. This is as valuable as an eyewitness's account of a case, even though that person's account may vary word-for-word from each telling of it. We must not overlook, either, the divinely-guided inspiration of Luke's account. In that light, he will record nothing more or less than what the Holy Spirit wanted recorded.

Peter's defense, in substance was this: "We have done a good deed. Are you who are guilty of murdering the Messiah going to punish us?" No wonder the rulers were in a place of great embarrassment. They had no charge against the apostles in the first place, and they could find no flaw in Peter's defense. The Sanhedrin did the only thing they could do if they were going to save face—they stalled for time, that they might consider their dilemma.[133]

The Council's deliberations achieve nothing. They cannot deny that a miracle has occurred (as in John 11:47).[134] Even so, the fact of this miracle means nothing to these men—such is the depth of their unbelief. Also, they dare not address Peter's stinging accusations. The best they can do, under the circumstances, is resort to threats and intimidations. Apparently, they think so highly of their ecclesiastic authority that they can "command" people not to speak a message that is confirmed by nothing less than *miraculous proofs*. This kind of reasoning is not only absurd, it is delusional, desperate, and shows the level of insincerity to which these men have sunk. One thing that *has* been accomplished, however, is they affirm the "name" of Jesus Christ is directly connected with the power to perform such undeniable miracles. Previously, the Jews attributed Jesus' power to Satan—a baseless charge which Jesus immediately destroyed (Matthew 12:24-29). In the present case, it seems they *know* this (healing of the lame man) was a heavenly miracle, but they are still unwilling to accept its necessary conclusions. At the end of this passage (4:22), we discover that the formerly lame man is "more than forty years old." This further adds to the credibility of the miracle. This is not a fraudulent claim; for decades, the people have known about this man's crippled condition.

---

133   Reese, *Book of Acts*, 182.

134   The account of the healing of the lame man is the first and lengthiest account of any healing in Acts. Stott (*The Spirit, the Church, and the World*, 103) notes five significant characteristics: the man's crippled condition was real and congenital, and apparently no doctor could heal him; this healing took place by a direct command given by Peter made in the name of Jesus Christ; the healing was instantaneous, not gradual; the healing was complete and permanent, not partial or temporary (3:16, 4:10); and the healing was publicly acknowledged to be "indisputable." Those who claim that the church is still performing miracles today would do well to compare what they *claim* to be modern miracles with those that are actually *performed* in the NT record.

His instantaneous healing cannot be attributed to anything short of a miracle—it cannot be explained away otherwise.

Peter's response to the Council bluntly implies that their court order *once again* stands in opposition to God, as when they falsely indicted His Son as a blasphemer. "You be the judge" (4:19-20) is an intentionally ironic statement, since these men represent the highest judgment in the land among Jews. If the question had been asked of them, "Which is right: to serve God or heed the words of men?" they would have replied, "To serve God." Yet, rather than carrying out the will of God, their judgment is blinded by fear of the people (Matthew 21:26 and John 12:42-43). Regardless, the apostles' position remains unchanged: "we cannot stop speaking about what we have seen and heard."[135] (Peter revisits this same thought in his own epistle years later; see 1 Peter 3:13-17.) This also provides a precedent for Christians today: we can endure immoral governments, unfair treatment from higher authorities, and even illegal imprisonment, but we must never violate the commandments of God in order to satisfy the threats and demands of mere men, regardless of how important those men think themselves to be.

Despite the apostles' defiance of their court order, the Council did nothing other than issue more threats, and then released the two men (4:21-22). Dr. Joseph Klausner, a Jewish scholar, provides an insightful observation here:

> This was the first mistake which the Jewish leaders made with regard to the new sect. And this mistake was fatal. There was probably no need to arrest the Nazarenes, thus calling attention to them and making them "martyrs." But once arrested, they should not have been freed so quickly. The events showed on the one hand that the new sect was a power which the authorities feared enough to persecute, and on the other hand

---

135   "This was an open defiance of the authority of the Sanhedrin, when it conflicted with the authority of God. This was also an implication that the authority of the Sanhedrin was in defiance of the authority of God. The Sanhedrin was to learn that there were some things that it could not do; it could not put to silence the apostles" (Boles, *A Commentary on Acts*, 71).

they proved that there was no danger in being a disciple of Jesus (he, of course, being the one who had saved them from the hand of their persecutors!).[136]

From this perspective, we can see that it is of greater benefit that the apostles *were* arrested than if they had simply been ignored by the powers that be. Clearly, the hand of God is in this situation. This is also evident in the fact that the Jewish Council has long since disappeared from existence, yet the church of Christ continues to grow even to this day.

The apostles' prayer (4:23-31)

Peter and John, upon their release, reunite with "their own companions," who are not specifically identified but must have at least included the other apostles. (The word "companions" [NASB] or "company" [KJV] or "friends" [ESV] is supplied by the translators, being implied rather than stated in the Greek.) Instead of preaching spiteful tirades against the Council, they simply hand the matter over to God in prayer. Some highlights of this prayer:

❑ Acknowledgement of God's sovereignty and creative power, as opposed to the moral blindness and very limited power of the Sanhedrin (4:24).

❑ Affirmation of the divine inspiration of David's prophecies (Psalm 2:1-2), which are in contrast to the selfish interests of the Jews (4:25-26).

❑ Four parties are mentioned as antagonists to Jesus Christ (at His trial and execution): Herod Antipas, Pontius Pilate (Luke 23:1-25),[137] "the Gentiles" (i.e., Romans), and "the peoples of Israel" (4:27).

❑ These parties aligned themselves against Christ, thinking that they were going to defeat Him, but instead they had unwittingly fulfilled

---

136 Quoted in Bruce, *The Book of the Acts*, 104.

137 "Pontius Pilate was appointed in AD 25 sixth *procurator* of Judaea [*sic*], which on the deposition of [Herod] Archelaus, AD 6, had been attached to the province of Syria. [In] AD 36, he was sent to Rome by Vitellius, governor of Syria, to answer a charge brought against him by the Samaritans" (Page, *The Acts of the Apostles*, 108; bracketed words are mine).

God's "predestined" purpose (4:28; see Ephesians 3:11-12 and Colossians 2:15).

❑ The apostles pray, in essence, "Frustrate their plans and allow us to continue to boldly proclaim Your message." The apostles indirectly acknowledge their human fear of the Jews' intimidation, but know that they have no reason to succumb to it (4:29; Luke 12:11-12).

❑ They also ask that God would continue to manifest His power among them, as it provides an irrefutable testimony of the divine source of their message (4:30).

This serves as a model prayer for Christians today who are being harassed and persecuted for exercising their faith in Christ. We are to pray for our enemies, but we are not to pray that our enemies will succeed in their wicked plans. Instead, we are to pray that Christ would intervene for the sake of His believers *in whatever way He chooses* and that our enemies' plans would be defeated. This perspective serves the best interest of all parties involved. Psalm 2 provides an excellent basis for this prayer, since David expressed the true nature of the situation (of those persecuted for their belief in God) most appropriately. "The kings of the earth take their stand" against God and His people (Psalm 2:2), but the Lord is not intimidated by their threats. He knows where He stands, and the tremendous power and authority He possesses. We see the same scenario expressed in Revelation: while the church faces enormous persecution, God sits in majestic repose in the center of the universe—not unconcerned for His people, but unthreatened by their opponents. What the Sanhedrin does not realize (or will not admit) is that they have *made* themselves God's opponents by rejecting Jesus as the Messiah.

God acknowledges this prayer by physically shaking their meeting place, strengthening the confidence of the apostles and other disciples (4:31). "Filled with the Holy Spirit" does not automatically mean "performing miracles *by* the Holy Spirit." This expression requires context in order to reach this conclusion. Without such context, it simply means, "They were encouraged by the Holy Spirit who indwelled them, as evidenced by their resolution and conversation."

The community of believers (4:32-37)

God noticeably responds to the people's prayer and the people visibly respond to God with charity. The apostles, in particular, continue boldly speaking of the resurrection of Christ, they being eyewitnesses (testifiers) of this factual and historical event. For now, the apostles also oversee the distribution of monies being collected. We have not yet seen the appointment either of elders or deacons to assist in this process. The idea being expressed here (4:32-37) is not that everyone with property (or other possessions) is selling everything they have and thus are impoverishing themselves in the process. Rather, *as the need arises*, those who are able to make contributions (by letting go of worldly possessions) respond to such needs. Such collective action *by* believers both here and elsewhere throughout the NT is always for the benevolence *of* believers. As Reese says:

> The rights of property ownership have not been abolished, nor is the individual holding of property declared to be wrong. Rather we find each of the brethren willing and anxious to use whatever they possessed for the eternal benefit of each and any of their brethren. They loved so much they were willing to give all they had if it would help the other fellow.[138]

We never see a collective action of the saints being used to help or financially support those outside of the church itself. (This latter action would be the responsibility of individual believers, to do as they purpose in their hearts.) Whatever money that the church collects, it spends on its own members or for the expressed purpose of evangelism.

---

138   Reese, *Book of Acts*, 192. Personally, I cannot help but wonder if the *teaching about the "restoration of all things"* (recall 3:21) might have sparked this open generosity as well. As we see later in the Thessalonian letters, Christians believed that Christ would return at any moment, such that some were abandoning their personal responsibilities in anticipation of that return—a decision that Paul strongly rebuked. Even so, if Peter (and the other apostles) truly believed that Christ would return at any moment, and this was preached among the people, then this further explains the immediate decision to sell property and donate the proceeds to a bunch of relative strangers. This remains only speculation, since there is nothing definite to support it in the present context, but (given the Thessalonian experience) is worthy of consideration. And, it takes nothing away from the spirit of generosity itself that we see being displayed here, since these people sold and donated as an act of faith in God *and* in order to serve the best interests of fellow believers.

Furthermore, there is no indication of a general disbursement of the monies collected to *each person* in the church, but only to those who are "in need." Whatever is happening here in this section is in response to a specific need, and is not meant to implement a standing policy of the church for all time. On the other hand, there will *always* be financial needs among the saints (and in the preaching of the gospel) that only the saints themselves are uniquely obligated and qualified to fulfill. The mission of the church is *not* to serve as a social institution, tending to the welfare of unbelievers. The church is a privately-owned, privately-held, and transcendent entity that neither caters to social agendas nor seeks to address social ills. Christ never told His church to accept as its moral responsibility the burden of "saving" or even rehabilitating the community in which Christians live, except by the godly influence and preaching of those believers. The mission of the church is summed up in *discipleship*, not community service. At the same time, it is noteworthy that the apostles did not take care of the physical needs of the believers in Jerusalem *miraculously*. In other words, they did not call manna down from heaven, as God did with Israel; they did not feed thousands of people with a few loaves of bread, as Jesus did. Rather, God has shown His ability to provide for His people (in the cases cited), but He wants His people to be necessarily and instrumentally involved in the process. He wants believers to experience the joy—and sacrifice—of giving to a spiritual family in honor of Christ: "It is more blessed to give than to receive" (cf. Acts 20:35). He also wants those who *receive* such gifts to experience the joy—and humility—of depending upon someone other than themselves for their provisions. This dependence ultimately is upon God, not men, since all gifts and blessings originate from Him (2 Corinthians 9:10-11, James 1:17). Such are some of the lessons implicit in the passage under discussion.

The phrase "common property" cannot mean that each member suddenly assumes ownership of all Christians' properties and goods; Acts 5:4, for example, prevents such conclusions.[139] No one is *forced*

---

139   One of the tenets of Communism is the ultimate and complete abolition of private property: all privately-held land is given over to the State, which then disburses food and resources to the people on an "as needed" basis. Some (including noted

to give up anything; these are freewill offerings which, if properly given and received, will take care of all physical needs among the saints. Joseph, a.k.a. Barnabas, a native of the island of Cyprus (thus, a foreign-born Jew), provides a personal example of such a freewill benevolence. He is the first among the saints (since Pentecost) who is specifically mentioned besides Peter and John. He will play an instrumental role in the development of Paul's missionary work in the chapters to come.

The *selling* of land is rather intriguing here, since the Law of Moses put great emphasis on the *retention* of inherited land.[140] Granted, these Jews are not selling *all* of their land (thus, not all or any of their actual inheritance), but we are already seeing a shift in emphasis from the *land* to the *people*. Ancient Israel, as a nation, had to have a place to live and call their own; the Christian community, however, needs no such earthly stake or possession in order to exist and function as God's people. That which was once protected by necessity can now be relinquished for a *better* inheritance (Philippians 3:20-21, Hebrews 11:13-16).

---

atheists) have accused the church of being communistic in practice, citing 4:32-35 as their "proof." Yet, nothing to support Communism is "proved" by this passage. The actions are voluntary, not forced; funds are collected for God's church, not a man-made State; and the funds are distributed as godly charity, not for a mere redistribution of wealth. Furthermore, the *intent* here is not to make everyone equally wealthy or poor, but to respond to genuine needs of the brethren because they *are* brethren and because this is the right thing to do in God's sight (1 John 3:16-18). "Christians give. Communists take. Christians love. Communists hate. Christians worship. Communists blaspheme. One of these societies is of God. The other is of Satan... See any difference?" (Coffman, *Commentary on Acts*, 63).

140   Land that belonged to a specific tribe was meant to remain perpetually with that tribe, and specifically with the family that owned it. The land of Israel was directly tied to (and a manifestation of) God's fulfillment of His promises to those who came out of Egypt. However, Israel's exile into Assyria and Judah's exile into Babylon made the continuation of land inheritance difficult if not impossible; all the tribes to the north, for example, lost their land through transpopulation—i.e., the bringing in of foreigners to occupy a conquered nation. Nonetheless, the selling of land remains a significant transition.

∾ Chapter 5 ∾
Ananias and Sapphira; the Apostles' Arrest

Ananias and Sapphira (5:1-11)

Ananias ("Jehovah has been gracious") and his wife Sapphira become the first recorded recipients of divine punishment toward any Christians (5:1-2).[141] This chapter is sometimes titled, "First Church Discipline," but really it is not the entire church either receiving or meting out the discipline; it is God Himself dealing with two people whose actions threatened to jeopardize the good being done by others.[142] It has also been titled, "First Church Sin," which also is very misleading and incorrect. It is not the *church* that is sinning (the implications of which are quite disastrous), but two people within the church. Again, their sin will be dealt with swiftly and appropriately, which tells us how God expects us to take care of any sin that is discovered in our own congregations.

Specifically, the sin involved here is *not* Ananias' keeping back some of the proceeds of the sale of the land. Rather, it is his deception of *pretending* to give the full price when in fact this was not done (5:3-4). Neither Ananias' money nor the property he sold to obtain it was required of him; no one forced him to let go of it; no one forced him to give any or all of the proceeds to the church. Once the deed is done, however, Peter confronts Ananias face to face. "Why has Satan filled your heart?"—eerily similar to what happened with Judas (John 13:2, 27). Satan cannot *make* a person sin, but he has the ability to tempt a man's heart; *how* he does this is not fully disclosed to us. Sin occurs not during the temptation itself but in the illegitimate response *to* that temptation.

---

141   Sapphria's name means "beautiful" or "jewel"—"A name found almost exclusively among the Jerusalem rich of the 1st century," which is an interesting side note to this account (Margaret H. Williams, "Palestinian Jewish Personal Names in Acts," *The Book of Acts in Its First Century Setting*, vol. 4, 95).

142   Incidentally, there are several parallels between this account and that of Achan; see Joshua 7. F. F. Bruce says: "The story of Ananias is to the book of Acts what the story of Achan is to the book of Joshua. In both narratives an act of deceit interrupts the victorious progress of the people of God" (Bruce, *The Book of the Acts*, 110).

While trying to deceive men, Ananias is summarily exposed by God and charged with the sin of *intent* and *action*. The deliberate intent to do evil as well as the evil act itself are both considered "sin" (James 1:13-15). "You have not lied to men but to God"—this is not to say that Ananias did not lie to men at all, but that the One to whom he is really trying to deceive is God Himself. So it is with all lies: a person may literally tell a lie to someone else, or he may simply try to deceive someone into thinking something is true when it is not. In either case, that person attempts to dupe God as well as his fellow man. Yet, the one who lies actually deceives himself into thinking that he will avoid accountability; "God is not mocked" (cf. Galatians 6:7). As indicated in the case of Ananias, God knows fully, accurately, and immediately the falsity of a person's heart.

Luke provides no record of Ananias' response, even if he gave one (5:5-6). "Ananias fell down and breathed his last"—a somewhat euphemistic way of saying that he suddenly collapsed and died.[143] The timing and manner of his death are not natural or coincidental, but are imposed upon him by God, not Peter. God's judgment against Ananias is swift and potent. Some today are critical of this, accusing Him of being rash or over-reactive. Yet the context supports God's decision (and we are not in a position to question it): the infant church can weather a great deal of *external* threats and pressure, but it is not yet prepared to deal with *internal* corruption. Such rottenness has to be excised immediately and properly so as to maintain the integrity of the group itself. "The young men ... buried him" (5:6): "It was the Jewish practice to bury the dead before sunset on the day of death."[144]

---

143   "Breathed his last" is from the Greek *ekpsucho*, lit., "yielded up (one's) spirit," or "gave up the ghost" [KJV] (see John 19:30 and James 2:26) (*Strong's* [electronic edition], #G1634).

144   JFB *Commentary*, on 5:6. Boles says: "The circumstances required a speedy burial; neither the place nor the circumstance would admit of much formal preparation for a funeral. It was customary among the Jews to bury on the same day that death occurred; coffins or caskets were not in use at that time, and they simply 'wrapped him round' with possibly his mantle that he had worn. This was done without delay and without sending his wife word" (*Commentary on Acts*, 79). But Gaertner rightly observes something more than just a practical matter: "Though it is true that burials in the first-century Palestine often took place the same day as the death, this burial seems particularly unceremonious. There is no mention of a funeral procession, no mourning, and apparently no effort to contact Sapphira. ...The lack of sympathy in this tragedy

How the church keeps this information from Sapphira, we are not told (5:7-10). It is possible that only a few people know what has *actually* happened (while the rest either know nothing or suppose that Ananias has merely died a natural death) and that these are silenced by Peter. Regardless, Sapphira is given a fair opportunity to provide a full confession of her participation in this crime. She, of course, does not do so, but lies just as her husband had lied; thus, his punishment now becomes her own. "Why ... have [you] agreed together to put the Spirit ... to the test?" (5:9)—to "test" God in this context means to question His decisions or ability. (Compare this with Malachi 3:10 and Matthew 4:7, for example.) Ananias and Sapphira questioned God's ability to *bless* them (if they had given the whole amount of the sale) and His ability to *detect* their trickery. It is one thing to ask God questions; it is a sin to question God by putting Him to the test (Numbers 14:22, Deuteronomy 6:16, Matthew 4:7, Acts 15:10, et al). Thus, God strikes her dead on the spot, and she is immediately buried alongside [lit., face to face (to)] her husband.

While God's judgment on Ananias and Sapphira came suddenly and without warning, the fact remains: this would not have happened if these people had not lied to God in the first place. God's divine response also foreshadows what is to come for *all* liars and deceivers, especially those who may presently masquerade as sincere believers (Revelation 21:8). It is not hard to imagine scenarios today parallel to Ananias and Sapphira's own situation:

- ❑ A Christian man publicly promises to donate a specific percentage of his earnings to the church—but later decides to spend that money on his credit card debt instead without disclosing this fact.
- ❑ Several families of a certain congregation pledge to offer extra support for a particular ministry of their church. Yet, soon afterward they leave that group and join a different one instead—leaving those who remain to shoulder this financial burden.

---

implies that the event was understood as God's judgment upon sin" (*Acts*, 108). See Jeremiah 16:1-7 for a comparable situation, where God told Jeremiah not to mourn for the people of Judah who receive divine judgment for their sins.

- ❑ A Christian woman promises to give her life to the Lord—and makes everyone think that she did—but she knows her allegiance is only half-hearted and yet she refuses to do anything about it.
- ❑ A Christian man makes a public commitment that he has entirely forgiven a fellow believer, yet he continues to exhibit bitterness and resentment toward that person.
- ❑ A Christian woman knowingly agrees to support a sinful behavior in which her husband has engaged; later, when their sin is discovered, she claims that she did this in order to be in "scriptural" subjection to her husband.

While we cannot always know about such deceptions, we can be sure that God does. In due time, He will reveal all that is hidden (Luke 12:2) and "will judge the secrets of men" (Romans 2:16). Men can be fooled, and false gods can detect neither sincerity nor insincerity, yet the God of heaven knows fully and accurately the heart of every person (John 2:24-25, Luke 6:8, 11:17, Hebrews 4:12-13, et al). F. F. Bruce rightly notes:

> [This] incident shows us, too, that even in the earliest days the church was not a society of perfect people. The narrator [Luke] refuses to idealize his picture of the primitive community, and lest his readers should over-estimate the unity and sanctity of the Christian body in those early days, he has put on record here one of those accounts which not only illustrate the honest realism of the Bible but serve as salutary warnings to its readers.[145]

"And great fear came over the whole church ..." (5:11)—this healthy fear for God's power and the apostles' position was the intended outcome of the manner in which this situation was handled. Some of this "fear" may be the realization that God does indeed know the hearts of men. Christians must fear God's great power to *destroy*, if indeed we stand condemned (Matthew 10:28); but we also must fear (revere) His great power to *save*, if indeed we have put our trust in

---

145   Bruce, *The Book of the Acts*, 112; bracketed words are mine.

Him (1 Corinthians 1:18). The fear brought about by God's discipline actually inspires both kinds of fear; the result is positive, not negative. We should consider, too, the positive effect of discipline carried out by the members of any given congregation toward one of their own impenitent members. If handled correctly, this can actually bring about a positive result for the entire group—regardless of whether or not the sinful person repents.

The Apostles' Arrest (5:12-42)

Miracles of the apostles (5:12-16)

The scene that Luke now describes (5:12) is reminiscent of the excitement and wonder generated by Jesus' own miracles of healing (Matthew 4:24-25, 8:16, 14:14, et al). These are performed "at the hands of the apostles." So far in Acts, it is the apostles alone who have performed any miracles; as yet, no one else has been given the power to do this. The miracles themselves are not exclusively performed upon *Christians* but "the people" in general. However, as a *result* of the miracles—and the preaching which accompanies them—many "men and women" believe in the gospel and are added to the church (5:14). While the apostles are the ones performing these signs and wonders, Peter remains the apparent leader among them. People believe they will be healed simply by having his shadow fall upon them; accordingly, they put the sick and paralyzed into the street in hopes that he will walk by (5:15; see also Acts 19:11-12). "Cots" are like small padded beds, usually belonging to wealthier people; "pallets" are thin mats that can be rolled up, and belong to the poor.[146] "But none of the rest dared to associate with them" (5:13)—i.e., the non-believing Jews who are not interested in becoming Christians are keeping their distance, likely because of what had happened to Ananias and Sapphira.[147] If God will strike people dead for insincerity, then only the sincere will choose to

---

146   JFB *Commentary*, on 5:15.

147   It has also been suggested that it was the Christians who were afraid of the apostles (see Boles, *A Commentary on Acts*, 82), but there is no indication for this elsewhere. The natural conclusion is that which is stated above: those sympathetic to the church—but who are unwilling to commit personally to its cause—show respect but remain aloof.

approach Him and call upon His name for salvation. Even so, those who do not believe hold the church "in high esteem" for the way that it is conducting itself. That esteem is not shared, however, by the members of the Jewish Council, as we will see next.

The apostles are arrested (5:17-42)

The Sadducees cannot sit back and watch what is happening any longer without taking action (5:17-18). "Sadducees, like many modern religions, don't care what you teach as long as it doesn't affect them"[148]—but they are clearly frustrated with the success and popularity of the church. They are also frustrated with their poor handling of their earlier arrest of Peter and John, which completely backfired against them. Just as Satan had filled the hearts of Judas and Ananias, so the Jewish rulers' hearts are filled with a satanic spirit of "jealousy" (see Matthew 21:15, Mark 15:10, Acts 13:45, and 17:5). Instead of arresting only Peter and John, they now arrest all twelve of the apostles. The Council's logic seems to be this: cutting off the head of the movement will cause it to collapse and fade away (as Gamaliel later implies in 5:36-37). They assume wrongly, however, that the apostles are the "head" of this movement rather than the power and authority of Jesus Christ (Colossians 1:18).

No amount of human effort—nor the walls of an earthly prison—can contain Christ's spokesmen if He determines otherwise (5:19-20).[149] "An angel of the Lord" is sent to free these men, even though the guards do not see these angels or the escaping apostles, and the prison doors are opened and then re-locked.[150] Upon their miraculous release,

---

148   Mitchell, "Acts," 4.6.

149   This scenario illustrates the *limitation* of the apostles' use of miraculous power. They could heal all kinds of ailments and diseases—even raise the dead (as we will see in chapter 9)—but they were not permitted to rescue themselves from a man-made prison. Miracles were used for God's purpose, not for oneself. By God choosing to rescue His apostles from prison apart from any human intercession, He proves (or, continues to prove) that the power to perform miracles does not originate with men, but with Him. God can do miracles whenever and however He chooses, but men can only do miracles when He permits them to do so. In either case, however, God's will is fulfilled.

150   Notice how God dispatches His "ministering spirits" (cf. Hebrews 1:14) whenever He chooses (see Matthew 1:20, 28:2-7, Luke 2:8-14, Acts 8:26, 10:3, 12:7,

the angel instructs the apostles, "Go …stand and speak …the whole message of this Life" (5:20). This serves as a kind of mission statement for the work of the apostles. This also serves as the responsibility of any Christian evangelist, to preach "the whole purpose" of God (cf. Acts 20:27)—not merely what is popular or easily accepted (2 Timothy 4:1-5). Thus, the apostles resume their preaching and teaching in the temple as before.

We cannot help but regard what happens next with a bit of humor (5:21-26). The Council convenes with all formality and seriousness, fully intending to reprimand and severely punish their prisoners. Yet, they are informed by their own officers that *the prisoners are not where they are supposed to be*. Not only is this extremely humiliating to all of the authorities, but it has them rattled and "greatly perplexed." When they are informed that the apostles are back in the temple "teaching the people" about Christ, the officers go and retrieve their prisoners "without violence," for fear of the people (see similar reactions in Matthew 14:5, 21:46, Luke 20:19, et al). This strongly suggests that the Christian community is of sufficient size and favorable reputation (recall 5:13) that it wields considerable clout in Jerusalem. Just as when Jesus was apprehended in the garden of Gethsemane, the apostles offer no apparent resistance to their own arrest.

Once the apostles are again presented before the Council, the high priest (likely Caiaphas) strongly rebukes them (5:27-28). Notice that no mention is made of *how these men escaped prison undetected*; this time, the Council purposely avoids bringing up anything that they themselves cannot explain. They focus instead on two things: their own human authority and their unwillingness to take any responsibility for Jesus' death. The Council—and especially the high priest—are incensed by Peter's accusation concerning the blood of Jesus ("[you] intend to bring this man's blood upon us"). It cannot be that the Council is saying, "We are not responsible *at all* for 'this man's' death," for many of its members most certainly plotted against Jesus (John 11:47-53), condemned Him to death with an alleged charge

---

and 27:23). These intercessions come at critical moments, when human effort will not work or when divine judgment is necessary (as in Acts 12:23).

of blasphemy (Matthew 26:62-66), and even asked for His blood to be upon their heads (Matthew 27:24-25). Their fierce contention is with the claim that Jesus was *innocent* (and thus they sentenced to death an innocent man) and that He is the *Messiah* (and thus they are responsible for executing God's Anointed). The apostles' case is airtight, yet the Council members resist admitting to any criminal action. Their hardness of heart is reminiscent of Pharaoh's hard heart in Exodus 7 – 10: as the evidence continues to increase, so does their unwillingness to accept that evidence.

Peter's initial response is succinct yet timeless: "We must obey God rather than men" (5:29). His following message is also brief but powerful (5:30-32): God "raised up Jesus" to be a prophet among the people (see notes on 3:22-26); the Council, however, raised up Jesus upon a cross. God raised Jesus in glory and honor; the Jews raised Him up as an object of shame and dishonor (see John 8:49, for example).[151] In other words, the Council, while professing to uphold God's honor, is actually antagonistic to Him (John 16:1-3). Nonetheless, "God exalted [Christ] to His right hand"—i.e., the Jews' efforts could not deter or overcome the will of God. "Prince and Savior" confirms what has been said before: it is necessary to believe that Jesus serves both of these functions, not one or the other. If He is "Prince" (or Lord), then He has the authority pronounce innocent those who have accepted the terms and conditions of salvation; if He is Savior, then He is the actual source and provider of that salvation (recall 4:12). "We are witnesses of these things"—a resounding theme of the apostles (1 John 1:1-3)—"and so is the Holy Spirit" (5:32). This latter witness is accomplished through the testimony of the apostles and the miracles that they have been performing. Thus, besides the testimony of men, Christ also has the testimony of God's Spirit (as He had promised in John 15:26-27 and 16:8-11). The next statement—"God has given [the Holy Spirit] to those who obey Him"—extends beyond the scope of the apostles, miracles, and the early Christian community. It refers instead to a pledge of salvation from God to believers of all time (see 2 Corinthians

---

151   "The verb [for "put to death"] is put in the perfect tense to indicate the deed has been done but the impact is still being felt" (Gaertner, *Acts*, 113; bracketed words are mine).

1:21-22 and Ephesians 1:13-14). It is an all-encompassing statement, in the same vein as John 17:20.

The following scenario (5:33-40) is similar to those who would later unblinkingly stare down the prosecution of the medieval Roman Catholic Inquisition. Peter and the apostles are, in the Council's eyes, ordinary and unlearned men; yet their convictions in Christ and sheer defiance of Jewish authorities have the Council members completely unhinged and unable to cope rationally with the situation. The Council's first impulse is to have the apostles executed, but they are restrained (at least in this case) by the calming advice of one of their own prominent members. Gamaliel the Elder (as he is known) is the most revered teacher of his day and the leader of the school of Hillel, a somewhat liberal-minded group of learned Jews.[152] Even though the Council is under the general influence of the Sadducees, the Pharisees (such as Gamaliel) have a much more favorable relationship with the people. For this reason, the Sadducees will often defer to their judgment before acting on their own. As Josephus will later note, "[The Sadducees] are able to do almost nothing of themselves; for when they become magistrates, as they are unwillingly and by force sometimes obliged to be, they addict themselves to the notions of the Pharisees, because the multitude would not otherwise bear them."[153] It is widely assumed that Saul (Paul), one of Gamaliel's most famous students (Acts 22:3), is present at this private meeting.

---

152   Bruce, *The Book of the Acts*, 124. He was actually the grandson of Hillel, one of the most influential (liberal) rabbis of this era (JFB *Commentary*, on 5:34). "He was interested in Greek literature and encouraged his students to study it. His teaching tended toward a more spiritual interpretation of the Mosaic Law.... Gamaliel was the first among seven teachers to receive the title *Rabban*, a higher form of the epithet, '*rabbi*,' which in the form *Rabboni* is applied to the risen Jesus by Mary Magdalene (John 20:16). "Rabbi" means "my teacher"; "rab" means "teacher" (Robertson, *Word Pictures*, 387). He was held in such esteem that it is related in the Mishna (*Sota* 9:15), that 'with the death of Gamaliel the reverence for the Law ceased and purity and abstinence died away'" (King, *At the Feet of the Master*, 60). "It has been imagined by some that he became a Christian: and why he did not become so is known only to Him who understands the secrets of the human heart. But he lived and died a Jew; and a well-known prayer against Christian heretics was composed or sanctioned by him. He died eighteen years before the destruction of Jerusalem, about the time of St. Paul's shipwreck at Malta, and was buried with great honor" (Conybeare and Howson, *Life and Epistles*, 48).

153   Josephus, "Antiquities," 18.1.4; bracketed words are mine.

Gamaliel's counsel is, in essence: Let's not do anything rash (5:34-39). He cites a couple of men of recent history—Theudas[154] and Judas, who both had spearheaded impressive campaigns against the Romans—whose followers dispersed once their leaders were killed. (The "census" referred to here is not the same as that in Luke 2:2, but was a few years later, ca. AD 6.[155]) Thus, his advice is: if the apostles' mission is of men, then it will run its course and dissipate over time; otherwise, not even the full determination of the Council will be able to stop it. We should remember that Gamaliel is a Pharisee in the midst of a Sadducee-controlled Council; as such, he is closer to the common people than are the aristocratic, Roman-supporting chief priests.[156] He is not willing to accept the conclusion that the apostles *are* from God (despite all the evidence supporting this), but he realizes that the Council cannot afford to overreact and threaten its reputation as a competent and legitimate court of law. "The only oversight in Gamaliel's statement is that he did not say *when* it will be overthrown. He and his colleagues may be

---

154 Josephus records that a magician named Theudas led a rebellion against Rome (ibid., 20.5.1), but this occurred some fourteen years after this present account. Some historians have thus criticized Luke for making an anachronism. But this assumes that Luke actually read Josephus, then misquoted him; or it assumes that Josephus' record is more reliable than Luke's. This is not to say that Josephus was indeed mistaken: two separate uprisings by the same name are possible; other explanations exist as well (see Coffman, *Commentary on Acts*, 116-117). In the end, we are not compelled to pit Luke against Josephus in this case; we are not forced to choose one over the other, as Robertson supposes (*Word Pictures*, 68). Luke's information stands on its own and is necessarily endorsed by both Paul and the Holy Spirit as being truthful and accurate. Kistemaker writes: "The historical accounts of Acts at times have a parallel in the works of Josephus. But this fact does not signify that Luke depended on Josephus to furnish him with historical details. On the contrary, a comparison of parallels from Luke and Josephus clearly indicates that the two writers relied on independent traditions" (*Acts*, 23). It should be noted, too, that Luke most likely finished his account in AD 62-63, whereas Josephus' account was not completed until AD 93.

155 Josephus, "Antiquities," 13.1.1.

156 Gamaliel's speech provides further clues about the Pharisees' perspective. It also shows Luke's concern for verisimilitude [lit., seeking the appearance of truth—CMS]. Although the Christians would not see themselves as a faction comparable with the followers of Judas or Theudas, Gamaliel compares these groups as a councillor [*sic*, and so hereafter—CMS] might plausibly do. He is the only counsillor we have met who has the slightest interest in discussing the Christians' claims, and this alone sets him apart from the chief-priestly councillors, just as the Pharisees of the Gospel, who loved to debate issues, were different from the chief priests there" (Steve Mason, "Chief Priests, Sadducees, Pharisees and Sanhedrin in Acts," *The Book of Acts in Its First Century Setting*, vol. 4, 150)..

dead and gone by the time this human thing, if it be human, is finally overthrown. The question for Gamaliel was as to how long he could wait."[157]

The Council accepts Gamaliel's wait-and-see advice, not because they are concerned with fighting against God (because they do not believe that these men *are* from God), but because they fear losing the support of the people (John 12:42-43). Instead of executing the apostles—which technically would require Roman approval (see John 18:31)—they have the apostles beaten. "Flogging" likely refers to a whipping or scourging of 39 lashes (so as not to violate the Law—Deuteronomy 25:3); even though the account here is brief and sanitized, such beatings are intentionally brutal and demoralizing.[158] After being further threatened "not to speak in the name [lit., according to the authority] of Jesus," they are released. It is impossible, of course, to reconcile the alleged objectivity of Gamaliel's counsel with the subsequent beating and threats: the one contradicts the other.[159] The apostles remain completely undeterred, however. They continue doing exactly what Christ had commissioned them to do, despite the threats of the Jewish authorities. Instead of cowering in fear or suppressing their ministry, the apostles rejoice that they could share in the sufferings of Christ (see 1 Thessalonians 2:14, 2 Thessalonians 1:5, and 2 Timothy 1:8). "Preaching Jesus as the Christ" (5:42) links the historical man Jesus, whom the Jews had crucified, with the long-awaited Messiah of biblical prophecy. Hester summarizes what is happening:

---

157   Lenski, *Acts of the Apostles*, 234.

158   It is amazing to see horrific beatings and executions reduced to such few words, as in the case of Jesus: "And they crucified Him" (Mark 15:24). It seems clear that the intent is not to sensationalize or even diminish such acts of torture, but simply to acknowledge them as real and historical. Even so, our imagination ought not to be limited to the words themselves, but we would do well—in appreciation of what such men endured for the Lord's sake—to put ourselves in the place of those being beaten, scourged, or even crucified. A sterile or sanitized version of suffering for what is right will leave us with entirely the wrong impression of what "suffering" is all about.

159   Lenski, *Acts of the Apostles*, 237. Boles rightly notes: "The members of the Sanhedrin may have felt that their honor was at stake, and that, if the apostles departed untouched, they themselves would be regarded as having proceeded against innocent men; hence, to save their honor and the honor of the court, and to make the impression that the apostles were guilty of some offense, they were scourged. This was a frequent, though a very disgraceful, punishment among the Jews" (*Commentary on Acts*, 93).

It is quite evident that a new force was at work in Jerusalem. The disciples had become a dynamic, courageous and aggressive company using every occasion for the propagation of their faith. Great numbers of people believed and were baptized. Miracles occurred with frequency and the whole city was stirred. The Jewish leaders who had thought when they crucified Jesus that they had stopped this movement discovered to their dismay that their difficulties had multiplied a thousand-fold. They didn't know how to cope with the situation, except with the use of physical force, but this did not stop these men. In vain the Sanhedrin met and deliberated and tried one measure after another, and still the movement swept on.[160]

---

160 Hester, *The Heart of the New Testament*, 240.

∽ Chapter 6 ∽
Appointment of Seven Servants; Stephen's Arrest

Appointment of Seven Servants (6:1-6)

"Now at this time ... a complaint arose" indicates that while the church is enjoying tremendous growth and the apostles are staring down the Jewish Council, trouble is brewing within the Christian community (6:1). "The daily serving {of food}"—or, "the daily ministration"—is not defined or accompanied with an explanation. Gaertner offers what is likely happening here:

> Two forms of benevolence were practiced by the Jews [at this time in history]. Every Friday relief officers would collect money for the poor in a box (*kupah*) and distribute enough for fourteen meals to those resident poor in the community. The second form was for poor strangers whose presence was temporary. The relief officers would go house to house to fill a tray (*tambuy*) with food and drink from which they would distribute to the poor. The description Luke gives here implies that the church had adopted a combination of these methods for "daily" distribution of food to widows.[161]

Regardless, it is important to recognize that the church is responding to a genuine and specific need; it is not simply feeding Christians who are hungry (but have other means by which to obtain food). A "Hellenist" formally refers to a person who has adopted and assimilated the Greek culture and philosophy into his lifestyle. In a much more general sense (as used in 6:1), "Hellenistic" simply refers to those (Jews) who were born abroad and who speak Greek as a primary language. "Hebrews," by contrast, are Jews born in Palestine (and eastward, even into the regions of former Babylonia) and speak Jewish Aramaic as a primary language. Most likely, in this case, the Hebrews far outnumber the Hellenists. The complaint [lit., murmuring or grumbling, as in John 7:12] specifically regards a failure to properly take care of the Hellenistic widows; the *implication* is that of favoritism and

---

161   Gaertner, *Acts*, 119; bracketed words are mine.

partiality.[162] Neither scenario is acceptable; both anticipate resentment and division. It is important to note that there is no actual proof of any *intentional* overlooking of these widows; nonetheless, immediate action is required in order to avoid tarnishing the image of the newly-founded church.[163]

Since we have no evidence that men have yet been appointed to the office of an elder, the twelve apostles themselves provide oversight for the church in Jerusalem. After the church is scattered beyond Jerusalem (Acts 8:4), this will change. Yet, the primary concern of the apostles is to attend to the spiritual and doctrinal matters of the church, not to "serve tables" (6:2-4). In other words, there are other capable men to whom this task can effectively and efficiently be delegated. This does not mean that the apostles refuse to serve tables, but that they have a different responsibility entrusted to them (similar to Paul's statement in 1 Corinthians 1:17: "Christ did not send me to baptize, but to preach the gospel"). It also does not mean that these men are to tend only to the mundane or utilitarian needs of the group, as many assume the sole function of deacons to be in modern churches. Their high qualifications of character necessarily imply that they are capable of—and expected to perform—far beyond such menial tasks.

It is *the congregation*—not a "men's meeting" or "committee" but *the entire group*—that is involved in the nomination and selection of these

---

162   In matters of ongoing financial assistance, we would expect these widows to conform to the requirements necessary for church support as described in 1 Timothy 5:3-16. However, the present situation (in 6:1ff) does not seem to indicate such a situation, but may much more likely be a temporary one brought on by the unexpected and prolonged stay of these women because of their conversion to the church.

163   Despite this account, "What is striking about our main source for early Jerusalem Christianity—the book of Acts—is that so little is said about socio-economic class distinctions. The wealthy are hardly noticed at all except for a few cases of extraordinary generosity. We cannot document that any of the High Priestly family or any of the governing elite were members of the earliest church. The lower class has the fewest references, although one could speculate that they had the largest representation. The submerged class enters the story only to indicate that the church is caring for them. The central figures are those that perform ministries of some kind, whether they come from the upper or lower class" (Fiensy, "The Composition of the Jerusalem Church," 229).

men.[164] The apostles, however, state the need for the selection, limit the selection to men "from among you," and specify the number of such men (seven). It is clear, too, that the apostles would not have appointed any men of whom they themselves did not approve. "Good reputation" indicates these men's good standing with the physical church; "full of the Holy Spirit" indicates their good standing with God as those who lead a holy life. This expression does not have any reference to the ability to perform miracles, but to the Spirit's visible effect upon their speech and conduct. Before the apostles lay their hands upon these men, we do not see any of the seven performing miracles. Immediately after the laying on of hands, however, we *do* see this. This is consistent with what we see later in Acts: with only two exceptions (the apostles, and then Cornelius and company), no one performs miracles prior to the apostles having laid hands on him. "And of wisdom"—not only are these men virtuous in character, they also exhibit mature and intelligent thinking. The task to which these men will be assigned (serving tables) is mundane, to be sure; however, they need to be qualified to represent the entire group in this public service.

---

164   This section is traditionally titled "the appointment of deacons" or "first church deacons," even though the word "deacon" is nowhere used in it. For this reason, some question whether or not the men being put forward actually become church deacons or are simply appointed as needed (like a temporary committee) to address a particular problem and nothing more. Furthermore, if these men *are* actual deacons, then they must be held to the same requirements as we find in 1 Timothy 3:8-13, meaning that these men must be married and have children (making Stephen's martyrdom all the more tragic). Another question then arises as to whether churches are allowed to appoint deacons in the absence of an appointed eldership. My thoughts, for what they are worth: First, after careful consideration, I find it unwarranted to call these men deacons in the same vein as what Paul describes in 1 Timothy 3:8-13. My conclusion is not absolute, but neither can be the opposite conclusion. The absence of the word "deacon," the temporary and limited nature of the situation at hand, and the fact that Philip (for one) so quickly leaves the church for Samaria (chapter 8) argues against the fixed role we would expect from an appointed deacon. Second, I know of nothing in the New Testament that prohibits a church from appointing deacons in the absence of appointed elders. No passage forbids it; no passage requires the one (elders) before the other (deacons); and we have no precedent one way or the other. It is tradition that compels us to think that we must have elders first, nothing more. Some argue that, since the twelve apostles serve as the Jerusalem church's elders, therefore this means that elders must be appointed first, then deacons. Even though I do agree (that the apostles are the early church's elders), the rest of the argument is presumptive and forced.

The men who are chosen (6:5) have names that are conspicuously Greek in origin[165]; however, it is also common for Jewish men to be known by a Greek name and a (corresponding) Jewish name in the case of some necessary connection with the Graeco-Roman world."[166] "Nicolas," however, is specifically identified as "a proselyte"—i.e., a Gentile convert to the Jewish religion, indicating that he also has been circumcised and (until his conversion to Christ) submitted himself to the Law of Moses. These men are not actually identified as deacons in this passage, but this is what they are by definition. ("Deacon" is transliterated from *diakonos*, which means "servant" or "minister," as in Mark 10:43 or Philippians 1:1; a form of this word is used in Acts 6:2 for "serve.") This is an appointment to a work, not an election to an office. Even if these men are appointed as literal church deacons, there is no such thing in the NT as the "office of a deacon," only that of an elder (1 Timothy 3:1). These men are presented before the apostles (6:6) who then lay their hands on them as a conferral of their approval *and* to bestow upon at least some of these men spiritual (miraculous) gifts (as evidenced by Stephen and Philip). The Holy Spirit's miraculous response also indicates His approval of what is being done here.

Stephen's Arrest (6:7-15)

The conversion of the priests (6:7)
As a side note, Luke informs us how prosperous the church has become, which is to imply that problems (like that which was just mentioned) are being dealt with and overcome. Furthermore, the priests are abandoning their status and ordination to become Christians. This shows how the gospel is eroding some of the ranks of its own opposition—the Jewish leadership itself. "Obedient to the faith" implies

---

165   Two of the early church "fathers" (Ireneus and Victorinus) apparently assumed, on the basis of the common name alone, that "Nicolas" later apostatized and became the ringleader for the "Nicolaitans" in Revelation 2:6, 15. This is absolutely without substantiation and is contradicted by other early church commentators (Bruce, *The Book of the Acts*, 129-130; Coffman, *Commentary on Acts*, 125-126).

166   A case in point would be Matthew [Greek, *Matthaios*], who was also known as Levi (Hebrew); compare Matthew 9:9 and Luke 5:27.

an objective and universal response to the body of sound doctrine that defines what actually is "the faith" in Jesus Christ (see Romans 1:5, 16:26, and 1 Peter 1:22). "The faith" indicates a standardized teaching of the apostles, which is the implementation of what Christ had instructed them to do (Matthew 28:19-20).

While "the priests" are often portrayed negatively in the gospels (because of their stubborn resistance of Jesus and His teaching), they are well-trained, well-schooled, and noteworthy men. The fact that "a great many" of them are accepting the gospel of Christ does not negate all of this training and experience but actually capitalizes upon it.[167] These men possessed a mastery of the Law and the Prophets—especially now that they see Jesus Christ as the fulfillment of these things. This provides an excellent scholarly backbone for the early church, and undoubtedly some of these men will serve as elders in the near future. At the same time, these men make a considerable sacrifice of their heritage, profession, and reputation among the non-believing priests, inasmuch as their loyalty now lies with Christ.

Stephen is accused and arrested (6:8-15)

Stephen's prominence is no doubt attributed to the great spiritual power imparted to him through the laying on of the apostles' hands (6:8). We are not to think that he abandoned his responsibility of serving tables in order to defend the faith; certainly he could do both tasks effectively (and so should any present-day deacon). It is clear, however, that the church is now facing opposition other than the Council itself. At this time, there are apparently hundreds of synagogues in Jerusalem.[168] "Freedmen" [Greek, *Libertinos*; lit., "Libertines"] usually indicates Jews who have been released from imperial constraint (i.e., forced slavery); for whatever reason, these men maintain this distinction and

---

167   "The Jewish historian Josephus [in *Against Apion*, 2.8] relates that in his day there were four priestly tribes and that each one of them numbered some five thousand members. 'These officiate by rotation for a fixed period of days.' On any given day, therefore, there were some five thousand priests in Jerusalem" (Kistemaker, *Acts*, 225; bracketed words are mine).

168   Robertson says there were 400 synagogues (*Word Pictures*, 75); Boles says 280 (*Commentary on Acts*, 99). It is safe to say that there were numerous synagogues, just as there were numerous nationalities of Jews in Jerusalem at this time.

use it as a basis of identity and solidarity. It has been suggested that Saul has sympathies for these Freedmen and their arguments, since some are from Cilicia, the region of his own birthplace.[169] This might also explain some of Saul's vehemence against the church—i.e., not only to preserve the Law (as he saw the situation) but also to justify the Freedmen's position.

Regardless, this fact remains: these men are unable to contend with Stephen either on an *intellectual* or a *doctrinal* level (6:10). "He spoke with such fearlessness, clearness of argument, understanding of the prophecy, and power of the Spirit that his speech was irresistible."[170] When dishonest men's logic fails them, they resort to misrepresentation, violence, and even murder; such is the case here. This is the first recorded occasion of the *people* being stirred up against a Christian (as opposed to merely the Sadducees). Both the "stirring up" of the people and the induction of "false witnesses" serves as an ugly precedent for future events, as we will see later in Acts. "Blasphemy" means sacrilege or the profaning (or speaking evil of) that which is holy. Stephen's alleged blasphemy against Moses refers to his having identified Jesus as the Christ [Messiah]; his blasphemy against God refers to his purported desecration of the temple ("this holy place"—6:13).[171] Both of these charges stem from the fact that the gospel of Christ will supersede the Law of Moses, the Jewish temple, and the priestly sacrificial system.[172]

---

169   F. J. Foakes-Jackson, *The Acts of the Apostles* (New York: Harper and Bros., 1931), 56; Robertson, *Word Pictures*, 76. Incidentally, "Cyrenians" are men from Cyrene (modern-day Libya) on the northern coast of Africa; "Alexandrians" are men from Alexandria, Egypt, which has (in Luke's day) the largest concentration of Jews in the world outside of Judea; "Cilicia" is a Roman province (in which Saul was born) that sits northwest of Syria, between the Tarsus Mountains and the Mediterranean Sea; and "Asia" refers not to the continent but the Roman province on the western side of the Anatolian Peninsula (modern-day Turkey), in which the seven churches from Revelation 2 – 3 will be founded.

170   Boles, *A Commentary on Acts*, 100.

171   Jesus *did* promise that "this temple" would be destroyed, but He referred His body, not the literal temple in Jerusalem (John 2:19-22). Yet, He also prophesied that the *literal* temple would be destroyed (Matthew 24:1-2, Luke 19:41-44). In either case, Jesus' words are *true* and (will prove to be) historically *accurate*.

172   It is critically important to understand that Jesus *never* changed the Law of Moses during His lifetime; He only expounded upon or explained it in ways that the people had not heard before. He clearly rejects any notion that He intended to violate

While the accusation is technically *correct*, it is also completely misunderstood and taken entirely out of context. Calvin observes:

> They accused Stephen of teaching that the form of the worship of God must be changed, and they saw this as a blasphemy against God and Moses. So their dispute with Stephen was over a matter of principle rather than facts. The question revolved around whether a person is dishonoring God and Moses when he suggests that the visible temple is the image of a more wonderful sanctuary [i.e., Christ] in which the fullness of God dwells [cf. Colossians 2:9] and teaches that the shadows of the law are temporary [cf. Colossians 2:16-17, Hebrews 10:1].[173]

Regardless, charges of blasphemy are most serious ones (Leviticus 24:16); the fact that the case is brought before the Council indicates the intensity of these Jews' contempt for Stephen's having humiliated them. "And they dragged him away" (6:12) indicates that they have abandoned all respect for Stephen's human dignity, since a man who has blasphemed God is regarded as no longer fit to live. There is no hint of a figure of speech here; they *literally* drag Stephen to his own trial. Since he has humiliated them, they apparently reason, they will humiliate *him* in this way.

This entire scene is reminiscent of Jesus' own arrest and trial before the Council. Alleged charges of blasphemy and conspiring to destroy the temple are once again dredged up, as they were in the trial against Jesus (compare John 2:19-22 and Matthew 26:60-66; see also Jeremiah 26:8-11). Even the use of "false witnesses" is reminiscent of Jesus' trial.[174] As for Stephen's face glowing "like an angel" (6:15), this might

---

the Law (Matthew 5:17-19) or "alter the customs which Moses handed down," although He did not always honor the man-made rabbinic traditions established long after Moses (Matthew 15:1-9, for example). The point is: we cannot say that Jesus "altered" the Law while at the same time affirm that He "committed no sin" (1 Peter 2:22), since *any* violation of the Law would be sinful. Furthermore, He could not be a worthy sacrifice for our sins if He Himself was a sinner.

173 Calvin, *Acts*, 92; bracketed words and citations are mine.

174 The hypocrisy of these Jews is evident in this simple fact: they will incite "false witnesses" to (allegedly) substantiate charges of blasphemy, yet being a false witness is

be just a figure of speech except that the context suggests otherwise. His angelic countenance is contrasted with the hardened and hate-filled countenance of his accusers and judges.

---

itself in direct violation of the Law (Exodus 20:16).

∼ Chapter 7 ∼
Stephen's Defense

Stephen answers charges of blasphemy against Moses (7:1-43)
Stephen's defense is the longest and most detailed speech recorded in Acts. Stephen himself represents a more important role *at this time* in the church's brief history than we can likely appreciate today. This is also the first time since the establishment of the church that someone other than Peter will give a defense for Christ.[175] This also marks a turning point in the relationship between the general public and the newly-formed church. Stephen's defense before the Council results in a persecution within Jerusalem, likely due to the blind zeal of Saul of Tarsus. It is the content of this defense—and the composure of Stephen himself—that ignites this persecution. He begins by talking about something near and dear to the heart of all Jews, namely, their own privileged history as God's chosen people. However, they do not see where Stephen is going with this until it is too late—and they will have no good answer to his conclusions once he gets there.

Stephen is brought before the Jewish Council (Sanhedrin)—the same group of men that condemned Jesus and threatened Peter and the rest of the apostles. The high priest (likely Caiaphas) simply asks, "Are these things so?" He is not about to incriminate himself with statements of his own; he wants Stephen to make his own self-incriminating statements. When given permission to speak, Stephen begins with essentially four responses to the charges of blasphemy against Moses:

❑ **First response (7:2-8):** Stephen affirms his high regard for the solemnity of God's covenant with the patriarchs (Abraham, Isaac, and Jacob) and the sons of Israel. The Promised Land (ancient

---

175   "This speech is commonly called Stephen's defence, or apology, but it is obviously not a speech for the defence in the forensic sense of the term. Such a speech as this was by no means calculated to secure an acquittal before the Sanhedrin. It is rather a defence of pure Christianity as God's appointed way of worship; Stephen here shows himself to be the precursor of the later Christian apologists, especially those who defended Christianity against Judaism. The charges brought against Stephen by the witness for the prosecution were garbled; Stephen sets forth here the arguments of which these charges were travesties" (Bruce, *The Book of the Acts*, 141; bracketed words are mine).

Canaan) was bequeathed to Abraham by divine decree; it was to be his physical inheritance by way of a covenant relationship between God and the patriarch. (Stephen quickly summarizes God's promises to Abraham as recorded in Genesis 12 – 17.)[176] This inheritance, however, would not be given to Abraham personally, but his posterity—and then only after "four hundred years" of enslavement and mistreatment in a "foreign land" (Egypt). The descendants of the twelve sons of Abraham's grandson, Jacob (Israel), will be the recipients of the promises made to their fathers. "Circumcision" was given as a sign of the covenant that guarantees this inheritance (Genesis 17), but the Jews have obsessively fixated upon circumcision as a status symbol of their unique relationship with God, which they assumed made them morally superior to all other men.[177]

❏ **Second response (7:9-16):** Jacob's sons were jealous of the attention he (Jacob) gave to the youngest, Joseph. As a result of this, they sold him into slavery and then lied about it to their father (Genesis 37). Yet, even though he was rejected by his own brothers ("the patriarchs"), Joseph was highly esteemed and protected by God. Because of a false accusation by Potiphar's wife, he languished in prison for up to 13 years. Yet, after interpreting Pharaoh's perplexing dreams—both the dreams and the interpretations being the result of divine intervention—he was elevated to the highest position in Egypt under Pharaoh (Genesis 39 – 41). Later, Joseph served as a type of messiah (savior) to his family, inasmuch as he provided for their welfare in Egypt to save them from an intense famine (Genesis 50:18-21). Jacob was buried in the tomb of Abraham in Canaan (at Machpelah; Genesis 50:13), and Joseph's bones were buried in Shechem, on the property which Jacob had

---

176   "The opening words of Stephen's defence imply that the people of God must be on the march, must pull up their tent-stakes as Abraham did, leaving national particularism and ancestral ritual, and go out where God may lead. In this Stephen blazes a trail later followed by Paul, and more particularly by the author of the Epistle to the Hebrews" (ibid., 143).

177   Paul will make the point later that circumcision actually preceded the Law of Moses, and that the initial promises to Abram (Abraham) were given while he was yet uncircumcised (Romans 4:9-13). Thus, while the Jews latched onto the value of circumcision as an act of righteousness in itself, Paul declares that the purity of one's heart is more important than an act performed upon the flesh (Romans 2:25-29).

purchased from the sons of Hamor (Genesis 33:19, Joshua 24:32). Both burials were signs that either predicted or confirmed that the promise God made with Abraham was genuine. Moreover, Stephen here begins to reveal a pattern of *Israel's rejection of men who have found favor with God*. This is merely an embellishment of Peter's last words before the same Council: "The **God of our fathers** raised up Jesus, whom **you had put to death**" (Acts 5:30, emphasis added).

❑ **Third response (7:17-37):** Stephen has specifically mentioned "the promise" twice so far (7:5, 17); this establishes another pattern, namely, that God works according to a specific purpose and reveals His plans to those who (are expected to) cooperate with them.

▪ Though accused of blasphemy against Moses, Stephen clearly demonstrates his loyalty to and respect for him as God's prophet. His reference to Moses' parent's refusal to obey Pharaoh's edict to kill all Hebrew males upon birth (7:19-21; Exodus 1:22 – 2:10) indirectly alludes to what Peter had already declared to the Council: "We must obey God rather than men" (5:29).

▪ Furthermore, God called Moses to be a deliverer of His people (Exodus 3:1-10), even though they had rejected him at first (Exodus 2:11-14). This calling was confirmed with a sign (the burning bush), and Moses' leadership was confirmed with numerous and unprecedented signs and wonders (7:36). This is another tacit allusion to the present situation: Christ's apostles' were identified by a sign of fire (recall 2:3) and then numerous miracles thereafter (2 Corinthians 12:12, Hebrews 2:3-4).[178] But as great as Moses was, he pointed forward to One even greater—the Son of God—and commanded the people to follow Him (Deuteronomy 18:15, 18, John 5:45-47, and Acts 3:22-23). Likewise, even though the apostles have demonstrated many signs, these have not been produced by their own power and authority, but Christ's (Acts 3:12-13).

---

178   Stephen does not mention it specifically, but the reason *why* Israel wandered in the wilderness for forty years was because of their having "ten times" failed to believe in God's ability to save them, even after He had successfully and single-handedly led them out of four hundred years of Egyptian bondage (see Numbers 14). Once again, Israel exhibits a pattern of rejecting not only Moses' leadership but also God's rescue of them.

- Stephen's point: Jesus Christ is neither a usurper of Moses' authority nor a blasphemer of God, since a blasphemer of God cannot perform genuine miracles (see John 3:2, 10:37-38). Therefore, it is not blasphemy to give allegiance to Him but is exactly what God's people are expected to do.

❑ **Fourth response (7:38-43):** Stephen then cites idolatry—the ultimate form of blasphemy—as being Israel's trademark violation of God's holy covenant. Even while God was delivering them from Egypt, the Israelites were clinging to their pagan gods and household idols (7:43). Their desire to return to Egypt translated to a lack of belief in God's ability to lead them. Their request for Aaron to make for them "gods who will go before us" is a direct violation of the first two of the Ten Commandments (Exodus 20:1-4)—commandments that they had promised to uphold (Exodus 19:8, 24:7).

- Thus, from the beginning the Israelites have established a clear pattern of rejecting God for other gods, just as they rejected those sent *by* God and chose lesser men over them.[179] This has culminated in their rejection of Christ [implied] and their having chosen a wicked man (Barabbas) instead (recall 3:14). So then, while there is no basis to the charge of blasphemy against Stephen, the charge against the entire nation of Israel has been confirmed by Moses himself.

- Stephen's quote in 7:42-43 is from Amos 5:25-27.[180] God has already removed the Israelites from their land (in exile to

---

179   This is particularly true with regard to Israel's (and Judah's) long history of resisting—and murdering—God's prophets and turning instead to false prophets and false visions; see Jeremiah 28 and Ezekiel 13, for example.

180   "Moloch" was originally an ancient sun-god of the Akkadians (ancient Assyrians), whose cultic worship was adopted by the Ammonites (under "Milcom"), Phoenicians, and other nations as well. Moloch (or Molech) worship often involved human sacrifice (see 2 Chronicles 28:3, 2 Kings 17:17, 21:6, and Jeremiah 19:4-5) and was expressly forbidden in the Law (Leviticus 20:2-5) (T. Nichol, "Molech," *ISBE* [electronic edition]). "Molech (as the name is elsewhere rightly spelt [*sic*]) means 'king.' He was an Ammonite deity to whom children were offered. The image is said to have been ox-headed, with arms outstretched (in which the children were placed) and hollow so as to be heated underneath: hence perhaps the phrase 'pass through the fire to Molech'" (Page, *The Acts of the Apostles*, 126). "Rompha" (or Rephan) refers to a worship associated with the planet Saturn, which also can be traced back to ancient Assyria (Bruce, *The Book of the Acts*, 154-155; Coffman, *Commentary on Acts*, 141-142; Max L. Margolis, "Chuin/Rephan," *ISBE* [electronic edition]).

Assyria and then to Babylon) for idolatry. Stephen's implication is that God will not tolerate an unfaithful people, but will take severe action again if they will not repent. This corresponds to Jesus' own predictions of divine condemnation against Jerusalem for her rejection of her King (Luke 13:3, 5, 19:41-44, 21:20-24, et al).

Stephen's argument is that it is the *Christians* who are following God, not the unbelieving Jews who idolized their Temple and Jewish heritage. The Jewish Council is following the example of the disobedient Israelites who, though they identified themselves with God, did not seek the will of God but instead stubbornly resisted Him. Stephen cites biblical and historical evidence to support his case; he will continue to do this until the Council refuses to hear anymore.

Stephen answers charges of blasphemy against the temple (7:44-50)
Stephen begins this next part of his defense by showing that God's glory and authority are by no means dependent upon a man-made temple. God waited patiently for *hundreds of years* for Israel to build a (permanent) temple (see Deuteronomy 12:5-7); His divine nature did not suffer in the least during that time. God also promised that He would *destroy* His temple if Israel turned away from Him (1 Kings 9:3-8). Regardless, God does not actually dwell in temples or anything made with human hands (Isaiah 66:1-2, Acts 17:24-25, et al); the heavenly sanctuary of God is one that has been made *without* hands (Hebrews 8:1-2, 9:11). "The argument seems to be that if the universe which God made could not contain him, how much less this temple which had been made by the hands of men. This is what Solomon said in his prayer at the dedication of the temple (2 Chron. 6:18)."[181]

God does not need temples made with hands, but He *did* commission the building of Solomon's temple. The purpose was not for God's benefit but that of the people of Israel. They needed a centralized and standardized system of Jehovah worship so that every person did not simply do what seemed "right in his own eyes" (cf. Judges 21:25) but instead submitted to the heavenly pattern. The temple system was

---

181   Boles, *A Commentary on Acts*, 115.

intended to define holy living for those in a covenant relationship with God *and* provide a physical point of reference for fellowship with God and the covenant community. By Jesus' day, however, this system had become corrupted by politics, power struggles, man-made traditions, fanatical religious fervor, and rebellion against God. What was intended for good had been hijacked by a corrupt group of elitists (the Jewish leadership) who used the temple for their own purposes. In so doing, they openly rejected any person—even God's Son—who challenged their authority or threatened their social, political, and religious positions within Jewish society. Thus, the Jews place an inordinate emphasis upon something which *God does not require*, yet they reject His Son whose allegiance He *does* require [implied].

These Jews pride themselves (as Jews continue to pride themselves today) as God's chosen people, yet they "have not known the Father" because they refuse to recognize Jesus as His Son (John 8:39-43). They put great emphasis on their status, and mistakenly believe that because they control God's temple in Jerusalem, therefore they are closer to God than all other people. In fact, if any non-Jew wished to worship God, he could only do so by going through *them* (another mistaken belief). God had made it clear that the Jews should not equate the presence of the temple in their midst with God's acceptance of their professed loyalty to Him (see Jeremiah 7:1-15 in particular). Likewise, Jesus made it clear that God showed great compassion to those outside of Israel (see Luke 4:23-28). Even so, the Jews have great and special advantages: covenantal promises, the Law of Moses, centuries of prophetic teaching and revelation, the Aaronic priesthood, the temple (see Romans 3:1-2, 9:3-5), and the fact that the *Son of God* walked in their midst and performed many miracles in their sight. These privileges were supposed to prepare the world for its Redeemer, not make those who received them proud, arrogant, and obstinate (see Matthew 11:20-24, Romans 10:16-21).

Stephen goes on the offensive (7:51-53)
In a masterful defense, Stephen has just turned the entire case on its head. He has proven that it is his *accusers* who are guilty before God, not him. By association, Stephen has just indirectly charged these

Jews with yet another form of idolatry: the worship of a man-made structure (the temple) and their subsequent blasphemy against the Son of God.[182] He now forcefully lands his entire argument: "You… are always resisting the Holy Spirit; you are doing just as your fathers did" (7:51; see Isaiah 63:10-11). The Holy Spirit has *always* been the voice of God's prophets; He has *always* been the source of divine inspiration. It is not surprising to have *Him* referenced whenever someone cites Old Testament prophecy, as Stephen does. (See also Mark 12:36, Luke 2:25-26, 1 Peter 1:10-12, Hebrews 3:7-11, 9:8, 10:15-17, et al.) "Stiff-necked" means obstinate, unyielding, insubordinate, and rebellious (as in Isaiah 48:4 or 65:2, which is quoted in Romans 10:21). "Uncircumcised" usually is a derogatory term for heathens and Gentiles (as in 1 Samuel 14:6, 17:26), whom the Jews held in contempt. Yet, Stephen applies this term to the Jews themselves with reference to their unholy disposition toward God and their persistent violation of His covenant (see Leviticus 26:41, Jeremiah 4:4, 6:10, and 9:25-26). Stephen purposely cites Moses himself ("So circumcise your heart, and stiffen your neck no longer"—Deuteronomy 10:16) as a stinging rebuke of their hypocrisy. While Stephen never once mentions Jesus in his defense, the implications are pointed and unmistakable. Just as the ancient Israelites persecuted and killed those who prophesied of Christ, so the Council has killed Christ Himself (Matthew 23:29-32). Just as ancient Israel rejected the law "as ordained by angels" (Galatians 3:19, Hebrews 2:2), so the Jews have rejected the gospel as ordained by God Himself (in Jesus Christ; see Hebrews 1:1-3).

The Council's response to Stephen's defense (7:54-60)

There is a reason why Luke (by inspiration) has dwelt upon the details of Stephen's trial. His defense showcases the illogic and illegality of the highest Jewish body of authority in Palestine—the Jewish Council (Sanhedrin). He has accurately proved through Israel's own history

---

182   "Stephen points to two problems with the [Herodian] temple when it came to be built. It had not been built according to God's pattern; its very form was an expression of human willfulness and disobedience. Worse, a temple 'made with hands' meant it was no different from idols, which were also said to be 'made with hands' (Ps. 115:4; cf. Is 46:6). The people preferred the golden-calf idol to Moses then, and they prefer the temple-idol now" (Barnett, *Early Christianity*, 220; bracketed word is mine).

that the Jews (as a nation) have systematically rebelled against God, His covenant, and His prophets. The present situation—i.e., the Jews' rejection of God's Son—is not an anomaly to this history but entirely consistent with it. To put it differently, nothing has changed: the ancient Israelites rejected their own leaders, violated God's covenant, and killed His prophets—and those to whom Stephen is speaking are doing the same thing (Matthew 23:28-36). Such impenitent action justifies the divine retribution that Christ promised would come upon Jerusalem (as a representation of the entire nation; see Luke 19:12-14, 27). Yet, it also vindicates the gospel of Christ as as legitimately superseding of the Jewish system.

Stephen's defense is unanswerable; the Council members are beside themselves with anger and frustration. Every time one of Jesus' disciples stands before them, *the disciple* gains the upper hand and it is *the Jewish authorities* who end up being put on trial! They are "cut to the quick" [lit., sawn through to the heart] and "began gnashing their teeth at him"—like a pack of frenzied, ravenous wolves ready to devour their prey (7:54). They have had enough; it is time for more serious, even extreme, action. Stephen's vision of "the glory of God" pushes them over the edge; they are bent now on nothing short of execution (7:55-56). (There is no reason to believe that anyone but Stephen himself sees this vision, but his response to it constitutes a statement of blasphemy, as far as they are concerned.) The Holy Spirit approves of Stephen; the Council calls for his death. Stephen has provided a multiplicity of evidences, to which the Jews have no rebuttal. Bruce offers what seems the most logical explanation of the "standing" of Jesus:

> It may be … that a standing posture is mentioned here because the Son of man at God's right hand is not only viewed as king and priest, but also—and this is most relevant to Stephen's special situation—as a witness. Stephen has been confessing Christ before men, and now he sees Christ confessing His servant before God [cf. Matthew 10:32]. The proper posture for a witness is the standing posture. Stephen, condemned by an earthly court, appeals for vindication to a heavenly court,

and his vindicator in that supreme court is Jesus, who stands at God's right hand as Stephen's advocate, his "paraclete."[183]

While Jesus stands at the right hand of God, giving approval to everything Stephen has just said, those who heard him cry out and cover their ears to avoid hearing any further alleged blasphemy. Apparently they have already rejected Gamaliel's "wait-and-see" approach. They come at him with "one impulse"—to kill him—without any deliberation, vote, or response to Stephen's defense. ("It is unclear who "they" are that rush upon him—the Council members, the elders and scribes who dragged him to the Council [recall 6:12], or other Jews listening to his testimony.)

Stoning is (at this time) the most common form of capital punishment, especially due to the abundance of stones in Palestine. "It was also a convenient way to express anger or hatred, and was often threatened even if it was not literally carried out (as in John 8:59, 10:31-33, 11:8, and Acts 14:5)."[184] According to the 2nd century Mishnah:

> When the trial is finished, the man convicted is brought out to be stoned. The stoning place was outside the court. ... When ten cubits from the stoning place they say to him, "Confess: for it is the custom of all about to be put to death to make confession; and every one who confesses has a share in the world to come." ... Four cubits from the stoning place the criminal is stripped. ... The drop from the stoning place was twice the height of a man. One of the witnesses pushes the criminal from behind, so that he falls face downward. [It is understood that the victim is also bound hand and foot before being pushed from behind.] He is then turned over on his back. If he die from this fall, that is sufficient. If not, the second witness takes the stone and drops

---

183   Bruce, *The Book of the Acts*, 168; bracketed words are mine. "Paraclete" is the Greek word from which "Advocate" is translated in 1 John 2:1.

184   J. C. Moyer, "Stoning," *The Zondervan Pictorial Encyclopedia of the Bible*, vol. 5 (Grand Rapids: Regency Reference Library, 1976), 524.

it on his heart. If this cause death, that is sufficient; if not, he is stoned by all the congregation of Israel.[185]

"If this was the statute in effect, Stephen's death appears procedurally lawless even by Jewish standards."[186] They remove their outward robes in order to free their arms to cast stones, and lay these "at the feet of a young man named Saul" (7:58)—our first introduction to the future apostle. This is Saul's way of saying, "I'll watch your things while you go and execute this heretic!" Watching their coats gives passive agreement; his "hearty agreement" is literally expressed in 8:1 and demonstrated in the persecution that he launches soon after Stephen's stoning.

While Jesus committed His spirit to the Father, Stephen commits his spirit to Jesus Christ (7:59; see Luke 23:46). "Lord, do not hold this sin against them!" cannot mean, "Automatically forgive them of this crime," since God forgives no one who will not seek His forgiveness through repentance and obedience to His will. Given the context, Stephen realizes that these men are acting out of human anger and emotion, not necessarily with intent to violate God's laws. This does not excuse their crime, but puts it in its proper light (as in Luke 23:34, Acts 3:17, and 1 Corinthians 2:6-8). In effect, it means, "Lord, when these men come to their senses and realize what they have done, do not withhold forgiveness from them even though they have committed such an awful crime." At this, "he fell asleep"—a euphemistic expression for "he died" (see John 11:11-13), which also is "an unexpectedly beautiful and peaceful description of so brutal a death."[187]

---

185   Quoted in Bruce, *The Book of the Acts*, 171; bracketed words are mine. Other accounts say that the large rock is dropped upon the victim's head, not his heart.

186   Mitchell, "Acts," 7.9. It was also a lawless act by Roman standards, since it was illegal for the Jews to execute anyone without the permission of the Roman governor (John 18:31). It has been suggested, however, that the authority of Pontius Pilate—who was most likely still governor of Judea and lived in Caesarea—was so weak among the Jews at this time that they [the Jews] simply disregarded him. Very soon after this, Pilate was recalled to Rome for his own crimes (specifically, the murder of a number of Samaritans at Mount Gerizim), and was replaced by Coponius (Kistemaker, *Acts*, 280; Josephus, "Wars," 2.8.1, and "Antiquities," 18.4.1-2).

187   Bruce, *The Book of the Acts*, 172.

Clearly, Luke gives Stephen and his trial more attention than any other person or subject so far in Acts. The recap of Israelite history that he provides is crucial in establishing God's case against the Jews, just as has been done in the Old Testament (see 2 Kings 17:7-23 and Ezekiel 20:1-44, for example). Stephen's defense also shows that all *future* Jewish persecution of Christians is unwarranted, illegitimate, and *not from God* (despite what they will think otherwise; see John 16:1-3). This sets the stage for what is to come in the rest of Luke's account of the early church. Stephen, then, serves as a pivotal transition between the early success and popularity of Christ's church among the Jews and the shifting emphasis toward those outside of Jerusalem, Judea, and the Jewish people themselves. To some extent, Stephen's brief but powerful ministry is a microcosm of Paul's own: once Saul (later called Paul) becomes a Christian, it is as if we are watching in him Stephen's ministry all over again, but in very slow motion.

⌒ Chapter 8 ⌒
Dispersion of the Church; Philip's Ministry

Dispersion of the Church (8:1-4)

Saul was briefly introduced in 7:58, and his story will soon become a major part of the book of Acts. He will also become one of the most significant and influential men of the church and all of human history. A zealous Pharisee, born of the tribe of Benjamin yet possessing Roman citizenship, he is initially a powerful threat to the early church, even though he must be quite young at this time (ca. AD 34).[188] "The ascription *young man* refers to a person aged twenty-four to forty. Probably Saul (Paul) was thirty."[189] The historian Philip Schaff writes:

> The intellectual and moral endowment of Saul was of the highest order. The sharpest thinking was blended with the tenderest feeling, the deepest mind with the strongest will. He had Semitic fervor, Greek versatility, and Roman energy. Whatever he was, he was with his whole soul. He was *totus in illis*, a man of one idea and of one purpose, first as a Jew, then as a Christian. His nature was martial and heroic. Fear was unknown to him—except the fear of God, which made him fearless of man. When yet a youth, he had risen to high eminence; and had he remained a Jew, he might have become a greater Rabbi than even Hillel or Gamaliel, as he surpassed them both in original genius and fertility of thought.
>
> Paul was the only scholar among the apostles. He never displays his learning, considering it of no account as compared with the excellency of the knowledge of Christ, for whom he suffered

---

188   "[I]t is sometimes alleged that being a Roman citizen required concessions to paganism incompatible with the strict Judaism which Paul and his family professed. But our sources tell us of nothing involving sacrifices to pagan gods, the imperial cult, or milder concessions. On the contrary, everything suggests that a Jew who was a Roman citizen continued to enjoy the privileges accorded to his people in that matter and that he did not run the risk of associating with hellenism [*sic*] on other points" (Simon Legasse, "Paul's Pre-Christian Career According to Acts," *The Book of Acts in Its First Century Setting*, vol. 4, 371).

189   Kistemaker, *Acts*, 280.

the loss of all things, but he could not conceal it, and turned it to the best use after his conversion. Peter and John had natural genius, but no scholastic education; Paul had both, and thus became the founder of Christian theology and philosophy.[190]

Saul is a Hellenistic Jew, whereas Stephen was a Hellenistic Christian; this is a significant point. Some have suggested, and with good reason, that Saul's persecution is really (only) against the Hellenistic Christians, not the entire church. (This may help explain why the apostles and Judean Christians remain in the city; see 9:29.) Filled with passion for his heritage and (albeit misguided) zeal for God, Saul instigates a general persecution against the church.[191] Saul (Paul), in his own words, tells us later that this was a particularly aggressive, violent, and vengeful action (see Acts 9:1-2, 22:19-20, 26:9-11, and 1 Timothy 1:12-13).

Saul's is the first organized persecution against Christians (8:1-3), and creates a difficult situation for the Jews on both sides—i.e., believers and non-believers alike. Just as the Civil War in America divided families and pitted brother against brother, so we must imagine the same scenario here: unbelieving Jews fighting against believing Jews, and families being torn apart by opposing allegiances (just as Jesus predicted; see Matthew 10:32-39). Those who bury Stephen imply through their "loud lamentation over him" (8:2) that his execution was

---

190   Philip Schaff, "St. Paul and the Conversion of the Gentiles: Paul Before His Conversion," *History of the Christian Church,* vol. 1 [electronic edition] (© 1910, Chas. Scribner's Sons; database © 2004 WORDsearch Corp.).

191   Some have argued that Saul was a member of the Sanhedrin (Council). "One of the necessary qualifications of members of the Sanhedrin was, that they should be the fathers of children, because such were supposed more likely to lean towards mercy. If this was the rule when Stephen was tried, and if Saul was one of the judges, he must have been married at the time" (Conybeare and Howson, *Life and Epistles,* 59, fn 6). These historians go on to say, however, that "if he was not a member of the Sanhedrin at the time of St. Stephen's death, he was elected into that powerful senate soon after; possibly as a reward for the zeal he had shown against the heretic. He himself says that in Jerusalem he not only exercised the power of imprisonment by commission from the High Priests, but also, when the Christians were put to death, *gave his vote* against them [Acts 26:10]" (ibid., 64). Thus, Saul may have been (or became) a member of the Council, but was not qualified to preside as a judge over its trials; he served only as a jury member.

unjust and unwarranted. Otherwise, mourning and lamentation is not allowed for those who are executed, based upon Moses' instruction to Aaron concerning Nadab and Abihu (Leviticus 10:6). "That these devout men would bury Stephen's body is equivalent to an avowal of their belief that he was innocent. Commonly, when a man was stoned to death on a charge of blasphemy, he would have no funeral honors, but instead would have been buried with 'the burial of an ass' [cf. Jeremiah 22:19]."[192]

Stephen's martyrdom serves as a breaking point between the traditional Jewish order and the newly-established church. Instead of finding favor with all the people as before (recall 4:21 and 5:13), the disciples are now being forced to surrender their freedom and even their very lives for professing allegiance to Jesus Christ. Indeed, Saul actively pursues Christians "house after house," pulling people right out of their homes and possibly the worship assembly in order to bring them to trial and even sentence them to death. So much for Gamaliel's "let's-not-do-anything-rash" or "wait-and-see" approach (recall 5:33-40): Saul obviously ignored it, likely because he did not think that it would work. In Saul's mind, heresy is heresy; it is not something that can be given time to run its course, but must be stamped out at once, however violently. F. F. Bruce comments: "He too was exceptionally far-sighted, and realized as clearly as Stephen did the fundamental incompatibility between the old order and the new. The temporizing policy of his master Gamaliel ... was not for him; he saw that no compromise was possible, and if the old order was to be preserved intact, the new faith must be stamped out."[193]

Saul (Paul) later will admit that he "acted ignorantly in unbelief" (1 Timothy 1:13), but at this time he truly believes that what he is doing serves the will of God. This can easily be repeated today: just because a person passionately acts upon or defends his faith does not mean that he is *correct* in what he believes to be true. Every false religious system that exists today has within it many people who zealously defend their

---

192   Reese, *Book of Acts*, 315; bracketed words are mine.

193   Bruce, *The Book of the Acts*, 172; bracketed word is mine.

supposed faith in God. Even Christians who claim to be preachers of "sound doctrine" may succumb to errors in their comprehension of Scripture or errors in reasoning, resulting in a passionately-fueled but misguided crusade "for the Lord."

As a result of Saul's persecution, many disciples in Jerusalem are scattered outside of the city and into the surrounding cities and regions.[194] What Saul ends up doing, however, is not what he intends: he intends to stamp out this alleged heresy; instead, he actually forces the gospel to spread, take root, and flourish elsewhere (8:4). Ironically, he will end up being one of those who *takes* it elsewhere. Albert Barnes has rightly observed:

❑ Persecution tends to promote the very thing it seeks to destroy.
❑ One of the best ways to make Christians active and zealous is to persecute them. (Group dynamics forces aside petty concerns and internal differences, and unites the group toward achieving a common goal or purpose.)
❑ It is right for all Christians to make the gospel known, whether or not as a result of persecution.
❑ It should be the mission or objective of all Christians to make their Savior known everywhere—through the testimony of their own speech, conduct, and commitment to God.[195]

There is no room for fence-riding, half-heartedness, or tepid faith in the midst of a persecution of the church: a person stands for Christ and accepts the consequences of that decision or he seeks to avoid all such consequences. For this reason, Acts 8:4 has been called the "hub" of the NT, since it so clearly designates the sharp break from a Jerusalem-centered church to (what will become) a universal church, and from Jews exclusively to (ultimately) Gentiles of every nation.

---

194 Christians are "scattered" like seeds tossed from the hand of a sower, to which the original Greek word for "scattered" actually refers (*Strong's* [electronic edition], #G1289). The word *diaspeiro* is that from which we also get "(The) Diaspora," the great scattering of Jews into the world following the exiles of both Israel and Judah.

195 Albert Barnes, *Barnes' Notes* (Grand Rapids: Baker Book House, no date), 138.

Philip's Ministry (8:5-40)

Philip's preaching in Samaria (8:5-8)

As Christians are dispersed abroad, they carry with them the good news (gospel) of Christ. Philip (later called "the evangelist"—21:8) is an example of someone who is not passively speaking to those with whom he comes in contact, but who embarks on a brief missionary journey throughout the land of Samaria (8:5). "The city of Samaria" likely refers to Sebaste, a rebuilding of ancient Samaria by Herod the Great.[196] It is about 35 miles north of Jerusalem.[197]

Samaria itself is a region generally despised by the Jews, since its inhabitants are not of pure Jewish stock, having intermarried with heathen nations (see 2 Kings 17:24-41). This intermarriage has rendered the land unclean, as far as the Judean Jews are concerned. The Samaritans do practice Jehovah worship, not at the temple in Jerusalem, but at their own place (Mt. Gerizim) and "in ignorance" (cf. John 4:20-22).[198] Jesus Himself had a mixed reception from the Samaritans (compare John 4:39-42 and Luke 9:51-56). Nonetheless, He credited Samaritans as being more genuine and compassionate than the purist Jews who freely condemned them (see Luke 10:33 and 17:16). The fact that the gospel is being brought to Samaria is a further fulfillment of Jesus' prophecy (recall Acts 1:8); the fact that this

---

196   "Sebaste" is the Greek form of "Augustus," since the city was named in appreciation for Augustus Caesar. Samaria was once the capital of the northern ten tribes of Israel, having been built by King Omri (1 Kings 16:23-24). It had been destroyed by the Assyrians in 721 BC, then rebuilt, and then destroyed again by John Hyrcanus in 120 BC (W. Ewing, "Samaria," *ISBE* [electronic edition]).

197   Philip "went down to the city of Samaria" from the perspective of Jerusalem. While Samaria was north of Jerusalem—and therefore, we would say that Philip went *up* to Samaria—it is also true that Jerusalem is higher in elevation than Samaria, and (among Jews) is ethically and religiously "higher" in caliber as well. Because the temple is in Jerusalem, that city is thought to be closer to God than the cities of the unclean heathens.

198   "Abraham came through the pass and camped near Gerizim at the oak of Moreh (Genesis 12:6). According to Samaritan tradition it was on this mountain that he prepared to sacrifice Isaac, and at Salem, not far distant, he met Melchizedek (Genesis 14:17ff)" (W. Ewing, "Gerizim, Mount," *ISBE* [electronic edition]). The "this mountain" reference in John 4:21 is most certainly Mt. Gerizim, "the cliffs of the mountain almost overhanging the Well of Jacob" (ibid.).

preaching is accompanied by miracles indicates that the Holy Spirit is behind this endeavor.

The ability to exorcise "unclean spirits" (demons) requires an otherworldly authority greater than that of the otherworldly demons themselves (8:6-8). In essence, this is the "finger of God" that Jesus mentioned with regard to this same activity (Luke 11:20). Philip's ability to perform miracles can, like Stephen's, be traced back to the transmission of such power through the laying on of the apostles' hands (recall 6:6). We have no indication that Philip himself can impart this power to others; in fact, the present account (with Simon) proves the exact opposite. The purpose for these "signs" is to point to the authenticity and power of the message being preached (1 Corinthians 2:3-5, 4:20, and 1 Thessalonians 1:5). We never see miracles being exercised *in place of* the message; rather, we see them accompanying and validating it (Luke 4:31-36, Hebrews 2:3-4).

Conversion of Simon the Sorcerer (8:9-13)

Simon the Sorcerer is not merely a magician but also a con artist; such is the practice of such men in those days (8:9). Originally, a "magician" was one who practiced the art of the Magi (see Matthew 2:1). The Magi rose out of Persia (and possibly India), and were obsessed with the study of philosophy, astronomy, medicine, etc. Later, however, the name came to signify any of those who made use of the knowledge of these arts, especially astrologers, soothsayers, necromancers (conjurers of the dead), fortune-tellers, and others. These men thought themselves able to predict the future by the positions of the stars, cure diseases with incantations, and interpret dreams.[199] While the practice of the Magi began as something seemingly noble, it later descended into a profit-earning enterprise, as well as an opportunity for self-exaltation, as is the case with Simon.

Magic has as much to do with duping the senses or manipulating the emotions of the audience as it does with illusion and sleight-of-hand. Magicians often used hallucinogens (often vaporized, the steam or

---

199   Barnes, *Barnes' Notes*, 139.

smoke of which is inhaled by the observer) to trick the mind into believing an illusion is authentic.

> It is not strange to find the gospel brought into direct conflict with magicians, for in the 1st and 2nd centuries there were a multitude of such persons who pretended to possess supernatural powers by which they endeavored to deceive men. They flattered the sinful inclinations of the human heart, and fell in with men's current ways of thinking, and required no self-renunciation at all. For these reasons the magicians found a ready belief on the part of many. ...The influence of such persons presented an obstacle to the progress of the Christian faith, which had to force its way through the delusions with which these sorcerers had surrounded the hearts of those whom they deceived. When the gospel came in contact with these magicians and with their works, it was necessary that there should be striking facts, works of supernatural power strongly appealing to men's outward senses, in order to bring them out of the bewilderment and deception in which they were involved, and to make them able to receive the impression of spiritual truth.[200]

Magic has long been associated with the acquisition of power through occultism or demonic assistance; for this reason, it is condemned in the Law of Moses (Deuteronomy 18:10-12). The Samaritans nonetheless think Simon to be something great; ironically, they associate his magic with God's power (8:10-11). Yet when Simon is confronted with *genuine* greatness (in the power of the Holy Spirit), he himself becomes a believer. He believes in the same gospel that other Samaritans believe in; he is baptized just as these others are baptized (8:12-13). His conversion underscores the genuineness of these miracles: if there had been anything fraudulent about Philip's "signs," then Simon of all people would have detected it immediately. As someone has said, it takes a con man to know a con man when he sees one. As it is, there is nothing false about Philip's demonstration of power. Simon's actions

---

200   John Rutherford, "Simon Magus," *ISBE* [electronic edition].

were for entertainment and personal profit; Philip's actions defy natural explanation and confirm the message of God which he is preaching.

Many Samaritans, too, believe and obey the message of God. The gospel of Christ is not just another form of Judaism (which they already practice in part) but a refreshing message of freedom and acceptance: these people enjoy the same fellowship with God as pure-blooded Jewish Christians do. "The good news of the kingdom and the name of Jesus Christ" (8:12) do not refer to two different messages, but one and the same. Some commentators assume that "kingdom" is synonymous with "church" here—and since it is here, therefore it must always be so.[201] Yet, this premise is not correct: the kingdom refers to the rule of Christ over *all* things and *all* authorities (in heaven *and* on earth) and is not limited to His headship of His church. It is true that a person who enters into Christ's church through obedience to His gospel also enters into His kingdom. He becomes a *child of the King* rather than merely a *subject of the King's universal domain*. In other words, in becoming a Christian, a person is brought (through an adoption process) into the family or household of the Father (1 Timothy 3:15); he is no longer a common slave, but an heir of God (John 8:35, Romans 8:14-17, Galatians 4:4-7, et al).

"Men and women alike" (8:12) indicates a profound equality of opportunity. As we have seen earlier (recall 5:14), women are able to respond to and participate in this "good news" along with the

---

201   Coffman, for one, cites Matthew 16:18-19, where Jesus says "I will build My church" and then gives Peter the "keys to the kingdom"; he concludes from this that Christ's "church" and His "kingdom" are indisputably interchangeable (*Commentary on Acts*, 157-158). In my understanding, such a conclusion is based upon a fundamental error: Peter was not given keys to open the door to Christ's *church*, as though he determined who could be saved or not; rather, he was given keys to the *kingdom of God*, in that he provided the *invitation* to be saved. In other words, he opened the door to two groups of people (first Jews, then Gentiles) so that they could give allegiance to the King (Christ) upon obedience to His gospel. Remember that it was the *Lord*—not Peter—who was adding to the number of the saved (Acts 2:47), and these people were added to Christ's *church*, the holy sanctuary of believers in the midst of Christ's universal *kingdom*. To be "in the kingdom" with reference to *salvation* means to be a Christian. These two things—kingdom and church—are most certainly related, but not interchangeable.

men.[202] Nowhere in Acts do we see the gospel preached to children; nowhere does the church assume an active role in teaching children, especially apart from children's own parents. Nowhere in Acts do we see children (of any age) being baptized. The gospel is an adult message: it is directed *to* adults, intended *for* adults, and carried out *by* adults. It requires an adult decision to accept the moral responsibilities and personal demands of the gospel of Christ. In order to remain true to the NT pattern, we can neither dumb down the gospel's message and responsibilities to accommodate children nor allow those to become Christians who are simply not mature enough to make such decisions. It should be noted that once a person believes, he is baptized (8:13)— i.e., immersed in water in the name of Jesus Christ.[203] We *never* see disciples being "made" apart from baptism (Matthew 28:19); we *never* see any long period of time between one's genuine belief in the message and his being baptized. Baptism is an expression of one's faith in the Lord, not an incidental ritual to be dealt with at some future time, if at all. It is a visible and necessary expression of belief and a prerequisite for forgiveness of sins (Acts 2:38, 22:16, and Romans 6:2-4). These Samaritans who receive the gospel of Christ and respond in obedience (baptism) become Christians; given the text, no other conclusion is possible. This is remarkable, too, given the great hostility that had previously existed between Jews and Samaritans (see John 4:9, 8:48, et al). Now we have a Jewish missionary baptizing Samaritans into the same church to which believing Jews already belong. Thus, there is not a Jewish church and a separate Samaritan church, but *one church* into which all believers are added. "Even Simon himself believed" and was baptized (8:13); we have no reason to doubt his conversion,

---

202   Just as they share in the blessings of the gospel, so women also share in its tribulations. Saul's persecution, for example, does not target only male believers, but "men and women" who are Christians (see Acts 8:3, 9:2, and 22:4). This equality of persecution is nearly unprecedented in Scripture.

203   This is a pattern seen consistently throughout Acts: see 2:38-41, 8:36-38, 10:48, 16:15, 16:31-33, 18:8, 19:1-5, and 22:16. Yet many denominationalists repeatedly reject the necessity of baptism in the conversion process. John MacArthur, for example, writes: "It [baptism] is important, however, and commanded of all believers following salvation, though it plays no part in it" (*Acts: 1 – 12*, 243; bracketed word is mine). It is impossible to follow his logic. The fact that it is "commanded of all believers" makes it a *necessary requirement* of all believers. Since God's commands must be obeyed, a person would be in violation of His command if he refused to be baptized.

despite what happens shortly.[204] Many newly-baptized believers have committed awful blunders and serious doctrinal errors. He "continued on with Philip," awestruck at the great power that the Holy Spirit revealed through this man.

Simon's attempt to purchase the power of God (8:14-24)

"Receiving the Holy Spirit"—in *this* context (8:14-16)—is a direct and inescapable reference to the ability to perform miracles through the power of the Spirit (1 Corinthians 12:4-11). Peter has already stated that everyone who obeys Christ receives the Spirit (5:32); *that* reception is in a completely different context than *this* one. These Samaritans had obeyed and were baptized; therefore they *did* receive the Spirit for the purpose of enjoying access to God through His (the Spirit's) renewal of the soul (Titus 3:5). But the visible manifestation of the Spirit, being demonstrated through miraculous gifts, is something that only the apostles can confer (8:17-18; see 2 Timothy 1:6); this latter fact is one of the main thrusts of this entire passage.[205] If this is not the case, then this passage—as well as the church's decision to dispatch Peter and John to Samaria—is completely unwarranted and inexplicable.[206]

---

204   Any insinuation that Simon only *pretended* to believe, or failed to be truly converted, must be rejected. The text is clear and unmistakable: in the same way that the Samaritans believed and obeyed the gospel, so did Simon. Calvin writes: "Simon's example plainly shows that not everyone baptized is given the grace that is represented in that rite" (*Acts*, 135). Calvin's premise wrongfully assumes that one who is baptized is immune to sin—a teaching of Calvinism ("perseverance of the saints"), not the gospel of Christ. We cannot question Simon's decision to become a Christian simply because he sinned so soon afterward; given this logic, many genuine believers today should be considered frauds as well. Furthermore, we cannot doubt *God's* work (grace in conversion) because we are disappointed with *human* effort (whatever happens after conversion). We must also keep in mind the very primitive understanding of the people to whom Philip is preaching, and their limited exposure to truthful teaching. These people have been immersed in their sinful culture for all of their lives; we should not expect a complete removal from their errors overnight. This is asking more of them—and Simon in particular—than we expect of ourselves or others today.

205   The obvious exception to this method is when the Spirit imparts such gifts without human agency, as He did with the apostles (chapter 2) and as He will do with Cornelius and company (chapter 10). Other than these two exceptional situations—which were both for very specific and non-duplicable reasons—all transmission of this power comes through the hands of the apostles as Christ's spokesmen and representatives.

206   "The conversion of the Samaritans was the conversion of people with a Jewish background and who practiced circumcision and basic elements of the Law of Moses.

There is no reason to believe that every Samaritan who became
a Christian also received the ability to perform miracles. It is not
necessary to perform miracles in order to be saved or even because
one is saved. Many commentators have maintained that the apostles
were "confirming" baptized believers (meaning: they are not *fully*
converted until this confirmation is carried out), yet "it is laying too
great a burden on the present passage to extract this meaning from
it."[207] There is no evidence in the NT that a "confirmation" was ever
instructed, performed, or required. It is appropriate to say that Peter
and John are linking together the community of believers in Samaria
with the community of believers already established in Jerusalem,
and that the visible power of the Holy Spirit confirms *this*. "Simply...
baptized in the name of the Lord Jesus" (8:16) does not mean that
this baptism is in any way inadequate for salvation or an incomplete
response on the part of the people to Christ's gospel. This only means
that *one* thing had been done but not yet the *other*; it does not mean,
however, that both actions are necessary for forgiveness of sins. Again,
nowhere in the NT is miracle-working a necessary requirement for
salvation in Christ.

With regard to the "receiving the Holy Spirit" phrase (8:17), the same
(or similar) words or phrases can be used to mean two different things.
It is the *context*, not a word or phrase itself, which determines the
accurate or full meaning of what is being said.

Philip begins a work there and many are baptized into the name of Christ. But was the
work legitimate? The Jerusalem church thought it was and sent Peter and John down
to check it out. When the two apostles arrived they received these believers into the
Messianic fellowship and God bore his own witness that they had been accepted by
him when he poured out miraculous power on them. **Raw Gentiles and Samaritans
were not regarded as parallel cases** [with reference to the conversion of Cornelius and
company—MY WORDS]" (McGuiggan, *The Reign of God*, 78; emphasis is his).

207   Bruce, *The Book of the Acts*, 182.

In one passage:	In another passage:
Apostle = one of the twelve hand-picked representatives of Christ (Luke 6:13, Romans 1:1)	**Apostle** = one appointed for a particular work or mission for the church (Acts 14:14, Romans 16:7, Galatians 1:19)
Baptism = the act of immersion in water for the purpose of becoming a Christian (Acts 2:38)	**Baptism** = a difficult ordeal (Luke 12:50); or, the Holy Spirit's approval of Jews (Matthew 3:11, Acts 2:1-4) and then Gentiles (Acts 10:44-45) for admission into the kingdom of God
Receiving the Holy Spirit = gaining access to the Father through the intercession of His Spirit (Acts 2:38, Ephesians 2:18)	**Receiving the Holy Spirit** = the impartation of miraculous gifts for the purpose of confirming the Word of God (Acts 8:17, 19:6, Galatians 3:2) or to signify God's approval of (a group of) people to be saved (Acts 10:47)
The kingdom of God = the reign and realm of Messiah (Christ) over God's kingdom for the purpose of salvation (Mark 1:15, Luke 9:62)	**The kingdom of God** = the ultimate and realized heavenly inheritance of the believer in Christ (Acts 14:22, Ephesians 5:5, 2 Peter 1:11)
Circumcision = a literal cutting of the male foreskin as a sign of covenantal standing with God (Acts 15:1)	**Circumcision** = the spiritual act of the sinful "old self" being "cut away" by Christ in baptism (Colossians 2:11-12)
Assembly = the gathering together of Christians on the first day of the week (1 Corinthians 14:26, Hebrews 10:25)	**Assembly** = a group of people who have come together for no religious purpose at all (Acts 19:32-41); or, the meeting of the Council (Acts 23:7)
Elder = a mature Christian man appointed by his congregation to be its overseer (Acts 14:23, Titus 1:5-9)	**Elder** = an older man, with no specific respect to his religious responsibilities (Acts 4:8, 1 Peter 5:5); or, a heavenly representative of God's people (Revelation 4:4, 10, et al)
Lord = Jesus Christ (Acts 2:36) or God the Father (Matthew 11:25)	**Lord** = a person of significant position or authority, as a ruler or Caesar (Acts 25:26, 1 Peter 3:6, Revelation 7:14)

In one passage:	In another passage:
Perish = the loss of one's soul (John 3:16, 1 Corinthians 1:18, 2 Thessalonians 2:10)	**Perish** = the loss of one's life (Matthew 8:25, 26:52); or, (adjectively) the nature of one's mortality or the temporal earthly life (1 Corinthians 15:42, 50-54, Colossians 2:22)
Sleep = an unconscious state of rest (Matthew 1:24, Luke 9:32, Acts 20:9)	**Sleep** = a state of (spiritual or mental) lethargy or inactivity (Romans 13:11, 1 Thessalonians 5:6); or, a euphemism for one's actual death (John 11:11-13, 1 Thessalonians 4:13)

We have already seen that Simon himself believed and was baptized just as the other Samaritans believed and were baptized. "The fact that he later went wrong… is something that followed. All that Luke intimates regarding this outcome is the fact that Simon was too much captivated by the miracles he saw. The probability is that he came to regard them as being in the same class with his own magical arts but far superior to what he had been able to produce."[208] Thus, Simon wishes to purchase this "authority," since it is popular in his day (as it is today) to acquire ecclesiastical *power* through the exchange of money (8:18-19). (Our modern word "simony" comes from this very account, and refers to the buying and selling of "ecclesiastical preferment."[209]) In fact, the Jews have long practiced the purchase of the office of the high priest with money and/or favors paid to the Romans; and non-Romans can purchase Roman citizenship with money (Acts 22:28).

However, Peter makes it clear: this power is not for sale; man-made wealth has no value in matters of the kingdom of God (see 1 Peter 1:18-19). "May your silver perish with you" (8:20) is a strong condemnation of both Simon's *heart* as well as the error of his *proposal.* "You have

---

208   Lenski, *Acts of the Apostles*, 322.

209   *Merriam-Webster's 11ᵗʰ Collegiate Dictionary* (electronic edition; © 2003 by Merriam-Webster, Inc., ver. 3.0). Lenski makes an insightful comment here: "We should note that Simon's story is told so fully because it is parallel to that of Ananias and Sapphira. Both stand out in the first church as glaring examples of the frightful attempt by means of money to obtain what can be obtained only by God's grace. So men still think they can buy honor in God's kingdom, yea, salvation itself, by means of money contributions to some church cause, whether they acknowledge their secret intent or not" (*Acts of the Apostles*, 329).

no part or portion in this matter" (8:21) underscores the fact that only the *chosen apostles*—and no one else—could impart these gifts.[210] "For your heart is not right before God"—because Simon is focused only on his own interests, not God's (see Matthew 16:23). "Gall" is greenish bile, probably of a poisonous plant (like wormwood); here, it implies a poisoning of the soul (8:23). "Bondage of iniquity" indicates Simon's allegiance to the ways of sinful men rather than the pure motives of a believer; he is thinking like a natural man of the world, not like a servant of Christ. Through this exchange, we also learn that Simon *can* be forgiven, but only through prayer (petitioning God for mercy) and repentance (a change in attitude and action). "The apostle was not so much wishing destruction on him as terrifying him by telling him that God's just vengeance was hanging over his head."[211]

"Pray to the Lord for me yourselves" (8:24)—to which one commentator responds, "Peter urged Simon to pray himself [because] Simon had no real concern for forgiveness."[212] This rush to judgment misrepresents both Peter's words and Simon's response to them. Rather, Simon seeks special intercession for such a grievous sin to avoid the severe judgment Peter levels against him. Tradition says that Simon

---

210 "The ability to perform miracles was not automatically or indiscriminately given to all believers. It *is* true that the Spirit would be 'poured out' upon *all* believers, regardless of status, gender, or nationality (Acts 2:17-18); it is *not* true that this would be accomplished without due process. The church itself did not choose this process, nor did the apostles, but it was the Holy Spirit who provided the manner in which the ability to exercise miracles was given: the laying on of the apostles' hands" (Sychtysz, *The Holy Spirit of God*, 131). On a related note, we should compare this rebuke with: Ezra's rebuke of (ironically) the Samaritans who wanted to help re-build the temple (Ezra 4:1-3); Azariah's rebuke of King Uzziah for wanting to burn incense to God (2 Chronicles 26:16-19); and Jesus' rebuke of Peter himself (Matthew 16:21-23). No matter how great we think our position to be, God puts limits on the scope of our knowledge of, or involvement in, things which we have no business to pursue further.

211 Calvin, *Acts*, 138.

212 JFB *Commentary*, on 8:24. MacArthur brazenly condemns Simon to hell. He says that Simon never really believed, but exercised a "false faith," and that his "faults kept him from genuine faith and left him in the position to perish eternally" (*Acts: 1 – 12*, 238-239). The emphasis of Simon's account, however, is not to dwell on Simon himself, but to show that the power of God will not be sold or extorted, and that the apostles alone have been given the ability to transmit that power through the laying on of their hands.

Magnus (as he is referred to) went on to practice a mixture of magic and Christianity, but there is no proof to this, only legend and hearsay. Nonetheless, such thoughts may lead us to negatively judge his heart. All we know for certain is what is said; this is our last encounter with Simon in the NT.

Conversion of the Ethiopian eunuch (8:25-40)

Peter and John capitalize on Philip's own success in evangelizing Samaria as they make their way back to Jerusalem (8:25). The Spirit has other plans for Philip, however: he is instructed to travel southwestward on a road to Gaza with no other stated objective (8:26-27).[213] But upon arriving at this road, he comes upon the caravan of a "court official of Candace, queen of the Ethiopians."[214] This man is a eunuch, likely castrated specifically for the purpose of serving on the queen's official cabinet. Since eunuchs cannot have sexual relations or father children, they also do not marry and thus can be wholly devoted to their careers.[215] Also, a eunuchs' loyalty lies with his master, since he depends upon him or her (and not his children) to care for him in later life. This Ethiopian is likely black and not a Jew, but is at the *very least*

---

213   "Desert" in this context does not necessarily mean a waterless region (like we think of deserts today), but a place with little or no human population. In fact, this area "has never been anything but a fertile plain called the plain of Philistia, having many pools and streams of water" (Coffman, *Commentary on Acts*, 169). Gaza, one of the oldest places mentioned in Scripture (Genesis 10:19), was once one of the five cities of ancient Philistia. "Palestine was divided into three divisions at this time—Galilee was the extreme northern division, Samaria was the middle division, and Judea the southern division. Gaza was in Judea. Gaza was about sixty miles southwest from Jerusalem, and had been destroyed in 96 BC, but was rebuilt, and was a city of importance at this time. Philip would pass west of Jerusalem on his way from Samaria and would intercept the road between Jerusalem and Gaza; this was a journey of from sixty to seventy miles" (Boles, *A Commentary on Acts*, 133). There were actually a couple of roads that led in this direction; Philip apparently took the most deserted one.

214   "Candace" [pronounced kän-*däk*-ay] is the royal title (like Abimelech, Pharaoh, Czar, or Sultan) of a dynasty of Ethiopian queens. "The king of Ethiopia was venerated as a child of the sun and regarded as too sacred a personage to discharge the secular functions of royalty; these were performed on his behalf by the queen mother, who regularly bore the dynastic title Candace" (Bruce, *The Book of the Acts*, 186).

215   On this point, consider what Jesus (Matthew 19:10-12) and Paul (1 Corinthians 7:32-35) say about an unmarried person's devotion to the Lord.

a Jewish proselyte.[216] This also would require him to be circumcised. His situation, then, is not fully comparable with that of Cornelius (in chapter 10). Other than this, we know nothing else about this man or his entourage. But we *do* know what he is reading—and that he is a genuine seeker of the truth.

Philip's arrival is, providentially, well-timed (8:28-39). The eunuch is reading aloud a key passage from Isaiah, but does not comprehend it. "Reading [manuscripts] in ancient times was almost invariably aloud. ... Beginners regularly read aloud; it requires considerable experience (not to say sophistication) to read silently, though this stage is reached more quickly with modern print than with ancient manuscript."[217] He wants to know the true identity of the person in the text of Isaiah 53:7-8. We must not assume that Christians alone are capable of comprehending Scripture (and that non-Christians are incapable of this), but the Scripture at hand *is* difficult to understand *without* the knowledge of Jesus Christ—knowledge which Philip has and is able to impart to the man. The Spirit instructs Philip to invite himself *to* the chariot; the eunuch then invites Philip *into* the chariot. "Beginning from this Scripture ... [Philip] preached Jesus to him" (8:35) is a powerful statement for several reasons:

❑ This confirms for us that Isaiah 53 *is indeed* a direct prophecy about Jesus.
❑ The origins of the gospel are indeed embedded in the oracles of the Jewish prophets, as Jesus Himself had declared (Luke 24:44-45, John 5:39, et al).

---

216   Some would consider him a "half-convert" to Judaism, since he could not participate in any holy assembly due to his emasculation (Deuteronomy 23:1). However, "he not only worshiped God in his local Jewish synagogue [in Ethiopia]; he also took his religion seriously and went on a pilgrimage to Jerusalem (compare John 12:20). Historical records show that numerous Jews had taken up residence in Egypt and Ethiopia. These Jews worshiped Israel's God and invited the Gentiles to their religious services, with the result that many Gentiles became God-fearers" (Kistemaker, *Acts*, 312; bracketed words are mine). Lenski, for his part, says that the Greek word for "Ethiopian" indicates the color (blackness) of skin, not just nationality; furthermore, "[t]he entire narrative points to the fact that this man was a Gentile" (*Acts of the Apostles*, 337).

217   Bruce, *The Book of the Acts*, 187; bracketed word is mine.

❑ The best interpretation of Scripture for *us* is to let an inspired man like Philip explain it. Since Acts is a work of inspiration, we have one inspired work (Acts) interpreting another inspired work (Isaiah), so that we can know for certain the latter work's meaning.

❑ What Philip preached is consistent with others who also preach the same gospel (Acts 10:36-43 [especially verse 43], 17:2-3, 1 Peter 1:10-12, et al).

❑ To "preach Jesus" means to preach His gospel ("good news"), since this is what Philip preaches both previously and afterward (8:12, 40).

❑ To "preach Jesus" means to communicate God's terms of salvation for the believer, and whatever conditions are required on the part of the believer under the general heading of "faith."

❑ Preaching Jesus is sufficient for one's obedience to God and conversion to a Christian. There is no need for catechism, a mandatory series of classes, or extra-biblical curriculum.

❑ This preaching necessarily *includes* instruction on baptism and its direct connection with salvation in Jesus. In other words, baptism is always at least one necessary demonstration *of* obedience. Boles rightly says: "No inspired preacher of the gospel then preached Jesus without preaching the baptism that Jesus commanded; no gospel preacher today can preach Jesus without preaching the command to be baptized."[218]

❑ This preaching is what Christians are expected to do when the Holy Spirit provides an opportunity to express "the hope that is in" us (1 Peter 3:15).

The *kind* of baptism that "preaching Jesus" involves is most definitely water baptism. Any reference to a so-called "Holy Spirit baptism" for salvation (as is popularly taught among modern charismatics and some evangelicals) is completely unfounded. Verse 37 is not included in the oldest (and thus more reliable) manuscripts of the NT, yet it does not contradict what would be expected of either the Ethiopian or Philip in this case.[219] Eunuchs (i.e., emasculated men) are, according

---

218   Boles, *A Commentary on Acts*, 138.

219   "The verse was introduced into the modern printed Greek texts by Erasmus [15th century Greek scholar], who thought it had been omitted through scribal error and that

to the Law of Moses, prohibited from participating in holy festivals or entering into the courtyard of the tabernacle (Deuteronomy 23:1). God's acceptance of this Ethiopian eunuch indicates that one's eligibility for full fellowship with Him and servitude in His kingdom is no longer based upon bodily perfection (compare Leviticus 21:17-23 and Isaiah 56:3-7). Both men "went down into the water," but only *one* man was baptized (8:38); both men walked into the body of water, but only *one* was immersed in that water for the purpose of becoming a Christian.[220]

After his baptism, the Ethiopian rejoices over his spiritual re-birth, while "the Spirit of the Lord snatched Philip away" for a different mission (8:39). This expression is difficult to interpret in any way other than the most obvious conclusion: Philip disappeared from the man's view and "found himself" elsewhere (8:40). "Azotus" is the ancient Philistine city of Ashdod, some 20 miles from where he likely met the eunuch and 54 miles from Caesarea Palestina (on Mediterranean coast). We do not hear of him again until Paul meets up with him in Caesarea after his third missionary journey (21:8).

---

it originally belonged to what Luke wrote. From Erasmus' text, it was included in the KJV" (Reese, *Book of Acts*, 340; bracketed words are mine).

220   Lenski claims, "We are left to suppose that the two men went to this water, and that the baptismal act was an application of water by pouring or by sprinkling. Those who make the words 'they both went down into the water' a part of the baptismal act in order to obtain immersion...prove too much" (*Acts of the Apostles*, 347). I strongly disagree with Lenski's imaginative interpretation of this passage. If anyone is "proving too much," it is Lenski himself. See further comments in the footnote on Acts 9:18.

∼ Chapter 9 ∼
Saul's Conversion; Peter's Ministry

Saul's Conversion (9:1-31)

Saul's encounter with Christ on the road to Damascus (9:1-9)

We are not told why Saul finds it necessary to go to Damascus to hunt down Christians. There are plenty of believers to pursue in Jerusalem and Judea. (Add to this that Damascus is a 150-mile, six-day journey from Jerusalem.) Something—divine intervention, if nothing else—drives Saul to pursue those in Damascus belonging to "the Way" (an early euphemism for the Christian faith). This shows, along with Luke's graphic portrayal ("breathing threats and murder"), the depth of the Jewish rulers' contempt for Christians at this time. It also shows that, besides Stephen, other Christians are being jailed and even executed for their faith. As stated earlier, this also defines the commitment level that is required of all believers: our lives may be taken away by the force of those who do not believe (Matthew 10:16-22, John 16:2-3); or we may need to lay down our lives for the sake of other believers (1 John 3:16).

Saul's "letters" refer to legal documents issued by the Jewish Council for the apprehension of Christians.[221] These people would be arrested, bound, and extradited to Jerusalem to stand trial as heretics before the Council. Saul is not traveling alone; likely, a number of men (temple guards?) accompany him in order to carry out his orders. Damascus, the oldest continually-inhabited city in the world (dating back to the time of Abraham; see Genesis 14:15), has the largest Jewish community in Palestine outside of Jerusalem.[222] King Aretas IV, father-

---

221   "By decrees of Julius Caesar and Augustus the high priest and Sanhedrin at Jerusalem had jurisdiction over Jews resident in foreign cities" (Page, *The Acts of the Apostles*, 136). "These letters are not addressed to the local officials of Damascus or the Romans but 'to the synagogues of Damascus' (Acts 9:2) and more specifically, 'to their [i.e., to the Jerusalem Sanhedrin's] brothers in Damascus (Acts 22:5). More than mere letters of commendation, they authorize the use of punitive measures to dissuade Jews from following the Way and specifically mandate the extradition of individuals to answer charges before the chief priests in Jerusalem (Acts 9:2, 21; 22:5). The central question here is whether the Jerusalem religious authorities could exercise jurisdiction over Jews outside of Palestine" (Brian Rapske, "Paul in Roman Custody," *The Book of Acts in Its First Century Setting*, vol. 3, 101).

222   "Damascus...bursts upon the traveller like a vision of paradise amidst a burning

in-law to Herod Antipas, is ruler of the city at this time. The date is approximately AD 35. Of this event, Conybeare and Howson write:

> No journey ever taken, on which so much interest is concentrated, as this of St. Paul from Jerusalem to Damascus. It is so critical a passage in the history of God's dealings with man, and we feel it to be so closely bound up with all our best knowledge and best happiness in this life, and with all our hopes for the world to come, that the mind is delighted to dwell upon it, and we are eager to learn or imagine all its details. The conversion of Saul was like the call of a second Abraham.[223]

Even so, some critics have attempted to reduce Saul's "road to Damascus" experience to a mere hallucination, epileptic seizure, sunstroke, lightning, or some other natural phenomenon. All such opinions fail miserably under any serious scrutiny. Others want to discredit the experience due to alleged discrepancies between the three accounts of this incident (see 22:3-16 and 26:9-18), but plain and logical explanations exist so as to dismiss all such criticisms and provide a unified explanation of "what happened" (see comments on 26:12ff). Saul's credentials, his zealous reputation as a Pharisee (see Galatians 1:13-14), the witnesses who accompany him, the lack of motive otherwise, etc., all support this account as being authentic, accurate, and historical.

As he travels toward the Syrian capital, Saul and his entourage are suddenly overwhelmed by "a light from heaven"—i.e., from above (skyward), (9:3-7). The brilliant, flashing light and powerful voice out of nowhere have a shocking effect on the entire traveling party. Everyone falls to the ground, though not everyone perceives what exactly is happening. Jesus says audibly, "Saul, Saul, why are you

---

and barren wilderness of sand; it is watered by the never-failing rivers Abana and Pharpar (which Naaman of old preferred to all the waters of Israel [2 Kings 5:12]), and embosomed in luxuriant gardens of flowers and groves of tropical fruit trees; hence glorified by Eastern poets as 'the Eye of the Desert' (Schaff, "St. Paul and the Conversion of the Gentiles: The Conversion of Paul," *History*, vol. 1 [electronic edition]; biblical citation added).

223   Conybeare and Howson, *Life and Epistles*, 68.

persecuting Me?"—a profound and rhetorical question, since Jesus most certainly knows (better than Saul himself) what is driving this man to do this. The question is not posed so that Saul will inform Jesus, but that Jesus might open Saul's mind to what has *really* been happening. Saul has been stubbornly stamping out "the Way," yet it may never have occurred to him that his fight is against an individual Person. "Saul, Saul" reminds us of "Martha, Martha" (Luke 10:41) or "Simon, Simon" (Luke 22:31) or "Jerusalem, Jerusalem" (Luke 13:34)—not a biting accusation, but rather an admonitory reproof from one in higher authority to a much lower subordinate. Saul asks, "Who are You, Lord?"—until Jesus identifies Himself personally, Saul may not know for certain who He is. Certainly, He is "Lord" (from *kurios*, a general term of great respect for one in authority), but we cannot imagine that Saul believed this to be the risen Jesus without being told this for certain. In his mind, Jesus was dead (or did he really believe this?), and this could be an angel of God.

Christ dispels all other notions, however, and identifies Himself: "I am Jesus" (9:5).[224] In this way, the Lord makes a direct connection between Jesus *the Man* and Christ *the Lord*—which is exactly what Peter had said earlier (in 2:36). Christ speaks to Saul directly; He uses no angel or human intercessor. "He [Saul] heard what they did not hear. He saw what they did not see."[225] In other words, Christ wants Saul's complete and undivided attention—and He most certainly has it. Perhaps nothing *less* than the appearance of Christ would have deterred such a stubborn and zealous man as Saul; on the other hand, this effort indicates how valuable Saul will be to the cause of Christ. In any case, Saul's persecution against "the Way" is a persecution against Christ (Matthew 12:30); thus Christ asks, "[W]hy are you persecuting Me?" In another account, Christ also tells him, "It is hard for you to kick against the [ox] goads [or, pricks]" (Acts 26:14, bracketed words are mine). The implication is: *this persecution of yours is going to hurt you,*

---

224   "In the Greek, Jesus is actually saying to Paul, 'Yes, indeed, I am Jesus.' Then he adds, 'whom you yourself are persecuting,' to emphasize the direct accusation" (Kistemaker, *Acts*, 332).

225   Conybeare and Howson, *Life and Epistles*, 74. Consider also 1 Corinthians 9:1 and 15:8, where Paul affirms that he had "seen Jesus our Lord" and that Jesus was "seen" by him.

not Me. If He has overcome the entire world (John 16:33) and death itself (Acts 2:24), certainly Christ will have no problem defeating Saul's comparatively insignificant campaign against the church.

As a result of this experience, Saul is temporarily blinded (9:8). We likely underestimate the magnitude of feelings, confusion, and conflicts he endures during his three days of darkness, fasting, and solitude.[226] This is something he never *ever* expected; he is forced to reconsider everything he has been taught and has believed. It is possible that what Saul has *really* been kicking against is his own inner doubts about what he was doing by persecuting the church; it is possible that the testimonies of Peter and Stephen have caused him to wonder whether "the Way" really *is* genuine. After all, he now knows that the One whom the Jews had crucified is *very much alive* just as His disciples had said.[227] Furthermore, the One whom Saul had condemned in his heart as a blasphemer has just confronted him, and he is helpless to offer an armed resistance or even a single argument against Him! With a single display of supernatural power and authority, Christ has reduced this most passionate foe into a helpless, bewildered, and disoriented man.

Saul (Paul) will later write, "I am the least of the apostles, and not fit to be called an apostle, because I persecuted the church of God" (1 Corinthians 15:9; see also 1 Timothy 1:12-16). He believed himself to be obeying God in persecuting the church; now he has been shown to be terribly mistaken. Gamaliel had predicted that if this "present case" is from God, then "you will not be able to overthrow" it, otherwise "you may even be found fighting against God" (recall 5:39). Indeed, this is Saul's sudden realization: he has not been fighting *for* God in his crusade against Christians, but *against* Him. It does not matter how truthful, sincere, or pious a person thinks himself to be: if his conclusions contradict the evidence God has provided, then he is wrong.

---

226   While Jonah spent three days in the darkness of the belly of the "great fish," and Jesus' body spent three days in the darkness of His tomb, so Saul spent three days in the darkness of his own conflicted mind, contemplating the profound realization of his encounter with the Christ.

227   Adapted from Chad Sychtysz, "The Conversion of Saul of Tarsus," *Biblical Insights* (vol. 11, no. 10: Oct, 2011), 14-15.

It is interesting to note what Christ does *not* tell Saul. He does not say, "Now stop persecuting Christians!" Instead, He tells him (in essence), "Focus your zeal and attention on the ministry that I am giving to you." In other words, Christ does not simply tell Saul to put an end to his bad behavior, but to engage in the work that God has planned for him. The same should be said today: we cannot just tell people, "Stop doing wicked things"; we must *especially* tell them, "Discover what 'good works' God has planned for you (cf. Ephesians 2:10) and throw yourself into that ministry." Certainly if one is to serve God appropriately, he must remove those wicked things that stand in contradiction to that service.

Ananias meets Saul (9:10-19a)
Saul has been led by his fellow travelers into Damascus, to the house of Judas (a man otherwise unknown to us). While Saul copes with his blindness and newfound information, Christ commissions another man to meet him and restore his sight (9:10). The irony is unmistakable: Saul had been going to Damascus to imprison men like Ananias, yet it is Ananias who is sent to Saul in order to free him from *his* prison of darkness and self-doubt. (Paul later describes Ananias to a gathering of unconverted Jews as "a man who was devout by the standard of the Law, and well-spoken of by all the Jews who lived there [in Damascus]"—Acts 22:12.) We are not told whether Ananias was converted in Jerusalem or Damascus (or somewhere else); we only know that he is now a devout Christian. The fact that Christ called upon him to deal with Saul speaks volumes for his good character.

Christ appears to Ananias in a vision, which is one of God's special ways of communicating with His servants (9:10). Ananias' response ("Here I am, Lord") is reminiscent of that of previous servants of God when they were called, such as Abraham (Genesis 22:1), Moses (Exodus 3:4), Samuel (1 Samuel 3:10), Isaiah (Isaiah 6:8), and others. At first, Ananias respectfully protests to the Lord at offering aid to a man who so viciously has assailed the church of God. Yet Christ makes it clear that Saul "is a chosen instrument of Mine" and will actually become His (Christ's) most outspoken servant (9:15-16). (Recall how the eleven apostles—and then Matthias—were all "chosen" by

Christ; Acts 1:2, 24-26.) Even so, the suffering that Saul will endure for the Lord will be even greater than whatever he has inflicted (or thought to inflict) upon the church. This is not Saul's *punishment* for his persecution as much as it is his *responsibility* for the stewardship that will be entrusted to him. Thus, Saul's life becomes paradoxical: his great learning and advancement in Judaism make him the most ideal and appropriate candidate for suffering for the cause of Christ, once converted to that cause.

Ananias finds Saul at the house of Judas on the "street called Straight" (9:11). Incidentally, all of the streets in ancient Damascus are characteristically crooked, except for one: a mile-long street simply called "Straight" (which is still in use today). Ananias does not meet a raging, vengeful, or desperate man "breathing threats and murder," but instead finds Saul to be a calm and changed man, determined to serve the Lord in whatever way Ananias instructs him.

> He [Saul] is in a depressed and wretched condition. Luke states only the outward facts. His fearful sin lay heavily upon him, and the Lord permitted it to crush him for three days. A good deal was required to grind down this mighty Pharisee and implacable foe of the gospel. Shut off from the world, blind, abstaining from food, with no one to help his soul's distress, his proud self-righteousness was conquered, and there remained only a sinner in the dust who ever after felt himself chief of all sinners.[228]

It takes physical blindness for Saul to "see the light," so to speak. He is the ideal person to bring the gospel to the Gentile world, but not while completely engulfed in his Jewish zeal without knowledge (cf. Romans 10:2). His training and skills are excellent, but his heart has not been right. He needed to spend some time in darkness, isolated from his preconceived notions and predetermined mindset, in order to realize the truth that he has been avoiding all along. This proves to us that one who possesses great learning and ability can still be spiritually blind if he refuses the "simplicity and purity of devotion to

---

228   Lenski, *Acts of the Apostles*, 358-359; bracketed word is mine.

Christ" (cf. 2 Corinthians 11:3). Many Jews of Jesus' day were men of great learning and status, yet remained "blinded" by their religious presumptions—a blindness and delusion influenced by Satan himself (see John 3:18-21, 9:39-41, and 2 Corinthians 4:3-4).

Ananias explains his visit to Saul: Christ has sent me so that your sight may be restored and you will be filled with the Holy Spirit (9:17). There is no indication up to this point that Saul *will* regain his sight; he may be thinking that his blindness is permanent. In any case, this meeting is undoubtedly tense, awkward, and intimidating for both men. We are not to think that these few words are *all* that Ananias says to Saul; in fact, there is no reason for Saul to be baptized unless he was specifically instructed to do this. Ananias simply does what he is told: he lays his hands upon Saul; it is Christ who removes Saul's blindness (9:18a).[229]

Upon his having been baptized, Saul receives the Holy Spirit (19:8b; recall 2:38, 5:32).[230] The fact is that *every* person who is obedient to Christ—as evidenced by one's baptism *into* Christ—receives the Holy Spirit (Acts 19:1-3, Romans 8:9, 1 Corinthians 6:19, et al). There is no reason to believe that Ananias imparted any *spiritual (miraculous) gifts* as we saw in 8:14-17; the context and wording are completely different. Ananias is not an apostle: like Philip, he has no authority to confer such

---

229   "The Greek does not indicate that 'scales' or 'something like scales' actually fell from his eyes, but that which Paul experienced was the 'falling away' of 'a sort of scale' or 'film,' which had previously obscured his vision" (Page, *The Acts of the Apostles,* 139).

230   Lenski, a staunch Lutheran, makes great effort to tell us that both the Ethiopian's and Saul's baptisms were carried out with water being poured over these men's heads. Having visited Damascus himself in 1925, Lenski explains that there was insufficient water in the city for one to be immersed, so Saul must have been "baptized" through this pouring method (*Acts of the Apostles,* 366-367). "A vessel filled with water was brought in," he says matter-of-factly, "some of the water was applied to Saul as Jesus had directed in Matt. 28:19, in the name of the Father, etc., and the blessed act was completed" (368). This is an amazing piece of deduction. First, he assumes that the city's water situation has not changed in 1900 years. Second, he literally re-defines the *word* "baptize" through his own insistence. Third, based upon this subjective re-definition, he explains what he thinks then must have happened. I appreciate Lenski's scholarship when in fact he employs it, but when he merely defends a Lutheran practice I am unable to accept his very biased conclusions. In order for Saul *or* the Ethiopian to be baptized, each man had to be immersed in water, since this is what baptism literally means in the Greek text. It is unnatural and unbiblical to conclude otherwise.

power upon anyone; like Simon, he has "no part or portion" in that ministry (recall 8:21).

Instead, Christ personally imparted this ability to Saul during his retreat into Arabia just prior to his meeting with the other apostles. If he received his apostleship *and* divine revelations from Christ (1 Corinthians 1:1, Galatians 1:11-12), it stands to reason that he could have received the ability to perform miracles directly from Him as well. In any case, what Ananias does for Saul is exactly what Christ instructed him to do—no more and no less. We must not assume conclusions that the text simply does not support.

Upon being baptized into Christ, Saul becomes a Christian. (He could not have become a Christian *until* or *unless* this baptism had occurred. He could not have obeyed Christ by refusing what is required of Him; see 22:16.) Because of this one man's conversion, the world has literally never been the same. This is not to discredit at all the efforts of the twelve apostles. These other men are courageous, committed, and of excellent character.

> Nevertheless these men did have limitations that precluded their doing what needed to be done. They were not trained in the schools of the time. In this sense they were unlettered. They were not acquainted with the world outside the confines of their own little land. They knew but little, so far as we know, of Greek philosophy, or Roman culture, or pagan literature and history. They knew nothing of life as it was in such Gentile cities as Ephesus, Corinth and Rome. If Christianity was to be introduced to the Roman world and win a place of recognition in competition with all the other philosophies and religions of the Gentile world it must be done by a man like Paul.[231]

It is true that other apostles will eventually leave the confines of Palestine; church tradition claims that Peter will go to Rome, John will

---

231   Hester, *The Heart of the New Testament*, 254-255.

go to Ephesus, Andrew (allegedly) will go to Scythia, etc.[232] But it may well be said that Saul (Paul) will open the door to these forays into the Empire and beyond. His status as one who sat at the feet of Gamaliel *and* as a Roman citizen gives him considerably greater advantage over the twelve—an advantage of which he never boasts, but one that is evident all the same. Because of this, the eminent historian Philip Schaff writes:

> [Saul] could argue with the Pharisees as a son of Abraham, of the tribe of Benjamin, and as a disciple of the renowned Gamaliel, surnamed 'the Glory of the Law.' He could address the Greeks in their own beautiful tongue and with the convincing force of their logic. Clothed with the dignity and majesty of the Roman people, he could travel safely over the whole empire with the proud watchword: *Civis Romanus sum* [full Roman citizenship]. This providential outfit for his future work made him for a while the most dangerous enemy of Christianity, but after his conversion its most useful promoter. The weapons of destruction were turned into weapons of construction. The engine was reversed, and the direction changed; but it remained the same engine, and its power was increased under the new inspiration.[233]

Nonetheless, some have questioned Christ's method of calling Saul in the first place. They accuse Him of giving Saul preferential treatment ("Why has Jesus never appeared to *me* in the way that He appeared to *Saul*? Why did He never appear to my now-deceased loved one in this manner? If He had, this person might have obeyed the gospel instead of being lost"). Such accusations fail to take into account at least two major points: first, Saul did not have the benefit that all of us have today in the form of a written record (the NT) and the sheer availability of that record (in printed Bibles); second, Saul's ministry is to be far different from that of any Christian today. His appointment

---

232   James M. Gray, "Simon Peter"; James Iverarch, "John, the Apostle"; C. M. Kerr, "Andrew"; all from *ISBE* (electronic edition).

233   Schaff, "St. Paul and the Conversion of the Gentiles," *History*, vol. 1 (electronic edition); bracketed words are mine.

to the office of an apostle (Romans 1:1, Galatians 1:1, et al) requires that he *see* and *hear* Christ in order to be an eyewitness of His resurrection (recall 5:32; see also 1 Corinthians 15:1-8). The nature of his ministry—and the extraordinary responsibilities and struggles that he will have to endure (see 2 Corinthians 11:22-29)—demand an extraordinary calling. It seems reasonable to say that if Christ needed another apostle like Saul *today*, then He would appear to that person in a way similar to how He did to Saul. The fact that no such appearances have been made necessarily proves that He needs no other apostles.

As for us, we have the written record of the gospel "once for all handed down to the saints" (Jude 3). We do not need a personal appearance by Christ to believe who He is, what He has done, and why we should obey Him. We need only to believe what is written, for this is the *purpose* of that written record in the first place (John 20:31). We should not expect—nor demand—some specially-delivered evidence that is beyond the proof God has furnished to *all* men through the resurrection of His Son (Acts 17:30-31). The record stands; it is available for all to read; we should not wait for something else to happen before believing it, nor is something else necessary for such belief.

Saul's preaching in Damascus and Jerusalem (9:19b-31)

Upon his conversion, Saul immediately begins to associate with other Christians in Damascus. His tradition of going to synagogue and the cultural ties he has to his countrymen do not simply terminate upon him becoming a Christian. There is evidence later in Acts which indicates that Saul (Paul) privately will participate in certain Jewish rituals. However, his purpose for going to synagogue has changed: now it is an opportunity to preach that "He [Jesus] is the Son of God" and "the Christ [Messiah]" (9:20, 22; bracketed words added). These are dangerous things to say; such acknowledgment incited the Jews to condemn Jesus (Matthew 26:63-66). Nonetheless, it is substantiated with syllogistic logic:

❑ The Messiah is to fulfill specific, divinely-revealed prophecies of Scripture.

❑ Jesus of Nazareth has fulfilled these specific, divinely-revealed prophecies.

❑ Therefore, Jesus of Nazareth must be the Messiah.

Gareth Reese adds here:

> The phrase "proving that this Jesus is the Christ" is instructive. "Proving" is from the verb *sumbibazo* which means to unite, to compare, to put things together. What Paul did was to make a comparison of the Old Testament prophecies and the facts from the life of Jesus; and then he would draw the inescapable conclusion that Jesus must be the promised Messiah, else how could the perfect agreement between the two be accounted for.[234]

"The Son of God" and "the Christ" are two different designations of the same person (Matthew 16:16, John 20:31). One refers to Jesus' divine nature; the other, to His role as the world's Redeemer ("the Lamb of God who takes away the sin of the world"—John 1:29). Both acknowledgments are necessary for salvation. Both also rise or fall together: if He is one, He must be the other; if He is not one, He cannot be the other. If (since) Jesus *is* the Son of God *and* the Christ, it necessarily follows that the only way to be in fellowship with God is through the redemption offered by Him (Jesus)—which is exactly what Jesus Himself had said (John 14:6). "According to the Scriptures" is the authoritative point of reference in Saul's preaching (see 1 Corinthians 15:1-4).

The people—Christians and non-Christians alike—are dumbfounded at the incredible reversal of Saul's beliefs. No doubt many see it as a possible trap; others simply do not know what to make of it; still others are likely very impressed with it. The people know that Saul originally came to Damascus with the full intent of arresting, imprisoning, and possibly even executing Christians (9:21). His change of heart is indeed perplexing to those who do not know of his experience on the road

---

234   Reese, *Book of Acts*, 364.

to Damascus. Even so, his mastery of the Old Testament coupled with his newfound knowledge that Jesus *the Man* is the Christ *of prophecy* provides him with a powerful and irrefutable means of "confounding the Jews" (9:22).

Shortly after his conversion, however, it appears that Saul leaves Damascus for an unspecified place in Arabia, then returns to Damascus, then after three years goes up to Jerusalem (Galatians 1:15-21). Luke therefore condenses a great deal of time between 9:22 and 9:23. There is no contradiction between the two accounts (i.e., Luke's and Paul's), but they do serve different purposes, and therefore highlight different details. "Nothing that Luke says here about the early period of Saul's life in Christ stands in direct conflict with the account in Galatians," since Luke is being "intentionally general."[235] Just as the twelve apostles needed time (three years) to prepare for their own ministries, Saul also needs time for preparation, reflection, and direct revelations from Christ (Galatians 1:11-12). "Arabia" is a broad and ambiguous description for a large region of desert and wilderness areas to the north, east, and south of Palestine. In ancient times, Arabia often referred to the Sinai Peninsula, but in Saul's day this region juts northward into the southern regions of Mesopotamia (a.k.a. the Fertile Crescent) to the east of Syria. After Saul's return to Damascus, the Jewish leaders are convinced that he is a traitor—or insane (as some thought about Jesus—Mark 3:21; see also Acts 26:24-25, 2 Corinthians 5:13)—and decide to destroy him. "After many days"—i.e., after a significant but unspecified amount of time—a plot is laid against his life, but "his disciples" (those who support Saul) inform him of this and help him to escape the city secretly "by night" (9:23-25).[236]

After his escape from Syria, Saul goes to Jerusalem where he encounters the same resistance and opposition that he experienced in Damascus

---

235   Gaertner, *Acts*, 160, 162.

236   In 2 Corinthians 11:32-33, Saul (Paul) says that even Aretas the "king" (of Arabia) is involved in this plot. Aretas was the father-in-law of Herod Antipas, but the two men had little liking for each other and engaged in a bitter border dispute in the years previous (Henry E. Dosker, "Aretas," *ISBE* [electronic edition]).

(9:26-28). (We are left to wonder how differently Saul views Jerusalem now—the center of Jewish heritage and pride, but also the city where God's Son was murdered; see Matthew 23:27.) The Christians in that city simply do not know what to make of him, and fear that he may be an impostor. Barnabas (recall 4:36), however, "took hold of him and brought him to the apostles," which implies that even some of the apostles initially have some serious misgivings about Saul's sincerity.[237] After this introduction, Saul enjoys fellowship with the church, and stays with Peter for fifteen days (Galatians 1:18-19). He also is able to move throughout the city with little interference—at least for a while.

Eventually, however, Saul becomes embroiled in discussions and disputes with the Hellenistic (Greek-speaking and possibly Greek-born) Jews within the city (9:29). These may well be the same Jews with whom Stephen had argued (recall 6:9-10). Just as they could not contend with the sound logic of Stephen, so they are unable to do any better against Saul. The reason for this is because it is really neither Stephen's nor Saul's logic being used against them, but that of the Holy Spirit. At this point, Saul becomes a lightning rod for controversy and confrontation. It is likely that his very presence in Jerusalem causes great (and avoidable) trouble, making it difficult for the other Christians there. "The same zeal which had caused his voice to be heard in the Hellenistic Synagogues in the persecution against Stephen, now led Saul in the same Synagogues to declare fearlessly his adherence to Stephen's cause. The same fury which had caused the murder of Stephen, now brought the murderer of Stephen to the verge of assassination."[238] Thus, he is sent away to Caesarea by which he can return by sea to his homeland—Tarsus in the Roman province of

---

237   In Galatians 1:18-19, Paul specifically says that he only saw Cephas (Peter) and "James, the Lord's brother." There is no contradiction between the two accounts, given Luke's general usage of the word "apostles."

238   Conybeare and Howson, *Life and Epistles*, 86.

Cilicia—which is well over 300 miles away (9:30).[239] He will not return again to Jerusalem for a number of years (Galatians 2:1).[240]

If we piece together what Luke records of Saul's (Paul's) early Christian history with what Paul also provides in Galatians, this is what appears to have happened:

❑ Saul is converted (ca. AD 35) in the several days between Christ's appearance to him and Ananias' visit. This culminates in his baptism in Damascus (Acts 9:1-19).

❑ Saul spends "many days" in Damascus thereafter, preaching and teaching that Jesus is the Son of God and practicing his new-found faith (Acts 9:20-22).

❑ After the Jews in Damascus form a plot against Saul's life, he escapes from that city and disappears for a while (Acts 9:23-25, 2 Corinthians 11:32-33).

❑ Likely it is at this point that Saul retreats into Arabia, both to contemplate his radical conversion, to immerse himself in his studies, and receive divine revelations (Galatians 1:17). It seems reasonable to assume that the "Arabia" mentioned here refers to Syrian Arabia (because of its proximity to Damascus), rather than the Sinai Peninsula far to the south of Jerusalem.

❑ After this time, Saul returns to Damascus—better trained and more prepared to deal with his ministry (Galatians 1:17).

---

239 Tarsus had already been settled for over a millennium before Saul was born there. Formerly a Hittite, then Persian, city, Tarsus was taken over by Alexander the Great, and became one of the leading centers of Greek scholarship in the world. "Saul's background in Tarsus uniquely equipped him for the work to which God had called him. Few others in the world at that time could have been what this man was. Saul was a devout Jew by family upbringing in Tarsus and rabbinic training in Jerusalem, a member of the Hellenistic world who was fluent in *koin* Greek both spoken and written, and a citizen of both Tarsus and Rome" (Barnett, *Early Christianity*, 262). William M. Ramsay devotes a great deal of his book, *The Cities of St. Paul: Their Influence on His Life and Thought, The Cities of Eastern Asia Minor* (Whitefish, MT: Kessinger Publishing, 2004) to a wordy but significant understanding of the history, geography, philosophy, politics, and religion of the city of Tarsus (85 – 244). His material provides far too much depth to reproduce in this commentary.

240 The "fourteen years" reference in Galatians 2:1 is almost certainly calculated from Paul's conversion, not from his escape from Jerusalem in our present text. Thus, it is actually about ten or eleven years after the present situation, not fourteen.

❑ "Three years later"—likely calculated from the time from his conversion in Damascus—Saul "went up to Jerusalem." Initially, he tries to associate with the church there, but they resist him due to his past history (Acts 9:26). It is not until Barnabas "took hold" of Saul that he is personally introduced to Peter and James (the brother of the Lord), and he spends "fifteen days" with Peter (compare Acts 9:27 and Galatians 1:18-19). (It is assumed that the other apostles are on missions elsewhere, just as Peter himself later pursued in Acts 9:32ff.)

❑ While in Jerusalem, Saul spends time reasoning and debating with the Judaists, and especially with the Hellenistic Jews—Greek-speaking, foreign-born Jews (as opposed to the Judean Jews who were born and raised in Jerusalem and its environs). These latter Jews, unable to reason against or accept what Saul is teaching, form a plot against his life, thus forcing him to leave Jerusalem.

❑ Next, Saul travels northward into Syria, then westward into the Anatolian Peninsula (modern-day Turkey) into his own home region of Cilicia, and specifically to the city of Tarsus (Acts 9:30, Galatians 1:21).

❑ Saul will remain in Tarsus for an indefinite period of time, until Barnabas seeks him out for the work in Antioch of Syria (Acts 11:22-26). Thus, he disappears for a number of years from the chronology of Luke's narrative at this point.

After the uproar over Saul ceases, the church "enjoyed peace," in spite of the turmoil and persecution that he himself had initiated following Stephen's martyrdom (9:31). It is possible, too, that the attention of the Jews has been re-directed from the Christians to the provocations of Emperor Gaius Caesar.[241] Insulted by Jewish repulsion of his delusional aspirations (since he claimed to be a brother of Zeus, and thus a divine being), Gaius orders that a statue of himself be erected in the Temple in Jerusalem. He sends Petronius, the distinguished Roman commander over Syria, to enforce this; thus, 18,000 Roman soldiers march into Jerusalem. Petronius, however, being moved by the Jews' willingness to

---

241 Gaius Caesar is also known as Caligula ("little boots"), a fond nickname given to him by his father, but which became a contemptuous name for him used by some of his military officers who had little respect for this depraved and self-infatuated ruler.

die rather than to allow such sacrilege, petitions Gaius to reconsider. The emperor is furious and commands Petronius to fall upon his sword; yet very soon afterward he (Gaius) is assassinated. News of this assassination travels faster than the news of his order, however, and Petronius is spared—and the statue is never erected.[242] All of this occurs during AD 39-41, which corresponds chronologically with Acts 9.

Peter's Ministry (9:32-43)

Peter's healing of Aeneas (9:32-35)

Luke abruptly ends his narrative concerning Saul (for now) and turns his attention to Peter's ministry (9:32). It seems apparent that the church in Jerusalem is becoming increasingly self-governed, allowing the apostles themselves to engage in various missionary efforts. Thus, Peter travels throughout Judea preaching the gospel, and winds up in Lydda. This is the ancient city of Lod (1 Chronicles 8:12), some 20 miles west of Jerusalem, on the Plain of Sharon near the Mediterranean coast. While there, Peter encounters Aeneas, a man who suffers from some kind of physical paralysis that prevents him from walking.[243] Peter heals him, giving all credit to the power of Jesus Christ (9:33-35). News of this miracle spreads throughout that area and many people "turned to the Lord" because of it. Incidentally, this is the first time "saints" [Greek, *hagios*, lit., "holy ones"] is used by Luke to describe Christians (see also 9:41, 1 Corinthians 1:2).

Peter's healing of Dorcas (9:36-43)

Joppa, a seaport on the coast (and the same city from which Jonah fled to Tarshish some 800 years earlier), is about 10 miles from Lydda. In that city, a well-respected woman named Tabitha (a.k.a. Dorcas) falls sick and dies (9:36-37). The fact that her friends have "washed

---

242   Josephus, "Wars of the Jews," 2.10.1-5; "Antiquities," 18:8.7-9.

243   The NASB uses the term "paralyzed"; older versions or translations use "palsy." Both words refer to the loss of sensation or the movement of any part of the body, and may include uncontrollable muscle spasms (tremors). This condition is debilitating, and can also be fatal (Alexander MacAlister, "Palsy; Paralysis; Paralytic," *ISBE* [electronic edition]).

her body"—in preparation for her burial—indicates that she is most certainly dead. "The disciples" in Joppa indicates that there *are* disciples in that city, likely due to the dispersion following the exodus from Jerusalem due to Saul's persecution (9:38). These people beseech Peter to come to Joppa without delay, and he agrees to do so. It is possible that he is summoned while the woman is still sick, but she dies before his arrival; if so, the situation is very similar to that of Jesus being summoned to heal Lazarus (John 11:1ff). We have no record so far of Peter raising anyone from the dead; thus, we should not assume that they are requesting him to do this. The fact that Luke records her death before he does the summons for Peter does not demand that the one followed the other, but that the two accounts are necessarily related.

Upon arriving in the "upper room" where Tabitha's dead body now lays, Peter is confronted with all of the stories and acts of kindness that this woman did when she was alive (9:39). Boles provides a moving account:

> Dorcas had made these [garments] and the widows were displaying them as an appeal to Peter to help them in some way. This presented a very vivid and pathetic picture; to see the prostrate body of Dorcas lying cold and stiff in death, and to see the work of her hands which had blessed and helped so many, and to hear the grief-stricken widows sobbing in sorrow for the loss of their friend and sister; it must have made a very strong appeal to Peter.[244]

Peter makes everyone leave the room, however, and prays over her—and God *brings her back to life* (9:40). Peter's kneeling by Tabitha's bedside and speaking life into her dead body is reminiscent of Jesus' healing of Jairus' daughter (Matthew 9:25-26); this scene is also reminiscent of Elijah's healing of the widow's son (1 Kings 17:20-23) and Elisha's healing of the Shunammite's son (2 Kings 4:32-37). Peter then "presented her alive" to all of her friends and fellow believers, and news of this spreads throughout the city (9:41). Again, many are

---

244   Boles, *A Commentary on Acts*, 158; bracketed word is mine.

convinced of the authenticity of the gospel message because of a miracle and thus they "believed in the Lord" (9:42). Following this, Peter spends "many days" in Joppa at the house of Simon the "tanner"—i.e., one who prepares skins (hides) of dead animals for leather (9:43). Tanners are typically looked down upon by Jewish purists, since tanners deal regularly with death (and the stench of death), rendering them unclean.[245] That Peter stays with a man of this profession indicates a reconsideration of his views regarding the Law and its ceremonial requirements (see Mark 7:18-19, Romans 14:14, and 1 Timothy 4:4-5). This also sets the stage for one of the most significant conversion cases in all of history.

---

245   The Law of Moses does state that one is rendered "unclean" if he touches the carcass of an unclean animal (Leviticus 5:2, 11:24); even if he touches the body of a clean animal that dies naturally (versus being slain), he will be unclean only until evening (Leviticus 11:39). We are not told what *kind* of animals Simon the tanner dealt with, but it is likely that his profession was generally frowned upon regardless, simply by its association with death.

❦ Chapter 10 ❦
Cornelius' Conversion

Cornelius' vision (10:1-8)

Caesarea Palestina (also known as Caesarea Maritima) was one of the most ambitious building projects of the ancient world. Since the Palestinian coastline had no natural seaport of any significant size, ships had to remain in deep water, battered by wind and waves. This situation also made getting cargo from the ships to land very difficult. King Herod (a.k.a. Herod the Great; reigned 37 – 4 BC), desperate to cull the favor—and trade income—of Rome, provided a solution: an artificial harbor with walls to buffer from the wind, as a safe haven for ships to dock. He named this "Caesarea," in honor of Caesar Augustus.[246] (This seaport took 13 years to build and was completed in 9 BC.) Below is a rendition of what it may have looked like (looking north) based upon historical accounts and existing physical ruins.

On another level, Caesarea serves as an intrusion of Roman influence into the heartland of the Jews. The Romans use the port as a sea entrance for bringing troops into Judea to enforce Roman laws and

---

246   "There was a standing quarrel between the Greeks and the Jews, as to whether it was a Greek city or a Jewish city. The Jews appealed to the fact that it was built by a Jewish prince. The Greeks pointed to the temples and statues. The quarrel was never appeased till the great war broke out, the first act of which was the slaughter of 20,000 Jews in the streets of Caesarea" (Conybeare and Howson, *Life and Epistles*, 607). See also Josephus, "Wars of the Jews," 2.18.1.

policies. This gives Rome an advantage to entice Judea to assimilate into the Empire, as is expected of all other vassal provinces. On the other hand, God uses Caesarea as a tool *against* the Romans in the spread of Christianity throughout the Empire.

> Rome chose Caesarea as the city to defeat God by Romanizing the people in God's city (Jerusalem). God, in ironic response, chose Caesarea as the city to defeat Rome by Christianizing Romans in this city of Rome (Cornelius). Said again, Caesarea did not infect God's city with Romanization, rather Caesarea infected Rome with Christianity! Paul's imprisonment here (Acts 23) made Caesarea the gospel's post office, with ships mailing his spiritual messages across the world. And, as further example of the futility of opposing God, God reached within the walls and made Rome's soldier His soldier.[247]

Thus, it is rather conspicuous that God chooses a Roman soldier in a Romanized seaport of the busiest sea in the entire world to spread His gospel "to the end of the earth" (Acts 13:47).

We do not know anything factual about Cornelius other than what is provided in this account (10:1-2). "Centurion" (*centurii*) originally referred to an officer in command of 100 soldiers. Later, this number was reduced to 60 or 80 men, while the *centurii* became a rank or military designation rather than referring to a literal number of men.[248] Often career soldiers, centurions form the backbone and stabilizing force of the Roman military. (Another famous yet unnamed centurion is the one who petitioned Jesus on behalf of his servant; see Matthew 8:5-13.) Polybius writes: "Centurions are required not to be bold and adventurous so much as good leaders, of steady and prudent mind, not prone to take the offensive or start fighting wantonly, but able when

---

247   Mitchell, "Acts," Appendix 9.1.

248   Ibid., Appendix 8.1. The Greek word for "centurion" in Acts 10:1 is actually *hekatonarches*, "the captain of one hundred men" (*Strong's* [electronic edition], #G1543). Whether this number (100) was taken literally or generally is not known for certain, since the usage of this designation changed over time.

overwhelmed and hard-pressed to stand fast and die at their post."[249]
The "Italian cohort" (or, battalion) is thought to refer to the infamous
legionnaires, a rather small but potent and deadly arm of the Roman
military that specifically guards the Emperor and other Roman officials.

Cornelius is likely a physically strong man and wields impressive
authority in the city of Caesarea. He is also praised as "a devout man,
and one who feared God," a man of prayer and one who monetarily
supports the Jews in his city.[250] It is conspicuous that a man of his
caliber needs to hear anything at all from Peter; many people today
would consider him a "good, moral person" and therefore justified
before God on this basis alone.[251] Yet, while Cornelius *is* a good,
moral person, generally speaking, he is not a *child of God*. He has not
been "born of God" (John 1:12-13); he remains a sinner in need of the
atoning blood of Christ. He could not remain "devoted to God" by
spurning the invitation to become a Christian. God certainly approves
of this man as a choice candidate for salvation, but he is not saved until
he obeys the gospel of Christ.

At "the ninth hour" (3 p.m.), Cornelius sees an angel of God "in a
vision" (10:3). This is not an actual dream as when one is sleeping,
but *is* dream-like in some respects. "Vision," in this context, refers
to an intense manifestation of a supernatural being (like an angel)

---

249   Quoted in Bruce, *The Book of the Acts*, 215. Polybius, a Greek historian
(ca. 203 – 120 BC), is famous for *The Histories*, which covers the rise of the Roman
Republic.

250   It is clear from this account—and its implications—that while Cornelius is a
devout *supporter* of the Jews, he is an uncircumcised Gentile rather than a circumcised
proselyte. This is what sets his situation apart from earlier Gentiles who have become
Christians (such as "Nicolas, a proselyte [i.e., a Gentile convert to Judaism] from
Antioch" [Acts 6:5] and the Ethiopian eunuch). This is why titling this chapter "First
Gentile Convert" (as has been previously done) is in error or misleading at best. "First
Uncircumcised Convert" would be a more appropriate title, as is the title chosen in this
commentary.

251   It is also conspicuous that the angel that spoke to Cornelius did not *himself* tell
the centurion what to do to be saved. In fact, we never see angels preaching the gospel
instead of men; they are messengers, not evangelists; they are ministers to the saints
(Hebrews 1:14), not preachers of the gospel. It is also true that whatever an angel *does*
communicate to men is never in contradiction to what men have been commanded to
preach as the gospel—and even if an angel were to do this, we ought not to listen to
him (Galatians 1:8).

or the unfolding of events. Cornelius unmistakably sees "an angel of God"—i.e., he sees a man-like figure that nonetheless has otherworldly characteristics. This angel describes Cornelius' devotion to God with reference to a priestly sacrifice: "Your prayers and alms have ascended as a memorial before God" (10:4; see Leviticus 2:2, 24:7, et al). Indeed, Cornelius prays during the traditional Jewish times of prayer even though he remains an uncircumcised Gentile. Cornelius is told to send for Simon Peter who is at Joppa, some 30 miles south of Caesarea (10:5-6).[252] What is impressive here is not only that Cornelius responds obediently to the vision, but that he is able to easily convince others (who had *not* seen the vision) of its credibility. Thus, he dispatches two of his own household servants as well as a very trustworthy soldier from among his own inner circle to send for Peter (10:7-8). While angels may be instrumental in bringing a believer together with the gospel message, the decision to receive and obey that message remains always with the believer, not the angel.

Peter's vision (10:9-16)

The next day, Peter is upon the housetop, also at a time of prayer (10:9). (Housetops in Peter's day, as in modern times in that same area, are flat and often encased with a parapet or low wall; see Deuteronomy 22:8.) He becomes hungry—the Greek indicates *very* hungry, having a strong desire to eat.[253] Suddenly, he "fell into a trance" (10:10); this is something different than a literal vision (in which a person "sees" something while fully cognizant of his actual surroundings). In a trance, a person has a kind of out-of-body experience (similar to what Ezekiel had—Ezekiel 8:1-3).[254] While in this state, Peter sees a spread-open sheet descending from the sky, filled with all sorts of animals, some of which are "unclean" for consumption according to the Law

---

252   Boles notes: "Philip the evangelist was in Caesarea (Acts 8:40). Why was not Philip called? We are not told; however, Peter had 'the keys to the kingdom of heaven' (Matt. 16:19), and he is to give by the Holy Spirit the conditions of salvation to the Gentiles; Peter is to open the door to the Gentiles" (*A Commentary on Acts*, 161).

253   *Strong's* (electronic edition), #G4361.

254   The Greek word for "trance" is *ekstasis*, lit., a displacement of the mind. It is the same word from which we get the English word "ecstasy" (*Strong's* [electronic edition], #G1611). Luke also refers to this trance as a "vision" (10:17), but only in the most general sense.

of Moses (10:11-12; see Leviticus 11). "Unclean" in this context does not mean *immoral* (or sinful) but *ritually unacceptable*. (However, if one is commanded for *any* reason not to eat these animals, then it *is* immoral or sinful for him to violate that command. The emphasis, then, is not so much on the animals themselves as one's obedience of the commandment concerning them.) God allowed certain "clean" animals for the Israelites for two major reasons: such animals are hygienic in nature (i.e., they are not animals of prey, carnivores, or omnivores)[255]; and this separation would distinguish the diet of the Israelite from that of the heathens (who ate indiscriminately and did not always drain the blood from their animals; see Leviticus 17:10-11).

In this trance, "a voice came to him" and said, "Get up, Peter, kill [lit., sacrifice] and eat!" (10:13). Remember that Peter is *very* hungry, and it appears that he is being given permission to eat of any of these animals. Yet, Peter's loyalty to the deeply ingrained teachings of the Law as well as his own conscience prevent him from accepting that directive—at least at first. God never instructs a person to violate his conscience, but it is also true that a man's conscience can be changed or re-trained to obey God more accurately. That this voice speaks three times (see Genesis 41:32) indicates its heavenly origin and its emphatic message: "What God has cleansed, no longer consider unholy" (10:14-16).[256] God did not change a *moral* law (see table below), but a ritual

---

255   Since some of the animals that the Israelites ate were also used in sacrifices to God, it was necessary that there be no association of these animals with an inappropriate means of death. In other words, animals that were not slain specifically *for* sacrifice could not *be* sacrificed. Animals that died naturally, were killed by other animals, or in which there was any putrefaction (i.e., rotting carcasses) could not be sacrificed. Thus, those classes of animals that *feed* on such carcasses could not be used for sacrifice. The dietary restrictions of the Jews served as one facet of the "barrier of the dividing wall" between Jews and Gentiles, which was abolished in the once-for-all sacrifice of Christ (cf. Ephesians 2:13-14).

256   God cannot "cleanse" *moral* abominations, since these are directly offensive to His holy nature. The fact that He can "cleanse" (or, remove the stigma of) dietary restrictions indicates that what rendered these animals "unclean" in the first place was not because of anything inherently *sinful* in consuming them. As the Law has been fulfilled in Christ, such distinctions are no longer necessary. Because of this, "unholy" in this context means "common" in contrast with that which is considered sacred *by application*. The reasons why these animals were previously *rendered* common (or, profane) was because of the Law, not because the mere eating of these animals would morally corrupt a person (see Mark 7:18-19, Colossians 2:20-23, and 1 Timothy 4:1-5).

observance of the Law of Moses. This indicates that that Law is being made obsolete and "ready to disappear" (cf. Hebrews 8:13).[257] We today are simply unable to comprehend the impact and scope of such a message; to a pious Jew, it seems to be in contradiction to what has been strictly reinforced for some 1,500 years. Yet, *regardless* of how offensive this idea might have seemed to a pious Jew, it is *not* offensive to God—and this fact alone is sufficient reason for Peter to reconsider everything he had previously come to believe. The prophet Joel predicted a great upheaval in the Jewish system (recall 2:16-21), but Peter has not yet seen the full manifestation of that upheaval—until now.

Moral Laws in Covenant	Ritual Laws in Covenant
Commanded by God	Commanded by God
Consistent with God's holy nature	Consistent with God's holy nature
Identical in every covenant of God	Different from covenant to covenant
Cannot change (timeless)	Can be changed, as God deems necessary
Universal (apply to all people in all covenants with God)	Limited to those within a specific covenant with God (non-assumable, non-transferable)
Define the expected or righteous behavior of those in covenant with God	Physical signs or observances that point to a spiritual reality

Peter meets with Cornelius in Caesarea (10:17-33)

While Peter is "greatly perplexed" [lit., filled with self-doubt; unable to make sense of (something)],[258] the messengers from Cornelius arrive at the door downstairs and ask for Peter (10:17-18). Meanwhile, the Holy

---

257   God allowed a 40-year transition period—between the establishment of Jesus' church and the destruction of Jerusalem (AD 30 – 70)—in which the gospel was preached to the Israelite nation. During that time, those Jews who heard the gospel were obligated to obey it, since everything in the Law of Moses anticipated this gospel and God's covenant with Israel was fulfilled by Christ Himself. Those who did *not* hear it were still obligated to obey the Law of Moses, since they knew of nothing else. Upon the destruction of Jerusalem—God's judgment against and break with the nation of Israel—it is only the gospel of Christ that He recognizes, since the Law could no longer be kept. Thus, the author of the Epistle to the Hebrews can speak of the first covenant as being literally fulfilled in Christ and at the same time "ready to disappear" all at once.

258   *Strong's* (electronic edition), #G1280.

Spirit informs Peter that these men have arrived, and to "accompany them without misgivings" or reservations since He has arranged for this meeting (10:19-20). The Spirit is directly instrumental in bringing together preachers and listeners, but intentionally does not provide all the specific details of their circumstances (recall 8:29). Thus, the Spirit reveals to Peter only what is necessary; the rest of what Peter needs to know will soon be self-evident. Peter presents himself to these men and is told only that he is to bring "a message" to Cornelius. Since it is too late in the day to travel all the way back to Caesarea, Peter hosts these Gentiles at this house in Joppa—something he might never have done previous to his vision—and then accompanies them to Caesarea on the following morning (10:21-23).

"Now Cornelius was waiting for them" (10:24)—in other words, we see a man excited and anxious to hear what message this man of God will bring. Not only this, but he has also "called together his relatives and close friends"—the dream situation of any evangelist! "So Cornelius has taught us by his example," Calvin notes, "that when God reveals himself to us we must not put out the light of his knowledge with sloth or fear, but we must rather take care to let our faith give other people light and show them the way."[259] Yet when Peter arrives, Cornelius bows to worship him—likely as a means of expressing deep respect and gratitude. Nonetheless, it is an action that Peter quickly rejects as inappropriate and unnecessary (10:25-26; see Revelation 19:10, 22:8-9). "This act of Cornelius' does all credit to his humble and willing spirit; but Peter's refusal to accept such an honor does equal credit to him."[260]

Peter confirms the awkwardness of this meeting by reminding the crowd of "many people" that it is "unlawful" for him to be there—i.e., it is in violation of the separation between Jews and Gentiles for him to socialize with them (10:27-28a). What Peter means by "unlawful" here indicates a violation of Jewish *custom* or *expectations*, not a violation of the Law itself. There is nothing in the Law that forbids a Jew to be

---

259   Calvin, *Acts*, 177.

260   Lenski, *Acts of the Apostles*, 412.

under a Gentile's roof, but the Jews believe that such social interaction will render them unclean and thus unable to participate in Jehovah worship (see John 4:9 and 18:28). Peter also makes it clear that he has understood the application of the visionary message that was given to him (10:28b-29). God has given His divine approval for him to "associate" with Cornelius as one who is also regarded as "holy" and "clean." Thus, all personal, ethnic, and social taboos are made irrelevant for the sake of a higher purpose—even though this purpose has not yet been revealed to Peter.

So then, Peter asks Cornelius, in essence, "Why am I here?" In response, Cornelius recounts his vision to him (10:30-33). "Cornelius not only commends Peter for his courage in breaking away from Jewish customs, but he takes no offense at the implied superiority of the Jews over the Gentiles; he tells Peter that his circle of close friends are [*sic*] present to hear the message from God that Peter has. This audience was fertile soil for the preaching of the gospel to the Gentiles."[261] As Cornelius explains the situation, Peter's mind opens up and he suddenly grasps the enormity of the situation before him.[262]

Peter's message to Cornelius (10:34-48)

Peter is no doubt astonished by what he has just heard! Even so, he is thinking clearly: "I most certainly understand {now} that God is not one to show partiality" (10:34). "Partiality" is a bias or favoritism based upon a personal or subjective system of evaluation. It is something men have long *assumed* that God has exercised, largely through a misunderstanding of His purpose for those with whom He seemed to favor (consider Deuteronomy 7:7-8, for example). Yet, the individual regard that God has for *all* men is foreshadowed in the Hebrew prophets (Isaiah 42:6, 49:5-6, 51:4, et al), inasmuch as He has been unveiling His universal gospel since the time of Abraham (Genesis 12:3). One of the great hallmarks of the gospel of Christ is its *impartial*

---

261   Boles, *A Commentary on Acts*, 170.

262   Consider the implications of Jesus' words to the apostles in Luke 24:45 in conjunction with what is happening. This informs us that the opening of their minds was not a one-time event but a continuous process that occurred on an as-needed basis.

regard for all people, since we have *all* sinned against God (Romans 3:23) and are *all* made "one in Christ Jesus" (Galatians 3:28; see Romans 2:9-11).

"But in every nation the man who fears Him and does what is right is welcome to Him" (10:35). This demands that reverence *for* God and obedience *to* Him are inseparable: if one claims to revere ("fear") God, he must also obey Him; if one claims to be obedient to God, he must also revere Him. This statement also denies the legitimacy of any religion that contradicts God's commandments, since this is *not* "right." No one comes to God except through Jesus Christ (John 14:6), and no one can learn of Christ except through His gospel ("the word"— Romans 10:17). Being "welcome" to God, in the context in which Peter uses it, *must* mean that a person is given permission to call upon His name for salvation (see Acts 2:21). It *cannot* mean that a sinner can have fellowship with God apart from having obeyed His gospel.

Jesus had promised that Peter would be given the "keys of the kingdom of heaven" (Matthew 16:19), and we see him exercising that responsibility here. In Acts 2, Peter opened the door to the Jews and invited them to enter into the kingdom of God through obedience to Jesus Christ. In the present case, Peter opens the door to these Gentile believers and invites them into this same kingdom through the same kind of obedience. In having the keys of the kingdom, Jesus did not mean that Peter can save (or condemn) whomever he wants, apart from or regardless of Christ. Rather, he has been chosen as Christ's spokesman for laying out the terms and conditions of salvation to both parties—Jews and Gentiles—in full compliance with what Christ had commanded *him*. In reality, it is Christ who holds all keys to all doors, "who opens and no one will shut, and who shuts and no one opens" (Revelation 3:7). Peter has a special responsibility entrusted to him; he does *not* have authority equal to Christ's.

Peter then outlines the general message of this gospel. (No doubt this message was actually longer than what is recorded here; Luke provides the highlights, not the entire script.) The essential message is as follows (10:36-43):

- ❑ Peace with God is accomplished only through His Son, Jesus Christ.
- ❑ Jesus was an actual flesh-and-blood person, not a myth or legend.
- ❑ Jesus demonstrated in His earthly ministry—the time between His baptism by John the Baptist and His resurrection—that He was indeed the Christ, the fulfillment of Jewish prophecy concerning the Messiah.
- ❑ Jesus was "anointed" with the Holy Spirit, by whose power He performed miracles, and especially miracles of healing (Matthew 4:23-25). To be anointed by God means to be chosen by Him for a specific ministry (as a prophet, priest, king, deliverer, etc.). Inasmuch as Jesus was given the Spirit "without measure" (John 3:34), His anointing was superior to that of all other servants of God.
- ❑ "Oppressed by the devil" indicates an enslavement to Satan because of sin, guilt, and the fear of judgment. In Jesus' day, this enslavement was physically manifested through disease, impairment, and demon possession. Jesus' mastery over and healing of these problems illustrated His power over Satan and the demonic realm (Luke 13:16, 2 Timothy 2:26, and Hebrews 2:14-15).
- ❑ "For God was with Him"—the miracles He performed proved this, as Nicodemus observed (John 3:2) and as Jesus Himself had said (John 5:36).
- ❑ The Jews put Jesus to death "by hanging Him on a cross," but "God raised Him up on the third day" (Matthew 12:39-40, 16:21, Acts 2:23-24, 4:10, et al).
- ❑ There are witnesses as to what has happened to Jesus, the foremost of whom are Peter and the other apostles. These men "ate and drank" with Jesus after His resurrection—i.e., they can testify that Jesus' bodily resurrection was real and not a myth or hallucination (1 Corinthians 15:3-8, 1 John 1:1-3). Cornelius has only heard of these events, but Peter and the apostles have actually seen them.
- ❑ Jesus commissioned the apostles to begin preaching the gospel of salvation in His name (Acts 4:12). In so doing, they also necessarily indict the Jewish authorities who orchestrated His execution.
- ❑ God is the "Judge of the living and the dead"—this has multiple meanings: "the living" can refer to those who already know God (the Jews), and "the dead" can refer to those who have no

relationship with Him (the Gentiles; see Ephesians 4:17-18). Or, "the living" can mean those who are *presently* in fellowship with Him (Christians), and "the dead" can refer to those who are *outside* of this fellowship (non-Christians; see Ephesians 2:1). Or, "the living and the dead" can be taken literally, since *all* men—regardless of whether or not they remain on this earth—are accountable to Him (1 Peter 4:5).

❑ All who believe in and obey this gospel will receive the forgiveness of sins, regardless of nationality or other earthly distinctions (Romans 10:11-13). This is the revealing of the "mystery" of the ancient prophets (cf. Ephesians 3:1-11).

Before Peter finishes speaking, God gives His divine stamp of approval to this message with a divine manifestation of His power (10:44). The expression "the Holy Spirit fell upon [them]" is to be understood in the present context and not as a standalone phrase. Peter says: "Surely no one can refuse the water for these to be baptized who have received the Holy Spirit just as we did, can he?" (10:47)—and many have supposed that the "we" here includes the six men who accompanied him to Cornelius' house (see 11:12). But there is zero substantiation for this; it is clear that Peter means "we" as in *we apostles*, and that his words are explanatory to the six men rather than including them. (John does the same thing in 1 John 1:1-4.) The purpose of this miraculous manifestation of the Spirit is not to save Cornelius and the others, but to *indicate God's wholesale acceptance* of uncircumcised Gentile people as candidates *for* salvation.[263] This is evident in the response of those Jews who accompanied Peter: the Holy Spirit has been poured out on *them* (Gentiles) just as He has been poured out upon *us* (Jews) (10:45-46).[264] (Their statement is not in contradiction to what we

---

263 As we have noted earlier, Cornelius was not literally the first Gentile to become a Christian; however, he *was* the first uncircumcised Gentile (who had not already become a proselyte of the Jewish religion) to become a Christian. Thus, this is a watershed moment in which a person did not have to go *through* the Jewish religion (so to speak) in order to come to Christ. It is at this point that this "barrier" is forever removed (cf. Ephesians 2:13-18).

264 Recall here Acts 2:16-21. The "pouring out" of the Holy Spirit was *manifested* by miracles, but is not *limited* to them. In both cases—Acts 2 and 10—the Holy Spirit acted independently of any human agency in order to reveal a *divine decision* as to who (as a group of people) was invited into the kingdom of God. The Holy Spirit's

have determined earlier, but is only a general reference to it.) We never see God "saving" people apart from their personal demonstration of faith in obedience to His Word; however, we do see God providing the evidence for one's faith and the opportunity to respond to His offer of salvation. Such obedience is tested when Peter commands these people to be "baptized in the name of Jesus Christ"—and they comply (10:47-48).[265] J. W. McGarvey offers excellent insight here:

> If Peter had finished his discourse, promising them the indwelling gift of the Holy Spirit on the terms which he had laid down on Pentecost, and had baptized them [in water], these brethren would have taken it as a matter of course that they had received the indwelling of the Holy Spirit, Acts 2:38. And if, after this, Peter had laid his hands on them and imparted to them the miraculous gift of the Holy Spirit, as in the case of the Samaritans, they would not have been greatly surprised. The considerations which caused the amazement were: first, that the Holy Spirit was "poured out" upon them directly from God, as it had never before been on any but the apostles, and, secondly, that this unusual gift was bestowed on [uncircumcised] Gentiles.[266]

---

unbidden manifestation of a miracle upon Cornelius that is consistent with that which was displayed upon the apostles themselves indicates a common acceptance of the two groups—Jews and Gentiles. Yet, while the *acceptance* is extended to both groups, the *power* (to serve as an apostle; to speak with apostolic authority; and to transmit the ability to perform miracles through the laying on of hands) remains with the hand-picked apostles. Despite the miracle, we never see Cornelius being given equal *power* or *authority* to that which was given to the apostles.

265 Many people misunderstand what is happening here. They assume that because Cornelius was speaking in tongues, therefore he was *already* saved. They assume also that he received the Holy Spirit (in a miraculous way) *because* he is saved. Yet, the situation here is the opposite of what Peter promised to the people in Acts 2:38: if you repent *and* are baptized, *then* you will receive the Holy Spirit—always in that specific sequence. Miracles are not a necessary part of salvation; they only provide God's endorsement of what is happening (or, what *ought* to happen). Thus, Cornelius was not saved *unless* or *until* he did exactly what the Jews had been told: repent [implied] and be baptized into Christ for the forgiveness of sins.

266 J. W. McGarvey, *New Commentary on Acts of Apostles,* vol. 1 & 2 (Delight, AR: Gospel Light Publishing Co., no date [orig. © 1892]), 1:213; bracketed words are mine.

Beasley-Murray says this: "In that case the gift of the Spirit without [water] baptism must be viewed as exceptional, due to a divine intervention in a highly significant situation, teaching that Gentiles may be received into the church by [water] baptism, even when they have not removed their uncleanness through circumcision and sacrifice."[267] There would be no need for this baptism if these people were already Christians; since baptism is commanded of them, they cannot become Christians until they are obedient to the command.[268]

---

267   Beasley-Murray, *Baptism in the New Testament* (Grand Rapids: Eerdmans Publishing, 1962), 108; bracketed words are mine.

268   We *never* see Christians being baptized in Acts; rather, we see believers who wish to *become* Christians being baptized for this very reason. If Cornelius (and company) was already a Christian when he was baptized, it violates what was commanded (in 2:38), every other instance of conversion in Acts, every teaching on baptism as a necessary requirement of salvation in the NT, and the logical explanation of what is happening in the present account. It is a shame that so much explanation has to be offered on this point when the conclusion is clearly evident, yet denominational teachings have so obscured and confused the situation that a lengthier response seems necessary in order to refute such false teachings. God has *one* method of salvation, not many, and it always involves water baptism.

∼ Chapter 11 ∼
Peter's Defense; The Church in Antioch

Peter's Defense (11:1-18)

Philip did not have to defend his preaching to the Ethiopian eunuch because he only spoke with him and did not enter his house. Furthermore, that man was a Jewish proselyte and not an uncircumcised Gentile. In the Jewish mindset, to enter a Gentile's house implies eating his unclean foods, endorsing his unclean lifestyle, and becoming unclean by unnecessary association with an uncircumcised man. Nothing in the Law of Moses forbids an Israelite to eat with a Gentile; however, sharing a common meal with one is too much for the purist Jewish mind to endure. Besides this, these Jews at Jerusalem have not seen what Peter saw nor heard what Peter heard; therefore, they are in a very different "place" than him.

The news of Cornelius' conversion spreads like wildfire. As soon as Peter returns to Jerusalem, he is confronted by "those who were circumcised"—i.e., Jewish Christians. They accuse him of doing something that he should not have done (11:1-3). Peter does not respond in an emotional way or by trying to justify himself. Instead, he provides a kind of "What would *you* have done?"-scenario to these men—that is, if they had been faced with what *he* had faced, would they not have responded the same way (11:4ff)? Peter explains that "the Spirit told me to go" (11:12), and that Cornelius had sent for him in obedience to his own angelic vision (11:14). In other words, this decision was not initiated by Peter but God, as further evidenced by the miraculous endorsement of the Holy Spirit (recall 10:44-46).

"At the beginning" (11:15) indicates that nothing like what happened in Acts 2 had happened since; this event (with Cornelius) is the only one of its kind, with the exception of what the apostles also experienced. "This also shows that the baptism of the Holy Spirit was not to convert people, for Peter would only have had to refer to any case of conversion to prove his point."[269] Peter also cites Jesus' own prediction about

---

269   Boles, *A Commentary on Acts*, 179.

being "baptized with the Holy Spirit" (11:16; recall 1:5) and further links this to the situation with Cornelius. Since Cornelius believed in the Lord *and* He approved of him as an acceptable candidate for salvation (and as a representative of *all* uncircumcised Gentiles), the Holy Spirit responded with His miraculous endowments (see Acts 15:7-11). The "gift" of the Holy Spirit, in this context, is directly related to miracles (as in 8:14-20), whereas the "gift" in Acts 2:38 is directly related to forgiveness of sins (salvation). While it is true that the Holy Spirit would not have given any gift to men to whom He did not *offer* salvation, the miracles themselves are no substitute *for* salvation—or Cornelius' necessary obedience.

Sometimes Christians are hesitant to accept another person's "conversion story" because it does not conform to their personal expectations. This happens today just as it happened in the present account. A legitimate conversion does not have to conform to your or my expectations, but it most certainly *must* conform to God's. We may *assume* our expectations are equal to God's, but we (people) have a bad habit of adding to or subtracting from God's terms and conditions based upon our personal convictions, traditions, prior religious teachings, "bad" experiences, fear, pride, etc. The Jews against whom Peter defends himself *think* that they alone were worthy candidates for entrance into God's kingdom; God has said otherwise, and the Holy Spirit has now proved otherwise by providing—without Peter's having invoked His power—miraculous substantiation of this decision. The Jews thus mean well, but they are mistaken; even Peter had to be re-trained through his own experience (i.e., God's vision of the animals being lowered on a sheet). It is God who dispenses grace and salvation, not people, church leaders, or churches themselves. We must never condemn one of whom God so clearly approves (Romans 9:22-26); we must never force someone to conform to our *personal expectations* for conversion as a mandatory requirement for that person to be saved by God. Forcing a person to comply with men in order to be saved (rather than merely complying with God) constitutes a false doctrine.

The Jews' response to Peter's account is subdued but agreeable. Their statement ("Well then, God has granted to the Gentiles also the repentance that leads to life"—11:18)—is probably more profound than even they realize at the time. As we will see in chapter 15, they may not have truly comprehended its full implications. Furthermore, probably no one yet foresees the great storms of conflict that the inclusion of Gentiles will bring to the church.

11:19-29 The Church in Antioch

Luke now resumes where he left off in 8:4, after Saul's persecution had scattered Christians all over Palestine and beyond (11:19). Phoenicia refers to the ancient realm on the Mediterranean coast to which the famous city-states of Tyre and Sidon belong. Cyprus is the island off the coast of Phoenicia to the west, and was likely first occupied by the early Phoenicians.[270] Antioch of Syria is nearly 200 miles north of Jerusalem. It was founded in 300 BC by Seleucus I Nicator (who also founded 15 *other* cities named "Antioch").[271] It sits on the Orontes River, some 15 miles from the port city of Seleucia. This city once served as the capital of the Seleucids, one of the dynasties that had received a one-fourth portion of Alexander the Great's empire.[272] When it had been absorbed by the Roman Empire (64 BC), Antioch was declared a "free city," meaning that it was able to operate with a self-governing (autonomous) status, as long as it paid its taxes, complied with Roman edicts, and kept the peace. With a large population and a crucial geographical location, Antioch ranked third in importance in the Empire "in magnitude and other marks of prosperity," after Rome and Alexandria.[273] This eclectic Gentile city seems to be an unlikely hub city for what is to come, but the church finds here a strong foothold,

---

270   The ancient Phoenicians were maritime explorers, and are believed to be responsible for significant early colonial establishments in Greece, Sicily, Spain, etc., the most notable being Carthage in North Africa (H. Porter, "Phoenicians," *ISBE* [electronic edition]). Because of this, there is something symbolic (if nothing else) in the spread of the gospel throughout Phoenician territory, since this represents a starting point for many other opportunities for preaching the gospel throughout the Mediterranean theater.

271   Conybeare and Howson, *Life and Epistles*, 101. He also founded nine other cities called Seleucia, and six called Laodicea.

272   Bruce, *The Acts of the Apostles*, 238.

273   Josephus, "Wars of the Jews," 3.2.4.

and in several ways this city eclipses Jerusalem as the focal point of missionary evangelism. The time now is about AD 41-42.

It is in the idolatrous, immoral, and pagan Antioch that the early disciples begin spreading the good news of God's salvation to the spiritually lost and otherwise hopeless Gentile population (11:20-21).[274] The result is phenomenal: the church grows so quickly and so large that the disciples begin seeking outside help. The apostles and other disciples who are in Jerusalem dispatch Barnabas to help with the church in Antioch (11:22-24). The apostles may feel that Barnabas (a Cypriot by birth) will be ideally suited for this particular work. It is also possible that certain apostles are no longer in Jerusalem but are on missionary journeys of their own.[275] "Barnabas was a good man, judicious, broadminded, and generous. He was of the tribe of Levi, spoke Greek, and was well qualified to mix with the people of Antioch; they could trust him to give wise counsel and to bring an accurate report to Jerusalem."[276] But Barnabas also sees that the task is too great for him alone. Thus, he leaves for Tarsus (northwestward to the province of Cilicia, 150 miles away from Antioch) to seek out Saul; upon finding him, the two men throw all of their ministerial efforts into the church in Antioch (11:25-26).[277]

---

274   We must assume that these men (those of Cyprus and Cyrene) did not precede what has just happened with Peter and Cornelius. It is inconceivable to think that God would have allowed such a passive inclusion of the "Greeks" in this case except for what happened in Caesarea. It is logical to assume that Luke first documented Peter's encounter with Cornelius for just this reason—i.e., to highlight the profound and far-reaching effects of that meeting. Also, the church in Jerusalem would never have sent Barnabas to help in a church work that the Jewish Christians (including the other apostles) had not already come to accept.

275   Lenski, *Acts of the Apostles*, 452.

276   Boles, *A Commentary on Acts*, 182-183.

277   It is unknown for certain what Saul had been doing for the last several years. "... In his letter to the Galatians he seems to indicate that he was preaching in Syria and Cilicia [Galatians 1:21ff]. Some commentators have suggested that it was during this period that he suffered some of the physical persecutions to which he later referred [2 Corinthians 11:23ff], and was disinherited by his family [Philippians 3:8?]" (Stott, *The Spirit, the Church, and the World*, 204; bracketed citations are mine). "It is likely that the briefer narratives for Saul's first fourteen years and the disproportionately longer narratives for the succeeding ten years are no accident; the lesser detail for the one and the greater detail for the other may reflect Luke's own view that God's future lay not with Israel but in the west, with the Gentiles. This theological understanding was not an

Like Barnabas, Saul also is well-suited for the work in Antioch. Having been born outside of Judea, in a city (Tarsus) immersed in Hellenism, he already has far more in common with other non-Judeans than do the twelve apostles. He understands their worldview; he has been confronted with their philosophy; he can meet them on their own level. On the other hand, his rabbinic training provides him with a scholarly comprehension of Old Testament scriptures for defending "the Way" as a fulfillment of what had been foretold in the Law and the Prophets. He is fluent in Greek and Hebrew—not just the languages, but also the socio-religious cultures. He is intelligent, well-educated, and personable. Thus, he is an ideal candidate for speaking with both Jews and Gentiles. We do not yet see him acting in an official capacity as an *apostle* (although it is clear that this ultimately will be his calling), but we do see him preparing for that role.

"And the disciples were first called Christians in Antioch" (11:26). Until now, "disciple" has almost exclusively been used to describe those who associated themselves with Jesus Christ. "Christian" [lit., follower of Christ] necessarily implies a new allegiance, no longer to the Law of Moses (in the case of Jews) or any pagan beliefs (in the case of many Gentiles).[278]

> When Gentiles began to listen to what was preached concerning Christ—when they were united as brethren on equal terms, and admitted to baptism without the necessity of previous

---

artificial construct. It was forged from the realities of Paul's own experience in ministry, as observed, reflected upon and finally narrated by the author of the book of Acts. Israel rejected Paul and his message, but the Gentiles welcomed him" (Barnett, *Early Christianity*, 249).

278 "'Christians' is from the Greek 'Christianous'; this termination was frequent in Latin in the early days; whether this name was derived from the Latin or not, the termination became common enough in Greek, and therefore there is no necessity to ascribe the name 'Christianos' to a Roman origin. Later 'Christianos' was modified to 'Chrestianos' (both words being pronounced alike). Each of the three languages has contributed to the formation of this word. The *thought* is Jewish, denoting the Anointed One; the *root*, Christ, is Greek; the *termination*, ianoi, is Latin. So in the providence of God, the same three nations whose differing dialects proclaimed above the cross, 'Jesus the Nazarene, the King of the Jews' [cf. John 19:19-22], now unite in forming a word which for all time shall be applied to those who follow Christ. Antioch, the center from which the gospel radiated among the Gentiles, has given us the common name, Christian" (Boles, *A Commentary on Acts*, 185; bracketed citation is mine).

circumcision—when the Mosaic features of this society were lost in the wider character of the New Covenant—then it became evident that these men [i.e., the missionary preachers— MY WORDS] were something more than the Pharisees or Sadducees, the Essenes or Herodians, or any sect or party among the Jews. Thus a new term in the vocabulary of the human race came into existence at Antioch… Thus Jews and Gentiles, who, under the teaching of St. Paul, believe that Jesus of Nazareth was the Saviour of the world, "were first called *Christians.*"[279]

Thus, Christians—Jews and Gentiles alike—are those who affirm Jesus' divinity, His authority, and His power to redeem souls. It should be noted, however, that the term "Christian" appears to be what *non-believing Gentiles* call the disciples, and is not yet a popular name that the disciples use to identify themselves. The unbelieving Jews would likely avoid the use of "Christian," since they did not believe Jesus to be the Christ; they instead use the term "Nazarenes." Paul, in all of his epistles, not once uses the term "Christian," but instead refers to believers as "saints," "brethren," or "fellow workers." (The word "disciple" does not appear in Scripture after Acts; "Christian" is used only once outside of Acts, in 1 Peter 4:16.)

We assume that Agabus (11:27-30) is the same prophet who later will predict troubles for Saul (Paul) in Jerusalem (in 21:10). "Prophet" (in the New Testament context, as in 1 Corinthians 14:1ff) is not necessarily one who foretells the future; more accurately it describes one who confirms the truth (or provides divine approval) of something, which can include but is not limited to future events. Agabus' prediction here of a great famine most certainly did come true; "all over the world" is understood to mean throughout the Roman Empire, not the entire globe. In fact, during the reign of Emperor Claudius (reigned AD 41-54), the Empire suffered several successive famines (according to accounts from that period of Suetonius and Tacitus), though one

---

279   Conybeare and Howson, *Life and Epistles*, 99.

of the most severe was centered in Palestine.[280] It might seem that the last thing the church needs to deal with is a large-scale famine, yet God does not spare His people from this. There are good reasons for this:

❑ It reinforces the fact that while Christians are "in Christ," they remain also in the physical world, and thus must continue to endure the difficulties of this world.

❑ It compels Christians to look "above" (cf. Colossians 3:1-2) for the time when they will be delivered from these difficulties.

❑ It forces them to depend upon God for their sustenance rather than themselves.

❑ It provides an opportunity for other Christians (who are unaffected by the famine, or who are able to contribute to the needs of others regardless of it) to rise to the occasion and give help to their fellow believers.

❑ It provides an opportunity for God to respond to these needs in whatever way He chooses.

The church in Antioch decides to send relief money in the care of Barnabas and Saul to Judea (ca. AD 46). (Given the dates, this account of the collection actually happens chronologically *after* the following account of Peter's imprisonment and Herod's subsequent death in AD 44; see notes on following section.) "In the proportion that any of the disciples had means, each of them determined to send a contribution..." (11:29)—i.e., this was an offering that was collected by those who volunteered to help (see Romans 15:27, 1 Corinthians 16:1-2, 2 Corinthians 8:8, and 9:5-7). This money is delivered not to the apostles in Jerusalem but to "the elders" (11:30), an office within the churches that appears without explanation (which implies its widespread use and common understanding in Luke's day). This tacitly implies a shift in the oversight of that church from the apostles exclusively to a structure of leadership that will become more familiar to us as the narrative continues (as in 14:23). This is also the first time that monies are collected by the disciples for purposes beyond their own church's needs (compare with 4:32-37).

---

280   Page, *The Acts of the Apostles*, 155; Lenski, *Acts of the Apostles*, 460.

This instance of church benevolence does not cover all situations that will arise in the future, but it does provide a structural precedent for how all such voluntary charity is to be handled. The donated money is not given to a third-party organization to distribute to those who solicit help; it is also not entrusted to *one* church to distribute to *all* the churches. Rather, it is brought directly from the contributors to the need itself—a practice from which Christians today have no good reason to deviate. It is also conspicuous that this money is distributed (as in 4:32-35) only to "the brethren" who are in need. It is not given to those who are *not* in need (as a blanket redistribution of wealth) or to those who are not "brethren." The money is collected *by* the saints and used for the direct benefit *of* the saints. This is the NT pattern concerning the church's collection and distribution of money.

～ Chapter 12 ～
Peter's Arrest and Deliverance

Peter's arrest and imprisonment (12:1-19)

Herod Agrippa I died in AD 44, so we can assign that date to the events in this chapter. (Herod is the grandson of Herod the Great—the Herod who was king during Jesus' birth—and reigned from AD 41-44.)[281] Peter is arrested in the spring of that year, at the time of Passover (12:4).[282] Why Herod singles out James and has him executed is a mystery to us, although it fulfills what Jesus predicted of this apostle (see Matthew 20:20-23 and Mark 10:35-40). James' martyrdom is described with the same brevity as Jesus' own crucifixion, and far less detail than was given to Stephen.[283] Bruce says, "That James should die

---

281   "[Herod Agrippa I] ruled with great munificence [i.e., lavish generosity—CMS] and was very tactful in his contact with the Jews. With this end in view, several years before, he had moved Caligula to recall the command of erecting an imperial statue in the city of Jerusalem; and when he was forced to take sides in the struggle between Judaism and the nascent Christian sect, he did not hesitate a moment, but assumed the role of its bitter persecutor, slaying James the apostle with the sword and harrying [i.e., harassing—CMS] the church whenever possible (Acts 12). He died, in the full flush of his power, of a death, which, in its harrowing details reminds us of the fate of his grandfather. ...With Herod Agrippa I, the Herodian power had virtually run its course" (Henry E. Dosker, "Herod Agrippa I," *ISBE* [electronic edition]; see also Josephus, "Antiquities," 19.8.2).

282   "Easter" in the KJV is a completely inaccurate translation here. The Greek word *pascha* is used exclusively for "Passover"; in the 29 uses of this word in the NT, all of them are elsewhere translated "Passover" in all of the more modern translations. The word "Easter" comes from "the Anglo-Saxon Eastre or Estera, a Teutonic goddess to whom sacrifice was offered in April, so the name was transferred to the paschal feast" (H. Porter, "Easter," *ISBE* [electronic edition]). The *tradition* of an Easter celebration was incorporated into a special observance of the Lord's Supper in the next few centuries after the apostles. The celebration as it exists today is a (highly commercialized) adaptation of ancient Catholicism, in which it was popular to marry pagan rituals with genuine Christian practices in order to reach a broader audience.

283   "With the sword" indicates that James was beheaded, which was a far more dignified execution than crucifixion. Usually, beheading was reserved for Roman citizens, while non-citizens and slaves were typically crucified. While James was not a Roman citizen, we are not told why Herod chose one method over the other. (Decapitation is also one of the four methods of execution among the Jews, the others being stoning, burning, and strangling [Boles, *A Commentary on Acts*, 188].) It is possible that he did not want to associate James's death with that of Jesus, so as not to create (another) martyr for the church; it is also possible that he wanted to send a message to the church by literally chopping the head off of its organization in an attempt to destroy it (recall Gamaliel's comments in 5:34-39). In the end, all such theories do not change the outcome of what happened.

while Peter should escape is a mystery of divine providence which has been repeated countless times in the course of Christian history, down to our own day."[284] McGarvey also adds:

> The death of James, the first apostle who suffered martyrdom, must have been a source of indescribable grief to the church in Jerusalem; and to an uninspired historian, it would have furnished matter for many pages of eloquent writing; what shall we think, then, of Luke as a writer, who disposes of it in a sentence of seven words in the Greek? Surely there is an indication here of some supernatural restraint upon the impulses of the writer, and it is accounted for only by his inspiration.[285]

Herod also arrests Peter with the intention of executing him in the same manner as he did James (12:3). He chooses not to do this, however, until after the Passover, so as not to profane the Jewish festivities (cf. John 19:31) and because it is politically expedient for him to avoid upsetting the Jews. The relationship between the Herodian kings and the Jews has always been tense at best, and sometimes outright hostile. However, the two parties need each other in order to get what they want: Herod needs the Jews' cooperation in order to remain king; the Jews need Herod's cooperation in order to escape full Roman occupation—and, in this case, to rally against the Christians, whom they regard as a heretical assault against the Law. Just as Pilate and Herod became friends over the execution of Jesus (Luke 23:12), so the Jews appear to befriend Herod whenever they need his help in carrying out their self-serving agendas.

Herod places Peter under the watch of sixteen soldiers who are likely Jews and not Romans (12:4).[286] It is very unlikely that all sixteen

---

284   Bruce, *The Book of the Acts*, 251.

285   McGarvey, *Acts of Apostles*, 1:232.

286   There is nothing in the text that compels us to think that these are Roman soldiers, even though they are called a *quaternion* (i.e., a group of four soldiers) in the Greek text and kept the same shifts that Roman soldiers kept. It is likely that Herod simply copied the Roman system and applied it to those soldiers under his charge. It is also unrealistic to think that Herod, a non-Roman official, would be able to sentence Roman soldiers to death (12:19). The persecution against the church is still, at this

men are on duty at the same time, but they are all responsible for this very special prisoner. Peter is chained to a guard on either side of him, kept in a (presumably) locked room with two stations of guards outside of his cell (12:6). "The situation looked extremely bleak, even hopeless. There appeared to be no possibility of Peter's escape. What could the little community of Jesus, in its powerlessness, do against the armed might of Rome?"[287] In other words, Peter cannot escape his imprisonment undetected with anything *short* of a miracle. While Peter awaits his seemingly certain execution, the church prays for him, just as we are told to pray for all who are imprisoned for their faith today (Colossians 4:2-4, Hebrews 13:3).[288]

Yet, just as before (recall 5:17-20), an angel of the Lord rescues Peter from certain death (12:7-10). In other words, Peter is delivered by *divine intervention*—the Lord's command, as carried out through His angel—rather than by human effort. The angel instructs Peter as to what to do, and Peter complies, though he is unaware at first that such actions are really happening. Peter's release seems dreamlike—due to its unexpectedness as well as its incredibleness—but it is hardly a dream. A person cannot dream his way out of a well-guarded prison; a dream

---

point in history, completely *Jewish* in nature, and thus it is Jews who carry it out. While Herod himself is not a Jew, his reasons for imprisoning Christians is all about placating the Jewish leadership, whose support he desperately needs for his own reasons. At the same time, Herod *does* use his Roman-given power to carry out his agenda.

287   Stott, *The Spirit, the Church, and the World*, 208. Obviously, Stott reflects the typical human disposition toward Peter's situation, and does not suggest that *God* was as helpless as some Christians regarded themselves. The church has seen Peter released from prison twice before; the question is not, "*Can* God deliver him?" but "*Will* He?" and then "*How?*"

288   Peter's situation (not his moral condition), while real and historical, serves as an allegory of the spiritual condition of one who is a captive of Satan, as all sinners are (2 Timothy 2:24-26). Peter is put into this prison by an unjust ruler, just as Satan is unjust and unrighteous. He is guarded, just as all of Satan's prisoners are prevented from escaping his lies and accusations on their own power. He is bound, just as Satan's prisoners are also bound with the chains of guilt, shame, bad habits, addictions, procrastination, and self-inflicted problems. He is asleep—a state of insensitivity, inactivity, and illusion—just as every sinner is "asleep" with regard to his moral responsibility to God (Romans 13:11, 1 Thessalonians 5:6). He is in darkness, just as the power of darkness belongs to Satan (Luke 22:53). He is unclothed, just as all sin and spiritual destitution represent a type of nakedness (Revelation 3:17-18). And he is condemned to death, just as all sinners are under the divine condemnation (John 3:18) (adapted from Coffman, *Commentary on Acts*, 243).

cannot account for other people seeing Peter outside of that prison; and a dream cannot explain Peter's physical absence in the jail cell the next morning, resulting in the death of sixteen guards. Once he is outside of the prison and in the city street at night, Peter realizes what has just happened ("Now I know for sure…"—12:11) and he immediately goes to the "house of Mary," where he knows that many disciples are gathered together.[289]

In 12:12, we are indirectly introduced to John Mark, who will later accompany Saul (Paul) and Barnabas on the first leg of their missionary journey (Acts 13:5). "John" is his Hebrew name; "Mark" is his Latin (Romanized) name. The size of his mother's home, as well as the presence of a servant girl (Rhoda), indicates an affluent family. Rhoda's excitement over hearing Peter's voice creates a somewhat humorous situation: she leaves Peter standing nervously outside while she runs to tell the others of his arrival (12:13-16). The brethren do not believe her at first, however. The sudden and inexplicable nature of the situation has left them unable to grasp its reality. (The scene is reminiscent of the apostles' reaction to the women who told them of Jesus' resurrection; see Mark 16:11-13.) Some of them remark, "It is his angel"—an implication that Peter is still under God's providential watch, or that he has died (and the angel is present to deliver the news).[290]

Meanwhile, Peter continues to knock at the gate, no doubt very much afraid of being detected. Once he is finally admitted into the home—to the amazement of the group—his stay is brief. He knows that it will only be a matter of time before the guards will search for him. He tells them to "report these things to James and the brethren" (12:17)—i.e., let the church in Jerusalem and its elders know that I have been

---

289 Peter's release from prison also compares to Israel's deliverance from Egypt: even though Israel was a slave nation in an "iron furnace" (Deuteronomy 4:20), God rescued this people from their imprisonment despite every human and physical obstacle that stood in their way. As in the case of one being rescued from the condemnation of his own sin, it is God who intervenes and does what men cannot do for a greater purpose than the mere release from prison itself.

290 Many people have since construed this to mean Peter's *guardian* angel. While the idea of guardian angels is popular among Jews at this time, the Bible does not teach the "guardian angel" concept as fact.

delivered by God's hand. "James" almost certainly refers to the physical brother of Jesus (Mark 6:3, Galatians 1:19), who is elsewhere in the city, but obviously is recognized even by Peter as being an influential leader in the church there (Galatians 2:9). "Then he left and went to another place"—the lack of information on where Peter goes is likely deliberate, so as not to implicate those who might render assistance to him and therefore jeopardize their own safety. It is possible, too, that Peter did not even tell those who are present in the house where he is going, so that if they are questioned, they can honestly say that they do not know where he is.

Herod had planned to execute Peter the next day, but his prized prisoner is inexplicably missing (12:18). ("No small disturbance" is Luke's way of drawing attention to the *great* disturbance this has caused; see also Act 19:23 and 27:20.) This is terribly embarrassing for Herod. First, he has proved to be no more useful than the Jewish Council in keeping Christians in prison. Second, he had hoped to use Peter's execution as yet another means of befriending the Jews (for his own political advantage). Third, the Jews now have another reason to despise him. Sadly, the guards who were given responsibility over Peter are led away to their executions (12:19). It is standard practice for those who have let their prisoner escape to be sentenced to whatever punishment their prisoner was to receive.[291]

> He [Herod] had to explain Peter's disappearance somehow, but to admit the miracle would generate extreme displeasure and quite possibly insurrection. To admit the miracle would be a *de facto* admission that Jesus was the messiah and king, ending his own reign. He could not prove the guards had accepted a Christian bribe, for why were they all still there, offering a ridiculous story? There had been no rescue by armed Christians.

---

291   "From the early days of the Empire, a penalty system ranging from corporal punishment without loss of rank to the death penalty was in force for guards who permitted the release or escape of their prisoners through neglect, drunkenness, sloth, avarice, or sympathy" (Rapske, "Paul in Roman Custody," 30).

Thus the sole alternative was to blame it on the hapless guards, regardless of the evidence, and this is what he did.[292]

In all this, it is quite conspicuous that Herod made no further search (that we know of) for Peter, but simply dropped his prosecution of him altogether. Immediately after this, Herod (understandably) leaves Jerusalem and returns to the palace built by his grandfather, Herod the Great, in Caesarea Palestina on the Mediterranean coast.

The death of Herod (12:20-25)
Herod Agrippa I has very strong political ties to Emperor Claudius, the two being good friends, and thus wields a considerable amount of power in Palestine. For some undisclosed reason (possibly over taxation of trade), Herod is "very angry" with the people of Tyre and Sidon, two sister cities on the Mediterranean coast in ancient Phoenicia, just north of Caesarea (12:20). (The Greek wording is very strong here, and implies that Herod is angry enough to go to war with these cities.[293]) Technically, Tyre and Sidon are outside of Herod's jurisdiction; they are under Syrian authority, as dictated by Rome. However, these cities serve as major seaports for Judea, and thus depend heavily on income generated (through trade and tariffs) from Herod's domain; thus, their prosperity is directly tied to Herod's cooperation. Furthermore, Tyre and Sidon's grain comes from the wheat fields of Galilee (an arrangement possibly dating back to the days of King Solomon; see 1 Kings 5:9ff), which is also under Herod's oversight.[294] Thus, "Grain

---

292   Mitchell, "Acts," 12.4. This situation is also similar to that of Daniel's friends whose lives were spared while the lives of King Nebuchadnezzar's servants were lost (Daniel 3:19-22).

293   *Strong's* (electronic edition), #G2371.

294   This situation reveals just how far from their ancient power and glory Tyre and Sidon have fallen. In the centuries past, Tyre (particularly) withstood sieges from several Assyrian rulers, King Nebuchadnezzar of Babylon, and Alexander the Great. The island city of Tyre, also known as "New Tyre"—an extension of the mainland city, which was known as "Old Tyre"—finally succumbed to Nebuchadnezzar's assault, but only after a 13-year siege. It also held off Alexander's siege for seven months, which is impressive in itself. Alexander, however, made sure that the island city would never be rebuilt, fulfilling Ezekiel 26:14 (H. Porter, "Tyre," *ISBE* [electronic edition]). In other words,

had become as political a factor in the ancient world as oil was to become in the twentieth century."[295]

The people of Tyre and Sidon send a delegation to Caesarea to "win over" Blastus, Herod's chamberlain, in order to gain favor with Herod himself.[296] (Bribery is common in such circumstances.) Herod agrees to make an official statement to these men in the theater he had built not far from his royal residence (12:21). The implication is that the people of Tyre and Sidon have agreed to Herod's demands, and thus he retracts any threats against their cities. According to Josephus, Herod wears a silvery-threaded robe that highly reflects the sun; thus, it gives him the appearance that he is radiating with glory. Because of this brilliance—and to stroke his ego—the people claim that the king is "a god and not a man" (12:22). Herod, for his part, does not correct or rebuke them. In other words, "He let these pagan idolaters make a pagan god of him and enjoyed it."[297] For this impudence and his many other crimes, Herod is immediately struck by God with intestinal worms. He lingers for five days in awful misery before succumbing to death at age 54.[298]

Yet, even though James has been martyred, the Jews have been humiliated with Peter's escape, and Herod has died an agonizing death, the church continues to grow and flourish (12:24). "The persecution,

---

the Tyrians have shown themselves to be bold and courageous in the past, but now (in the case of Herod Agrippa I) they beg a rather petty provincial "king" not to go to war with them.

295   Bruce W. Winter, "Acts and Food Shortages," *The Book of Acts in Its First Century Setting*, vol. 2, 61).

296   A chamberlain is technically an officer who is put in charge of the king's bedroom [lit., the "chamber" wherein the king has "lain"]; more generally, he is a close political confidant or private attendant to the king.

297   Lenski, *Acts of the Apostles*, 487.

298   Josephus, "Antiquities," 19.8.2. Clearly, many men and women have since received glory for themselves that was due God, and yet He did not inflict them with worms. While Herod's crimes are great, his crimes against God's people are especially offensive. While David withheld from killing King Saul because he (Saul) was God's anointed (1 Samuel 24:6, 2 Samuel 1:13-16), Herod has no problem executing one of God's anointed apostles. God's judgment against this monstrous individual also serves as a precedent for the divine judgment that awaits all people who murder His people or declare war upon His church.

rather than stopping Christianity, served rather to further it."[299] Stott sums it up well:

> The chapter opens with James dead, Peter in prison and Herod triumphing; it closes with Herod dead, Peter free, and the word of God triumphing. Such is the power of God to overthrow hostile human plans and to establish his own in their place. Tyrants may be permitted for a time to boast and bluster, oppressing the church and hindering the spread of the gospel, but they will not last. In the end, their empire will be broken and their pride abased.[300]

Saul and Barnabas, having completed their earlier mission (recall 11:29-30), leave Jerusalem and return to Antioch of Syria. John Mark is now mentioned in person, inasmuch as he will play a dubious role in what will become Saul's (Paul's) first missionary journey.

---

299   JFB *Commentary*, on 12:24.

300   Stott, *The Spirit, the Church, and the World*, 213.

∽ Chapter 13 – 14 ∽
First Missionary Journey

Introduction to this section

Chapters 1 – 12 in Acts deal primarily with: the preaching of the gospel in Judea and Samaria; Peter's influential role as a leader in the church; and Jerusalem as the central hub of the early church. Chapters 13 – 28 provide a definite shift in emphasis. From this point forward, Luke narrates: the preaching of the gospel outside of Judea and Samaria; Saul's (Paul's) pivotal role in the development of a worldwide church; and Syrian Antioch as a kind of home base from which Saul's journeys will all begin. (Neither section in Acts is exclusive to these things, however; we are recognizing dominant themes, not absolutes.) While the church most certainly began with Jews in Jerusalem, it was never intended to remain there. God had long predicted that *all* "the nations" (Gentiles) would hear His message of salvation and be granted entrance into His kingdom equal to that which He granted to the Jews (see Isaiah 49:5-6, 51:4, and John 10:16).

When we say "*first* missionary journey," we should note that this is not the first missionary effort in Acts. Philip engaged in a journey of his own in Acts 8, as did Peter in Acts 9. It does mean, however, that this is the first journey for Saul and Barnabas. "Missionary" is our word, not Luke's; as such, it is merely descriptive in nature, not doctrinal. In the context of Acts, this word simply refers to an organized evangelic effort intended to spread the gospel throughout the Roman Empire. As such, it has no connection with modern "missionary" efforts that focus on improving the physical welfare of indigenous people (i.e., building houses, founding schools, providing fresh water, food, vitamins or medicine, etc.). Saul and Barnabas are not traveling abroad to help people with their secular lives; their objective is entirely spiritual in nature, and their journey is directly commissioned by the Holy Spirit. There are inferences elsewhere that others have already gone ahead of Saul and Barnabas, but there has not yet been a systematic or collaborative effort to propagate the gospel. "Christianity had by this time spread beyond the boundaries of Palestine, but the church had no organized missionary effort. It was from the church at Antioch that the first teachers were sent forth with the purpose of spreading the gospel of Christ and organizing local churches."[301] Furthermore, it establishes Saul's (Paul's) apostolic authority within the church, and especially his ministry to the Gentiles (Galatians 2:7-9, 1 Timothy 2:7). The year this journey begins is circa AD 45.

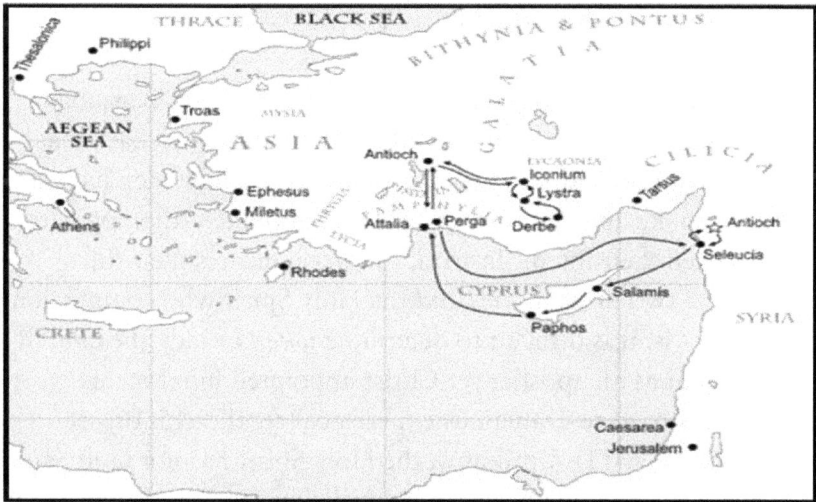

The Holy Spirit commissions Saul and Barnabas (13:1-3)

Several prominent men served in the church in Antioch (13:1); "prophets and teachers" reminds us of 1 Corinthians 12:28 or Ephesians 4:11ff.[302] "Ministering to the Lord" usually alludes to a priestly function, but in the present case has to do with taking care of the work of the Lord in Antioch, likely preaching, teaching, and overseeing benevolence (13:2). "Fasting" is something that the people of God do on special occasions; here, the occasion may be

---

301   JFB *Commentary*, on 13:1.

302   "Simeon who was called Niger"—Simeon is his Hebrew name, Niger ("black") is his Latin name, likely indicating that he is dark-skinned and possibly from Africa. Some have assumed that this is the same Simeon who bore Jesus' cross (Luke 23:26), though there is little to substantiate this. "Lucius of Cyrene" may be one of those men mentioned in Acts 11:20. Cyrene is a city of Libya in North Africa. It is believed that Manaen was a foster-brother (per the Greek) to Herod Antipas, not Herod Agrippa I (Boles, *A Commentary on Acts*, 200). Regarding "prophets and teachers," these are two distinct works; all prophets are teachers by definition, but not all teachers receive revelations from God as prophecies. Teachers expound upon Scripture and communicate the fundamental teachings of Christ; prophets are not bound by Scripture or known teachings, and speak to the church by way of divine revelations made to them (Kistemaker, *Acts*, 454).

the expectation of a divine message from the Holy Spirit, as foretold by one of their prophets. Indeed, the Holy Spirit does provide this message: "Set apart for Me Barnabas and Saul..." Likely, these words are conveyed through one of the prophets in this church, but it is one of the very few recorded instances in which the Holy Spirit has actually uttered His own words to people.

The laying on of hands here (13:3) is *not* to commission Barnabas or Saul as apostles; this act "imparted no qualification to Barnabas and Saul which they did not already possess."[303] These men have no authority to make apostles; there is nothing in the text that indicates that this is even their intent. Instead, this act indicates their full support to the two missionaries *and* the Holy Spirit who commissioned them. The fact is, it is difficult to determine *when* exactly the church recognized Saul as an apostle, yet Christ appointed him for this office upon his road-to-Damascus experience (recall 9:15-16; see 1 Corinthians 15:6-11). Until now, the Holy Spirit has not used Saul in this capacity; the pressing need for evangelizing the Gentile world has necessitated this, however. In all of Acts, there is a conspicuous absence of overseeing boards, missionary societies, central headquarters, etc. that are common to man-made religions today in order to conduct missionary work. There is also a complete absence of any account in which Christ personally chose Barnabas in the same way He did the eleven apostles (after Judas' suicide), then Matthias, and then Saul himself (recall 1:2, 24-26, and 9:15). This means that Barnabas, while called an "apostle" in the general sense, is not inducted into the *office* of an apostle as the twelve apostles and Saul have been.

Saul and Barnabas in Cyprus (13:4-12)

Seleucia is an ancient seaport and Roman naval base about sixteen miles from Antioch (13:4). Cyprus (a.k.a. Kittim from ancient times; see Numbers 24:24, Jeremiah 2:10, Daniel 11:30, et al) is an island in the Mediterranean, about sixty miles from the Syrian coast—a full day's travel by boat. It is considered the fabled birthplace of the Greek goddess Aphrodite [Roman name: Venus], although others claim that this goddess simply walked out of the sea. The island nation of Cyprus

---

303   Bruce, *The Book of the Acts*, 261.

has been under the oversight of a proconsul (a type of governor) since 22 BC. Since Barnabas is a native of this island (recall 4:36), he is probably well-familiar with its layout and culture; this makes it a natural beginning point for the entire journey. Salamis and Paphos are on opposite ends of the island, about 85 miles apart.

> Paphos was a city at the western end of the island, and served as the Roman capital of the island. It had a small harbor, which at times offered no shelter from the prevailing winds. There was a celebrated temple there in which Aphrodite (Venus) was worshipped. The worship was notorious for the licentiousness of the harlot-priestess who served in the temple.[304]

In an aside, Luke mentions that "they also had John [Mark] as their helper" (13:5), the word "helper" literally referring to a subordinate oarsman, or an assistant of any kind.[305]

In Paphos, Barnabas and Saul encounter two very different men: Elymas,[306] a Jewish magician, and Sergius Paulus, the Roman proconsul of Cyprus (13:6-8).[307] The proconsul is an "intelligent" man, though not possessing the same spirit as Cornelius; his intelligence has

---

304   Reese, *Book of Acts*, 461.

305   *Strong's* (electronic edition), #G5257.

306   "Elymas" is an Aramaic translation of "magician" (or "sorcerer"), not of "Bar-Jesus" (Coffman, *Commentary on Acts*, 258; Gaertner, *Acts*, 206). "The Greek word translated 'sorcerer' is *magos*. The magi were originally a Median priestly caste, but in later Greek and Roman times the word was used more generally of practitioners of all sorts of magic and quackery. The latter sense is required here; a Jew, even a renegade Jew (as this man was), could not have been a member of the magian [*sic*] priesthood. Luke calls him a false prophet, not in the sense that he foretold things which did not come to pass, but in the sense that he claimed falsely to be a medium of divine revelations. When Luke says (v. 8) 'Elymas the sorcerer (for so is his name by interpretation),' he cannot mean that Elymas is the interpretation of Bar-Jesus, but that 'sorcerer' (Gk. *magos*) is the interpretation of Elymas; Elymas is probably a Semitic word with a similar meaning to Gk. *magos*" (Bruce, *The Book of the Acts*, 264).

307   The title of "proconsul" for this man was, for centuries, disputed; in fact, many commentators believed Luke to be mistaken in his use of this office. Yet, he has since been vindicated through archaeological evidence and the discovery of ancient coinage bearing his name and title. Thus, it is Luke and not his critics who has been vindicated for his accuracy and attention to detail (McGarvey, *Acts of Apostles*, 2:7, fn. 1).

nonetheless taught him to be tolerant of new ideas and philosophies. He desires to hear the word of God, but the magician seeks not only to prevent this, but to "turn the proconsul away from the faith" (13:8). Thus, the magician is not a passive unbeliever but is wholly antagonistic to the teaching of the gospel, as Saul makes clear in his rebuke of him (13:10; see also 2 Timothy 3:8). The synonymous phrases in Paul's accusations against Elymas—"full of all deceit and fraud," "son of the devil," "enemy of all righteousness," and one who "[makes] crooked the straight ways of the Lord"—all describe the same kind of person.[308]

It is conspicuous that Saul's first exercise of miraculous power is a *punishment* (rather than, say, a healing) and involves *blinding* a false teacher (since Saul himself was blinded by Jesus for a time).[309] This is the first time we have seen Saul exercise such authority; Luke is clear to ascribe the *source* of that authority, however, to the Holy Spirit (13:9). Elymas claimed to have great power (like Simon the sorcerer did), yet this is nothing compared to the Spirit's power. After all, it is not Elymas who blinds Saul, but the other way around. The result of this bold reproach is that the proconsul believes in the gospel that Barnabas and Saul have preached (3:12). The historians Conybeare and Howson observe:

> This blinding of the false prophet opened the eyes of Sergius Paulus. That which had been intended as an opposition to the Gospel, proved the means of its extension. ...We cannot doubt that when the Proconsul was converted, his influence would make Christianity reputable; and that from this moment the

---

308   "The task of John the Baptist as of all prophets and preachers is to make crooked paths straight and to get men to walk in them. This false prophet was making even the Lord's straight ways crooked. Elymas has many successors" (Robertson, *Word Pictures*, 182). Lenski adds: "A devil's son is not only his offspring but one in whom the devil's characteristics reappear" (*Acts of the Apostles*, 505).

309   This is not to suggest that Saul himself was literally a false teacher. False teachers (as defined in the NT, such as in 2 Peter 2:1-3) are those who *know* the truth yet teach the opposite of it (or a perversion of it) as a means of self-advancement. This hardly describes Saul's situation in his persecution of Christians. At the same time, blindness does figuratively indicate that a person is going in the *wrong direction*—whether intentionally (as Elymas) or not (as Saul), and that he is given an opportunity to see the error of his ways. Saul's blindness led to a change of heart; we have no indication that Elymas' blindness brought about any lasting change in *his* heart.

Gentiles of the island, as well as the Jews, had the news of salvation brought home to them.[310]

"Paulus" [lit., "little one"] is the Latin name for "Saul"; being adopted into the Greek language, it is simply rendered "Paul" (13:9). All Roman citizens have two, if not three, names: a family (or given) name, a Latin or Romanized name, and sometimes a Greek name. Since he is entering into a predominantly Gentile world, it is to Paul's advantage to use his Latin name rather than his Hebrew one. "Luke presents this new name in a remarkable way; the 'also' does not mean that the name 'Paul' was given now for the first time, but that he had always had it."[311] Luke thus refers to Saul as "Paul" from this point forward. It is also clear that the prominence of Barnabas to this point is now eclipsed by Paul, as Luke will mention Paul first in nearly all future narratives of this journey. Thus, "Barnabas and Saul" will now almost always be "Paul and Barnabas."[312]

Paul and Barnabas in Antioch of Pisidia (13:13-52)
The simplicity of the narrative may offer the appearance of an easy and carefree journey (13:13). The truth is, however, that travel by sea or road is very difficult at this time in history, even under favorable conditions. Paul later recounts such dangers (2 Corinthians 11:23-28), some of which he may well have endured during this first missionary journey. After leaving the island of Cyprus, Paul and company land in Perga, a city in the Roman province of Pamphylia. There is no record that they spend time here, but they will on their return trip (see 14:24-25). From Perga to Antioch of Pisidia is about 110 miles, with the Taurus Mountain range in-between the two cities. It is possible that

---

310   Conybeare and Howson, *Life and Epistles*, 120.

311   Boles, *A Commentary on Acts*, 202.

312   At least two exceptions exist: in 14:14, Barnabas is mentioned first, due to the way that the Lycaonians viewed him (as the chief god, Zeus) whereas they viewed Paul as merely a messenger of the gods (because he was doing most of the speaking). Also, Barnabas is mentioned first in written correspondence from the apostles to the church in Antioch (15:25), due to Barnabas's longer and more established relationship with that group than what Paul enjoyed. The change in name "occurs more naturally immediately afterwards when Saul stands forth by himself and becomes the principal actor" (Lewis, quoted in Ramsay, *St. Paul the Traveller*, 87).

the physical difficulty of the journey is the very reason for which John Mark deserts them upon reaching the mainland. Others speculate that he (Mark) is afraid of malarial sickness common to the lowlands of Pamphylia.[313] Still others believe that Mark objected to preaching the gospel specifically to Gentiles.[314] In the end, his abrupt departure is simply not explained to us; all we know is that Paul strongly disapproves of it (see 15:38-39).

North of Pamphylia is the province of Galatia, named after the ancient Gauls who settled there some two hundred years earlier. Galatia was made an official province in 25 BC, though its borders are not always universally recognized. Pisidia is a southern region within this province; Antioch is named "Pisidian Antioch" to distinguish it from the several other "Antiochs" in existence at this time (13:14).[315] There are numerous Jews in this city, since 200 years earlier Antiochus the Great moved 2,000 Jewish families there.[316] Paul and Barnabas locate

---

313   We do know that Paul suffered from some kind of sickness when he came into Galatia (Galatians 4:13). "Sir William Ramsay suggested that Paul suffered from 'a species of chronic malaria fever' (which the ancient Greeks and Romans both knew and feared); that it involved 'very distressing and prostrating paroxysms,' together with stabbing headaches 'like a red-hot bar thrust through the forehead' (perhaps his 'thorn in the flesh'); and that it was his fever which necessitated leaving the enervating climate of the low-lying coastal plain, in spite of the rigorous climb involved, in order to seek the bracing cool of the Taurus plateau some 3,500 feet above sea level. Perhaps it was this hurry which explains why the missionaries did not stay to evangelize Perga, which they did on their return journey" (Stott, *The Spirit, the Church, and the World*, 221-222). Most commentators, including Stott, admit that they do not know for certain why Mark deserted Paul and Barnabas. In my opinion, for what it is worth, the matter involved an *irresponsible* decision on Mark's part (as Paul saw it), which explains why he was so upset at him later (15:36-39). This seems far more plausible than the mere fear of a sickness.

314   Kistemaker, *Acts*, 466. But this theory does not explain why John Mark later joined his cousin Barnabas on a missionary tour to Cyprus, especially when Barnabas himself has been fully agreeable to teaching Gentiles ever since his own ministry in Antioch.

315   Sir Wm. Ramsay, based upon coinage from this era and other historical details, claims that Antioch of Pisidia was made a Roman colony in AD 25. "It was thus placed in the highest class of provincial cities: it was made, so to say, a piece of the Imperial city, a detached fragment of Rome itself, separated from Rome in space, but peopled by Romans...who were of equal standing and privileges in the eye of the law with the citizens of Rome" (*The Cities of St. Paul*, 269).

316   Reese, *Book of Acts*, 469.

a Jewish synagogue, which becomes a standard practice when entering new missionary fields (cf. Romans 1:16, "to the Jew first..."). "The synagogues throughout the Roman Empire were the centers of Judaism; and, in many of these, there were devout souls 'waiting for the kingdom of God,' and this fact naturally directed the feet of the first Christian missionaries to the synagogues wherever they went."[317] After prayers and readings (from the Pentateuch and the Prophets) are finished, the two men are invited to address the congregation (13:15). No doubt Paul's credentials as one who has sat at the feet of Gamaliel (Acts 22:3) are sufficient to warrant this invitation.[318]

Taking full advantage of the opportunity, Paul gives what we would call a *sermon* to those who have assembled at this synagogue (13:16ff). "Men of Israel" refers to Jews; "you who fear God" [lit., God-fearers] refers to circumcised Gentile proselytes who are present (see 13:26, 43). It is possible (given 13:48) that uncircumcised Gentiles are also listening, or have this sermon relayed to them soon afterward. Paul's sermon follows the basic pattern of Peter's sermon to the Jews in Jerusalem—without the pointed accusations. The substance of this lesson is as follows:

❑ **13:16-22** Paul recounts the general history of the origin and development of the nation of Israel, from its 400-year stay in Egypt to the time of King David—another 450 years.[319] The emphasis

---

317   Coffman, *Commentary on Acts*, 262.

318   "It was the duty of the rulers of the synagogue (*archisunagogoi*) to select the readers and the speakers for the service... Any rabbi or distinguished stranger could be called upon to speak" (Robertson, 186). Ramsay adds: "It cannot be supposed that the Rulers would have invited any chance stranger to speak in public. We must therefore conclude either that Paul and Barnabas took their seats in some special place, showing thereby that they desired to address the people, or that previously they had made known to these Rulers their character and mission as teachers: perhaps both of these preliminaries had been observed" (*The Cities of St. Paul*, 297).

319   Some have been critical of Paul (or Luke) for the "four hundred and fifty years" reckoning, since it seems at first to contradict the 480 years mentioned in 1 Kings 6:1. But the cited number of years all depends on the starting and ending point of the calculation. Paul most certainly knows the reference from 1 Kings; but he does not use the exact same parameters for determining the span of years here mentioned. "Paul ventures to give a round number for the period that began with Jacob and his children entering Egypt and ended with the Israelites receiving their inheritance in Canaan.

is on what God did for His people (Israel): He chose Israel out of all the other nations; He single-handedly delivered them out of Egypt; He destroyed the seven Canaanite nations that occupied what became His inheritance to Israel; and He gave them judges to govern the new Promised Land. Not satisfied with this latter decision, Israel wanted to be like all the surrounding nations and have a king of their own (1 Samuel 8:4-6). So they demanded a king, and God gave them Saul of Benjamin, a disappointing man who nonetheless mirrored the morally weak character of the people. After this, God appointed another king, David, whom He called "a man after My heart" (1 Samuel 13:14, Psalm 89:20). This brief recounting of Israel's early history indicates that Paul, given what he is about to say, is in no way ignorant of, nor indifferent toward, the plight of Israel or God's providential oversight of this people.

❑ **13:23-26** Paul introduces Jesus as the direct fulfillment of the promise to David (2 Samuel 7:12-13, Psalm 89:19-29), and of other promises (Deuteronomy 18:15ff, Isaiah 9:6-7, et al). Jesus is not just another prophet, but the Savior of Israel; the well-known prophet John the Baptist confirmed this (John 1:19-27). Though some thought that John himself was the "coming one," he (John) refuted this and identified Jesus as that one. It was Jesus, and not John, whom God "brought to Israel" to save that people from their own spiritual ruin. The "message of this salvation"—the Jews' invitation into the kingdom of God—was thus proclaimed throughout Jesus' ministry (Mark 1:14-15).

❑ **13:27-31** The Jewish leaders (of Jerusalem), however, did not recognize Jesus as Messiah, even though the Scriptures prophesied of Him (John 5:39-47). Because of such unwarranted ignorance, they gained Roman consent to have Jesus put to death on a cross [lit., tree or wood, to allude to Deuteronomy 21:23; see Galatians 3:13]. This, too, was a fulfillment of Scripture (13:29). In other words, these things were predetermined by God, not accidental or coincidental (recall 2:22-23). Jesus was thus executed by

---

God told Abraham that his descendants would be oppressed in a foreign country for 400 years (Gen. 15:13). Add to this number the 40 years the Israelites spent in the desert and allow 10 years for the conquest of Canaan; the total comes to 450 years" (Kistemaker, *Acts*, 470).

crucifixion, and His body entombed; "But God raised Him from the dead" (13:30)—a fact confirmed by many witnesses. The resurrected Jesus then appeared to His disciples for a period of time (forty days; recall 1:3). Paul does not mention Jesus' ascension in this speech, yet he shows himself to be very familiar with the facts of His ministry, trials, and crucifixion. This is the first time we have heard him present these facts personally; this also may be the first time that his present audience has heard this information.

❑ **13:32-37** Paul uses the exact same argument as Peter did on the day of Pentecost concerning David's prophecy of Christ's resurrection (recall 2:24-31). This may not seem to be such a relevant argument to us today, largely because we do not appreciate the influence of David's prophecies as these people did. Even so, it is an accurate and persuasive one, especially since no Jew will dare to question David's inspired words (from Psalm 2:7 and 16:10). (Remember, too, that "David" is the code word for Messiah in OT prophecy; see Isaiah 11:1-2, Jeremiah 30:9, Ezekiel 34:23-24, et al.) Even though David wrote the psalms cited, Paul gives credit to God's Holy Spirit for providing them ("He has spoken"; "He also says"). In other words, the providential care for Jesus' entombed body is yet another fulfillment of divine prophecy—and another proof that Jesus is the "Holy One" of Israel and the intended recipient of those promises given to David's heir (Isaiah 55:3).

❑ **13:38-41** Forgiveness of sins has *never* been proclaimed through any one person, not even Moses, until Jesus Christ (Luke 24:46-47). While Jews assume that they will be forgiven through their observance of the Law, the Law is (by itself) unable to forgive anyone. Law cannot pronounce anyone "free" once that person violates what it commands. As great and revered as the Law of Moses has been among the Jews for centuries, the gospel of Christ is in every way superior to it (Romans 8:1-3). The Law foreshadowed the *need* for a once-for-all sacrifice for sins but could not *provide* that sacrifice; "it is impossible for the blood of bulls and goats to take away sins" (cf. Hebrews 10:1-10). Paul knows that this news may sound too wonderful—or incredible—to be true, but he warns these people not to discount this message, since it has been proved to be authentic by supernatural works of God.

Many scoffing and mocking Israelites in Habbakuk's day refused to believe in a Babylonian invasion, yet God said that it *would* come and it *did*. (Paul quotes from Habakkuk 1:5.) So it is in the present case: just because this news sounds foreign to the ear does not mean it is impossible; just because Paul's words do not support one's personal beliefs does not make them untrue or irrelevant. Indeed, the present Jewish generation scoffed and mocked Jesus' claim to be the Messiah, yet judgment is coming upon it—this time, not from Babylon, but from the Son of Man Himself (Matthew 24:27-30).

Paul's message is well-received by some but condemned by others (13:42-45).[320] Many of the people beg Paul and Barnabas to continue their teaching. On the next Sabbath, "nearly the whole city assembled to hear the word of the Lord" (13:44). This may not be an exaggeration; it indicates how hungry many of these people are for the good news of Christ's redemption. But other Jews, who may have belonged to the sect of the Pharisees, are jealous of the attention and reception that these missionaries are receiving. Their "blaspheming" is no doubt their rejection of Jesus' divine nature, a denial that God was the power behind Jesus' miracles (see Matthew 12:24, John 8:48, 52), and/or a denial of His resurrection. Whatever it is specifically, the Jews' words are contradictory to Paul's, forcing the people to choose between the two. Division between those who believe and those who blaspheme will become the hallmark of every instance in which the gospel is preached from here forward in Acts. Thus, we should expect no different response from any general audience today to whom the gospel is preached.

Paul sharply rebukes these unbelieving Jews, laying at their feet the responsibility for their own condemnation (13:46-47; see John 3:18-21). "It was necessary" that Jews hear the message of salvation *first*, since this is the promise of God's covenant with Israel, as dictated by Jesus Himself (Isaiah 2:2-3, Luke 24:47). "Since you repudiate

---

320 "The consequences resulting from accepting or rejecting the teaching of the apostles are the same consequence as accepting or rejecting the teachings of Jesus. These are the same teachings from the same heavenly source" (Mark Turner, *Paul of Tarsus: Apostle to the World* [self-published, no date], 35).

it"—since you reject what God has offered you—"we are turning to the Gentiles [lit., nations]." In rejecting God's invitation into His kingdom, these Jews render themselves "unworthy" of life with God—a strong condemnation, but one that they have brought upon themselves. God responds to their hardened rejection of the gospel of Christ by giving what He promised them (the Jews) to people who will appreciate it (see Romans 9:22-33, 15:8-12). At the mention of God's salvation to the Gentiles—that is, salvation *apart* from conforming to the Law of Moses—these Jews are further incensed, while the Gentiles themselves are grateful for such news (compare with Luke 7:28-30). No longer regarded as second-class believers (from the Jewish perspective), these Gentiles are now given an opportunity to be *on par* with any Jew who also believes in Jesus Christ (Galatians 3:26-29). Indeed, there is not a "Jewish church" and a "Gentile church," but "one new man"—a singular, unified body of believers—through the atoning blood of Christ and the sanctifying work of God's Spirit (cf. Ephesians 2:13-18).

The word "appointed" [a military term; lit., placed in a certain row, position, or order] (13:48), if taken out of context, seems to support Calvinism (a.k.a. The Doctrine of Predestination). At first glance, it appears that God has predestined these people to be saved *no matter what* (what Calvinists call "sovereign election"). But this would violate the free will of all those who hear the gospel. If God has already selected those who are saved, and they cannot decide otherwise, then why is Paul required to preach a message of salvation to them? Calvinism makes *all* preaching of the gospel irrelevant (see Acts 26:16-18, 2 Timothy 2:24-26). Furthermore, this would contradict what Paul just said to the Jews in 13:46 ("since *you* repudiate it and judge *yourselves* unworthy"—emphasis added), which clearly leaves the decision of believing or rejecting in the hands of each *person*, not God. What this verse *does* mean, then, is that God has invited such people into eternal life, and as freely as some Jews reject that invitation, so some Gentiles accept it. The grace of God, powerful as it is for salvation, cannot function apart from the exercise of *personal faith* in such grace (Ephesians 2:8). Faith cannot be forced by God, and grace cannot be forced by man.[321]

This "appointment," then, is conditioned upon an individual's belief in God—i.e., human choice in the matter—and not divine will alone.[322] God most certainly foreordained the salvation of the Gentiles *as a people*; He did not, however, foreordain each individual person to be saved or lost. Calvinism attempts to turn the entire situation on its head, claiming that the only reason *why* certain people believe is because God appointed them to eternal life—thus, the entire decision to be saved (or not) is in God's hands. Thus, it assumes erroneously that those who are *saved* bear no responsibility for their salvation, whereas those who are *lost* bear full responsibility for their rejection of the gospel. (This latter aspect is intended to soften the ugly but necessary implication of Calvinism, that is, that God is fully responsible for sending people to hell only because *He* rejected *them*, not because *they* rejected *Him*.) This position is illogical, unbiblical, and indefensible.

---

321   John Calvin (*Acts*, 229) writes, "This verse teaches that faith depends on God's choice," and that "God's election"—i.e., His divine appointment of those who will be saved before such people are even born—"is the cause of faith and salvation," and thus "nothing remains for worthiness or merits." It is true that our "merits" cannot produce salvation, and that our salvation is not predicated upon these alone. But Calvin is seriously confusing the *role* of human works in the process of salvation with the *sole dependence* upon these works to do what God alone is able to do—that is, forgive sins and justify the human soul. Calvin first *assumes* that men are born in sin (ibid., 182) and that God has *pre-chosen* those whom He wants to save ("the elect"), then builds his understanding of the entire gospel of Christ around this. Calvin is virtually silent, however, on God's having also chosen (as a necessary implication) those who will be sent to hell simply because He did not *want* to save them—a teaching which violates the entire purpose for and message of Christ's gospel.

322   See McGarvey (*Acts of Apostles*, 2:29-33) for an excellent exposition of this passage. The Greek word (*tasso*) for "appointed" is the same word rendered "determined" in Acts 15:2; in both contexts, it indicates a decision of the human mind, not an immutable sovereign decision of God. If only a certain number of people were (are) appointed by God to have eternal life, then all the rest are appointed by God to be eternally lost: the same decision to appoint *one* number also rejects all who are *beyond* that number. Yet, in reality, "All who believe in Christ, repent of their sins, and are baptized into him are 'ordained,' 'disposed,' 'determined,' or 'destined' to eternal life. It does not matter which translation one accepts, the meaning is that those who accept Christ may enjoy redemption in him. Accepting Christ is an act of one's own will" (Boles, *A Commentary on Acts*, 218).

The Jews who reject the gospel show their true colors by purposely inciting others to act maliciously toward Paul and Barnabas (13:50). These people included "devout women of prominence" and "leading men of the city"—Gentiles who are either proselytes to the Jewish religion or sympathetic to the Jewish cause.[323] It is likely that Paul suffers personally at their hands (cf. 2 Timothy 3:11); it is possible that he and possibly Barnabas are beaten as part of this "persecution." Yet, to reject God's prophets is to court divine judgment. Shaking the dust off of one's feet (13:51a) implies symbolically that the city is under divine condemnation (Matthew 10:14-15, Acts 18:6)—specifically, this only applies to those who are persecuting them. Those who have believed, however, continue to rejoice in their newfound salvation (13:52). As a side note: the influence of the unbelieving Jews, as well as the misunderstanding of those Jews who *did* believe, will certainly mislead these people over time. It is for this reason that Paul later speaks of those who have "so quickly deserted" this gospel of salvation for a Jewish "version" of that gospel—a version that forces them to obey Jewish law and a salvation by works—in his epistle to the Galatians (1:6-9, 3:1-5, 5:1-4, et al).

Paul and Barnabas in Iconium (14:1-7)

Departing from Pisidian Antioch, Paul and Barnabas journey next to Iconium (13:51b, 14:1). This is a trip of about 60 miles, with mountains and difficult terrain separating the two cities. Iconium is a principal city of this region, being recognized by Claudius, the Emperor of Rome at this time; later in history it will be awarded honorary Roman status by Emperor Hadrian.[324] The same strategy that was

---

323   "Strabo [a Greek geographer contemporary with this timeframe—MY WORDS], who was intimately acquainted with the social position of the female sex in the towns of Western Asia, speaks in strong terms of the power which they possessed and exercised in controlling and modifying the religious opinions of the men. This general fact received one of its most striking illustrations in the case of Judaism. ...The Jews contrived, through the female proselytes at Antioch, to win over to their cause some influential members of their sex, and thorugh them to gain the ear of men who occupied a position of eminence in the city. Thus a systematic persecution was excited against Paul and Barnabas" (Conybeare and Howson, *Life and Epistles*, 144-145).

324   Coffman, *Commentary on Acts*, 274. There is some dispute, however, to which region Iconium actually belonged—whether Lycaonia (as is generally assumed) or Phrygia (as implied in 14:6, and by Xenophon's historical account) (see W. M. Calder, "Iconium," *ISBE* [electronic edition]). In the end, it really does not matter, since

used in Antioch is now used here: Paul and Barnabas try to reach as many Jews (and Gentile proselytes) as they can through the synagogue assembly. "Greeks" (14:1-2) refers to Greek-speaking proselytes to Judaism; "Gentiles" likely (in contrast) refers to those who have not been proselytized, but who hear the message of the gospel nonetheless. "The brethren" likely refers to those who believe in Christ and have become obedient to this message.

Every success Paul and Barnabas enjoy is ultimately threatened with resistance: "The Jews who disbelieved stirred up the minds of the Gentiles and embittered them against the brethren" (14:2).[325] This indicates an *organized* opposition (i.e., a few men deciding for many others) rather than an *individual* one (i.e., each man deciding for himself). Not only do these Jews not want to accept Paul's gospel, they do not want anyone *else* accepting it, either. This puts these Jews in the position of deciding what the Gentiles ought to believe rather than allowing them to think for themselves (implying a moral superiority over these people). Even though Paul and Barnabas produce miracles in the sight of these men (14:3), the Gentiles still refuse the gospel of Christ in favor of the propaganda of disbelieving Jews. Thus, some Gentiles accept the testimony of the Jewish leaders over the supernatural proofs performed at the hands of the missionaries.

As a result of this negative campaign, "the city was divided" (14:4), even as Jesus' own countrymen were divided over Him (John 7:40-43). "The Jews who disbelieved"—lit., who *disobeyed*—create an unnecessary obstacle here. The difference between disbelief and disobedience is indistinguishable in this context; "To disbelieve the

---

the final decision does not affect the credibility of the narrative or the events that it describes.

325   "The account of Paul's work at Iconium is couched in very general terms—a period of successful work, followed by a riot and expulsion from the city. But even in this vague outline it is clear that the circumstances were markedly different from what happened at Antioch [of Pisidia]. The Apostles resided a considerable time at Iconium ["Therefore they spent a long time there"—14:3]; the stress laid on this point implies that they stayed there longer than at any other place on this journey. Future history shows that Iconium was one of the most influential seats of the new religion in Asia Minor" (Ramsay, *The Cities of St. Paul*, 370; bracketed words are added).

word of God is to disobey God."[326] Sadly, these Jews poison the minds
of some of the Gentiles so as to turn them from the purity of the gospel
(cf. 2 Corinthians 4:3-4).[327] Incidentally, this (14:4) is the first occasion
in the NT in which Paul is referred to as an "apostle," though the word
here is used in the *general* sense (as "one sent") rather than referring to
the *office* to which Christ has appointed him (as used in Romans 1:1,
1 Corinthians 1:1, 2 Corinthians 1:1, Galatians 1:1, et al).

The tension created over Paul and Barnabas' preaching reaches a
critical level: the unbelieving Jews threaten to stone them (14:5). No
doubt the official charge is blasphemy (based on Leviticus 24:16); yet
clearly they are also motivated by fear of the loss of control of the
masses and by envy (see Mark 15:10). In order to preserve the newly-
formed group of believers, the apostles have no choice but to leave
the city (14:6-7).[328] "Lycaonia" is an ethnic region[329]; "Lystra" and
"Derbe" are cities within that region; these cities are in what is officially

---

326   Robertson, *Word Pictures*, 204.

327   "It must be observed that there was no ruling oligarchy in Iconium, like the
Roman colonists in Antioch. Iconium was a Hellenic city, where the power lay in the
hands of the whole body of citizens. In Antioch Paul's Jewish enemies accomplished
their object by appealing privately to the oligarchy through the ladies of high rank
who were within the influence of the Synagogue. In Iconium they gained the same end
by gradually working on the feelings of the masses" (Ramsay, *The Cities of St. Paul*,
371). This distinction also affects the different ways in which Paul and Barnabas are
driven out of each city: one, as a religious persecution; the other, through the threat of
execution.

328   "The actions of Paul and Barnabas bring up the question: When should a
preacher run, and when should he stay and fight? We have seen in the second verse that
when the opposition increased, the boldness of Paul and Barnabas increased and caused
them to continue there a long time. Now we are told that they fled. It is not wrong to
flee when your life is in danger, and when by staying you can do no more good. There
is not any reason for sticking your neck in the guillotine unless you are forced to do
it. One of the first laws of human life is self-preservation. God expects us to preserve
ourselves unless truth, honesty, and integrity are involved. Certainly, if the time ever
comes when one is forced either to deny Jesus or die, his line of duty is clear. But under
such circumstances as here in Iconium, when one sees that there is no more possibility
of doing good, and there is evidence that life is at stake, then it is time to get out"
(Reese, *Book of Acts*, 501).

329   "Lycaonia is situated on a mountainous plateau in the southern part of Asia
Minor at an elevation of thirty-three hundred feet. It borders the Taurus Mountains and
was part of the Roman province of Galatia. 'Lycaonia is a flat, dry, and almost treeless
plain, extremely dusty at the end of the summer, and inhospitably cold in winter'"
(Kistemaker, *Acts*, 509).

known as Galatia, but are more locally referred to as Phrygia. (Some
of the borders of these regions are recognized by Roman jurisdiction,
while others are recognized by ethnicity; thus, it is sometimes difficult
to determine which city belongs to what region or province.)

Paul and Barnabas in Lystra and Derbe (14:8-20)

The Lycaonians are a fierce and primitive people, highly superstitious,
and idolatrous. "The very name Lycaonia, interpreted traditionally as
Wolf-land (the local legend derived it from a man named Lycaon who
had been transformed into a wolf), faithfully represented the character
of the inhabitants."[330] Lystra is some 40 miles from Iconium; Derbe is
some 60 miles beyond Lystra.[331] Paul's celebrated healing of a certain
lame man (14:8-10) is reminiscent of Peter and John's healing of the
lame man in Jerusalem (recall 3:1ff). This man has also been lame from
birth, and is listening intently to Paul's preaching. "He had faith to be
made well" (14:9) means simply that he *believed* in God's power to heal
him (as in Matthew 9:22, Luke 7:50, or 17:19). This faith is evident in
the fact that the man stands up as soon as he is told to do so, whereas
the lame man in Jerusalem had to be further persuaded by Peter. Some
versions read, "...to be saved," since this is a correct translation from
the Greek. Yet, the context focuses on his physical healing—his being
made well or whole—rather than being saved from his sins. Even so,
it may be that this man sought *spiritual* salvation and Paul responded
first with *physical* healing. In any case, this man's healing was complete
and instantaneous, unlike the fraudulent and theatrical "faith healings"
performed today.

The people respond as they have been conditioned to believe—
namely, that Greek gods have come down to visit them (14:11-13)!

---

330   Edward Plumptre, quoted in Coffman, *Commentary on Acts*, 278.

331   "Little is said about Derbe in the Book of Acts, and little is recorded of it in
other ancient documents. It was one of the rudest [as in, primitive—MY WORDS] of
the Pauline cities, education had made no great progress in it, and therefore it was not
fitted to produce a strong impression on the history of the Church or of Asia Minor. Its
inscriptions are late in date, and show little trace of contact with the Roman world"
(Ramsay, *The Cities of St. Paul*, 399). The actual site of Derbe was not discovered until
1956 (David French, "Acts and the Roman Roads of Asia Minor," *The Book of Acts in
Its First Century Setting*, vol. 2, 51).

(People today still point to false powers [i.e., ghosts, the occult, alien encounters, "blind forces of nature," etc.] to explain things they cannot understand otherwise.) "Zeus" and "Hermes" are Greek names, though we should have expected Roman [Latin] names (as the KJV uses); yet the use of Greek names for mythological gods in this area has been substantiated through recent archeological finds. The Lycaonians refer to Barnabas as Zeus [Latin: Jupiter]—the chief of the Greek gods—possibly because his physical presence is more imposing or his personality is more charismatic than Paul's. They refer to Paul as Hermes [Latin: Mercury]—the messenger of the gods—because he is the primary speaker of the two men.[332] The pagan priests bring to the two missionaries ritually-decorated animals to be sacrificed in their honor.

Paul and Barnabas at first are unaware of what is happening because they do not know the Lycaonian language.[333] Once they learn of the true meaning of the commotion (14:14ff), they do their best to suppress the excitement by explaining that they are mere men, even though their message is indeed from the God of heaven—a "living God," not the product of ancient mythology (see Galatians 4:8-9, 1 Thessalonians 1:9). This God is not only the Creator of "the heaven [i.e., sky] and the earth and the sea," but He continues to provide food and sustenance for all people by way of these created realms (14:15). Paul and Barnabas explain that previously, in ancient generations, God allowed people to "go their own ways" (14:16)—i.e., He did not provide specific revelation concerning Himself—yet the "witness" of nature, the provision of seasons and harvests, and His general beneficence have been sufficient to prove that He is "good" to all people (14:17). Paul's argument here is more general than that in Romans 1:18-

---

332   "Mercury (*Hermés*) was the messenger of the gods, and the spokesman of Zeus. *Hermés* was of beautiful appearance and eloquent in speech, the inventor of speech in legend. Our word hermeneutics or science of interpretation comes from this word" (Robertson, *Word Pictures*, 210).

333   "...The crowd's use of Lycaonian explains why Paul and Barnabas did not grasp what was afoot until the preparations to pay them divine honours were well advanced" (Bruce, *The Book of the Acts*, 291). In fact, this is the only instance in Paul's missionary journey in which a native language is even mentioned. It is obvious, too, that just because the apostles occasionally spoke in foreign languages as a demonstration of the Spirit's power, this miracle did not allow them to speak or understand *all* foreign languages at any given time.

20, where he declares that the ancients were "without excuse" for their deliberate ignorance of God's divine nature. Yet, both accounts conclude the same things: "nature" did not just happen, but was once created and continues to be sustained by God; and the food that the earth provides is not the result of fictitious gods invented by men, but is completely dependent upon God's power and goodness. Only "with difficulty" are Paul and Barnabas able to talk the people out of sacrificing animals in their honor, no doubt to the displeasure of the local priests who are prepared to carry out their cultural duties. The fact that these missionaries tear their robes on this occasion demonstrates how serious they are about their protest to such designations and their accompanying sacrifices.

The lapse of time between 14:18 and 14:19 is unknown to us, but it has to be many days, possibly even weeks. News has to travel from Lystra back to Iconium and Antioch, and then certain Jews have to travel from those cities to Lystra—a journey of up to 130 miles (six or seven days on foot). The hatred and hostility of these men is clearly evident: without any formal charge, trial, or due process of law, "they stoned Paul and dragged him out of the city, supposing him to be dead" (14:19; see 2 Corinthians 11:25, Galatians 6:17). It appears that these Jews instigated this assault and may have even carried it out on their own, but the people of Lystra consented to it. This shows the fickle and unpredictable nature of these people: one moment, they call Paul a "god" because of the genuine power he demonstrated before their own eyes; the next moment (so to speak), they let Paul be stoned at the instigation of men who have shown them no power and who are not even from their city.[334] Incidentally, because Paul is a Roman citizen, the city officials themselves can face trial before Caesar and even be executed if this crime is reported to Rome.[335]

---

334   "The Jews who took part in this had no scruples against profaning the streets of a pagan city by such a murderous act; but in their perpetration of an identical thing in the martyrdom of Stephen, they scrupulously refrained from killing him within the city. Satan had indeed blinded such men" (Coffman, *Commentary on Acts*, 283).

335   Reese, *Book of Acts*, 595.

We later learn that Timothy lives in Lystra (see 16:1-2); he may be one of those who gazes over Paul's broken body, wondering what will become of him (14:20; see 2 Timothy 3:11). But Paul is not dead: he stands up, battered but alive! Some critics have suggested that Paul was merely "pelted" with rocks, and that Paul fell down "stunned."[336] But the wording is the same as what is used to describe the stoning of Stephen (recall 7:58) which was nothing short of a public execution. If so, then this account necessarily implies miraculous intervention in order to spare Paul's life—or bring him *back* to life.[337] The Jews are no amateurs at stoning people, and they will not leave their victim for dead unless they truly believe that he *is* dead. Likewise, a man who has just been stoned *to death* will not be able to get up on his own power and—the next day—begin a journey of some 60 miles (by foot?) to Derbe. What happens in Derbe is not recorded, other than that Paul and Barnabas do indeed journey there. Derbe lies on the edge of the Galatian frontier, backed up against the Taurus Mountains; across these mountains is Tarsus in Cilicia, Paul's place of birth.[338]

The journey back to Antioch (14:21-28)

After reaching Derbe and (it is implied) establishing a work there, the missionaries retrace their steps, even revisiting those cities that acted hostile to them, and encouraging those who have obeyed the gospel of Christ (14:21). "Through many tribulations" (14:22) is somewhat

---

336 Foakes-Jackson (*The Acts of the Apostles*, 128), for example, is one of these critics. Lenski says, "It is not difficult to see what had happened: a stone had rendered Paul unconscious, and he remained so until this time" (*Acts of the Apostles*, 583)—to which I ask, "How do you *know* that?" F. F. Bruce, though not supporting the "stunned" theory, does only say that Paul's escape from death has only "a flavour [*sic*] of miracle about it" (*The Book of the Acts*, 296). I am not certain what he means by that expression, but it seems to avoid a full admittance of miraculous intervention.

337 It would not be unreasonable to think that Paul, in his near-death experience, at this time had his vision of Paradise (2 Corinthians 12:2-4). The difference between what he saw and what people today claim to "see" in their own near-death experiences is that Paul's was confirmed by inspiration as a revelation of God, whereas other experiences lack any such substantiation and may well be nothing more than a shared phenomenon of the human psyche when faced with mortal trauma.

338 The ruins of Lystra were discovered in 1885. Derbe was lost to history, except for its mention in Acts, until recent archeological discoveries in the 1950s unearthed physical evidence of its existence (Gaertner, *Acts*, 222; Coffman, *Commentary on Acts*, 284).

of an understatement, given what Paul and Barnabas have thus far endured.[339] It is possible that Paul and Barnabas themselves are amazed at the fierceness and tenacity of men's resistance to the gospel; or, it may be that Paul now sees from the other side, so to speak, what it feels like to be the *recipient* of such hostility rather than the one who *incites* it (recall 9:1-2). Regardless, this statement is part encouragement and part explanation. It is encouragement to remain faithful and even joyful despite the hostile resistance of unbelievers (1 Thessalonians 1:6-7, 1 Peter 4:12-13). It is also an explanation as to *what happened* to Paul when he was stoned and left for dead: this did not detract from the authenticity and quality of the message preached to them. Instead, it underscores the fact that Christians must be willing to suffer for what is right (see Philippians 1:27-30). This explanation is, no doubt, for the sake of the new churches, not Paul's mere observation. It is a response to the implied question, "If these men are facing such resistance, then how do we know that what they say is true?" Paul reminds the new converts that hostility toward heavenly truth is going to accompany the preaching of that truth (2 Thessalonians 1:4-5). "Indeed, all who desire to live godly in Christ Jesus will be persecuted" (2 Timothy 3:12).

Paul and Barnabas also appoint elders [Greek, *presbuteros*] in every city's church (14:23); this becomes the expected practice of missionary work wherever congregations are established (Titus 1:5).[340] Church

---

339   In most cases (from Acts 2 forward), entrance into the kingdom of God is posed as a future promise (as in 2 Timothy 4:18 and 2 Peter 1:10-11), whereas entrance into Christ's church ("in Christ") is stated as a present reality, albeit spiritual in nature (as in Ephesians 2:4-7). No sinner will enter into the eternal kingdom of God unless he is first baptized into the body of Christ (His church). Whoever is given entrance into Christ's church is also promised entrance into the heavenly kingdom. However, this latter promise is contingent upon one's being "faithful until death" (cf. Revelation 2:10), not simply because he has been baptized into Christ. If one will not suffer for Christ, then he forfeits this opportunity (Romans 8:16-17, 2 Timothy 2:12). Put another way: the church is in the process of being added to *now* as people continue to be baptized into it; the kingdom is what Christ's church will enter into in the *future*, after having been fully assembled and prepared for its otherworldly glory (see Ephesians 5:25-27, Revelation 19:7-9, and 21:1-5).

340   The Greek word for "appointed" (*cheirotoneo*) literally means "to extend the hand (as in a vote)," but generally means "chosen" or "selected," as in 2 Corinthians 8:19 (which uses the same Greek word) (*Strong's* [electronic edition], #G5500). "Since the New Testament does not tell us how the elders were appointed, it seems that any method which promotes unity and does not violate a principle may be used" (Boles, *A*

elders provide leadership, organization, and spiritual oversight. "…
Christians can no longer count on the use of the Jewish synagogue.
They must have an organization of their own."[341] "Fasting" is nowhere
commanded of Christians, but neither is it discouraged. The purpose
of fasting is to deny one's carnal appetite in deeper pursuit of spiritual
nourishment (Matthew 5:6, in principle; see John 6:27). Put another
way: it is an "affliction" or "humbling" of the body for the purpose of
engaging in spiritual communion with God (as in Leviticus 16:29-31).
It is amazing that, despite all the Jewish persecution against Paul and
Barnabas, multiple churches are still established in this area.

In any case, the emphasis here as the first journey closes is optimistic
and encouraging. Luke chooses not to dwell upon the negative
encounters but on the positive results of the missionaries' preaching.
Upon reaching Antioch of Syria (which serves as a home base for the
missionaries), Paul and Barnabas relate their adventures to the church
and are highly commended for their faithfulness and courage. "They
began to report all things God had done with them and how He opened
a door of faith to the Gentiles" (14:27)—in essence, this "door" had
been closed to the Gentiles previously, but now things have changed.[342]
Paul clarifies the situation in Ephesians 3:4-7:

Commentary on Acts, 229)—a pragmatic summary of the situation.

341   Robertson, *Word Pictures*, 217. Stott adds: "These are the reasons why Paul
believed that the churches could confidently be left to manage their own affairs. They
had the apostles to teach them (through 'the faith' and their letters), pastors to shepherd
them, and the Holy Spirit to guide, protect, and bless them. With this threefold
provision (apostolic instruction, pastoral oversight and divine faithfulness) they would
be safe" (*The Spirit, the Church, and the World*, 237).

342   John Calvin tries to explain this verse in the context of Calvinism (a.k.a. the
Doctrine of Predestination)—not to *prove* it (since nothing in the NT can prove
Calvinism to be true), but in *light* of it. He says that all the "elect" have an "inward"
calling (election) of the Spirit which, when united with the "external" calling
(preaching) of the gospel, becomes a faith that *God* creates within that person apart
from any decision of his own (*Acts*, 246). Thus, what the Calvinist calls "faith" is
not a human response to "hearing…the word of Christ" (Romans 10:17) and that
person's obedience to *what* he hears (as is consistent throughout the book of Acts), but
refers instead to God making him "born" of God before that person does *anything* in
response to the Word.

... When you read you can understand my insight into the mystery of Christ, which in other generations was not made known to the sons of men, as it has now been revealed to His holy apostles and prophets in the Spirit; to be specific, that the Gentiles are fellow heirs and fellow members of the body, and fellow partakers of the promise in Christ Jesus through the gospel, of which I was made a minister, according to the gift of God's grace which was given to me according to the working of His power.

This journey has taken about two years to complete, possibly even more; in the process, Paul and Barnabas have traveled some 1,200 miles across land and sea.[343] They will spend at least another year in Antioch before heading out on a second journey.

---

343   "Paul and Barnabas had traveled the twelve hundred eight miles and had established more than half a dozen churches within the two or three years that they were gone on this journey" (Boles, *A Commentary on Acts*, 231).

∼ Chapter 15 ∼
Council in Jerusalem

The need for a council (15:1-2)
We should consider the monumental transition we have witnessed
thus far in Acts. Stephen's defense before the Council (chapter 7)
underscored the failure of Israel to properly receive her Messiah.
Instead of fidelity to their covenant with God, the Jews—especially
many of their leaders—chose jealousy, betrayal, and murder. As
a testimony of *God's* faithfulness to this covenant, the gospel is
nonetheless offered to the Jews first. (This privilege continues only
until the end of the Jewish system in AD 70; after this, the order of who
hears the gospel first or second will be irrelevant.) Regardless, we see
a definite shift in focus from the Jews to the Gentiles, as seen over a
period of several years:

❑ During His ministry, Jesus instructed His disciples to preach only to
   the "lost sheep of Israel" (Matthew 10:5-6).
❑ He referred to Israel as His "sheep," but indicated that the plan of
   salvation will include "other sheep" as well (John 10:14-16; see
   Isaiah 49:5-6).
❑ He told the Samaritan woman that a time was coming when
   physical location and *ethnicity* will be irrelevant in worship of God
   (John 4:21-24).
❑ He warned the Jews that if they refused His preaching, they will be
   denied participation in the kingdom of God (Matthew 8:11-12),
   and the invitation will be instead given to a "nation producing the
   fruit of" the kingdom (Matthew 21:43).
❑ He instructed His disciples to begin their preaching in Judea, but
   to ultimately take the gospel into "the remotest part of the earth"
   (Acts 1:8).
❑ We see the fulfillment of Jesus' words through the spread of the
   gospel to the Samaritans, then the Syrians, and then the Gentiles in
   regions far beyond Palestine (in Acts 8 – 14).
❑ Later, Paul declares that salvation is for *all* men, "to the Jew first,
   and also to the Greek" (Romans 1:16, 10:11-13). This universal
   salvation is the "mystery of Christ" that is revealed through
   apostolic teaching—a "mystery" that has been hidden from men

until now but has always been part of God's "eternal purpose which He carried out in Christ Jesus our Lord" (Ephesians 3:1-12).

❑ He also declares that salvation *and* punishment will be given to the righteous and the wicked, respectively, without regard for national status (Romans 2:9-11).

While profound and unprecedented, this transition is still not an easy one. Indeed, "no age … of Christianity, not even the earliest, has been without its difficulties, controversies, and corruptions."[344] Even so, it is challenging for us to appreciate just how awkward and uncomfortable it is for the first generation of Jewish Christians to accept Gentiles as equals in the Lord. This is compounded by their struggle to accept the fact that the gospel has superseded the Law of Moses—a law that they exclusively have possessed for some 1,500 years.[345] For the unbelieving Jews, these two problems appear insurmountable: God would never allow another people to share in the Jews' status, and He would never abandon the Law of Moses until or unless Messiah comes. Thus, their rejection of Jesus *as* the Messiah (Christ) drives all other actions and reactions. Because of this rejection—and the self-serving nature of their leadership—the Jews feel justified in persecuting the church as an illegitimate and heretical movement that must be stamped out of existence.

"Some men came down from Judea and began teaching the brethren, 'Unless you are circumcised…, you cannot be saved'" (15:1). "The brethren," we will soon discover, refers to the church in Syrian Antioch (15:30). The date of this incident is circa AD 50. The fact that this teaching attempted to redefine the terms and conditions of *salvation*

---

344   Conybeare and Howson, *Life and Epistles*, 160.

345   "They could not conceive, as yet, that this divinely given law, which had been in existence so long, and for the preservation of which their fathers had suffered so much, could be disregarded by any who would be heirs of eternal life" (McGarvey, *Acts of Apostles*, 2:54). We should clarify, however, that the reason *why* the Law of Moses was "superseded" was not because it was suddenly terminated in order to accommodate the gospel of Christ. Rather, it was *fulfilled* in Christ; its purpose has been satisfied in Him. It was a promise (or "shadow"—Hebrews 10:1) of things to come, but once that promise had been fulfilled, it was no longer binding. Its obsolescence allowed for a better ministry with better promises—promises of an eternal life, not merely ritual cleansing or national preservation as before (cf. Hebrews 8:6, 9:11-14).

(differently than what the apostles and others have preached) makes it a doctrinal matter and not one of mere human opinions. Since salvation comes *from* God, the terms of salvation—what is required of men as well as what is not required—is determined *by* God, never by men (or churches or religious institutions claiming to speak for God). These men are saying, in no uncertain terms, that *no one* can be saved apart from "circumcision," which represents (as a synecdoche) obedience to the entire Law of Moses. These men want to impose that which has been fulfilled and thus superseded *by* Christ upon those who are *in* Christ—something which they have no reason or authority to do.

For this reason, Paul and Barnabas had a "great dissention and debate" with these teachers who have come from Jerusalem to Antioch (15:2). This extremely important matter has to be addressed directly and conclusively, inasmuch as it threatens to undermine all the progress that has been made in the ministry to the Gentiles in Antioch and beyond. If the gospel is viewed as just another version of Judaism, then Gentiles are nothing more than second-class citizens as before. (Judaism has always forced a kind of glass ceiling over the Gentile proselytes, since no matter how Jewish these converts become, they cannot escape the fact that they are *not* Jews.) Paul and Barnabas thus aggressively oppose any teaching that mandates conformity to *Judaism* as a means of salvation in *Christ*. "[They] were not willing to see this Gentile church brow-beaten and treated as heretics by these self-appointed regulators of Christian orthodoxy from Jerusalem."[346] This is also why the subject occupies dominant attention in several of Paul's epistles (Romans, Galatians, Ephesians, and Colossians). The division is not merely a religious one; it also affects the Jews' and Gentiles' social identities.[347]

These men who "came down from Judea" to Antioch are Jewish

---

346   Robertson, *Word Pictures*, 223; bracketed word is mine.

347   "Jerusalem was the metropolis of the Jewish world. The exclusive feelings which the Jews carried with them wherever they were diffused, were concentrated in Jerusalem in their most intense degree. It was there, in the sight of the Temple, and with all the recollections of their ancestors surrounding their daily life, that the impatience of the Jewish Christians kindled into burning indignation" (Conybeare and Howson, *Life and Epistles*, 165).

Christians, yet maintain their association with the sect of the Pharisees (15:1, 5). They have a mistaken view of Christianity; they see it as an extension—rather than a supersession—of what they had already been practicing.[348] In their eyes, "Christianity, instead of being the purest and holiest form of Judaism, was rapidly becoming a universal and indiscriminating religion, in which the Jewish element would be absorbed and lost."[349] If these are the same men (or, the same *kind* of men) referred to in Galatians 2:4, Paul calls them "false brethren" who are trying to "bring us into bondage" by subjecting everyone again to the Law of Moses (see Galatians 3:1-3 and Philippians 3:1-3).[350] These Jews believe, in essence, that the only way one can truly have fellowship with God is to live like a Jew and thus receive circumcision. Thus, one of the first false doctrines with which the early church had to contend was the alleged marrying of Judaism with Christianity.[351] Church historian Philip Schaff says:

> The Jewish converts at first very naturally adhered as closely as possible to the sacred traditions of their fathers. They could not believe that the religion of the Old Testament, revealed by God himself, should pass away. They indeed regarded Jesus as the

---

348   "This controversy arose because many believed that the Messianic blessings were available to Gentiles *only if they became Jews*. This makes the point that the 'gospel of the kingdom' was peculiarly related to the Jew. Had there been no Isaiah 2:2-4 (and more like that), that conviction would never have arisen. It was precisely *because* the OT and the Gospels related the kingdom peculiarly to the Jews that this debate raged at Jerusalem. The Pharisaic party went beyond 'peculiarly related' to 'exclusively related.' They didn't mind Gentiles sharing in Messianic blessings *provided* they became Jews" (McGuiggan, *The Reign of God*, 71).

349   Conybeare and Howson, *Life and Epistles*, 165.

350   "From this judicial sentence upon them we ascertain that when they despaired of destroying the church by persecution from without, they deliberately confessed Christ and came into the church for the purpose of controlling it from within. It was their design to keep the church under the bondage of law, and thus prevent it from very seriously modifying the state of things among the Jews in which the Pharisees were the predominant party. Partisan zeal, the bane of their former life, was still their controlling passion" (McGarvey, *Acts of Apostles*, 2:59).

351   While circumcision is indeed a regulation of the Law of Moses (Leviticus 12:2-3), its *practice* and *association* as a covenant practice began with Abraham, not Moses (Genesis 17). This is Paul's argument in Romans 4:10-12: the Jews used circumcision to define themselves as keepers of the Law, yet God gave circumcision to Abraham some 500 years before the creation of the Israelite nation.

Saviour of Gentiles as well as Jews; but they thought Judaism the necessary introduction to Christianity, circumcision and the observance of the whole Mosaic law the sole condition of an interest in the Messianic salvation. And, offensive as Judaism was, rather than attractive, to the heathen, this principle would have utterly precluded the conversion of the mass of the Gentile world. The apostles themselves were at first trammeled by this Judaistic prejudice, till taught better by the special revelation to Peter before the conversion of Cornelius.[352]

The council in Jerusalem—our terminology, not Luke's—is the only one of its kind in Acts. It should be noted that it is the church in Antioch that dispatches Paul and Barnabas to Jerusalem, not the other way around (15:2).[353] Jerusalem remains the headquarters of the remaining eleven apostles, but it is also where this "party of the circumcision" is centered (cf. Galatians 2:12). It is very likely, too, that the Judaizing teachers who came from Judea to Antioch refuse to recognize Paul's apostolic authority. This situation requires a meeting of the original apostles along with Paul, to make certain that all of these men (the apostles) are in agreement—and to prove this agreement to the churches (see Galatians 2:6-9). Coffman rightly observes: "The notion that Paul needed their approval in any manner is wrong, except in the limited sense of his hoping to retain the unity of the Christian movement. Paul did not need the 'council'; they needed him."[354]

The council is convened (15:3-12)

For their journey from Antioch to Jerusalem (about 250 miles), Paul and Barnabas follow the Mediterranean coastline down to ancient Phoenicia (i.e., the cities of Tyre and Sidon; see 21:1-4) and then cut eastward through the region of Samaria (15:3). In the process, they visit

---

352   Schaff, "St. Paul and the Conversion of the Gentiles: the Synod of Jerusalem," *History*, vol. 1 (electronic edition).

353   In Galatians 2:2, Paul says that he went to Jerusalem for this meeting "because of a revelation." There is no contradiction between the two accounts, however: it may well be that *because* of this revelation the church in Antioch *dispatched* him to Jerusalem. The situation does not have to be made more difficult than this.

354   Coffman, *Commentary on Acts*, 291.

with several of the churches that have been established in these areas and share with them the great success they have enjoyed in spreading the gospel to the Gentiles.[355] Generally speaking, the church in Jerusalem is also supportive of Paul and Barnabas (15:4), which implies that the apostles and elders there have already endorsed their preaching to the Gentiles (see Galatians 2:7-10).[356]

Even so, there is division among the Jewish Christians over what is *required* for salvation. "It appears that the Judaizers, immediately upon the conclusion of the wonderful account of the first missionary journey, take an opportunity to point out what they regard to be a serious defect in the ministry of Paul and Barnabas among the Gentiles."[357] If it is *truly* "necessary" for all believers to be circumcised and uphold the Law of Moses (15:5), then this teaching must become a requirement for *all* believers for all time; yet whatever is "necessary" for salvation must be dictated by God and not men. "The apostles and the elders came together to look into [lit., perceive or attend to] this matter" (15:6) does not mean that the decision will be left up to them, but that they are investigating the facts and not jumping to any conclusions. Several times throughout Acts we see that the Holy Spirit allows Christians to *work through their problems*—even problems in understanding doctrinal teaching—rather than render an immediate decision for them. "The apostles" and "the elders" are not put on par with each other with regard to authority; this simply indicates an assembly of church leaders coming together to analyze the situation.

The fact is: the Holy Spirit has *already* answered the question over whether or not circumcision (i.e., observance of the Law of Moses) is

---

355   In reference to Acts 26:20, several commentators claim that there is no record of Paul ever preaching "throughout all the region of Judea." Yet the present passage (15:3) does allow for such preaching. It is also true that while Paul may not have *personally* preached throughout the entire region of Judea, his personal influence and the influence of his teaching certainly did encompass it.

356   There is no mention of Titus accompanying Paul to this meeting, as stated in Galatians 2:1-3. Again, there is no contradiction in the accounts, just one recorders preference of details over another's. As stated earlier, it is plausible that Titus and Luke are blood brothers, and it may be that Luke did not want to show any favoritism to his brother by mentioning him in his (Luke's) narrative.

357   Reese, *Book of Acts*, 532.

necessary. The fact that He provided miraculous proof of His *divine acceptance* of Cornelius and company—i.e., men who were neither circumcised nor bound to the Law—is conclusive in itself. What is common to all believers is their baptism into Christ, not physical circumcision (1 Corinthians 12:12-13).[358] All people—regardless of nationality, physical distinctions, or gender—are saved by grace and through faith. Grace is a divine gift of God; it cannot be earned or deserved. Faith is a work of human obedience; it is absolutely required (Romans 1:16, 2 Corinthians 5:7, Hebrews 10:35-39, 11:1-2, 6, et al). Those who demonstrate faith in God (by obeying what His gospel requires of them) are blessed with God's grace, which includes *everything* He does for believers that they cannot do for themselves with respect to salvation. No person is saved by *faith alone* (human effort by itself) any more than he is saved by *grace alone* (God acting *instead* of human effort); rather, it is the one working *through* the other, which is what Paul says: "by grace you have been saved through faith" (Ephesians 2:8-9).[359]

Peter grasps this point and clearly and concisely states the matter: Gentiles are saved in the same way Jews are—by divine grace through obedient human faith (15:7-11). It is God who made this "choice," not himself or any other man; the Holy Spirit Himself "testified" to this decision. "They [the Judaists] were refusing to accept that which God had accepted, or they were rejecting those whom God had accepted."[360] Peter also dispels any false hope that the Law of Moses offers spiritual

---

358   The insistence of circumcision upon all *male* believers also contradicts the unity of the body of Christ ("there is neither male nor female; for you are all one in Christ Jesus"—Galatians 3:28). This implies that the inheritance promised to believers only comes through *male believers* in the same way that the land inheritance among Israelites only came through Israelite men. Yet, Christ sees no gender distinctions between believers; the promise of an inheritance is the same for all faithful believers (Galatians 3:29). (The context here is spiritual, not physical; our earthly, marital, and social distinctions still apply.) Christians are united as "one new man" (cf. Ephesians 2:15) in fellowship with Christ *and* each other, but we are also united in doctrine—the legitimate basis *for* that fellowship.

359   This does *not* mean that grace and faith are equal in scope, power, or performance; it only means that both are *necessary* for salvation. For further study on "grace," I strongly recommend my book, *The Gospel of Grace* (Louisville, KY: Religious Supply, 2008); go to www.booksbychad.com.

360   Boles, *A Commentary on Acts*, 236, bracketed words are mine.

liberty to either Jews *or* Gentiles: the teaching of justification by law is "a yoke which neither our fathers nor we have been able to bear" (15:10; see Galatians 5:1-4). "But we believe..." (15:11)—i.e., Peter speaks on behalf of the other apostles; this is their clear and unified understanding. "We are saved through the grace of the Lord Jesus, in the same way as they also are"—i.e., we apostles are saved through the same method of salvation as were Cornelius and company; there is no distinction between the two groups (Romans 10:11-13). Christ is the source of salvation, not the Law of Moses, or law-keeping of any kind. Once a person sins against God, his only means of being reconciled to Him is through Jesus Christ. Peter's words—the last of his that are recorded in Acts—silences the debate itself. As the people listen to Paul and Barnabas recount all the work that God has done among the Gentiles (15:12), the conclusion is unavoidable: circumcision (or, any binding observance of the Law of Moses) is *not* "necessary" for salvation.

As stated earlier, this council has been convened for the purpose of defining the *doctrinal* terms of salvation. Now that this matter has been settled, there is no reason to reconvene to discuss it further. Likewise, now that the gospel has been "once for all handed down to the saints" (Jude 3), there is no reason to add to, subtract from, or modify it in any way.[361] Paul even places a divine curse upon anyone who would attempt to change the gospel that he preached to all men (Galatians 1:8, Colossians 1:23). We have in the NT everything that God needed us to know in order to have fellowship with Him through His Son, Jesus Christ. There is no reason to have more councils, other doctrines, modified gospels, different "faiths," or different methods of salvation; in fact, any departure from the NT pattern represents a violation of what Peter and Paul have preached and what the Holy

---

361   Calvin says, "All the holy synods, from the beginning, have assembled for the same purpose: that eminent men who know God's Word might decide controversies, not as they please, but according to God's authority" (*Acts*, 251). While there is nothing wrong with Christians coming together in a given church to deal with controversies within their own group, Calvin (among others) oversteps the context of this Jerusalem council. No council or synod today has any right to change what God has commanded in His gospel, nor do "eminent men" have any right to define that gospel differently than how it has already been defined in the NT record. Furthermore, no group of men, however well-intentioned it may be, has any right to decide *for the entire brotherhood* how a given controversy among Christians ought to be handled. We have the gospel; it is a sufficient authority for all teaching *and* settling of controversies.

Spirit has adamantly maintained is *true* and *necessary*. To assume that we can convene modern councils to continue or duplicate what was done in Jerusalem is to ignore the reason for and context of that special meeting.

The council's letter and its reception (15:13-35)

In the absence of any other antecedent, "James" (15:13) must be the same person as mentioned earlier in 12:17. He has apparently become a man of great distinction; Paul later refers to him as one of the "pillars" in the church in Jerusalem (Galatians 2:9). "If this were a present-day board meeting, we would say that James was acting as its chairman, and it was left to him to summarize the whole presentation."[362] Despite his high reputation, James is not usurping the authority of the apostles here; he merely addresses the meeting with a solution—one which will require the apostles' and (more importantly) the Holy Spirit's approval. He begins by giving his personal endorsement to what Peter has just said (15:14). ("Simeon" is the Aramaic form of "Simon," who is Peter; see John 1:42.) He then declares that Peter's statements are in full agreement with what has already been prophesied in Scripture (15:15-18). Specifically, he quotes from Amos 9:11-12, which predicts that the spiritual restoration of Israel will include the Gentiles ("nations").[363] The "tabernacle of David"—really, the house of Israel over which David reigned as king, and/or the royal lineage of David itself (since both meanings apply)—had fallen from power and glory due to the people's sins and God's subsequent judgment. But God promised to restore Israel (and David) "after these things" or "in that day" (after God's anger against Israel has been satisfied). The prophecy is symbolic in nature (as in Isaiah 2:1-5, 4:2-6, 11:1-9, et al), and refers to the *spiritual* restoration or rebuilding of Israel in the context of Christ's church. The final clause of James's citation is not actually from Amos, but (likely) Isaiah 45:21. James did not say, "I quote from Amos," but that "the prophets agree, as it is written."

---

362   Reese, *Book of Acts*, 540.

363   James cites from the Septuagint Bible, a Greek translation of the original Hebrew text. Paul and the author of Hebrews also cite heavily from this, since it is widely popular among Greek-speaking people.

Inasmuch as Christ's church is a fulfillment of Amos' prophecy, it also follows that the Gentiles will be made a part of His church on equal footing with Jews, so that the entire group may be made into "one new man" (cf. Ephesians 2:13-18). James's counsel is to advise Gentile believers by way of a written letter to abide by four general teachings (15:19-20, discussed below). "For Moses from ancient generations has in every city those who preach him" (15:21)—meaning: the moral and spiritual teachings of (the Law of) Moses will not be abandoned, since there remains many Jews in the world who will continue to teach them. This is not an endorsement of Judaism; it is merely a practical observation. What the Gentiles are being instructed to do is in harmony with what Jews everywhere already practice.

The idea of communicating these things in a letter was well-received by the apostles, elders, and the rest of the church in Jerusalem (15:22). Furthermore, it "seemed good" to them to have this letter delivered by Paul and Barnabas, since this issue directly affected their missionary work among the Gentiles. The group also asked that two other "leading men among the brethren"—Judas (surnamed Barsabbas) and Silas (a.k.a. Silvanus)—accompany the missionaries. The letter is written, and says or implies the following information:

- ❏ The ministry to the Gentiles carries the full endorsement of *all* the apostles (15:23). Likewise, it is fully endorsed by the elders of the church in Jerusalem. In effect, the salutation says: "From the brethren *here* (in Jerusalem) to the brethren *there* (in Antioch, Syria, Cilicia, and abroad)—we are *all brethren* in the Lord." Paul underscores this unity and equality in his letter to the Galatians: "There is neither Jew nor Greek, there is neither slave nor free man, there is neither male nor female; for you are all one in Christ Jesus" (Galatians 3:28).
- ❏ Any teaching that demands circumcision and the observance of the Law for salvation is *not from the apostles* ("we gave no instruction" to them—15:24). This clearly distinguishes between such teachers and the apostles themselves.[364]

---

364 "In spite of its rich diversity of formulation and emphasis in the New Testament, there is only one apostolic gospel. We must resist modern theologians who set the New

❑ Those men "of our number" (i.e., Jewish teachers from Jerusalem) who are trying to impose a distinction between Jewish Christians and Gentile Christians, or who are trying to impose additional requirements upon the Gentiles that goes beyond the gospel message that they have believed, have "no instruction" from the apostles to say such things (15:25). Their false representation of the gospel of Christ is stirring up all sorts of unnecessary grief within the body of Christ. Such men are "disturbing" and "unsettling" the souls of Gentile believers.[365] Thus, these false representatives are purposely subverting the sound teaching the Gentiles had once received.

❑ The apostles and elders in Jerusalem determined—with the Holy Spirit's approval—to compose a letter to clarify what *is* required among all believers. This letter commends Barnabas and Paul, as well as Judas and Silas, all of whom will serve as credible witnesses to the authenticity of the letter and their own approval of its contents (15:26-28).

❑ The letter requires "four essentials" to be observed, which will keep the Gentiles from sinning against God *and* facilitate social fellowship with Jewish believers, since these things are also offensive to them. It is not meant to be an exhaustive list by any means; it is also not meant to replace the gospel teaching they have already received, but to supplement it, as needed. It addresses some of the elemental things that Gentiles struggle with due to the pagan or polytheistic culture which they had once practiced (and still may have strong influence over them), namely (15:29):

▪ **Abstinence from the pollution of idols or things sacrificed to idols.** Eating meat from an animal that has been sacrificed to an idol is not sinful in itself (see 1 Corinthians 10:23-33, for example). However, participating in the *cultural feast* of this

---

Testament writers at variance with each other, and who talk about Pauline, Petrine, and Johannine positions as if they were incompatible gospels. Even Paul and James, who were reconciled at the Council, can be reconciled in their New Testament letters too. They taught the same way of salvation" (Stott, *The Spirit, the Church, and the World*, 256).

365   The Greek word for "unsettling" (*anaskeuazô*) means literally "to pack up (baggage)," as though to carry it to another place; the idea here, then, is that these false teachers are taking believers to where they do not need to go (*Strong's* [electronic edition], #G384).

sacrifice can create a stumbling block to the unlearned Gentile believer, since he may incorporate "sacrifices to demons" with his worship of Christ (cf. 1 Corinthians 10:19-21) or by partaking of this meat he may defile his conscience (Romans 14:13-23).[366]

- **Abstinence from blood**—specifically, the eating of blood (in meat) or any drinking of blood (as part of a religious ceremony). Gentiles are not as hygienic or discriminating about their foods as Jews are, and may not care (until now) whether or not blood is still in the meat they consume. The prohibition against eating blood was first given to Noah (Genesis 9:4), and was later codified in the Law of Moses (Leviticus 17:10-12). It is not a ritual requirement but a moral command that transcends any law given exclusively to the Jews, since blood represents a sacred element of life and atonement.

- **Things strangled**—because killing an animal in this manner does not allow the blood to properly drain from its flesh. Thus, it appears that the method of death (strangulation) is not so much the issue as is how it renders the meat unfit for consumption among believers. This instruction also is undoubtedly "to prevent participation in heathen sacrificial feasts."[367]

- **Fornication**—i.e., any sexual improprieties, perversions (e.g., incest, homosexuality, bestiality, etc.), or adultery. These are moral crimes against the body (1 Corinthians 6:15-18) and are not to be tolerated among Christians (1 Thessalonians 4:1-7), even though they are commonly practiced throughout the

---

366   Reese describes this in far more detail: "A heathen decides he will worship his favorite deity. He selects an animal for the sacrifice, usually an ox. The ox was taken to the heathen temple, where the tail was cut off, and the tail would be burned on a sacrificial altar. The rest of the animal was then roasted and used for a feast. All the worshipper's friends were invited. What this group would not eat was given to the priests in charge of the idol's temple... [and may be sold] to the local butcher. In fact, some idol's temples had a butcher shop right next door, and it was operated as an adjunct of the temple. The butcher would in turn offer the meat for sale to the housewives and townspeople, with the profit going to the temple where the meat was originally offered in sacrifice to the idol. ...[Thus] abstaining from the contamination of idols means, 'Do not go to the idol's temples and participate in the feasts held there!'" (*Book of Acts*, 545-546).

367   Edward Bagby Pollard, "Strangled," *ISBE* (electronic edition).

Roman Empire. "From the beginning it had been known to the patriarchs that it was sinful to have any responsible connection with idols, or to indulge in fornication."[368]

These four "essentials" are timeless and universal: they still apply to all Christians today, regardless of one's nationality or culture. "If you keep yourselves free from such things, you will do well" (15:29)—obviously, these are not the *only* things from which believers are to abstain, but the emphasis seems to be upon specific practices or behaviors that prevent Jews and Gentiles from enjoying full fellowship with each other in the Lord. It is as if the apostles are saying, "We [Jews] have made great concessions to receive you [Gentiles] as equals in the Lord; now you need to do your part not to purposely undermine that fellowship with these heathen practices." While the Jews and Gentiles are equals "in Christ Jesus" (cf. Galatians 3:28), nonetheless it remains true that the Gentiles ("the branches") owe their gratitude to those Jews who remained faithful to God from one covenant to the next ("the root" of the olive tree) (cf. Romans 11:18). Thus, both parties have a responsibility to each other in order to "preserve the unity of the Spirit in the bond of peace" (Ephesians 4:3).

This letter is sent initially to Antioch of Syria by way of Paul, Barnabas, Judas, and Silas (15:25-27); this is the "they" in 15:30.[369] The reception of the letter in Antioch is very favorable. "They rejoiced because of its encouragement" (15:31)—i.e., because it validated their good standing with the Lord. It also vindicated the work of Paul and Barnabas: "The church at Jerusalem recognized the great danger that

---

368   McGarvey, *Acts of Apostles*, 2:67.

369   "Frequently the question has been raised as to why Paul never mentions these decrees in his letters. Some critics have charged that he does not mention them because he did not know about them, thus impugning the credibility of Luke's account in Acts 15" (Gaertner, *Acts*, 243). Such baseless assumptions focus on one small detail—or an alleged omission of one—to the exclusion of the significant amount of evidence that *is* provided. Given such reasoning, we might call *all* of Luke's account into question—or Paul's epistles—because he does not mention any of Paul's epistles, and Paul's epistles do not mention Luke's historical account. But charging one man or the other (or both) with a serious omission overlooks the purpose for and inspiration of each man's writing. It also is a purely subjective accusation, and as such it assumes much and proves nothing.

Paul and Barnabas had suffered, as they are described in this letter as 'men that have hazarded their lives for the name of our Lord Jesus Christ' [citing the KJV—CMS]. They recognized the courage and heroism of Paul and Barnabas; they in fact also proved the sincerity of Paul and Barnabas."[370] No doubt Judas and Silas are sent to corroborate Paul and Barnabas's own testimony (to prove that the letter was not a forgery), and as representatives of the church in Jerusalem in particular. Since these two men are also "prophets," they are able to provide inspired confirmation of these things as well as additional teaching (15:32). After a while, "they"—presumably Judas and Silas— returned to Jerusalem (15:33). (Verse 34 is not included in the oldest manuscripts, and is thought to explain Silas' presence in Antioch for what happens next. Regardless of this verse's dubious authenticity, it does not matter: even if Silas had left Antioch, he could have just as easily returned upon Paul's request.) Meanwhile, Paul and Barnabas remain in Antioch to resume the work in which they had previously engaged (15:35).

Preface to the second missionary journey (15:36-41)
Paul's second journey—he being the prominent figure in all the detailed journeys of Acts since chapter 13—begins quietly, without the ceremony of the first (recall 13:2-3). "After some days Paul said to Barnabas, 'Let us return and visit the brethren in every city in which we proclaimed the word of the Lord, and see how they are'" (15:36). The decision to return to already-established congregations appears to be Paul's idea, but it may well be the Holy Spirit who prompts this mission. The year is now circa AD 51.

Luke's account of Paul and Barnabas's heated dissention regarding John Mark adds to the genuineness and brutal honesty of this narrative (15:37-41). The Greek word for "sharp disagreement" (or "contention") implies a provoking or stimulating of something: here, it is used in a negative sense; in Hebrews 10:24, it is used in a positive sense ("...stimulate one another..."). It is likely that Barnabas argues from an emotional perspective, since Mark is his blood relative (Colossians 4:10). For Paul, the matter is much more practical: Mark's

---

370   Boles, *A Commentary on Acts*, 243.

earlier desertion (recall 13:13) makes him undependable in Paul's eyes; "A man who failed once at a crucial time might well fail again."[371] Regardless, the two men cannot agree upon a decision, and thus they go their separate ways. Paul chooses "Silas"—the same man mentioned in 15:22—as his new traveling partner.[372] (The Latin version of his name is "Silvanus," as used in 2 Corinthians 1:19, 1 Thessalonians 1:1, etc.) This decision to take Silas will prove providential since both Paul and Silas have Roman citizenship, and they will use this to their advantage. What is conspicuous to us is that the Holy Spirit does not intervene in the dispute between Paul and Barnabas, but allows the two men to work out their problem themselves.

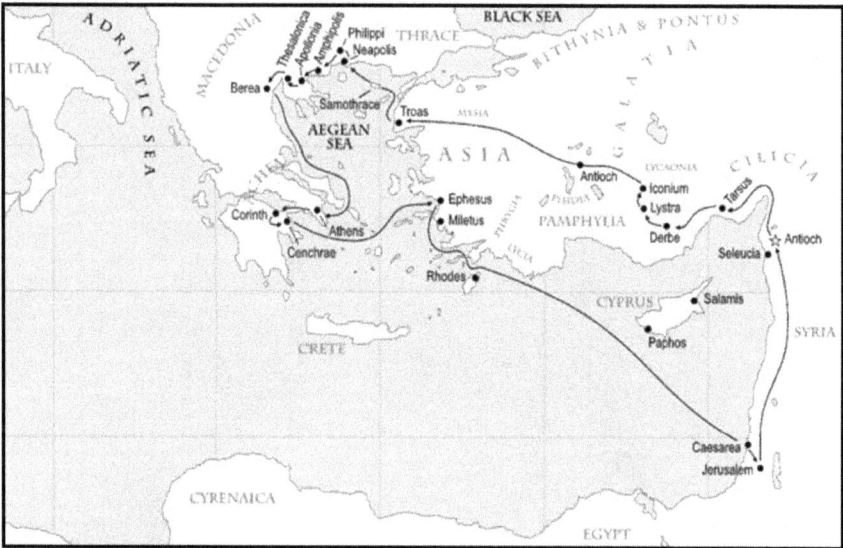

While Barnabas and Mark return to Cyprus—and this is the last that we hear of either one of them in Acts—Paul and Silas travel northwestward from Syria into the province of Cilicia, then apparently

---

371 Lenski, *Acts of the Apostles*, 634.

372 "The relationship between Paul and Silas is different from that of Paul and Barnabas. Luke never calls Silas an apostle, yet he refers twice to the apostle Barnabas. Silas accompanied Paul not as an equal but as a subordinate. By contrast, Paul always regarded Barnabas as his equal and in earlier days as his leader and mentor" (Kistemaker, *Acts*, 571). By "his equal," I assume Kistemaker to mean equal as a missionary partner, not having equal apostolic authority. Otherwise, this is an insightful observation.

cross the Taurus Mountains into Galatia.[373] "While the separation of Paul from Barnabas and John Mark was unpleasant, it did not keep both men from their service to God. The separation allowed two teams of missionaries to carry the gospel of Christ ... [which] resulted in spreading the influence of the church father than ever before."[374]

---

373   Ramsay's remarks here are worth considering: "Barnabas here passes out of history. The tradition, as stated in the apocryphal *Periodoi Barnabae*, a very late work, was that he remained in Cyprus till his death; and the fact that Mark reappears at a later stage without Barnabas, is in agreement. At any rate his work, wherever it was carried on, did not, in Luke's estimation, contribute to work out the idea of the organised [*sic*] and unified Church. That idea was elaborated in Paul's work; and the history is guided by Paul's activity from the moment when he began to be fully conscious of the true nature of his work. Others contributed to the earlier stages, but, as it proceeded, all the other personages became secondary, and Paul more and more the single moving genius" (*St. Paul the Traveller*, 176). This assessment may ascribe too much to Paul and too little to the other apostles, but it does acknowledge the great influence Paul had on the early church. We should not forget, either, that a good half of what we call the New Testament was written by him. Even so, it is Christ who is the real "moving genius" behind all the church's identity and success, including His selection and providential oversight of such men like Paul to carry out His work (cf. Acts 9:15-16).

374   Turner, *Paul of Tarsus*, 70; bracketed word is mine.

∼ Chapters 16 – 18 ∼
Second Missionary Journey

From Galatia to Philippi (16:1-15)

Upon entering into Galatia, Paul and Silas visit two of the churches that Paul and Barnabas had founded on the first missionary journey, namely, the churches in Derbe and Lystra. It is here in Lystra that we are introduced to Timothy for the first time, although it is very likely that the two men had already met on Paul's first visit (16:1-2). This young man (in his early 20s?) has from childhood received excellent instruction from his Jewish mother and grandmother (2 Timothy 1:5, 3:15), but his father was a Greek.[375] This means that Timothy is not a full-blooded Jew; however, Jews determine ethnicity through the bloodline of the mother, not the father. He is, as far as anyone would consider him at this time, a Jew.

Timothy, while young, still has a remarkable reputation in this area, and will continue to warrant high respect from the churches elsewhere as well, as is evident in Paul's epistles. "Paul wanted this man to go with him…" (16:3)—the reasons are not stated for this here, but we discover in his epistles that Paul looked upon Timothy as his "beloved son" and a "kindred spirit" (cf. 2 Timothy 1:2 and Philippians 2:19-22). This is particularly significant since Paul has no family—and thus no son—of his own. In order to take him along, however, Paul circumcises Timothy. "This implies that Timothy's father had not accepted the Jewish religion. No Jewish mother was permitted to circumcise her son against the wishes of a Gentile father."[376] This circumcision has no bearing upon Timothy's salvation, nor is it a requirement of the gospel; this act also does not violate the decision

---

375   In 16:3, the word "was" in the expression "…his father was a Greek" in the original language implies that his father was no longer living (Bruce, *The Book of the Acts*, 322).

376   JFB *Commentary*, on 16:3. On the other hand, Kistemaker writes: "The Jews considered a mixed marriage illegal…. Timothy's mother had married a Greek even though she knew the Scriptures. As a daughter of Abraham, she had not fulfilled the law, for she neglected to have her son circumcised. Although the Christian brothers in Lystra and Iconium spoke well of Timothy, the Jews took offense because Timothy was not circumcised. The Jews regarded him to be outside the covenant God had made with Abraham and his descendants" (*Acts*, 578).

reached during the council in Jerusalem. "The conduct of Paul here was an instance of his accommodation to Jewish prejudices, and did not involve any departure from his previous views of Christian duty and Christian liberty."[377] Schaff says:

> ... But how could Paul consistently afterwards [i.e., after the council in Jerusalem—MY WORDS] circumcise Timothy? The answer is that he circumcised Timothy as a Jew, not as a Gentile, and that he did it as a voluntary act of expediency, for the purpose of making Timothy more useful among the Jews, who had a claim on him as the son of a Jewish mother, and would not have allowed him to teach in a synagogue without this token of membership; while in the case of Titus, a pure Greek, circumcision was demanded as a principle and as a condition of justification and salvation.[378]

In essence, Paul did this only to prevent Timothy's *un*-circumcision from being a stumbling block to the Jews among whom Timothy would be working to spread the gospel.

As they retrace Paul's earlier journey through the southern Galatian region, the missionaries deliver copies of the letter (from Acts 15) to all the churches (16:4). This indicates the unity of teaching that is to be expected among all churches of Christ (1 Corinthians 4:17, Ephesians 4:1-3). It is impressive to see that these churches are not only still in existence but are growing and appear to be doing well, despite the pressure they receive from Jewish unbelievers (16:5).[379]

---

377 Boles, *A Commentary on Acts*, 252.

378 Schaff, "St. Paul and the Conversion of the Gentiles: the Synod of Jerusalem," *History*, vol. 1 (electronic edition).

379 "There are several explanations for the lack of a detailed description of Paul's work at this time. Some think it was because Luke (the writer) had not yet joined the group. Others maintain that Luke was anxious to bring his written record to the time of Paul's activities in Europe. Possibly the general theme of the development of the Christian church from Jerusalem to Rome made Paul's short time in Phrygia and Galatia of relatively little importance in that context" (JFB *Commentary*, on 16:6).

After passing through Phrygia and then Galatia, Paul and Silas (and now Timothy) are "forbidden" by the Holy Spirit to enter into the Roman province of Asia Minor (16:6).[380] We are not told why the Holy Spirit thus prevents them, but some plausible answers may be considered:

❑ That region was not yet as ready to receive the gospel as it will be in a few more years (when Paul goes to Ephesus on his third journey).

❑ Paul himself is not ready for what awaits him in that region; he needs more experience and preparation first.

❑ The Holy Spirit knows that the gospel will be far better received (under the current conditions) in the places that He is directing the missionaries to go.

❑ There are factors in either place (or both) of which we are not informed, that we do not need to know, and which the Holy Spirit chose not to reveal for His own reasons.

Paul and company then desire to go north into Bithynia in the direction of the Black Sea, but the Spirit (specifically, "the Spirit of Jesus") also prevents this (16:7).[381] Thus, they travel westward along the upper edge of (the province of) Asia, through a region known as Mysia, and drop down into the city of Troas from the north (16:8). (Troas,

---

380   Asia Minor is on the westernmost end of the Anatolian Peninsula (modern-day Turkey). It includes the seven cities named in Revelation 2 – 3, Colossae, and other cities not mentioned in the New Testament. "Asia Minor (as the country was called to distinguish it from the continent of Asia), or Anatolia, is the name given to the peninsula which reaches out between the Black Sea (*Pontus Euxinus*) on the North and the Mediterranean on the South, forming an elevated land-bridge between central Asia and southeastern Europe. On the Northwest corner, the peninsula is separated from Europe by the Bosporus, the Sea of Marmora and the Hellespont. On the West the peninsula borders on the Aegean Sea, whose numerous islands tempted the timid mariner of ancient times on toward Greece. ... On the East it is usual to delimit Asia Minor by a line drawn from Alexandretta to Samsun, but for the purposes of New Testament history it must be remembered that part of Cilicia, Cappadocia and Pontus (Galatia) lie to the East of this line" (W. M. Calder, "Asia Minor," *ISBE* [electronic edition]).

381   "This is the first and only time the NT contains the phrase 'the Spirit of Jesus.' Elsewhere, the Spirit is called 'the Spirit of Christ' (Rom. 8:9; 1 Pet. 1:11) and 'the Spirit of Jesus Christ' (Phil. 1:19). The use of the title 'Spirit of Jesus' in Acts shows the unity of action between Jesus and the Spirit that permeates this book. During the days of Jesus' earthly ministry, the disciples were directed by Jesus; now, after his resurrection and ascension, by 'the Spirit of Jesus'" (JFB *Commentary*, on 16:6).

a Roman colony, is thought to be the site of ancient Troy, where the legendary Trojan Wars were fought.) Luke obviously joins the travelers at this point, since he now includes himself in the narrative (16:10ff, the first of the "we" sections in Acts). We are given no information as to how Luke heard the gospel or when he became a Christian, but it is necessarily implied throughout this narrative and Paul's epistles that he most certainly *is* one. While he is with Paul, Luke becomes a firsthand observer of the following events rather than a mere recorder of them.

While in Troas, Paul sees a heavenly vision of a man in Macedonia (modern-day Greece) pleading for him to come to the aid of people there.[382] This is often referred to as the "Macedonian vision" (16:9). Macedonia has a rich heritage: centuries earlier, Philip of Macedon controlled the gold mines there which financed the military campaign of his son, Alexander the Great, who conquered much of the known world in the 4th century BC. Here also is where Brutus and Cassius, who fought against Octavian (nephew of Julius Caesar), were defeated in 42 BC. Octavian's victory provided his ascension to power as the first emperor of Rome; his title later became Augustus Caesar. Macedonia is across the Aegean Sea from Troas, and will be the first European soil visited during any of Paul's missionary journeys.

---

382 "Paul did not infer his Macedonian origin from his words, but recognised [*sic*] him as a Macedonian by sight. Now, there was nothing distinctive in the appearance or dress of a Macedonian to mark him out from the rest of the world. On the contrary, the Macedonians rather made a point of their claim to be Greeks; and undoubtedly they dressed in the customary Greek style of the Aegean cities. There was, therefore, only one way in which Paul could know the man by sight to be a Macedonian—the man in the dream was personally known to him; and, in fact, the Greek implies that it was a certain definite person who appeared... The idea then suggests itself at once, that Luke himself was the man seen in the vision; and, when one reads the paragraph with that idea, it acquires new meaning and increased beauty" (Ramsay, *St. Paul the Traveller*, 203). As much as I like this proposal, I cannot endorse it completely. Another way in which Paul could have known that the man in his vision—and let us not forget that it *was* a heavenly vision—is that God identified the man to him, however He chose to do so. Perhaps this is also the case in which Peter, James, and John immediately knew that it was Moses and Elijah who were talking to Jesus during His transfiguration (Matthew 17:3). In any case, Paul is certain that the man in his vision is indeed a Macedonian, and that his beckoning the missionaries to "come over...and help us" is indeed a message from God.

Paul wastes no time in responding to the vision (16:10-12). "Immediately" the missionary party sets out through the Aegean Sea to Macedonia, stopping only briefly at a small island called Samothrace.[383] The winds are very favorable for them, expediting their travel. They land in Macedonia at a seaport called Neapolis ("new city"), then travel by foot on a Roman highway called the Egnatian Way (*Via Egnatia*) for about ten miles until they come to Philippi. Philippi is a Roman colony, which means that its citizens have the same rights and privileges of those who live in Rome, while the city itself is self-governed (autonomous). The official language here is Latin, though its citizens are also fluent in Greek.[384] The city also serves as a Roman garrison, and is filled with retired military officers and other Roman loyalists. Such people are used to making difficult commitments. No wonder Paul later commends them so highly (in his Epistle to the Philippians), giving no indication that they have strayed from his teaching at all. The missionaries will remain in Troas "for some days" (16:12), meaning that they are not just passing through (as they did with Neapolis, for example).

As is his custom, Paul looks for a Jewish synagogue on the Sabbath, but cannot find one (16:13). According to Jewish tradition, at least ten male heads of household are required to establish a synagogue; the implication, then, is that the Jewish population here is small.[385] It is possible that Emperor Claudius' banishment of Jews from Rome (AD 49-50; mentioned in Acts 18:2) has also diminished the Jewish presence in Roman colonies such as Philippi as well. All that Paul and Silas can find are some Jewish women who have gathered just "outside the gate" (of the city) on the banks of the Gangites River.[386] Thus, they "sat down and began speaking" to them. "Sitting was the Jewish attitude

---

383   Samothrace is "an island in the Aegean Sea about half-way between Troas and Neapolis. It is about eight miles long, and six across, very mountainous, with some of its peaks being 5000 feet above sea level. The island can be seen from both continents; from Troas and from the hills between Neapolis and Philippi" (Reese, *Book of Acts*, 573).

384   Lenski, *Acts of the Apostles*, 652.

385   Bruce, *The Book of the Acts*, 331.

386   This gate has been discovered through archaeological excavations (Mitchell, "Acts," 16.4).

[lit., physical posture—MY WORDS] for public speaking; it was not mere conversation, but more likely conversational preaching of an expository character."[387]

"And a certain woman named Lydia..." (16:14)—there is no indication that this woman is herself a Jewess; her name is a common one in Greek and Latin. Luke identifies her simply as "a worshiper of God." If she is not a Jewess, her presence among the Jewish women may indicate that she is a proselyte to the Jewish religion. We do know that she is a seller of purple fabrics, which are used by royalty and nobles as a symbol of their status. The purple (or deep blue and/or deep scarlet) dye is produced from the secretion of mollusks that live in the eastern Mediterranean Sea; only one drop of dye can be acquired "from a small vessel in the throat of each shellfish," making this dye difficult to obtain and therefore expensive (Revelation 18:12, 16).[388] Thyatira, in Asia Minor, is famous at this time for its manufacture of purple-dyed garments. Lydia has originally come from there to find a ready market in Philippi; the implication is that she is rather wealthy. But even more importantly, this woman will be credited with being the first European convert as a result of Paul's missionary journeys.

"The Lord opened her heart to respond..." (16:14)—quite simply, she hears the gospel call (see 2 Thessalonians 2:14), it convicts her heart, and she responds favorably to it.[389] Consistent with previous conversion accounts, she is thus baptized into Christ, along with her

---

387   Boles, *A Commentary on Acts*, 256.

388   Lenski, *Acts of the Apostles*, 657. He goes on to say: "Purple cloth of all kinds would be in high demand in this colony with its many Romans. It formed the trimming of the white Roman toga as well as of the tunic; the rich wore purple (Luke 16:19); prominent ladies loved the royal color; rugs and tapestries contained much rich purple; and besides it was used by court officials for state robes and by emperors and their courts" (ibid.).

389   Calvinists insist that this is "proof" of Calvinism, that is, that unless God opens a person's heart, he (or she) will not be able to respond to His gospel. This does not "prove" Calvinism or any other "ism" of men; it simply means that Lydia was convicted by the things she heard—facts and evidence that God provided (as in Matthew 16:17)—and she, being a woman of sincerity and integrity, could not help but respond in the way that she did. Any Calvinistic belief that God chooses who will be saved (and, by necessity, who will be lost) is completely absent from this passage, just as it is from the rest of the NT.

household, in obedience to this message.[390] As an act of gracious
hospitality, she insists that Paul and his companions stay at her house
for a time (16:15). "And she prevailed upon us" indicates that the
missionaries' first answer is "no thank you," not wanting to impose
upon her, and possibly because she is (apparently) a single woman—
either never married or (more likely) a widow. Regardless, she is able to
persuade them to take her up on her offer. Her lodging may provide the
best food and most comfortable accommodations that these men have
enjoyed so far on their long and difficult journey.

Paul and Silas' arrest in Philippi (16:16-24)

On one particular walk to the place of prayer by the river, Paul
encounters "a certain slave-girl having a spirit of divination" who
cries out after him, "These men are bond-servants of the Most High
God, who are proclaiming to you the way of salvation" (16:16-17).[391]
"Spirit of divination" [Greek: *pneuma puthona*] literally refers to the
name of the region (Putho) where Delphi, the sanctuary of the famous
oracle, is located (in central Greece). Thus, those who practice fortune-
telling or soothsaying are called Pythons. (In Greek mythology, Python

---

390   We must not impose our *present* understanding of "household" upon this
ancient context. In the ancient world, "household" was hardly limited to one's spouse
and children; it necessarily included servants and other dependents of the head of the
household (Bruce, *The Book of the Acts*, 331). "There is nothing here to show whether
Lydia's 'household' went beyond 'the women' employed by her who like her had
heard the preaching of Paul and had believed. ...In the household baptisms (Cornelius,
Lydia, the jailer, Crispus) one sees 'infants' or not according to his predilections or
preferences" (Robertson, *Word Pictures*, 253). Yet, it is neither logical nor conclusive
that Lydia's *children*—if indeed she even had any—were baptized, as those who
promote infant (or child) baptism contend. The precedent in Acts so far has been
"men and women" (Acts 2:18, 5:14, 8:3, 8:12, and 9:2); there has been no mention
of children being baptized, or of any church action involving children (in the form
of teaching, benevolence, or otherwise). The burden of proof lies upon those who
dogmatically insist that "household" *must* include infants and children, and that it
cannot be otherwise, in the absence of any direct or positive teaching on this subject.
Not only this, but without any mention of a husband, one is unable to determine
conclusively whether or not Lydia even *had* children. Thus, this account presents an
even weaker argument for advocates of child baptism than before.

391   "In tracing the life of St. Paul we have not as yet seen Christianity directly
brought into conflict with Heathenism. ...But as we travel farther from the East, and
especially through countries where the Israelites were thinly scattered, we must expect
to find Pagan creeds in immediate antagonism with the Gospel; and not merely Pagan
creeds, but the evil powers themselves which give Paganism its supremacy over the
minds of men" (Conybeare and Howson, *Life and Epistles*, 229).

was a monster-dragon that lived in a cave on Mt. Parnassus, north of Delphi.) Delphi is where people go to hear their fortunes told, by way of elaborate rituals involving smoke and hallucinogenic fumes. There, the priestess ("Pythia") inhales fumes of burning incense, and then allegedly speaks in "tongues." A poet or priest standing nearby interprets the gibberish, and thus delivers the "prophecy"—for a handsome fee. This slave-girl who confronts Paul likely practices something similar to this, although the source of her power is clearly demonic, not drug-induced. F. F. Bruce rightly contrasts Lydia's heart that was opened to the Lord and this girl's heart which is imprisoned by a demonic spirit.[392] Stott says:

> You could not sink much lower in public estimation than to be a female slave. She owned nothing, not even herself. She had no possessions, rights, liberty or life of her own. Even the money she earned by fortune-telling went straight into her masters' pockets. ... She had lost her identity, her individuality, as a human being. If socially she belonged as a slave to her masters, psychologically she belonged to the spirit which controlled her. She was in double bondage.[393]

Despite the demonic entity that possesses her, what this slave-girl *says* is true. (Demons, we have seen in the gospel accounts, are not always wrong in what they *say*, but they are always wrong in what they *do* and in what they *are*.) Nonetheless, the source of this information is hardly the kind of advertising appropriate for a minister of God.[394] Paul is

---

392 Bruce, *The Book of the Acts*, 332-333.

393 Stott, *The Spirit, the Church, and the World*, 270.

394 "The idea was universally entertained that ventriloquism [i.e., the demon speaking through the slave-girl] was due to superhuman influence, and implied the power of foretelling the future. The girl herself believed this; and in her belief lay her power. Her words need not be taken as a witness to Christianity. 'God the Highest' was a wide-spread pagan expression, and 'salvation' was the object of many vows and prayers to that and other gods" (Ramsay, *St. Paul the Traveller*, 215; bracketed words are mine). Even so, in the present case, the girl (being most certainly under demonic influence) does speak the truth, regardless of whether or not one listening to her distinguishes between God's power and paganism. On the other hand, Paul's response to her may be largely because he wanted to end all speculation: *she* exercises the will of a demon, whereas *Paul* exercises the supreme power of the God of heaven.

"greatly annoyed" [ASV, "sore troubled"] at this spectacle (16:18). He tolerates this girl as long as he can ("for many days") but reaches a point where he can endure her no longer. It is wrong to conclude that he deals with this girl simply because she is an annoyance; rather, she is interfering with his preaching of the gospel of Christ. How Paul deals with this demon is nearly identical with how Jesus exorcised demons (see Luke 4:33-36, for example), the exception being that Jesus commanded demons with His *own* authority and no one else's, whereas Paul defers to Jesus' authority and not his own. "And it came out at that very moment"—Luke does not treat this as a "so-called" demon possession, but an actual one. The power and authority of Jesus Christ is always supreme to that of any demon, and it cannot do anything but obey Him.

Of course, once the demon leaves, so does the girl's ability to make her masters money, and these men are understandably very upset over this (16:19). (Luke's deliberate wording directly connects the two situations: as the demon has gone out from the girl, so the men's "hope of profit" has gone out from her as well.) Thus, they "seize" or physically grab Paul and Silas and haul them before the legal authorities, charging them with violating imperial edicts (16:20-21). Roman law forbids the introduction of any new religion (or, a *religio illicita*, an "illegal religion") or strange gods, except what is assimilated from nations conquered by Rome and added to the Empire.[395] The men add a personal insult as well; in essence, "*We*, being Romans, do not have to tolerate *these men*, who are only Jews." "As part of the Roman minority of the city, the owners had legal advantages over the native populace. The girl was business property that had been 'damaged' by these intrusive Jews, and the owners wanted retribution meted out."[396] Thus, the charges are political and economical in nature, not religious.

---

395   "Cicero wrote, 'No person shall have any separate gods, or new ones; nor shall he privately worship any strange gods, unless they be publicly allowed.' Virgil has, 'Care was taken among the Athenians and the Romans that no one should introduce new religions.' The Christian religion was permitted in the empire since it was thought of, in the first years, as being just another sect of Judaism" (Reese, *Book of Acts*, 584).

396   Mitchell, "Acts," 16.8. Rapske adds: "The contrasting phrasing 'being Jews' and 'who are Romans' emphasizes the accusers' assumed legal and social superiority on comparison with the accused" ("Paul in Roman Custody," 120).

"No Roman magistrate would deal with abstract theological questions [cf. 18:15]: religion only became a subject for the magistrate when it (1) might tend to create a breach of the peace..., (2) or tend to the encouragement of illegal acts, especially to the formation of secret sects, organizations, &c."[397]

There is no formal trial, no inquest, and no due process; this is nothing short of "mob justice."[398] (However, in ancient times, public participation in such matters is not only typical, but expected.[399]) Thus, Paul and Silas are stripped to the skin and beaten with rods (16:22-23).[400] "The lictors [policemen] were the official attendants upon the chief magistrates in Rome and other Roman cities. They carried as symbols of office bundles of rods, with an ax inserted among them under certain circumstances—the *fasces et secures*—denoting the magistrates' right to inflict corporal and capital punishment."[401] The missionaries are then placed in stocks, which forces their legs apart in extreme discomfort, and also forces them to lie on their backs (which have just been severely beaten and are bruised and lacerated). Roman jails are nothing like our relatively clean and comfortable American prisons. The "inner prison" (16:24) denotes a place that holds several men at once, usually chained together; it is often below ground, pitch black, reeks of stale air and the stench of human excrement, and is either stiflingly hot or bitterly cold, depending on the season.[402] "For

---

397   Page, *The Acts of the Apostles*, 186; bracketed words are mine.

398   Coffman, *Commentary on Acts*, 317.

399   Mitchell, "Acts," 16.9.

400   "The treatment is consistent with the juridical and social assessment of the apostles...; i.e., that Paul and Silas were low-status individuals safely presumed by accusations alone to be guilty of criminal behaviour" (Rapske, "Paul in Roman Custody," 125).

401   Bruce, *The Book of the Acts*, 336; bracketed word is mine. "Lictors" literally means "rod-bearers" (ibid., 340, fn. 60). Consider Paul's own words on this subject in Romans 13:1-4.

402   "'The inner prison' was the third compartment of the prison. In a Roman prison there were usually three distinct parts: (1) the communiora, or where the prisoners had light and fresh air; (2) the interiora, shut off by strong iron gates with bars and locks; (3) the tullianum, or dungeon, the place of execution or for one condemned to die. Not only were they put in the inner prison, but their feet were placed 'in the stocks.' Usually the 'stocks' were fixed so that the arms and legs, and even necks of the

a Jew, the prison—and particularly the Gentile prison—was a place of profound uncleanness. …Further contributing to the distress and unhealthy conditions [of prison] was the prison officials' lack of interest in even a modicum of prisoner hygiene."[403]

The Philippian jailer's conversion (16:25-34)

Paul and Silas are then given over to the charge of a certain unnamed jailer. This man's only concern is that prisoners put in his charge do not escape. His initial treatment of the missionaries indicates no compassion or concern for them, since it is he who puts them in a most uncomfortable and painful situation. Philo, for example, has nothing good to say about jailers of this time:

> And as those who associate with good men are improved in their disposition by such association…, so also do they who are living with the wicked take the impression of their wicked ways; for habit is a very powerful thing to put a force upon nature, and to make it resemble itself: now keepers of prisons live among thieves and robbers, and housebreakers, and men of insolence and violence, and murderers, and adulterers, and plunderers of temples, from every one of whom they contract some wickedness, and collect a sort of contribution: and from their manifold mixture, make up one thoroughly confused and wholly polluted iniquity.[404]

Despite all this pain and humiliation, Paul and Silas pray and *sing hymns of praise to God* in the hearing of the other prisoners (16:25).[405]

---

prisoners were confined; but here only the feet were placed in the stocks. 'Stocks' was an instrument of torture as well as confinement, consisting of heavy pieces of wood with holes, into which the feet were placed in such a manner that they were stretched widely apart so as to cause the sufferer greater pain" (Boles, *A Commentary on Acts*, 261-262).

403   Rapske, "Paul in Roman Custody," 214, 216; bracketed words are mine.

404   Philo, "De Iosepho," *The Works of Philo*, trans. C. D. Yonge (Peabody, MS: Hendrickson Publishers, 1993), 83-84. Philo (ca. 20 BC – AD 50) was a Jewish expositor of the Law of Moses and an essayist on Jewish life, religion, and philosophy.

405   "It was midnight, not merely in that jail, but throughout the great pagan empire also, a midnight of morals, humanity, and justice, as well as that of night; but within the inner dungeon there were songs of praise to the true God and suffering saints who

Suddenly, God responds to their prayers and songs with "a great earthquake" that opens of all the jail doors and releases all the inmates' chains. This is not a mere tremor, but a violent shaking—strong enough to compromise the integrity of the posts and hinges of the prison doors (16:26). Being roused from his sleep, the jailer sees the open doors and supposes that the prisoners have all escaped.[406] Since he will most certainly be executed for this, he sees no recourse but to take his own life (16:27). Suicide, in these times, does not have the disturbing, criminal stigma that it has for us today; it is an acceptable if not honorable course of action—in many cases, it is a personal *responsibility* rather than a crime. "Stoicism had made suicide popular as the escape from trouble like the Japanese *hari-kari*."[407]

Thankfully, Paul stops the jailer from doing any harm to himself (16:28-30). As much pain as this jailer has caused the missionaries (by putting them in the stocks), and as simple and unrefined as this man likely is, Paul still shows love for his soul and does not want him to be forever lost. This reveals the sincere nature of Paul's preaching (see 1 Corinthians 9:22). Trembling for perhaps several reasons—the earthquake, his brush with death, and his respect for these men of God—the jailer asks, "Sirs, what must I do to be saved?" Paul answers, "Believe in the Lord Jesus...."[408] It is difficult to ascertain exactly what the jailer means by being "saved"; it is unlikely that it means what we think, that is, saved from the wrath of God (Romans 5:9). It is possible that he had heard the words of the demon-possessed slave-girl; it is also

---

offered themselves to the Father in prayer" (Coffman, *Commentary on Acts*, 318).

406   "Why did not the prisoners run away when their fetters were loosed? ...An earthquake strikes panic into the semi-oriental mob in the Aegean lands; and it seems to me quite natural that the prisoners made no dash for safety when the opportunity was afforded them. Moreover, they were still only partially free; and they had only a moment for action. The jailor was also roused by the earthquake, and came to the outer door; he was perhaps a soldier, or at least had something of Roman discipline, giving him presence of mind; his call for lights brought the body of *diogmitai* or other class of police who helped to guard the prisoners; and the opportunity was lost" (Ramsay, *St. Paul the Traveller*, 221). It should be noted here that Sir Ramsay spent a great deal of time both touring and studying the land and culture of which he speaks.

407   Robertson, *Word Pictures*, 261.

408   The Greek is more effective: "*Kurios* [plural: "lords"], what must I do...?" "Believe in the *Kurioi* [singular: Lord]...."

possible that he desires salvation of a different nature than that of his *soul*.

> It is surely, however, a mistake to imagine that the jailor's inquiry had reference merely to temporal and immediate danger. The awakening of his conscience, the presence of the unseen world, the miraculous visitation, the nearness of death—coupled perhaps with some confused recollection of the '*way of salvation*' which these strangers were said to have been proclaiming—were enough to suggest that inquiry which is the most momentous that any human soul can make: '*What must I do to be saved?*'[409]

In any case, Paul immediately directs the jailer to the Lord Jesus, the Source of all salvation, and "spoke the word of the Lord to him" that very night (16:32). In response to this kindness, the man washes Paul and Silas' wounds; in response to the message itself, he himself is washed of his sins in baptism (16:34; see 22:16 and 1 Peter 3:21). Likewise, just as Paul feeds this man with spiritual food, so he feeds Paul and Silas with food from his own store.[410] This clarifies for us what it means to "believe in the Lord Jesus" for salvation. It does *not* mean (as is popularly taught today), "Just ask Jesus to come into your heart to be your personal Savior." Not a single person was ever "saved" through this method in Acts; no apostle ever taught such a method; no such method is found anywhere in the entire NT. Rather, "believe" means (in the context of salvation through Christ), "Be obedient to *whatever* is required of you to demonstrate your faith in Jesus' ability to save your soul."[411] This includes, but is not limited to, immersion

---

409   Conybeare and Howson, *Life and Epistles*, 237.

410   Under any other circumstances, "A jailor would never have fed his prisoners out of his own larder, much less at such an hour. Once during the day and only for needy prisoners was the usual pattern of distribution, and the ration would certainly have been simpler and less substantial if given at all" (Rapske, "Paul in Roman Custody," 214).

411   There is not a single standalone verse in the NT that details *every specific requirement* for calling on the name of the Lord for salvation. God, in His wisdom, forces us to investigate thoroughly this subject, not just read a verse of Scripture about it. Furthermore, not every person is at the same level of understanding with regard to the instruction; thus, a teacher of the gospel may have to start in a different place for

in water (baptism) for the purpose of the forgiveness of sins (recall 2:38). The jailer could not have known what it meant to "believe" in Christ until he was taught this; this teaching necessarily includes being baptized into Christ (just as it did when Philip taught Jesus to the Ethiopian; recall 8:35-38).[412]

Paul and Silas' release from the Philippian jail (16:35-40)

"Now when day came..." (16:35)—this is reminiscent of 5:21ff and 12:18, where men had determined a certain course of action against God's apostles, only to have His miraculous intervention *change* those circumstances. Luke does not say why the magistrates so quickly changed their minds, but there is little doubt that the earthquake may have shaken their confidence as well as the prison. It may be that they realized that their treatment of Paul and Silas was hasty and unjustified. It is necessarily implied that the two missionaries voluntarily returned to their prison cell to await whatever would happen next. At this time, the jailer tells them that the magistrates have sent word to release them (16:36). It is apparent that the jailer does not act alone in this entreaty, but that the "policemen" are with him.

It is at *this* time that Paul chooses to reveal his and Silas' Roman citizenship (16:37). This is more significant than we might realize: to chain, wrongfully beat, or imprison a Roman citizen is to dishonor the authority of the Emperor himself who *protects* such rights. Because of their carelessness, the Philippian magistrates can face criminal charges *themselves* before the Roman tribunal.[413] (Likewise, to *pretend* to have

---

one person than he will for another. "As the late J. H. Childress said, 'If one were to ask how to get a Ph.D. degree, a college graduate might be told one thing, a high school graduate another thing, and a boy in grammar school something else, with all of the various answers being strictly true" (Coffman, *Commentary on Acts*, 320).

412   Regarding the "with his whole household" phrase, see footnote and comments on 16:15 and 18:8.

413   "To subject a Roman citizen to an unlawful punishment was a serious offense, and was severely punished by law. If the prisoners pressed charges, the magistrates could be stripped of their office, and would never be allowed to hold office again. In 44 A.D., by order of the emperor Claudius, the people of Rhodes lost their own privileges of citizenship because they did not regard the fact that some prisoners they executed by crucifixion were Roman citizens who by law were exempt from such a mode of punishment. The punishment could even be more severe. Dionysius of Halicarnassus

Roman citizenship is punishable by severe torture or even execution.[414])
Paul says, in essence, "They have publicly treated us as guilty; let them
now publicly declare that we are innocent." The officials wish to keep
this matter quiet; Paul forces them to do otherwise.

Paul's claim implies legal incompetence on the part of the city officials;
thus, they are eager to make him go away and not press charges of his
own. It is for this reason that the magistrates personally plead with Paul
and Silas to leave the city (16:38-39). The men do eventually leave, but
they take their time doing so, stopping first at the home of Lydia. "The
brethren" (16:40) could refer to Lydia, her household, and Luke and
Timothy; or it could imply that a small church has been established in
Lydia's own home. It is most interesting that, while Paul and Silas were
the ones tortured, *they* are the ones comforting the brethren! "Paul's
insistence on an official apology may have served to some degree as
a protection to the members of the church which had been planted
in Philippi during the period of his stay there."[415] Since the "we"
references end here until 20:5, we logically assume that Luke stays
behind in Philippi; and possibly Timothy does as well, rejoining the
missionary party in Berea.[416]

Paul and Silas in Thessalonica (17:1-9)
Paul, Silas, and perhaps Timothy continue traveling down the Egnatian
Way, an old Roman military road. No record of evangelism is recorded
in either Amphipolis or Apollonia, possibly because of the absence of
any Jewish synagogues there (17:1). Thessalonica is separated from
Philippi by a hundred miles and two mountain ranges.

---

wrote, 'The punishment appointed for those who abrogated or transgressed the
Valerian law was death, and the confiscation of his property" (Reese, *Book of Acts*,
595).

414   Robertson, *Word Pictures*, 264.

415   Bruce, *The Book of the Acts*, 341.

416   So surmises Conybeare and Howson (*Life and Epistles*, 242). Timothy is not
mentioned at all in the Thessalonian affair, but his presence resurfaces in Berea (17:14).
Even so, this is not conclusive proof one way or the other.

Thessalonica was a prominent city of the Macedonians, boasting a population possibly as high as 200,000 people. It was allegedly named by the Macedonian king Cassander (ca. 315 BC) after Thessalonica, the half-sister of Alexander the Great. However, some maintain that it was named after Philip of Macedon himself in honor of his victory over the armies of Thessaly. (Formerly it had been known as Therme.) When Rome incorporated Macedonia as one of its official provinces in 146 BC, Thessalonica became Macedonia's capital city. In 42 BC, it was made a "free city," which means that it could maintain its own government and appointed political leaders, as long as it did not violate the laws of Rome.[417]

Thessalonica is nestled at the base of Mt. Olympus, the alleged home of the Greek pantheon. It is a large metropolis, yet because it is "free," it has no direct Roman oversight or military garrisons. "Besides being a commercial center, the city in Paul's day was the capital of Macedonia and served the entire province as an administrative center."[418] Because of its proximity to both land and sea trade routes, Thessalonica is strategically suited for the spreading of the gospel.

Paul's "custom" is always to present the gospel to the Jews first (cf. Romans 1:16); to accomplish this, he goes to where the Jews assemble—the synagogue (17:2). One of the most difficult teachings of the gospel for Jews is that the Messiah (Christ) must suffer, be killed, and be raised from the dead (see Luke 24:25-27, 45-47). In their understanding, Messiah will be a political and military leader as well as a redeemer; He will throw off the yoke of heathen government (Rome) and make Israel a sovereign and powerful nation. Under the rule of Messiah, Israel will become the center of the world, Jerusalem the world's capital, and the Jews the world's greatest people. Given such grandiose views, the idea of a Suffering Savior whose kingdom is heavenly in nature (and not an earthly one) is difficult for them to accept. Thus, Paul spends much time providing evidence—from

---

417 Sychtysz, *1 & 2 Thessalonians Study Workbook*, 2. I recommend this study workbook as a companion to the events described here in Acts 17.

418 Kistemaker, *Acts*, 612.

Scripture *and* historical events—that Jesus the *Man* was indeed Christ the *Son of God* (17:3). "Explaining" literally means "opening up (the mind)," which is necessary in order for these people to see the truth.[419] "Unless Paul's listeners are ready and willing to see that the person and work of Christ fulfill the scriptural prophecies, the Bible remains a closed book to them."[420]

Some Jews are persuaded and believe; likewise, some of the Greeks who worship God (but are not proselytes to the Jewish religion) also believe (17:4). "Prominent [or, chief] women" indicates that in Macedonia the women have a higher social standing and greater influence than in Judea. Certain unbelieving Jews, however, keep their minds closed and react out of fear and jealousy. They recruit (hire?) men from the marketplace—apparently men who will do anything for a price—to incite an uproar against the missionaries (17:5). "Mob" indicates a crowd of people, but usually one that takes on a life of its own. The fact that these unbelieving Jews are purposely willing to utilize "wicked men" to cause trouble for Paul speaks very negatively concerning their motives (despite their claim to be God's people), faith in their own beliefs (by calling upon wicked men to fight for them), and confidence in God's protection of their religion (versus taking matters into their own hands).

We do not know anything about this man "Jason," but he is introduced naturally, as though well-familiar to Theophilus, the original recipient of this account (17:5). Jason may be a believer who is boarding Paul and Silas; it is possible that a church has been established in his home.[421] In any case, Jason is literally dragged (so the Greek reads) to

---

419   *Strong's* (electronic edition), #G1272.

420   Kistemaker, *Acts*, 613.

421   "The gathering of Christian believers in private homes (or homes renovated for the purpose of Christian gatherings) continued to be the norm until the early decades of the fourth century when Constantine began erecting the first Christian Basilicas. For almost three hundred years the believers met in homes, not in synagogues or edifices constructed for the sole purpose of religious assembly. ...Furthermore, the 'house' gave the early believers an inconspicuous place for assembly. It was private. For this reason, Rome found it expedient to tolerate the Christian presence and, at the same time, the Christians had a means by which to distinguish themselves from outsiders. From the earliest accounts in Acts it is clear that the early believers differentiated between

the city authorities.[422] The alleged charge against Paul and those (like Jason) who support him is: "These men ... have upset the world"— which is *truthful* but highly misrepresented (17:6). They add another charge: "...They all act contrary to the decrees of Caesar, saying that there is another king, Jesus" (17:7). This is only partly true: the gospel does *not* teach rebellion to human government, but quite the opposite (see Romans 13:1-2, 1 Timothy 2:1-4, and 1 Peter 2:13-14). Jesus *is* a greater King than Caesar, but in a completely different context than that in which Caesar operates. This charge is quite similar to what was said during Jesus' trial before Pilate (John 19:15). However, these men are not interested in having the matter clarified; they have one intention, and that is to put an end to this teaching altogether (17:8).[423] Jason is compelled to provide a "pledge," a monetary bond that promises no further trouble (i.e., from rioting) (17:9). Unfortunately, to protect Jason and the new converts, Paul and Silas are forced to leave Thessalonica; in fact, the terms of the bond may stipulate this.

Paul and Silas in Berea (17:10-15)

Under the cover of darkness, Paul and Silas leave Thessalonica and travel to Berea [also spelled Beroea], an attractive city on the edge of the mountains, where there is abundant water, trees, and gardens (17:10). It is about 60 miles from Thessalonica, and a few miles off of the main highway. Luke calls the Jews there "more noble-minded"

---

activities which were appropriate in the private gatherings and the public spheres of daily life. The house acted as a boundary marker much like the synagogue in the Diaspora" (Bradley Blue, "Acts and the House Church," *The Book of Acts in Its First Century Setting*, vol. 2, 120-121).

422 "This word [for "authorities," *politarchas*] does not occur in Greek literature and used to be cited as an example of Luke's blunders. But now it has been discovered [in 1835] in an inscription on an arch in the modern city preserved in the British Museum. It has also been found in seventeen inscriptions (five from Thessalonica) where the word or the verb *politarche* occurs. It is a fine illustration of the historical accuracy of Luke in matters of detail" (Robertson, *Word Pictures*, 271; bracketed words are mine).

423 "The charge brought against Paul was subtly conceived and most dangerous. The very suggestion of treason against the Emperors often proved fatal to the accused; and it compelled the politarchs to take steps, for, if they failed to do so, they became exposed to a charge of treason, as having taken too little care for the honour of the Emperor. Many a man was ruined by such a charge under the earlier Emperors" (Ramsay, *St. Paul the Traveller*, 230).

because (he implies) they do not accept Paul's conclusions at face value but research these things themselves, "examining the Scriptures daily" (17:11). This process convinces many Jews to obey Jesus as the Christ, as well as "a number of prominent Greek women and men" (17:12). "It was inevitable in Jewish evangelism," Stott observes, "that the Old Testament Scriptures should be both the textbook and the court of appeal ...Paul 'argued' out of the Scriptures and the Bereans 'examined' them to see if his arguments were cogent [i.e., valid]. And we may be sure that Paul welcomed and encouraged this thoughtful response."[424]

As when Jews from Pisidian Antioch and Iconium went well out of their way to cause trouble for Paul (recall 14:19), so now Jews from Thessalonica come to Berea (17:13) just to stir up the people against him "like hunters upon their prey."[425] Paul, being the lightning rod of all such antagonism, is immediately escorted by some of the newly-converted brethren to Athens (Greece), while Silas and Timothy remain behind to further strengthen the new church. Yet, once Paul is in Athens, he sends for Silas and Timothy to join him (17:14-15).

Paul in Athens (17:16-34)

Athens is one of the most renowned cities of the Roman Empire, touted as the intellectual capital of the known world (17:16). Founded 1,500 years before Paul's visit (originally as an Egyptian colony), Athens has a famous university to which students from all over the Empire come to learn of Hellenistic (Greek) literature, philosophy, rhetoric, art, and mathematics. Many famous warriors, statesmen, poets, and philosophers come from or have studied here. Athens also boasts some of the most advanced architecture of its day. It is also a city literally filled with idols, shrines, altars, and memorials (to idols)—a city engulfed in idolatry. Petronius, a contemporary Roman satirist, wrote: "It is easier to find a god than a man there."[426] Coffman writes: "It is the arrogant and sophisticated intellectual center of the whole empire;

---

424   Stott, *The Spirit, the Church, and the World*, 275; bracketed word is mine.

425   Conybeare and Howson, *Life and Epistles*, 263.

426   JFB *Commentary*, on 17:16.

and the significant thing in this chapter [Acts 17] is that Christianity was preached in the very eye of Greek culture, a culture which through absorption by Rome was destined to change the character of the whole empire."[427]

The "market place" [Greek: *agora*] is one of Athens's most famous locations (17:17). Men from all over the world congregate here to share ideas, philosophies, theories, and fables. The pervasion of idols and shrines in this city agitates Paul's spirit and compels him to be especially vocal of the gospel, both within and outside of the synagogues there. In fact, it is one of the few times we see him engaging with the general public: he goes to the market place and reasons with whoever will listen to him.[428] (This is the same market place in which Socrates taught several centuries earlier.) However, "Paul was not concerned with removing the idolatrous art from the city, but with removing the worship of idols from men's hearts."[429]

"Epicurean and Stoic philosophers" (17:18) refers to two of the most celebrated philosophies of ancient Greece. Both philosophies came about as a result of (or reaction to) the changing conditions of the Grecian world.

> The conditions for the rise of Epicureanism and Stoicism were political and social rather than intellectual. Speculative thought had reached its zenith in the great constructive ideals of Plato, and the encyclopaedic [*sic*] system of Aristotle. Criticism of these would necessarily drive men back upon themselves to

---

427   Coffman, *Commentary on Acts*, 346; bracketed citation is mine.

428   "The mere Jew could never have assumed the Attic [Athenian] tone as Paul did. He was in Athens the student of a great university [Tarsus], visiting an older but yet a kindred university [Athens], surveying it with appreciative admiration, and mixing in its society as an equal conversing with men of like education. This extraordinary versatility in Paul's character, the unequalled freedom and ease with which he moved in every society, and addressed so many races within the Roman world, were evidently appreciated by the man who wrote this narrative, for the rest of Chapter XVII is as different in tone from XIII as Athens is different from Phrygia. Only a writer who was in perfect sympathy with his subject could adapt his tone to it so perfectly as Luke does" (Ramsay, *St. Paul the Traveller*, 238; bracketed words are mine).

429   Coffman, *Commentary on Acts*, 336.

probe deeper into the meaning of experience, as [Immanuel] Kant did in later times [18th century]. But the conditions were not propitious to pure speculation. The breaking up of the Greek city-states and the loss of Greek independence had filled men's minds with a sense of insecurity. The institutions, laws and customs of society, which had hitherto sheltered the individual, now gave way; and men demanded from philosophy a haven of rest for their homeless and weary souls. Philosophy, therefore, became a theory of conduct and an art of living.[430]

Epicurus (342 – 270 BC) taught that suffering and pain can be avoided by seeking excessive sensuous pleasure. Death is not to be feared since the soul dies with the body, and there is no eternal judgment, no hell, and no god with any interest in this world. "The Epicurean deity, if self-existent at all, dwelt apart [from the world], in serene indifference to all the affairs of the universe. The universe was a great accident, and sufficiently explained itself without any reference to a higher power. ... As there was no creator, so there was no moral governor."[431] Epicurus defined philosophy as "a daily business of speech and thought to secure a happy life," and his particular brand of philosophy has been described as "egoistic hedonism."[432]

Stoicism (derived from *stoa* ["porch"], where students once assembled to hear this doctrine) was the concept of Zeno of Cyprus (ca. 336 – 264 BC). He taught that "God" (or "Fate") indwells the material universe, and is also the "eternal reason" of and for this universe.[433] There really is no personal freedom in life, since all of life is determined by a world governed by necessity—in essence, by the eternal Fate/God. Life's highest gratifications are self-denial and self-sufficiency; passions and affections are to be ignored and restrained; emotions—even intense pleasure or pain—are to be subdued and neutralized. "The Stoic philosophers taught that virtue was its own reward, and vice its own

---

430 T. Rees, "Epicureans," *ISBE* (electronic edition); bracketed words are mine.

431 Conybeare and Howson, *Life and Epistles*, 285; bracketed words are mine.

432 Rees, "Epicureans," *ISBE* (electronic edition).

433 Dirk Baltzly, "Stoicism," *Stanford Encyclopedia of Philosophy* (http://plato. stanford.edu/entries/stoicism), cited October, 2015.

punishment; that pleasure was no good, and pain no evil."[434] Man's highest quest is to attend to his *duty*; this makes the Stoics proud and self-sufficient people. However, when this duty is done, or when it cannot be done any longer, then there is nothing left to live for. "…[R]eason was the guide and decided what was good and what was evil. He who followed reason was perfect and sufficient in himself. When reason saw no more in life, it dictated suicide as the most reasonable thing."[435] Thus, suicide is a final expression of the Stoic belief system. Self-inflicted death is simply a practical means to remove oneself from an otherwise hopeless situation.

Paul is derogatorily regarded as an "idle babbler" [Greek, *spermologos*, lit., "seed picker"] that picks up bits and pieces of philosophy from here and there (17:18). To them, his gospel is simply a blend (or plagiarism) of various beliefs and teachings that have been repackaged and renamed—"a ragbag of other people's ideas and sayings."[436] Ramsay's lengthy quote is worthwhile here:

> This term was used in two senses—(1) a small bird that picks up seeds for its food, and (2) a worthless Fellow of low class and vulgar habits, with the insinuation that he lives at the expense of others, like those disreputable persons who hang round the markets and the quays [enclosed docks alongside the water] in order to pick up anything that falls from the loads that are carried about. Hence, as a term in social slang, it connotes absolute vulgarity and inability to rise above the most contemptible standard of life and conduct; it is often connected with slave life, for the *Spermologos* was near the type of the slave and below the level of a free man; and there clings to it the suggestion of picking up refuse and scraps, and in literature of plagiarism without the capacity to use it correctly. In ancient literature plagiarism was not disapproved when it was done with skill, and when the idea or words taken from another

---

434   Boles, *A Commentary on Acts*, 277.

435   Lenski, *Acts of the Apostles*, 713.

436   Stott, *The Spirit, the Church, and the World*, 282.

were used with success; the literary offence [*sic*] lay in the ignorance and incapacity displayed when stolen knowledge was improperly applied.[437]

"Strange deities [or, gods]" is from *xenos diamonian*, lit., "foreign demons." This is "strange" to them because it refers to a literal resurrection that has already occurred—allegedly, the stuff of fables and folklore, not of credible truth. "Demons" to ancient Greeks usually refer to god-like entities that intercede for humans (see 1 Corinthians 10:20); thus, it does not actually refer to satanic demons as we use the word today, although some Greek demons are indeed evil.[438] It seems that these men are trying to reconcile Paul's seeming patchwork gospel with their own polytheistic understanding of the world. The Athenians might be thinking, too, that Paul spoke of *two* deities, Jesus and Anastasia ["resurrection" is translated from the Greek word *anastasis*], since Anastasia is the name of one of their own gods.[439]

The Aeropagus [lit., "Mars Hill"] (17:19) is perhaps one of the most celebrated tribunals in the Roman Empire.[440] ("Mars" is the Roman god of war that is based upon Ares, the Greek god of war.) The Athenians often gather at this place to hear and judge the many ideas and philosophies that trickle into their city from all over the world. The purpose of this is not to choose one or reject the other, but simply to

---

437   Ramsay, *St. Paul the Traveller*, 242-243; bracketed words are mine. Despite the slang term employed here, we cannot overlook the fact that the Athenians do allow Paul an opportunity to speak on Mars Hill, something that they would not do for one who was of a low class of society. Thus, while they may well question Paul's philosophy (as they see it), they respect his credentials as a learned man. On the other hand, the manner in which he is so invited—they "took him" or laid hands on him—might suggest that some of these men hold him in contempt, and wish to put his beliefs on a kind of public inquisition in order to discredit him through his own words. In any case, it does not appear at all that Paul is being put on trial, but he is being called upon to defend before the authorities what he has been saying to the general public.

438   Ironically, what Catholics refer to as "patron saints" the ancient Greeks would call "demons."

439   Bruce, *The Book of the Acts*, 351.

440   The Greek here is not clear as to whether the actual *hill* is meant, or the place where the court *of* the Aeropagus met; the fact that he "stood in the midst of the Aeropagus" (17:22) indicates the latter, although the traditional view holds to the former (see Robertson, *Word Pictures*, 283; Kistemaker, *Acts*, 628; et al).

be entertained by participating in the public debate (as Luke implies; 17:20-21). The bantering rhetoric is not to make converts, or even to be taken too seriously; since everything is questioned, therefore nothing is absolute. The Greeks of this day have a saying: "What's newer?" Demosthenes, 400 years prior, had rebuked his fellow Athenians for idling away in the Forum, listening to the latest news of Philip of Macedon, when they should have been preparing for war against him instead. In other words, this has been a pastime of theirs for centuries. There is one serious aspect to the Athenians' inquiry of Paul, however: it is their duty (as they saw it) to determine whether or not his teaching constitutes a threat to their state.[441]

Paul's speech, known familiarly to us as "the sermon on Mars Hill," reveals a masterful handling of this difficult and awkward situation (17:22-31). With remarkable tact and simple logic, he refutes the conclusions of the Athenians concerning their gods while simultaneously appealing to their intellect. In his argument, he demonstrates that the premise of a single, all-powerful, and universal God is both rational and superior to their empty mythologies and philosophies. Once this premise is accepted, the resurrection and judgment of Christ become natural and necessary conclusions. The major points of Paul's "sermon" are as follows:

❑ **17:22-23** Paul begins by finding *something* with which he can commend the Athenians with regard to their spiritual perspectives: "you are very religious in all respects." "Religious" in the Greek means literally "superstitious" or "demon-fearing," not necessarily pious or sincere.[442] In essence, he says: "At least you pay prolific homage to demons (intercessory gods), which is evident through your many shrines and idols." The Greeks, being highly superstitious, are careful not to offend even gods they do not know; thus, they have erected an idol inscribed with, "TO AN UNKNOWN GOD." Yet, not only are they ignorant of this God— the One who is greater than all others—but even their *worship* of

---

441   Kistemaker, *Acts*, 629; Bruce, *The Book of the Acts*, 352.

442   From *deisidaimonia*, "having a fear of (or, reverence for) the gods" (*Strong's* [electronic edition], #G1175).

Him is in ignorance. In effect, Paul rebukes their low estimation of him [Paul] and his gospel. In essence, he says, "You call me a preacher of 'strange deities,' but there's nothing stranger than worshiping an unknown god!"

❏ **17:24-26** Paul explains that this all-powerful God does not depend upon humans for His existence *or* His power. (This is in sharp contrast with the Greek gods, which do not even exist except for the constant attention and worship of humans.) Not only this, but the God of heaven gives life to men and dictates the course and boundaries of human existence. He is not dependent upon Greek gods, the Fates,[443] a Fate/God, or anything else (see 1 Kings 8:12-13, 27). God does not need anything from *men*, but men most certainly depend entirely upon *Him* for their very existence. And, because He is the Creator and Sustainer of *all* men, therefore no race of men is superior to another, with respect to our common relation to Him.[444]

❏ **17:27-28** The expected *response* of men is to "seek God," because this is the highest pursuit of one's life *and* because God will make Himself known to those who do this (Hebrews 11:6). God has determined the "appointed times" and "boundaries" for man because He has the right (as the Creator) to impose such limitations upon His creation (17:26). Yet, He expects men to "find Him" because He has made man "in His image" (Genesis 1:27) and it is only fitting that the created being should desire the fellowship of his Creator. At the same time, God allows each person the free will to make his own decision concerning this. Paul states God's true intention, regardless of how people respond to it. This is also an implied response to the Epicurean and Stoic beliefs as to what is the "greatest good": it is not to seek unbridled pleasure *or* bleak

---

443   The "Fates" (or *Moirai*, "the apportioners") were the white-robed personifications of destiny. They allegedly controlled the thread of the lives of every person, and therefore determined the course of human history. The three personages are thus named Clotho ("the spinner" who wove the thread), Lachesis ("the allotter" who determined the thread's length before it was cut), and Atrophos ("unturnable," the cutter of the thread) (http://www.theoi.com/Daimon/Moirai.html).

444   "The oneness and brotherhood of the whole human race are affirmed here... Paul thus challenged the snobbishness of every major division of ancient civilization. The Jews classified all men as Jews and Gentiles; the Romans classified them as citizens and non-citizens; and the Greeks viewed the whole world as either Greeks or barbarians" (Coffman, *Commentary on Acts*, 341).

asceticism, but to seek *God*. Indeed, every living person exists because of the life God has imparted to him (Romans 1:20). Paul quotes from Aratas, a Stoic philosopher of Cilicia (315 – 240 BC) and Cleanthes (300 – 220 BC), another Stoic, who wrote: "They fashioned a tomb for thee, O holy and high one—the Cretans, always liars, evil beasts, idle bellies! But thou art not dead; thou livest and abidest forever; for in thee we live and move and have our being."[445] (Paul also quotes from this in Titus 1:12.) Such quotes prove that Paul is well-read and well-educated in secular philosophy as well as the Hebrew Bible.

❑ **17:29** Each man naturally takes on the look of his parents, but all human beings reflect their Creator in the fact that they are *alive* and *intelligent*. Man-made idols do not impart anything to men, since *they* are created by *men* and not the other way around. Thus, man's Creator—a Life-giving and self-sufficient God—cannot be merely a glorified human (as the Greeks often depicted their gods). Human nature has already exceeded the nature of stone idols or mythological gods, but seeking the Unknown God brings men to a far superior nature than they could have achieved otherwise—"the Divine Nature" [Greek, *Theios*]. While it is impossible for men to make an image of this God, they themselves are made "in His own image" (Genesis 1:27).[446]

❑ **17:30-31** Finally, since God does exist and since He has authority over all things (by virtue of His having *created* all things), all men

---

445 Quoted in Reese, *Book of Acts*, 632.

446 Stott's lengthy quote is worth reading: "All idolatry, whether ancient or modern, primitive or sophisticated, is inexcusable, whether the images are metal or mental, material objects of worship or unworthy concepts in the mind. For idolatry is the attempt either to localize God, confining him within limits which we impose, whereas he is the Creator of the universe; or to domesticate God, making him dependent upon us, taming and taping him, whereas he is the Sustainer of human life; or to alienate God, blaming him for his distance and his silence, whereas he is the Ruler of nations, and not far from any of us; or to dethrone God, demoting him to some image of our own contrivance or craft, whereas he is our Father from whom we derive our being. In brief, all idolatry tries to minimize the gulf between the Creator and his creatures, in order to bring him under our control. More than that, it actually reverses the respective positions of God and us, so that, instead of our humbly acknowledging that God has created and rules us, we presume to imagine that we can create and rule God. There is no logic in idolatry; it is a perverse, topsy-turvy expression of our human rebellion against God" (*The Spirit, the Church, and the World*, 287).

will be held accountable to Him for their actions in this life. In ages past ("times of ignorance"), God's revelation to men was limited and general; thus, He "overlooked" [KJV, "winked at"] many of man's indiscretions. This cannot mean that God pretended that men did not sin, for He does not pretend anything, and every sin is an offense against His holy nature that requires divine justice. However, it does mean that God was merciful toward their spiritual ignorance and (thus) did not hold men to the degree of responsibility as He does today.[447] "Things have changed now since Christ has come with a full knowledge of God and has revealed God's will to man."[448] The proper *response* to this gospel requires repentance of all behavior that is sinful to Him and (by implication) honoring Him in a manner worthy of His divine nature (Romans 2:4, 2 Peter 3:9). The fact of this future accountability (or, divine judgment; see Hebrews 9:27) is substantiated by the factual resurrection of His Son from the dead ("a Man whom He [God] has appointed")—a miracle that proves His sovereign authority over all things physical and spiritual. In fact, no greater "proof" could be offered to validate this message.

The Greeks listen to Paul with interest until his mention of the resurrection of the dead.[449] At this point, however, some "sneer" while others claim to want to hear more (17:32). "The Epicureans did not believe in immortality in any form, while the Stoics accepted the concept of the soul enduring beyond the grave, but never in a bodily existence. In Greek philosophical reasoning there was simply no room for a resurrected body."[450] In any case, they do not charge Paul

---

447 In Luke 12:47-48, Jesus declared (through an illustration) that those with greater knowledge of God's will be held to a higher standard of responsibility and accountability. Few people today can claim ignorance of God's Word since the Bible and its influence are practically universal. This does not mean that we will be judged more harshly than those in the ancient world who had little access to information about God, but that we will *all* be judged proportional to what we do know.

448 Boles, *A Commentary on Acts*, 283.

449 To Athena, the patron goddess of the city of Athens, is attributed these words: "Once a man dies and the earth drinks up his blood, there is *no resurrection*" (Aeschylus, *Eumenides*, quoted in Bruce, *The Book of the Acts*, 363-364).

450 Gaertner, *Acts*, 280.

with any crime (17:33). But some *do* listen and take to heart what he has said, being convinced of the gospel. One of these is Dionysius, a judge of high rank (which is what is meant by "Aeropagite"—17:34); another is "a woman named Damaris," of whom we know nothing else; "and others with them" indicates a proportionately small number of believers. Sadly, for all of the intellectual learning that is the pride of Athens, very few people are actually interested in heavenly truth. Put another way: these people appear to love the *concept* of truth (as a sophistic interest) rather than the factual and practical truth as revealed by God.

As a side note, it is interesting to examine Paul's speech to the Athenians—or, at least as much of it as has been preserved—compared to what he will preach to, say, the Corinthians. To the Corinthians, Paul wrote, "I determined to know nothing among you except Jesus Christ, and Him crucified" (1 Corinthians 2:2). Yet, to the Athenians, Paul said very little about Jesus and nothing about His crucifixion. This reveals that it is permissible—even necessary—to exercise discretion and selectivity in choosing what to say about the gospel under limited circumstances. Paul has a very small window of opportunity to speak with the Athenians; he knows where they are coming from (idolatry and philosophy); he knows which hot buttons need to be pushed, so to speak; he knows that Christ's *crucifixion* to this well-learned and (relatively-speaking) intellectual group will be "foolishness" to them (see 1 Corinthians 1:22-23). He knows what they need to hear: God is not an idol; Greek philosophy cannot fulfill man's longing for fellowship with his Creator; there *is* an afterlife, and a judgment of the soul; etc. His stay in Corinth, however, will be longer (about eighteen months), giving him plenty of time to expound upon *all* aspects of the gospel message (as he will in Ephesus, where he remains for about three years; see Acts 20:27). A different society than the Athenians, the Corinthians are immersed in fornication, sexual deviancy (effeminacy and homosexuality), and petty "strivings" for power, self-promotion, and the approval of men. Thus, they will need to hear that, as Christ died on the cross, so they need to die to the world's "fleshly" pleasures.

(No single situation was exclusive to either city; we are simply comparing some of the dominant *emphases* from one city to the next.)

Regardless, it remains true that if the Athenians will not hear about the resurrection of the Son of God, they also will not care if He had been unjustly crucified. Their problem ultimately is that they trust in human wisdom to "save" them, but refuse to recognize the true nature of their problem: their sin against the Creator. He is as yet "unknown" to them *not* because they have no information about Him, but because they are unwilling to *hear* that information. So it is with an untold number of people today.

Paul in Corinth (18:1-17)

Corinth is one of the great trade cities of the ancient world, strategically located on the isthmus between the Ionian and Aegean Seas. It is also the capital of Achaia (Greece). Its glory days, however, are already behind it by the time Paul appears (18:1; ca. AD 50-51). The Peloponnesian War in Greece (5th century BC) contributed to its decline, and three centuries later it was involuntarily put under Roman jurisdiction. Julius Caesar rebuilt the city in 44 BC and "Romanized" it two years later, allowing many Roman freedmen (ex-slaves of various sorts) to move there. Because of this, its official language was made Latin, despite the prominence of Greek-speaking citizens. Despite its decline from earlier golden years, Corinth is one of the wealthiest and most populated cities of ancient Greece. It is also one of the most immoral and materialistic cities of the Empire; thus, to refer to something as "Corinthian" is to speak of it derisively. Pagan idolatry is heavily promoted, especially that of Venus (Aphrodite), but also Apollo and Asclepius.[451]

In AD 49 or 50, Emperor Claudius had ordered all Jews to leave Rome, since they were thought to be the source of much rioting in that city (18:2-3).[452] Many of these Jews sought work in the economical centers

---

451   Bruce, *The Book of the Acts*, 347; Gaertner, *Acts*, 283-284; et al.

452   Kistemaker, *Acts*, 649. "This action by Claudius Caesar (AD 41-54) is described by Suetonius, the Roman historian who wrote biographies on the twelve caesars

of the Empire; among these were Aquila and his wife, Priscilla. Aquila is a "native of Pontus," a Roman province north of Bithynia. "Tent-makers" can mean more generally "leather workers." It is common practice for scribes and rabbis to learn a trade by which to support themselves when necessary.[453] Paul stays with this couple and works alongside them for a time, at least until his fellow travelers arrive from Macedonia.

As Paul enters into Corinth, he begins his missionary work by speaking in the Jewish synagogues before moving on to the Gentiles (18:4). Upon the arrival of Silas and Timothy, Paul devotes himself full time to the work of preaching the gospel. It is possible that these men bring financial support from the Macedonian churches, which relieves Paul from the burden of tent-making. It is certain that they bring a great amount of personal encouragement, so that Paul can throw himself fully into the work of an evangelist. The core of Paul's preaching to the Jews is to testify (as in 17:3): "...that Jesus [the Man] was the Christ [the Son of God]" (18:5, bracketed words added). But for the most part, the Jews reject Paul's preaching; Luke rightly equates such rejection to "blasphemy" against God (as in 13:45). For this reason, Paul levels a curse upon them ("Your blood be upon your own heads!"—18:6). "I am clean" means "I am innocent of any

---

beginning with Julius Caesar. His *Life of Claudius* speaks of riots in Rome that were instigated by 'Chrestus.' Most scholars take this name as a misspelled reference to Christ, indicating that Jewish and Christian tensions in Rome produced the action by Claudius. Orosius, a church historian, later fixed the date for this edict between AD 49 and 50. These calculations are very valuable in determining the date of Paul's visit to Corinth" (Gaertner, *Acts*, 284).

453   Bruce, *The Book of the Acts*, 367. Turner adds: "According to Jewish custom, Saul [Paul] would learn an occupational trade before entering his religious profession. All Jews, even wealthy and academically learned men, were taught a trade. The Jewish law, after the exile, held that a father who taught not his son a trade, taught him to be a thief. The trade Saul developed was tent making. Tents constructed in this time period were made from the hair of goats. Tentmakers were common among Jews who lived in Tarsus. Saul would learn this trade then progress at the age of thirteen to Jewish schools of sacred learning in the city of Jerusalem" (*Paul of Tarsus*, 11; bracketed word is mine). This is the popular explanation, but some historians find it improbable. "The maker/repairer of tents and other leather products, carrying his bag of cutting tools, awls, sharpening stone and such, presents a more consistent and credible picture" (Brian M. Rapske, "Acts, Travel and Shipwreck," *The Book of Acts in Its First Century Setting*, vol. 2, 7).

wrongdoing against you, especially of preaching any heresy." Such language puts Paul in a role similar to Ezekiel, as a "watchman" who is warning the Jews of God's judgment against them (Ezekiel 3:16-21). Since these people are not listening, they bear the guilt of their own sin (see Leviticus 20:9-16 and 1 Kings 2:36-37 for more uses of this expression). "From now on I will go to the Gentiles" means that Paul has fulfilled his obligation to provide the Jews with first opportunity to receive the gospel of Christ, and now he will offer this message to the Gentiles in Corinth.

Even so, a man named Titius Justus—whose house is adjacent to the synagogue Paul has just left—gives sanctuary to Paul (18:7). Luke calls Titius "a worshiper of God" [lit., a God-fearer], the description he gives to Gentiles who worship God but are not circumcised (18:7; recall 10:2). Crispus, the *leader* of the synagogue, is also convicted by the gospel, dealing a severe indictment against the Jews who rejected it (18:8). Crispus is one of the few people that Paul personally baptizes in this city (1 Corinthians 1:14). "With all his household" simply cannot be used as a doctrinally-binding affirmation of the baptism of infants or children, since:

❑ This violates the "men and women" recipients of the gospel so far (recall 2:18, 5:14, 8:3, 8:12, and 9:2).

❑ This fails to acknowledge the adult responsibility (self-denial, sacrifice, and lifelong commitment; cf. Matthew 16:24) that the gospel message requires of anyone who responds to it.

❑ This assumes that Crispus *had* infants or young children in his household.

❑ This assumes that if he did, these would be included in the phrase "household" in the present context (i.e., those who can hear the message of truth and provide an intelligent and discerning response to it; cf. Ephesians 1:13, Colossians 1:5-6, et al).

❑ This assumes that infants and children are even eligible for conversion to Christ—i.e., that they can "believe in the Lord" on a level required by Jesus, the apostles, and the inherent demands of the gospel.

- ❑ This assumes that infants and children *need* to become Christians, which further assumes that they are indeed in sin (and condemned by God), which even further assumes that they are morally responsible to God and/or born in sin (per the Doctrine of Original Sin, which defies biblical teaching).
- ❑ This assumes that infants and children need to put their "old self" to death in baptism and be "born again" (cf. Romans 6:4-6, John 3:5)—even though they are not yet old *or* dead to God in sin (cf. Ephesians 2:1) nor have they become personally and morally responsible to God (unless we accept the false "Original Sin" premise).
- ❑ This assumes that infants and children are being baptized for reasons which they do not fully understand, and may not even be *able* to understand, and then are recognized on par with all adult believers.
- ❑ This makes a doctrinal assertion concerning the baptism of children from a number of very weak, presumptuous, and outright untenable assumptions.

"And many of the Corinthians when they heard were believing and being baptized" (18:8b). In keeping with the pattern so far, those who *believe* are also being *baptized*: baptism is the necessary and appropriate response to "believing." This also means that whenever we read of Christians who have "believed," it necessarily implies that they have also been baptized in accordance with that belief. Once again, no one in the NT is recognized as a Christian who has not been baptized into Christ (or, clothed with Him; see Galatians 3:26-27).

It appears that, despite these success stories, Paul is still hesitant and reserved in his preaching (18:9-10). He has faced considerable resistance in other places, leading to his own physical harm; these experiences create a kind of fear to which many of us simply cannot relate. Heavenly visions are not regularly given to the apostles; only at critical times or for critical decisions does God seem to provide them. Thus, the fact that Christ admonishes Paul in a vision necessarily implies that he is experiencing a great deal of pressure and intimidation in Corinth. Yet, the Lord offers great consolation and protection, allowing Paul to speak boldly without fear of physical harm. (Numerous times in the NT we are told "do not fear" or "do not be afraid." This reveals how common human fear is even among believers.) His confidence greatly emboldened by this vision, Paul spends a remarkable year and six months in this city (18:11). However, while Christ promised that no physical harm would come to Paul, He never promised the absence of *trouble* for him (18:12-17). The Jews are not going to back down quietly after being rebuked by this heretic (as they no doubt consider Paul to be). We know for certain that Lucius Junius Gallio is the proconsul (governor) of Achaia from AD 51-52, giving us a definite historical time-stamp for these next events. Gallio was born in Spain; he is a very intelligent, mild-mannered, and amiable administrator. His more famous brother, Seneca, is tutor and advisor to Nero, even after the young Nero becomes emperor (in AD 54). Later, Nero will order Seneca to commit suicide; Gallio, too, will fall victim to Nero's growing instability and is either killed or forced to commit suicide.[454]

The Jews, in their contempt for Paul, drag him before Gallio's tribunal (18:12).[455] Their charge is that Paul "persuades men to worship God contrary to the law" (18:13)—that is, contrary to the Law of Moses. (This is ascertained through Gallio's immediate response to the situation in 18:15—i.e., "your own law," not *Roman* law.) Yet Gallio will hear neither their complaint nor Paul's defense: his job is to arbitrate imperial law, not matters of religion (18:14-15). "His answer was that of a man who knew the limits of his office, and felt that he had no time to waste on the religious technicalities of the Jews."[456] Trying to reach a peaceful conclusion *for* the Jews over matters concerning *their* religion is a fruitless and exasperating task. Thus he

---

454   A. Rupprecht, "Gallio," *Zondervan Pictorial Encyclopedia*, 2:648-649.

455   This tribunal ("judgment seat" or "court") is from the Greek word *bema* (*Strong's* [electronic edition], #G968). "The *bema* was located on the south side of the marketplace in Corinth. Modern archaeologists have discovered the raised platform made of blue marble which held the seat on which the judge sat for civil cases such as this one. This judgment seat must have been very impressive. Later when Paul writes to the Corinthians he will tell them 'we must all appear before the judgment seat (*bema*) of Christ' (2 Cor 5:10)" (Gaertner, *Acts*, 288).

456   Conybeare and Howson, *Life and Epistles*, 328.

refuses their petition altogether, "and he drove them away from the judgment seat" (18:16) since they would not leave otherwise. Gallio's decision indirectly vindicates Paul's innocence and the legality of his gospel: a Roman official has just ruled (in essence) that there is nothing that Paul is saying or doing that violates Roman law. It is very possible that Gallio simply does not distinguish Christianity from Judaism, and therefore sees no need to weigh judgment on the matter. Regardless, this ruling of innocence to breaking Roman law will be the same decision that Felix (Acts 24) and Festus (Acts 26)—both governors of Judea— and even Emperor Nero will also reach. Yet, it will take years of time and Paul's own imprisonment for this exoneration to be realized.

Immediately after this, "they all took hold of Sosthenes, the leader of the synagogue, and began beating him" in view of Gallio (18:17). While some commentators believe that it is the Jews who begin beating Sosthenes (their own synagogue leader), the context more correctly suggests that the *lictors*—Gallio's policemen—are the "they" in this passage, not the Jews.[457] This also gives a better understanding of the statement, "And Gallio was not concerned about any of these things"— i.e., the plaintiff (Sosthenes) has been turned over to the police; they are in charge of him. This is their (the lictor's) punishment of the one who brought a frivolous charge before the proconsul of Achaia, and/or because he would not leave the tribunal when he was told to.[458]

The second missionary journey ends (18:18-22)

"Many days" after this incident, Paul finally leaves Corinth on his own free will and begins the long journey back to his home base in Antioch of Syria (18:18). Luke mentions that Priscilla and Aquila join his entourage, which also includes Silas and Timothy, and possibly

---

457   Lenski, *Acts*, 760; Boles, *A Commentary on Acts*; 291; Reese, *Book of Acts*, 651; Mitchell, "Acts of the Apostles," 18.5; et al. For what it is worth, I agree with these men's assessment and conclusion.

458   "The Jews 'lost' the case in that they were unable to proceed. They had unwittingly provided others with the opportunity to vent their anti-Jewish feelings against the new ruler of the synagogue in sympathy with the imperial action of recent times. The indifference of the governor to this is in harmony with the spirit of and the action of [Emperor] Claudius in recently evicting Jews from Rome (Acts 18:2, 17)" (Bruce W. Winter, "Acts and Roman Religion," *The Book of Acts in Its First Century Setting*, vol. 2, 100).

Erastus, Gaius, and Aristarchus (see 19:22, 29). It is possible that Paul carries with him donations from the Gentile churches to bring to Judea, and thus it is wise to travel with a group for security reasons. Regardless, travel in this time period is difficult and dangerous under any circumstances, and for this reason alone it is advisable to travel in numbers. "Cenchrea" is the actual seaport of Corinth, some two miles away; we learn later (Romans 16:1) that a church is established there. What Paul's "vow" is, we are not told; it cannot be a Nazirite vow, for this would prevent him from drinking "fruit of the vine" for the Lord's Supper (see Numbers 6:2-3). Perhaps it is a vow of gratitude to God for His having delivered Paul, as He promised to do.[459] In any case, there is nothing to prohibit Paul from making a personal vow to God, as long as he does not impose this specific vow-keeping upon the church as a test of fellowship.

When the traveling party arrives at Ephesus, Paul spends some time reasoning with the Jews in that city, but his intention is to head for home (18:19-21). (Remember that on his first missionary journey, the Holy Spirit prevented Paul from entering into this region; now, the reasons for that prevention are no longer relevant.) He promises to return, if possible, and leaves Priscilla and Aquila there. Indeed, Paul *will* return to Ephesus, and will stay there for about three years (see 20:31). Finally, Paul sails to Caesarea Palestina, and goes "up" to visit the church in Jerusalem, then "down" to Antioch. (The "up" and "down" references are always used in this way when speaking of Jerusalem, regardless of any north or south directions.) His entire second missionary journey has taken about three years to complete.

---

459   Reese, *Book of Acts*, 653.

∽ Chapters 19 – 20 ∽
Third Missionary Journey

The third missionary journey begins (18:23-28)
(To facilitate the organization of Acts into chapters, this passage is included in the "Chapters 19-20" section of Acts, although clearly we have not yet reached the nineteenth chapter.) Paul's third journey begins without ceremony: it is simply time to return to the missionary field (18:23). He spends "some time" in Antioch, then left to "strengthen" the mainland churches established on his first journey. The year now is circa AD 54. No specific traveling partner is mentioned for this journey, but it is very likely that a few men do accompany him (see 19:22), and several others will join him before he returns home (see 19:29 and 20:4), including Luke himself (since the "we" references resume in 19:6ff). Once again, Paul takes a land route from Syria over the Taurus Mountains into Galatia, then continues on a northwesterly course to Antioch of Pisidia. Later he will drop down into Ephesus (19:1), but for now the narrative focuses on Priscilla and Aquila's encounter with Apollos in Ephesus.

Apollos (likely the shortened form of Apollonius) is a learned Jew from Alexandria, Egypt, one of the greatest cultural and intellectual centers of the Roman Empire (18:24). This city also has at this time the largest population of Jews in the world outside of Jerusalem (one-third of the city is Jewish). Apollos is referred to as being "mighty in the Scriptures," meaning, he is well-versed in the Hebrew Bible and can also expound upon it with proficiency. Apparently he is quite the orator and a skilled debater, no doubt being educated in Greek rhetoric (i.e., the style of skillful and influential speech); he is eloquent, intelligent, and teachable. As yet, he is only familiar with the teachings of John, which continued in time only until John's execution by Herod (Matthew 14:1-12). Thus, Apollos is only familiar with the early ministry of Jesus, and not His death, burial, and resurrection. Nonetheless, he speaks boldly in the synagogue about what he *does* know (18:25-26a).

When Priscilla and Aquila hear him, however, they pull him aside privately and explain to him more fully what has happened since the preaching of John the Baptist (18:26b). No doubt their message is similar to what Peter spoke to Cornelius and company (recall 10:36-43). The discreet manner in which they handle this situation allows Apollos to retain his dignity (by not challenging or embarrassing him in front of his listening audience) and gives him opportunity to ask questions and receive answers. It is important to recognize here the nature of the problem: this is not a mere disagreement over opinions, methods, or unimportant details; this is a doctrinal matter for which there is only one correct answer. Priscilla and Aquila are not asking Apollos if he would mind reconsidering his message; they are *telling* him—tactfully, but certainly—that his message is out of date and therefore lacks critical information, especially concerning salvation in the name of Jesus.[460]

Apollos himself shows maturity in that he does not respond by trying to save face, being argumentative, or rebutting the two teachers. He is not interested in personal ambition; he is sincerely seeking to preach the truth, whatever it may be. Thus, he updates his teaching to include the fact that Jesus is the Messiah (Christ) (18:27-28). Filled with enthusiasm for the Lord, he then determines to go to Achaia (most likely to the city of Corinth, given Paul's several references to him in 1 Corinthians). "The brethren" in Ephesus give him not only their blessings but also write letters of commendation for him. His ministry there apparently becomes quite successful.[461] "Apollos was so 'mighty'

---

460   "The beauty of Priscilla's character lies in the fact that she never thrust herself forward, never asserted herself, or made her superiority felt. She was loyally true to Paul's teaching that the husband is the head of the wife. Aquila had found a pearl among women. Priscilla is the direct opposite of Sapphira. The one stimulated her husband to all that was good, the other helped her husband on to his destruction. Priscilla is the example our women need so much today when so many thrust themselves beyond their proper sphere and often do not know where to stop" (Lenski, *The Acts of the Apostles*, 774). While Lenski's assumptions about Priscilla are insightful, and likely correct, we cannot support them with Scripture.

461   "In this city [Corinth—CMS] of rhetoricians and sophists, the erudition and eloquent speaking of Apollos were contrasted with the unlearned simplicity with which St. Paul had studiously presented the Gospel to the Corinthian hearers. Thus many attached themselves to the new teacher, and called themselves by the name of Apollos, while others ranged themselves as the party of Paul (1 Cor. 1:12)—forgetting that Christ could not be 'divided,' and that Paul and Apollos were merely 'ministers by whom they had believed' (1 Cor. 3:5)" (Conybeare and Howson, *Life and Epistles*, 368).

[in the Scriptures] and the rabbis so weak for they know the oral law better than the written (Mark 7:8-12)."[462]

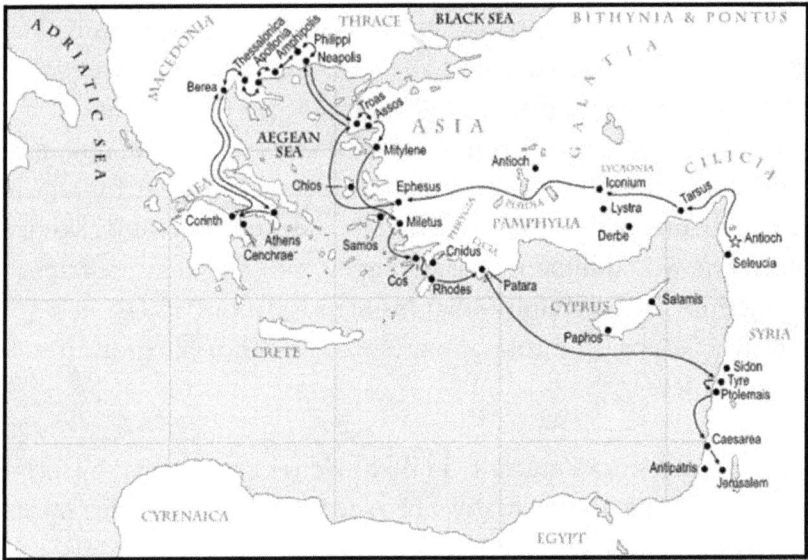

Paul's encounter with disciples of John in Ephesus (19:1-7)

Ephesus is one of the most powerful commercial and political cities in Asia Minor. The city also boasts one of the Seven Wonders of the ancient world—the impressive Temple of Diana [Greek: Artemis]—which makes it an important religious center of the pagan world as well. (More will be said on this temple and the worship of Diana shortly.) The population of Ephesus at the time of Paul's visit is approximately 200,000 people, which includes a large colony of Jews.[463] It is a "free city," which means that it can conduct its own politics and affairs which do not contradict imperial laws of Rome. The city is positioned on the mouth of the Cayster River; its harbor, however, regularly clogs with silt and must be dredged from time to time which is a difficult, expensive, and time-consuming effort. (Today,

---

462 Robertson, *Word Pictures*, 309; bracketed words are mine.

463 "The population of the city in the Roman period is generally estimated at between 200,000-250,000. This would probably make Ephesus the third largest city in the Empire after Rome and Alexandria" (Paul Trebilco, "Asia," *The Book of Acts in Its First Century Setting*, vol. 2, 307).

the ruins of Ephesus are far inland, since the silt build-up eventually overwhelmed any efforts to remove it.[464])

Apollos remained in Corinth as Paul traveled through the "upper country" (of Asia Minor, having come from the east through Galatia and Phrygia). "Some of the Christians there preferred Apollos's teaching to Paul's (1 Cor. 1:12; 3:4) because it was doubtless influenced by Greek philosophy Paul consciously avoided (1 Cor. 2:1-5)."[465] This cannot mean that Apollos is adding Greek philosophy to the gospel (something Paul cannot tolerate), but has reference to Apollos' oratory *style* of teaching which is similar to that of the philosophers. Meanwhile, Paul encounters "about twelve" disciples (cf. 19:7) who apparently are not affiliated with any other group. "Disciples" in this context cannot be construed to mean "Christians," since no one can be a Christian until or unless he is baptized into Christ (Galatians 3:27).[466] Perhaps Paul thinks at first that these men *are* disciples of Christ, given their devotion to God; yet it soon becomes clear that they are only disciples of John the Baptist, not Christ (see Matthew 9:14, where disciples of John and disciples of Christ are also identified separately).

Paul asks, "Did you receive the Holy Spirit…?" and the men answer, "No, we have not even heard whether there is a Holy Spirit" (19:2). Paul's question, however, indirectly underscores the Holy Spirit's prominent involvement in one's conversion to Christ. "In a word, they were still living in the Old Testament which culminated with John the

---

464   William Ramsay, *The Letters to the Seven Churches* (updated edition), ed. Mark W. Wilson (Peabody, MA: Hendrickson Publishers, 1994), 169-170. Ramsay's entire physical and historical description of Ephesus is worthy of note (151-171).

465   JFB *Commentary*, on 19:1.

466   Coffman titles this section in his commentary, "Christians Who Needed to Be Re-Baptized" (*Commentary on Acts*, 361). This misrepresents the situation here entirely—a rare misstep for him. The process by which a person is *made* a Christian (i.e., baptism) cannot be repeated; re-baptism in the context of salvation is foreign to the NT. It *is* true, however, that people might have been baptized into *one* thing (or for *one* reason) and then are later baptized into *another* thing (or for *another* reason), which is the case here in 19:1-5. These men are not re-baptized into the same thing or for the same reason. The *method* is the same (i.e., literal immersion in water), but everything else has changed. As far as one's salvation is concerned, God only recognizes "one baptism" (Ephesians 4:5).

Baptist. They understood neither that the new age had been ushered in by Jesus, nor that those who believe in him and are baptized into him receive the distinctive blessing of the new age, the indwelling Spirit."[467] Paul then explains to these men that their discipleship to John naturally leads to a far more important discipleship to the Messiah. Identification and allegiance to Him requires baptism in His name (or, by His authority). (No doubt Luke records only a summary of this explanation and not the entirety of it.) Paul necessarily links together *believing*, *baptism*, and the *reception of the Holy Spirit* for the purpose of salvation (19:2-3). These are not three disconnected actions, but are inseparable parts of conversion. In other words, one cannot be converted to Christ who does not believe in Him, is not baptized into Him, and (thus) has not received God's Holy Spirit as a result of this belief and baptism. Paul necessarily implies here that he has no concept of a Christ-follower (i.e., Christian) who has not been baptized into Christ. Until Paul baptizes them, "These twelve [men] were accordingly regarded as not having been baptized at all; and now for the first time they received real baptism."[468] "When they heard this, they were baptized in the name of the Lord Jesus" (19:5), which is the only appropriate response to the *preaching* of Jesus.

This account underscores the fact that John's baptism was not a special method of *salvation*, but was designed "to turn the hearts of the fathers back to the children, and the disobedient to the attitude of the righteous, so as to make ready a people prepared for the Lord" (Luke 1:17). John the Baptist spoke of the Spirit, but made it clear that his baptism was not for the purpose of *giving* the Spirit; it was for repentance in anticipation of the One who *would* give the Spirit (Luke 3:3, John 7:39). The Jews who accepted John's baptism were supposed to have done so *in preparation for* receiving the baptism of the Messiah when He had ascended to power (19:3-4). Thus, it was "a baptism of expectation rather than one of fulfillment."[469] In other words, John's baptism was to renew an existing covenant that God had with His

---

467   Stott, *The Spirit, the Church, and the World*, 304.

468   McGarvey, *Acts of Apostles*, 2:153.

469   Bruce, *The Book of the Acts*, 386.

people (Israel), not to establish a new and different covenant that was inaugurated with the blood of Christ (Hebrews 9:13-26).

This account also underscores baptism's distinct and objective purpose: it is a demonstration of faithful obedience upon which Christ provides the believer with forgiveness of sins, entrance into His church, and the right to be thereafter identified with Him. It also indirectly proves only *one* baptism is relevant—that which serves as this demonstration of faithful obedience (Ephesians 4:5). The objective is not merely "baptism" itself, as in, "any baptism will do." Rather, the objective is to participate in the *one* baptism in direct response to the terms and conditions of a covenant relationship (fellowship) with God through Jesus Christ.

> No one can become a Christian without being baptized into Christ. This is all we can teach, because this is all the New Testament has instructed us to teach. This sounds, of course, jarring and even offensive to the person who thought he (or she) *was already* a Christian (but simply missed a step in the conversion process). All I can do is point that person back to the Bible: What does it say? How does it read to you? If Christ said that you cannot enter the kingdom of God without being born of water *and* the Spirit (John 3:5), then a person who is not yet born of water is also not born of the Spirit, and is not in this kingdom. This does *not* mean that he has purposely deceived anyone, or that everything he learned up to this point is for naught. It simply means: there is something else that God requires, and until this is fulfilled, then the intended objective has not yet been reached. ...
>
> Will you come to a better understanding of baptism over time? I hope so! I know that I have—over and over again—and I trust that everyone who becomes a student of the Bible does so. But this new knowledge does not require a "new" baptism; it simply reinforces the *need* for and the powerful *symbolism* of your baptism. God always leads us from the simple to the complex, from the elementary figures to the far more sophisticated ones,

and from child-like faith to wisdom and maturity. All of us begin on an elemental level, and *after this* we move toward greater spiritual understanding (Hebrews 6:1-3). You are growing *in* Christ, not stepping *outside* of Him in order to grow. Whatever you learn *after* your baptism only adds depth and dimension *to* that baptism; it does not require you to redo it.[470]

"When Paul had laid his hands upon them, the Holy Spirit came on them" (19:6)—there are two very important considerations here: first, the *method* which is used to impart the miraculous power of the Holy Spirit to these men; second, the *purpose* for which this is done. The method here is exactly the same as that performed by Peter and John in Acts 8:14-17. Since Paul is an apostle of the church and appointed by Christ for this very purpose, he has the authority and the ability to lay his hands on people to impart spiritual (miraculous) gifts. As to the purpose of this transaction, we see that it is altogether different than what was necessary for their conversion. In order to become Christians, these men had to be baptized in water by the authority of Jesus Christ; in order to receive miraculous gifts of the Spirit, they had to have an apostle of Christ lay his hands upon them. One action (baptism) was for salvation; the other (laying on of hands) was to manifest God's approval of that first action. Boles accurately states: "This was not a baptism of the Holy Spirit; no human agency or administrator had any part in the baptism of the Holy Spirit."[471] The fact that these men can speak in tongues and prophesy by the power of the Spirit is proof positive of God's *approval* of what Paul has done (in teaching and baptizing them) and what these men have done (in receiving and being baptized according to this teaching). We simply cannot accept the idea that the Spirit would have given such power to these men regardless of any impropriety in this process.

---

470   Sychtysz, *Being Born of God*, 252-253.

471   Boles, *A Commentary on Acts*, 299.

Paul's ministry in Ephesus (19:8-20)

As is his usual custom upon entrance into a city, Paul goes to the place where he will find the highest concentration of Jews: the synagogue (19:8). For three months, he tries persuading the Jews of Ephesus to become Christians. The "kingdom of God" is no doubt as misunderstood among these Jews as it is today among Christians and non-Christians alike. The Jews see themselves as being preferentially and automatically ushered into the kingdom simply because they *are* Jews, yet Paul teaches that one's entrance into the kingdom requires submission to its King, Jesus Christ. No one is "fit for the kingdom" (cf. Luke 9:62) who refuses to obey Him and give Him full allegiance. The gospel, kingdom of God, Jesus Christ, and baptism in His name are *inseparable* with regard to salvation, in that a person must submit to *all* of them if he wishes to be saved. The *kingdom of God* refers to the authority and scope of Christ's reign over His Father's kingdom. The *church* refers instead to the body of believers who have submitted to Christ's kingship. Thus, the *kingdom* and *church* are certainly related but not interchangeable. No one can be loyal to the King (or His kingdom) without being a member of His spiritual sanctuary of believers (His church).

But not all Jews want to hear this good news (19:9a; see Hebrews 4:2). "Hardened" means to resist the truth; "disobedient" means to violate or sin against that truth. "Speaking evil of the Way" manifests both the hardening and disobedience of the human heart in its rejection of God's will. "As the Jews resisted the truth, they gradually became more and more callous to it; and the more they were hardened, the more they were disobedient.... The same sun will melt wax but it will harden clay. It depends on the substance it strikes. So it is with the Gospel."[472] "The Way" is an early reference to the gospel teaching (recall 9:2; see also 19:23, 24:14, and 24:22).[473]

---

472   Reese, *Book of Acts*, 674.

473   It is interesting to note that John the Baptist's proclamation to the Jews was to "make ready *the way* of the Lord" (Matthew 3:3, emphasis added). After Jesus' kingship had been secured and His church established, "the Way" becomes the *correct response* to John's message—i.e., not merely a baptism of repentance for those under the old covenant, but a baptism into a new covenant altogether. This "Way" is unique and exclusive: it is not to be compared to any other; it cannot be duplicated; no one can

If Paul is going to make any further progress, it will be necessary to remove the newly-converted disciples of Christ away from the negative influences of unbelieving Jews (19:9b). This puts into practice what Jesus Himself had said: "Do not give what is holy to dogs, and do not throw your pearls before swine, or they will trample them under their feet, and turn and tear you to pieces" (Matthew 7:6). There comes a time when it is clear that certain people simply are not interested in hearing the truth, and so expending more time trying to *teach* them "the truth" is pointless and exhausting. This does not mean that Paul is unconcerned for those Jews who resist his preaching (see Romans 9:1-3 and 10:1), but he also realizes his limitations. If the apostle Paul has such limitations, then we should recognize that we will (in our own preaching of the gospel) as well.

For this reason, Paul rents (or is given loan of) a "school of Tyrannus," which may be similar to a lecture room or hall, in order to continue his teaching (19:10).[474] He teaches daily "for two years," which is a considerable period of time, and this teaching has a profound effect on the heathen communities in the province of Asia (modern Western Turkey). Paul later says that he spent a total of three years in Ephesus (20:31), which may include the three months prior to using the school of Tyrannus (and other time that Luke did not record; see 19:22), and therefore may be a rounded figure. "So that all who lived in Asia heard the word of the Lord, both Jews and Greeks" (19:10) is a fair statement, given the ideal proximity of Ephesus on the convergence of two major trade routes (east-west and north-south). Paul no doubt enjoys a regular audience of local residents as well as the many travelers that passed through the city for commerce and other reasons.

---

enter into fellowship with God in any other "way" but this one (cf. John 14:6).

474   "The name 'Tyrannus' is a common one, and means 'tyrant.' We know nothing about this Tyrannus; we do not know whether he was a heathen [i.e., Gentile] or a Jew" (Boles, *A Commentary on Acts*, 301; bracketed word is mine). Kistemaker adds: "The Western text [an old and sometimes paraphrased translation of the NT from the Greek—CMS] adds the interesting note that Paul held discussions 'from the fifth to the tenth hour,' that is, from 11 a.m. to 4 p.m....There is reason to believe that the additional note of the Western text is authentic, yet translators hesitate to make it part of the New Testament text. They question why this piece of information, if it is genuine, has been deleted from the major manuscripts" (*Acts*, 684).

"God was performing extraordinary miracles by the hands of Paul..." (19:11)—the credit for this power is given to God, yet clearly Paul is His "chosen instrument" (cf. 9:15). It is significant that these miracles are considered "extraordinary" even in a world already saturated with charlatans, magicians, magic arts, and so-called divine oracles. The miracles Paul performs are both real and powerful, and offer irrefutable authenticity to his message. As noted earlier, miracles are not performed *apart from* or *instead of* the message: the one (genuine miracle) leads necessarily to the other (heavenly message). We have already seen similar demonstrations of this power by the hands of Christ (Matthew 4:23-24) and Peter (Acts 5:14-16). "Handkerchiefs or aprons" (19:12) may refer to Paul's own (that he uses in the course of his work as a tent-maker) or it could refer to those which are given to Paul to touch, which are then carried to those who are sick or demon-possessed. This is parallel to (but different than) the people in Jerusalem who sought healing from Peter's shadow falling upon them (recall 5:15).

One of the most powerful miracles one can perform is exorcism: the removal of an evil spirit from a person's body (see Luke 4:33-37). The reason for this is because such action requires authority over not only the physical or human realm but also the spiritual or unseen realm. "Exorcist" [Greek: *exorkizo*] means "(to cast out through) exacting an oath."[475] Jesus, Peter, and Paul were not literal exorcists (as practiced among the Jews) because they did not use oaths, spells, or ceremonial adjurations to remove demons; they simply commanded the demons to leave their hosts. "The method of Jesus in dealing with demoniacs was not that of the exorcists. While it is said (Matthew 8:16) that He 'cast out the spirits with a word,' it is abundantly clear that the word in question was not ritualistic but authoritative."[476] Jesus Himself said that He cast out demons "by the Spirit of God" (Matthew 12:28), not through some elaborate ritual. Nonetheless, some Jews of this time do practice exorcism (though we have no evidence of it being successful) and are highly regarded because of this. They stroll from place to place "like modern Gypsy fortune-tellers," seeking opportunities to use their

---

475   Robertson, *Word Pictures*, 317; *Strong's* (electronic edition), #G1844.

476   Louis Matthews Sweet, "Exorcism; Exorcist," *ISBE* (electronic edition).

powers.[477] Upon seeing Paul's great success by invoking the name of
Jesus (see Romans 15:18-19), Jewish exorcists also appeal to this name
(19:13). There is a difference in how the "name" is used here, however.
Paul legitimately appeals to Jesus' authority; the Jewish exorcists use
Jesus' name as part of a kind of magical spell or procedure.[478] The
Jewish exorcists essentially practice magic, not miracle-working; "and
as this account discloses, the city of Ephesus proved to be a storehouse
of magical scrolls."[479]

"Sceva" is a Jewish priest otherwise unknown to us, but his seven sons
all practice exorcism (19:14-16). These men try to cast out a demon
using (as a special charm) the name of "Jesus whom Paul preaches."
This backfires, of course; "like an unfamiliar weapon wrongly handled
it exploded in their hands."[480] The demon does not bow to the mere
use of a name, but only to the power and authority *behind* a name: "I
recognize Jesus, and I know about Paul, but who are you?" The Greek
uses "you" emphatically, as with a tone of contempt.[481] In other words,

---

477   Robertson, *Word Pictures*, 317.

478   "You shall not take the name of the LORD your God in vain" (Exodus 20:7) is
a law of morality, not ritual; therefore, it is timeless and universal command. Yet, these
Jewish exorcists see no problem with using the name of God's Son—a Divine Being—as
a means of self-promotion (thus, "in vain"). Certainly many examples exist today
where people are still using the name of Jesus Christ in order to further their man-made
religion, self-serving agenda, and personal profits. All such usage violates the moral
injunction against desecrating the holy name of God. Of all people, those who claim to
"know" God (because they claim to be Christians) ought to know better, and incur a
stricter judgment because of this (Luke 12:48, James 3:1).

479   Kistemaker, *Acts*, 687. Conybeare and Howson write: "The worship of Diana
and the practice of magic were closely connected together. Eustathius says, that the
mysterious symbols, called 'Ephesian Letters,' were engraved on the crown, the girdle,
and the feet of the [image of the] goddess [in the temple of Diana]....When pronounced,
they were regarded as a charm; and were directed to be used, especially by those who
were in the power of evil spirits. When written, they were carried about as amulets....
The study of these symbols was an elaborate science; and books, both numerous and
costly, were compiled by its professors" (*Life and Epistles*, 371, bracketed words are
mine).

480   Bruce, *The Book of the Acts*, 390.

481   Reese, *Book of Acts*, 679. Also, "'I know' is from 'genosko,' with respect to
Jesus, and from 'epistomai,' with respect to Paul; so the verbs are different, and carry
a different meaning" (Boles, *A Commentary on Acts*, 303). In essence, the demon says:
"I have intimate *awareness* or *perception* of Jesus' power, and I have *knowledge* of the
work of His servant, Paul, but *you men* are strangers to all of this."

"*You have no authority to use this name in this way.*" Demons are not stupid; they will not submit to any human for any reason. Only Christ's power is superior to theirs, and they are stronger than men. This is manifested visibly in the account of Sceva's seven sons being attacked and overwhelmed by one demon-possessed man—in essence, by the demon (or "evil spirit") itself. "Naked and wounded" indicates that these men are maliciously beaten and humiliated and not just running away unharmed. This account has a profound and convincing effect on those who hear of it—not only because of what happened to these men, but also what the demon confirmed about Jesus and Paul (19:17).

The city of Ephesus is inundated with sorcery and magical arts. Yet, spells are thought to be only as good as the secrecy of how they are practiced. The usage (and pronouncement) of certain names, putting words in certain orders, and/or making supplication of powerful invisible entities give the spell its potency. But certain Ephesian sorcerers, magicians, astrologers, etc., recognize the inferiority of their own magic and spells when contrasted with Paul's exercise of the genuine power of God. We do not know exactly what is meant by "confessing and disclosing their practices" (19:18), but it seems clear that these men are acknowledging the counterfeit nature of their practices as a means of renouncing them. We may not appreciate the significance of burning books of magic "in the sight of all" (19:19), but this is a profound act. Books are the source of spells, enchantments, recipes, incantations, and power; they contain the secrets of the sorcerers and magicians' practices; and they are difficult to produce and expensive to obtain. By publicly burning their books of the occult, these men admit that *these things are now worthless to them*—and to anyone else as well. Lenski notes: "[Fifty thousand pieces of silver] was a lot of money to be consigned to the flames. It was one of the best investments these believers ever made."[482] This also admits that the gospel message of Christ is worth *more* to these men than these once-prized possessions. "Pieces of silver" refers to silver coins; while it is difficult to determine this amount in today's money, it is substantial.[483]

---

482   Lenski, *Acts of the Apostles*, 798; bracketed words are mine.

483   "Books were generally burned in antiquity by rulers or others who found the books offensive, seditious, or dangerous, in order to repudiate the contents of the books

These three things—Paul's extraordinary miracles, the incident with the sons of Sceva, and the burning of the books of magic arts—indicate the gospel's great success in this region (19:20). No wonder, then, that Demetrius and his fellow silversmiths are genuinely concerned about the economic impact this will have upon their business, as we will see in the next section.

Paul's future intentions (19:21-22)

"These things" (19:21) refers to Paul's teaching at the school of Tyrannus and the sorcerers-turned-Christians' burning of their books of magic, both of which occurred in the same space of time. After leaving Ephesus, it is Paul's intention to visit Jerusalem after taking a circuitous route through Macedonia and Achaia. The purpose is twofold: first, to encourage the churches in those regions; second, to collect benevolence from them to bring to Jerusalem (2 Corinthians 8:1-6). His desire, however, is ultimately to visit Rome, then Spain (see Romans 1:11-15, 15:22-28). Some time has passed since we last heard of Timothy, but he has since joined Paul in Ephesus. Paul sends Timothy and Erastus (2 Timothy 4:20) ahead of him to Macedonia as he remains for a while longer in the province of Asia. Many commentators believe that at this time Paul writes (what we call) First Corinthians. It is now circa AD 57.

The riot in Ephesus (19:23-41)

Paul's stay in Ephesus has not been an easy one. Prior to the riot (which is covered next), he says that he "fought with wild beasts in Ephesus" (1 Corinthians 15:32) and that he faced "many adversaries" there (1 Corinthians 16:8-9); after the riot, he felt the "sentence of death" upon him (2 Corinthians 1:8-10). Wherever the gospel prospers, Satan is always there waiting to inflict as much damage as he can against the church and its preachers. In the present case, Satan finds a willing servant in Demetrius, a silversmith whose livelihood depends largely on selling household idols to the many world travelers who come to Ephesus to pay their respects to Diana/Artemis. ("Diana" is the Latin name for this goddess; Artemis is the Greek name.) Artemis of the

---

concerned" (Trebilco, "Asia," 315). The fact that these book are burned *not* because they have been confiscated by civil authorities but *voluntarily* is significant.

Ephesians[484] is sometimes represented with a triple face, and often with multiple breasts, indicating that she is a fertile source of blessings. (Goddesses of fertility and reproduction are common in the ancient world.)

> This city was renowned throughout the world for the worship of Diana, and the practice of magic. Though it was a Greek city, like Athens or Corinth, the manners of its inhabitants were half Oriental. The image of the tutelary goddess resembled an Indian idol rather than the beautiful forms which crowded the Acropolis of Athens: and the enemy which St. Paul had to oppose was not a vaunting philosophy, as at Corinth, but a dark and Asiatic superstition. The worship of Diana and the practice of magic were closely connected together.[485]

Years before, a fallen meteorite had been brought into the temple of Artemis. This rock became mystically associated with the goddess, and thus the Ephesians believed that it emitted supernatural powers. The priests of Artemis are eunuchs; virgin priestesses and a lower order of slaves known as "temple sweepers" maintain the temple. "Wild orgiastic exercises," frenzied dancing, ceremonial prostitution, and even human sacrifice describe the activity within its walls.[486]

The temple of Artemis, considered to be one of the "wonders" of the ancient world, certainly is impressive.[487] This structure, which took

---

484 Diana (Artemis or Cybele) of the Ephesians is not the same as Diana of the Romans or Artemis of Greek mythology, the daughter of Zeus and sister of Apollo. She is, however, the same as Astarte in Phrygia and Ashtoreth in Canaan (2 Kings 23:13) (Mitchell, "Acts of the Apostles," 19.6). Artemis of the Ephesians is a mother-goddess, a female figure "with arms extended in a gesture of welcome or invitation; from the waist down her legs are wrapped in cloth much like an Egyptian mummy, and this is covered with tier under tier of heads of lions, stags, oxen, bees, flowers, and corn" (Reese, Book of Acts, 687).

485 Conybeare and Howson, Life and Epistles, 371.

486 Robertson, Word Pictures, 325; Reese, Book of Acts, 687.

487 "Like the city, it [the temple—CMS] dates from the time of the Amazons, yet what the early temple was like we now have no means of knowing, and of its history we know little except that it was seven times destroyed by fire and rebuilt, each time on a scale larger and grander than before. The wealthy king Croesus supplied it with

over 200 years to complete, is 425 feet long and 220 feet wide; its roof is supported by one hundred and twenty-seven 60-foot-tall columns, each column being gifted by a king. The middle of the roof is open to the sky; beneath this opening sits the image of Artemis. The roof, doors, and paneling are of the choicest cedar; its interior is decorated with gold; the columns, foundation, and walls are of pure white marble. (Soon after Christianity swept through Asia Minor, temple worship fell into such decline that Pliny, writing to Emperor Trajan some fifty years later, spoke of deserted temples, neglected idol worship, and hardly a single person purchasing sacrificial animals. The temple of Artemis was later plundered and destroyed by the invading Goths during the reign of Emperor Gallienus, AD 263. Some of the materials were salvaged and used, ironically, in the construction of the mosque of St. Sophia in Constantinople [modern Istanbul] and some Italian cathedrals.[488])

"No small disturbance" is Luke's trademark way of drawing attention to the fact that what follows is a *major* disturbance (19:23). Demetrius, a silversmith, instigates a riot in Ephesus that engulfs nearly the entire city, and Paul is his target. Silversmiths organize themselves into trade guilds (which are similar to our modern labor unions) in order to regulate prices, guarantee employment, and prevent unwanted competition. Thus, Demetrius is not just a lone, angry entrepreneur; as a guild member, he has a number of powerful contacts and fellow craftsmen to call upon. Not only this, but he uses to his full advantage the ignorance and superstitious gullibility of the pagan-minded populace (19:24-27). We must also remember that it is not only the silversmith's trade that is being threatened by the gospel, but also a great deal of revenue that is brought into Ephesus directly because of

---

many of its stone columns, and the pilgrims from all the oriental world brought it [sic] of their wealth. In time the temple possessed valuable lands; it controlled the fisheries; its priests were the bankers of its enormous revenues. Because of its strength the people stored there their money for safe-keeping; and it became to the ancient world practically all that the Bank of England is to the modern world" (E. J. Banks, "Ephesus," *ISBE* [electronic edition]). Later, however, the influence of Christianity would overwhelm the pagan worship of Diana. When the temple of Diana was later destroyed, no one bothered to rebuild it. The Cayster River overflowed its banks and buried (in AD 263) the temple site; no one knew where it was until it was discovered and excavated in 1870 (ibid.).

488   Conybeare and Howson, *Life and Epistles*, 422ff.

Artemis worship. ("Artemision," the month on the Ephesian calendar which corresponds roughly to our April or May, is a month of holy pilgrimage to Ephesus by worshipers of Artemis.[489])

Demetrius lays out his argument against Paul (19:25-27), revealing a candid admission to the true nature of his character as well as his trade. He is not interested in the truth; he is interested in making money. His complaint is not really about religion; it is about economics. One's *economic* investment in his religion (however virtuous or not the religion itself) determines the content of what he believes as well as the level of commitment he has in that religion.[490] By creating such uproar over Paul's preaching, however, the silversmith inadvertently provided a great deal of advertising for it. "Demetrius not only exaggerated his statements to his fellow craftsmen, but he also exaggerated the effect of Paul's work."[491]

What begins as an isolated protest quickly swells into a city-wide riot. The people begin to cry out, "Great is Artemis of the Ephesians"—a chant that continues for at least two hours (19:28; see 19:34). Mob mentality does not have to be logical or systematic; people are swept into it simply by the sheer energy (and confusion) that it creates (19:29). Gustave Le Bon (*The Crowd*) describes what we refer to today as "mob mentality":

> Whoever be the individuals that compose it, however like or unlike be their mode of life, their occupations, their character, or their intelligence, the fact that they have been transformed into a crowd puts them in possession of a sort of collective mind which makes them feel, think, and act in a manner quite different from that in which each individual of them would feel, think, and act were he in a state of isolation.

---

489   Tribelco, "Asia," 321. He adds that the celebration of Artemision "likely included athletic, theatrical, and musical competitions" (ibid.).

490   Even so, "When religious devotion and economic interest were simultaneously offended, a quite exceptionally fervid anger was engendered" (Bruce, *The Book of the Acts*, 398).

491   Boles, *A Commentary on Acts*, 308.

In the collective mind [of the crowd] the intellectual aptitudes of the individuals, and in consequence their individuality, are weakened.

A crowd scarcely distinguishes between the subjective and the objective.[492]

The city's theater into which the mob moves is huge, capable of seating 25,000 or more people, and is often the site of gladiatorial fights.[493] Gaius and Aristarchus (see 20:4) are dragged into it; Paul wants to go there, perhaps to rescue them, but is wisely restrained.[494] It is possible that Paul would be killed if properly identified among such a wild mob. "Asiarchs" (or, "chief officers of Asia") is the title of ten wealthy and prominent men chosen annually to preside over the athletic games of the province. It is impressive that they are identified as friends of Paul, and indicates just how deeply the gospel has penetrated into the Hellenistic culture of Ephesus.[495] A man named Alexander is "put forward" by the Jews to calm things down, but since he is a Jew (and the pagans do not always make a distinction between Jews and Christians), the people refuse to listen to him (19:33-34). The riot loses sight of its original purpose, and, like all such unguided or misguided crowds of men, becomes nearly hysterical in nature.

It is no doubt that great effort is required to quiet the people, but the "town clerk" manages to do so (19:35). He is a magistrate (judge) of great authority, a representative of Ephesus to Rome in legal matters, a keeper and administrator of the city's papers and archives, and a highly-

---

492   Gustave Le Bon (1841 – 1931), *The Crowd: A Study of the Popular Mind* (Atlanta, GA: Cherokee Publishing Co., 1982), 6, 8, 22; bracketed words are mine.

493   Robertson, *Word Pictures*, 326.

494   "Gaius" mentioned here is most likely a Macedonian, like Aristarchus; the "Gaius" mentioned in 20:4 is from Derbe. Gaius was a common name at this time, and it is unlikely that the name here refers to the same person. It is also unlikely that either of these men are the same "Gaius" to whom John writes (3 John 1).

495   McGarvey, *Acts of Apostles*, 2:165. Bruce adds: "That these men were friendly to Paul indicates that imperial policy at this time was not hostile to Christianity, and that the more educated classes did not share the antipathy to Paul which the more superstitious classes felt" (*The Book of the Acts*, 400).

respected and very public figure. His prudent speech (19:35-40) is here summarized:

☐ Ephesus is the "guardian of the temple of the great Artemis" and its sacred image; no one is directly disputing this. "Thirteen cities in Asia participated in the worship of Diana, but Ephesus held the special responsibility and honor of caring for the temple."[496]

☐ Given this, there is no justification for the mob's complaint. (It is impressive how the silversmiths and crowd of worshipers feel the need to rise to their god's defense. They offer zero confidence that Artemis herself will retaliate against Paul, or will show any power at all to protect herself. As with all false gods, the power lays with the people, not the god itself.)

☐ Those who have been put forward (Gaius, Aristarchus, Alexander, and possibly others) have not done anything worthy of this disturbance. They are neither robbers nor blasphemers.

☐ Any genuine legal grievances should be taken to the proper civil authorities.

☐ This mob scene constitutes an "unlawful assembly" and a "disorderly gathering" which jeopardizes the free-governing status of Ephesus—and threatens martial law by Rome [implied]. In other words, this is *not* the way for the citizens of Ephesus to conduct themselves.

Having said this, the town clerk "dismissed the assembly" [lit., the *ekklesia*, the same word from which "church" is translated] (19:41). Incidentally, "disorderly gathering" (or, "uproar") implies not just a mass confusion but also carries the additional meaning of *conspiracy*—in this case, a treasonous act against Rome.[497]

The journey through Macedonia (20:1-6)

The "uproar" in Ephesus signals to Paul that it is time for him to move on (20:1). He assembles "the disciples" in that city together in order to

---

496   JFB *Commentary*, on 19:35. "These people were so proud of this temple that they refused to write the name of Alexander the Great on it, even though he had offered them all of his eastern countries in return" (ibid., on 19:28).

497   Kistemaker, *Acts*, 706; *Strong's* (electronic edition), #G4963.

say goodbye, not knowing when (or if) he will ever see them again (cf. 20:25). Paul has already sent Timothy and Erastus to Macedonia (recall 19:22), and his plan is to join them there.

Luke condenses a great deal of time and detail into a few verses (20:1-5). From Ephesus, Paul takes a northerly route to Troas, then crosses the sea to arrive in Macedonia. There, he works his way from Philippi southward on the Roman highway (*Via Egnatia*) through Amphipolis, Thessalonica, and Berea—the cities of Macedonia. Then "he came to Greece," namely, the city of Corinth. (There is no indication that Paul ever returns to Athens. It is thought that "Second Corinthians" is written while Paul is in Macedonia, and "Romans" during his present stay in Corinth.)   After three months in Corinth, Paul plans to sail to Syria (Antioch), but "the Jews"—those Jews who resist the teaching of the gospel—plot to take Paul's life, perhaps while he is on the ship. Thus, Paul decides instead to take a land route through Macedonia and then head southeastward to Troas across the sea. He is accompanied by several men: Sopater of Berea, Aristarchus and Secundus of Thessalonica, Gaius of Derbe, Trophimus of Ephesus (21:29), and Tychicus of Asia (possibly of Ephesus). "Sopater" may be the "Sosipater" mentioned in Romans 16:21; "Gaius" is most likely *not* the same man to whom John writes his third epistle decades later (3 John 1). These men are likely escorting Paul because of the benevolence money he is collecting from the Macedonian and Grecian churches for the saints in Judea.[498] (Later, Titus and two other unnamed disciples will participate in transporting

---

498   "One of the biggest mysteries in Acts has to do with this collection. Though it is obvious from Paul's letters that he considered the collection a major priority of this period in his ministry, Luke is completely silent about it" (Gaertner, *Acts*, 316). In a footnote, Gaertner refers to a theory by K. F. Nickle (1966) who "suggests that the money may have been confiscated by the Roman authorities who considered it illegal" (ibid., 316, fn. 8). There are a number of things about Paul's ministry which Luke does not mention; likewise, there are a number of things that Luke mentions that Paul does not. (As I have noted earlier, Luke does not even mention any of Paul's epistles, yet we know that they exist.)   This does not present a "mystery," as though we should suspect some kind of problem in either case. We certainly do not need to invent stories (like Nickle did) in order to rectify a problem that is not even proven to exist. It is reasonable to say: Luke did not mention the collection for reasons that we do not know, and do not have to know, whereas Paul's letters verify that this collection was "sanctified by the Holy Spirit" (Romans 15:16) and therefore completely successful.

Corinth's contribution to this same cause; see 2 Corinthians 8:6-24.[499])
These men go on ahead of Paul to Troas; meanwhile, Paul tarries in
Macedonia, no doubt to encourage the brethren in that region.

The crossing of the Aegean Sea from Neapolis [implied; recall 16:11]
to Troas takes five days—a great deal of time, indicating the winds are
contrary to the voyage (20:6), unless this time includes the travel from
Philippi to Neapolis. In Philippi, Paul picks up Luke, who includes
himself in the narrative (designated by the "we" and "us" pronouns).
"The days of Unleavened Bread" refers specifically to the seven-day
period of time immediately after Passover (Leviticus 23:4-8). This
may be a reference to the time of year (springtime) and nothing more.
Thus, it is probably the spring of 58. On Paul's first visit to Troas
(recall 16:7-11), he apparently did not engage in any missionary work;
on this occasion, however, he says that "a door was opened for me
in the Lord" (2 Corinthians 2:12). Paul had written a strong letter to
the church in Corinth ("First Corinthians") and was awaiting word
from Titus, whom he had sent there. Titus was supposed to meet up
with Paul, possibly in Troas and most certainly in Philippi; fear that
something had happened to him keeps Paul moving forward through
Macedonia until the two men finally reunite in Troas—and Titus brings
good news about Corinth (2 Corinthians 7:5-7, 13).

Paul in Troas (20:7-12)

Both Jews and Romans observe the same day (our Sunday) as "the
first day of the week." This "first day" has significance elsewhere in
Scripture:

❏ It is not only the *first* day of a new cycle of days (i.e., a new week),
but it is also the *eighth* day after the previous cycle of seven days.
This is significant because the number eight in Scripture often refers

---

499   Some find it strange that Luke would not mention Titus specifically, especially
since he (Titus) was such a close companion of Paul's. William Ramsey has suggested
that Titus was actually Luke's close relative, possibly even his brother, and that the
"we" section (beginning in 20:5) actually includes Luke *and* Titus (Ramsay, *St. Paul
the Traveller*, 59, 390). F. F. Bruce (*The Book of the Acts*, 406), James Coffman
(*Commentary on Acts*, 383), and others find this a plausible explanation.

to a new beginning, life, power, dynasty, or season.[500]

❑ It is the day Jesus rose from the dead (Matthew 28:1ff).

❑ It is the day of Pentecost, the same day in which the power of the Holy Spirit was manifested through the twelve apostles (Acts 2:1). Pentecost is always on the day after the (seventh) Sabbath following Passover (Leviticus 23:15-16); therefore, it is always on the first day of the week (our Sunday), which is also the *eighth* day after the previous cycle of seven days as well as a *type* of "eighth day" after seven Sabbaths.

❑ It is the day in which the disciples regularly met (1 Corinthians 16:1-2 [implied]). This has also been substantiated by secular authorities (such as Pliny) who wrote *about* Christians but did not have any involvement with them.[501]

❑ It is "the Lord's day," which alludes to Jesus' resurrection (Revelation 1:10). (Those who doubt this connection have yet to come up with a better explanation of John's phrase in the passage cited.)

There is no better or more natural conclusion than that this "first day of the week" is the typical and expected day of assembly for the saints. "Writings still extant from the early second century and onwards force one to accept the fact that the day of worship for the early Christians was Sunday, and that, too, long before Constantine officially changed the day for the whole empire."[502] "When you meet together" is when the Lord's Supper is taken (expressed negatively in 1 Corinthians 11:20, since the Corinthians were violating this intention). "Break bread" in this context must mean partaking of the Lord's Supper (Acts 2:42, 1 Corinthians 10:16); it is awkward and meaningless for Luke to refer to this as a common meal. Instead, it is clear that Paul and

---

500   Circumcision was performed on the eighth day (Genesis 17:12); the first-born animals were sacrificed to the Lord on the eighth day (Exodus 22:30); Israelites were considered ritually clean on the eighth day after seven days of uncleanness; the Jubilee was a type of "eighth" day following seven cycles of Sabbath years (Leviticus 25:10-13); David was the eighth son of Jesse (1 Samuel 17:12); Jesus gave eight "blessed" statements to describe the nature of those in the kingdom of God ("Beatitudes"; Matthew 5:1-12); etc.

501   Coffman, *Commentary on Acts*, 386.

502   Reese, *Book of Acts*, 734.

these disciples have come together with the specific intention of taking communion together.

Having limited opportunity, Paul's message to the disciples is longer than he (and the others) might have first intended, especially since he and his traveling companions have plans to leave for Jerusalem "the next day" (20:7). Eutychus has the unfortunate distinction of being the first person on record to fall asleep during a sermon. There is ample reason for this: if he is a slave (as is likely), he has probably worked the entire day and is already tired; the hour is late; and smoke from "many lamps" make the room stuffy and stale (20:8).[503] Regardless, he falls asleep and, because he is sitting on the sill of an open window, also falls to the street below. Luke is present here and, as a physician, is able to ascertain the facts: this young man is not merely unconscious, but dead (20:9). Paul's comment ("for his life is in him") is no different than Jesus' comments concerning Jairus' daughter (Mark 5:35-43). It is not meant to imply that Eutychus is not really dead, but that his death is not permanent: his life will resume. Paul's putting his body over the dead man's in order to restore him (20:10, 12) is reminiscent of how Elijah and Elisha both brought young men to life who had died (1 Kings 17:21, 2 Kings 4:34-35).

"And when he [Paul] had gone back up [to the upper room], and had broken {the} bread and eaten, he talked with them...until daybreak" (20:11, bracketed words added). There are two plausible explanations here:

❑ "Broken {the} bread" has nothing to do with "to break bread" in 20:7; the two statements speak of two separate actions. (There is no definite article in the Greek before "bread" in 20:11; thus, instead of reading "broken *the* bread," it is simply "broken bread.") The first action is the taking of the

---

503 Incidentally, the "many lamps" also indicates that these Christians had nothing to hide; everything was out in the open and exposed by the light (as Paul later implies; see Acts 26:26, "this [teaching of the Christian religion—CMS] has not been done in a corner." This also contradicts charges against the early Christians that they were engaging in secret and illicit practices (immorality, blood sacrifices, and even cannibalism—through a misunderstanding of the Lord's Supper).

Lord's Supper—this is the intent for having been "gathered together." The second action is a common meal. This same separation occurs in Acts 2:42 and 2:46: "breaking of bread" is the communion; "breaking bread from house to house" are common meals.

❏ "Broken {the} bread" has a direct *antecedent* in 20:7, where this is first mentioned; it is the communion or Lord's Supper. Thus, despite Paul being the only one mentioned as having "eaten" in 20:11, it is assumed that the entire church partook of the Lord's Supper together with him at that same time.

According to the first explanation: Paul joins the church in Troas to observe the Lord's Supper, and they do so; then Paul speaks until late; Eutychus falls out of the window and is resuscitated by Paul; then everyone returns to the upper room to partake of a common meal; finally, Paul continues to speak until the early morning hours. According to the second explanation: Paul joins the church in Troas to observe the Lord's Supper, but this is (inexplicably) delayed until after he speaks at length, and it is late; then Eutychus falls out of the window and is resuscitated; then everyone returns to the upper room and observes the Lord's Supper and immediately afterward enjoys a meal together; finally, Paul continues to speak until the early morning hours. The first explanation seems the most plausible, given the limited information we have to work with.[504] The second position creates problems that are difficult to resolve. For one, Paul is the only one mentioned who (after the midnight talk) is actually mentioned as having "eaten." This is an odd way to describe a memorial that is intentionally meant to be shared among believers, as Paul himself stresses in 1 Corinthians 11:33. For another, the circumstances here—that is, Paul's opportunity to speak, the unusual length of his message, and the interruption of Eutychus' fall—have supposedly delayed the Lord's Supper until the late hour. Some commentators thus

---

504   "It seems better to conclude that this [in 20:11—CMS] was not the Lord's Supper, but that it was a common meal which Paul ate in preparation for his expected departure. It is mentioned with particular reference to Paul, not to the worshiping company; hence, we conclude that the Lord's Supper had been observed at an earlier period of the meeting, and therefore, on the first day of the week, as they had met for that purpose on that day" (Boles, *A Commentary on Acts*, 320).

make creative attempts to prevent the Lord's Supper from technically occurring on a Monday (since it is after midnight that these disciples partook of it). At least one has suggested that this meeting really began on Saturday night, since by Jewish reckoning the new day begins after sundown, not after midnight.[505] This seems forced and speculative, and there is no need for it. Even if this second explanation is legitimate, the *intention* of the meeting is to partake of the Lord's Supper on the day (and time) in which the meeting convened; circumstances having interfered with this, forcing it to be later than expected, does not change that intention and does not set a *new* precedent (see Numbers 9:1-14, in principle). Furthermore, Paul's apostolic approval of this action trumps any of our own speculations or contrived scenarios.

Paul's meeting with the Ephesian elders (20:13-38)

Paul travels by land from Troas to Assos, whereas some or the rest of the traveling party journeys by sea to this same place (20:13-14). ("We" indicates that Luke is still in accompaniment.) The distance from Troas to Assos is forty miles by sea (because the ship has to follow the coastline) yet only twenty miles by land. For reasons not stated, Paul chooses to walk rather than sail. Assos, Mitylene, Chios, and Samos are all small seaports or islands along the coast of Asia Minor as one heads southward (20:15). Miletus is a growing seaport which nearly rivals Ephesus in trade volume; it also boasts a magnificent temple to the Greek god Apollo. It was one of the great Ionian settlements in Asia Minor, and provided an excellent place from which the ancient Greeks settled many other colonies in the Mediterranean Sea and Black Sea in the 8th to 6th centuries BC. It came under Roman rule in 133 BC, and remains commercially important to the Romans because of its strategic position.[506]

Paul may well be in a depressed state of mind right now: the churches in Corinth and Galatia are experiencing problems; he knows hardships lay ahead of him in Jerusalem; he has the constant burden of safeguarding the money entrusted to him as well as ensuring the safety

---

505   McGarvey, *Acts of Apostles*, 2:182.

506   R. C. Stone, "Miletus," *Zondervan Pictorial Encyclopedia*, vol. 4, 225-227.

of his traveling companions; he has had death threats against him; and he is no doubt weary from traveling. His intention, however, is to reach Jerusalem by Pentecost (20:16), which allows him no time to tarry in any one place for very long. (The date for Pentecost is calculated as being fifty days after the Sabbath which immediately follows Passover; see Leviticus 23:15-16.) For this reason, instead of entering into Ephesus, Paul has the elders of that church meet him in Miletus (20:17). "As the crow flies, Ephesus was only thirty miles north of Miletus, but the rather circuitous road was longer. It must have taken about three days for a messenger to travel to Ephesus and bring the elders back to Miletus."[507] This expedites Paul's travel time, but also gives him valuable opportunity to speak with these men privately and candidly.[508]

Paul's opening comments to these men (20:18-21) indicate some of the strenuous hardships and labors that he has experienced in bringing the gospel to these people. Yet he does not speak with regret, but impresses upon them the sincerity and genuineness of his ministry. It is possible that these comments are also intended to counter some of the accusations of the "false apostles" in Corinth—men who claim that Paul's preaching is "unimpressive" and that his intent is only to make money (see 2 Corinthians 2:17, 10:10, and 11:13). This explains the several times that Paul says "you know" or "you remember" or "you are witnesses." These men can testify that Paul's ministry has been honorable and authentic.

"I did not shrink from declaring to you anything that was profitable" (20:20)—i.e., Paul did not preach a partial gospel or speak only on selected topics, but provided the Ephesians with *everything* that God had intended them to know. "Solemnly testifying to both Jews and Greeks" (20:21)—this is in agreement with his commission from Christ (26:16-20) and is what Paul preaches everywhere (Romans 1:16,

---

507 Stott, *The Spirit, the Church, and the World*, 323.

508 Gaertner rightly observes: "No other Pauline speech in Acts sounds so much like his letters [than this one to the Ephesian elders]. The simple reason for this is that in Acts the speeches of Paul thus far have been to non-Christian audiences. The speech in Antioch of Pisidia (13:16-41) was before a Jewish crowd in the synagogue. The speech at the Areopagus (17:22-31) was before a pagan audience. Only now do we find a speech by Paul which is addressed to fellow believers" (*Acts*, 320; bracketed words are mine).

1 Corinthians 4:17). This teaching was both public (in the assemblies of the church) and private (in people's own homes, or in one-on-one discussions). This provides a precedent for the work of ministers today. "Repentance" is one of the core proclamations of the gospel message (Luke 24:47); "faith in our Lord Jesus Christ" includes any act of obedience that is required for establishing and maintaining fellowship with God through Christ.

"And now…" (20:22ff)—instead of talking about what *they* know, Paul now speaks about what *he* knows. He is well aware that difficulties await him in Jerusalem, but apparently he does not know exactly what these are. "Bonds and afflictions" indicates being physically restrained and persecuted. There is an ominous sense of finality in Paul's tone: he does not fully expect to live through whatever awaits him. Nonetheless, he is determined to go to Jerusalem to face these trials; he has a "course" to finish and a ministry to fulfill (see 2 Timothy 4:6-7). "Self-preservation was not a motive highly esteemed by Paul; his main concern was to fulfil the course which Christ had marked out for him, bearing witness to the good news of God's free grace in Christ."[509] "The gospel of the grace of God" (20:24) and "preaching the kingdom" (20:25) are in essence the same message: only through submission to the King (Christ) can one become an heir of His kingdom (i.e., as a citizen in good standing), wherein mercy and grace are received. Paul does not mention Christ's church here (as the sanctuary of such believers), nor does he have to; the distinction between the kingdom of God and the church of Christ has already been established. Whoever enters the kingdom under the terms and conditions of Christ's gospel must enter specifically into His church—the "body" of those who have been redeemed by His blood. "Kingdom" implies authority and power (as of a king); "grace" implies kindness and forgiveness (as of a high priest). It is most appropriate that Paul implies both the *kingship* and *priestly office* of Christ in the same context.

Paul does not believe he will see the Ephesians again (20:25). "This was not necessarily a prediction, but it was what Paul expected."[510]

---

509 Bruce, *The Book of the Acts*, 414.

510 JFB *Commentary*, on 20:25.

Thus he declares, "I am innocent of the blood of all men. For I did not shrink from declaring to you the whole purpose [ASV, "counsel"] of God" (20:26-27).[511] The "whole purpose" involves the full instruction necessary for entering into and maintaining fellowship with God. This involves at least: the terms and conditions of entering into a covenant relationship with God; a clear understanding of the "mystery of the faith" (cf. 1 Timothy 3:9); the sacrifice and mediation of Christ; the work of the Holy Spirit in the believer's life; the demands of discipleship; and the responsibility each Christian has toward the growth of the church "for the building up of itself in love" (cf. Ephesians 4:16). This verse (20:27) serves as a kind of personal mission statement for all ministers of the gospel, and is reminiscent of God's charge to Ezekiel as the "watchman" of Israel (see Ezekiel 33:1-9). Robertson notes: "One of the saddest things about the present situation is the restlessness of preachers to go elsewhere instead of devoting themselves wholly to the task where they are."[512]

Paul's tone now changes: "Be on guard for yourselves and for all the flock" (20:28). Church leaders must give constant vigilance to maintaining "sound doctrine" (cf. 1 Timothy 4:6, see Titus 1:9). Furthermore, elders have the responsibility to "shepherd" their own flock, in which they must resist all forms of injustice, self-promotion, and abuses of power (1 Peter 5:1-4). "Which the Holy Spirit has made you overseers"—i.e., the "office of overseer" (cf. 1 Timothy 3:1) is authorized by the Holy Spirit; He has provided both the legitimacy of this office and the pattern for its usage. The solemn responsibility entrusted to overseers is underscored by the price that has been paid for the flock: the blood of Christ. "The idea of the death of Christ being a purchase price is a distinctive emphasis in Paul's epistles"[513]—this is true with regard to the whole church as it is with regard to the individual believer (1 Corinthians 6:20). Peter later echoes this same thought: "...knowing that you were not redeemed with perishable things like

---

511   "'The whole counsel of God' means all the counsel of God that concerned Paul's work as a preacher of the gospel and an apostle of Christ" (Boles, *A Commentary on Acts*, 326).

512   Robertson, *Word Pictures*, 348.

513   Donald Guthrie, quoted in Kistemaker, *Acts*, 733.

silver or gold..., but with precious blood, as of a lamb unblemished and spotless, the blood of Christ" (1 Peter 1:18-19; see also Revelation 1:5-6, 5:9).

The abuse of power, corruption of integrity, exploitation (of a group's weakness), and conflicts of interest are real and constant threats to any congregation. Such abuses often originate in the *leadership* of a given group, which may include (but are not limited to) its elders. The corruptions of leadership always trickle down to the rest of the group. Or, if the leadership is weak, then it is ripe for being manipulated by the dominant and most vocal members of the group. In any case, Paul outlines what inevitably *will happen*—unless it is checked (20:29-31):

- ❑ **"Savage wolves will come in among you"**: Opportunists who have no vested interest in or spiritual concern for the flock will infiltrate the congregation and take full advantage of its members (see Matthew 7:15). Often such men prey on the weak and insecure, since these are the easiest to manipulate and deceive, in an attempt to erode the support of the group's leadership.
- ❑ **"Not sparing the flock"**: Such men see "the flock" as something to exploit for their own gain—i.e., something to rob, plunder, or cannibalize. This is the exact opposite of what an elder's concern should be. His responsibility is to feed, nurture, and guard the flock, not use it to advance his own agenda (1 Peter 5:1-3).
- ❑ **"And from among your own selves"**: Not all church problems are from external sources; more often than not, it is internal dissensions and cancers that destroy a group's effectiveness. External pressure (intimidation, harassment, and persecution) actually forces the church to circle the wagons, so to speak, and rally together around a common cause. Internal threats, however, erode the unity and collective trust of the group, causing it to fracture or collapse from within. "Your own selves" is not an accusation against these actual men to whom Paul is speaking, but is a reference to men of their office (i.e., from the eldership).
- ❑ **"Speaking perverse things"**: All apostasy begins with false or misleading information, which requires a departure from or a maligning of the truth (2 Timothy 4:3-4, 2 Peter 2:1-3). "Perverse"

means "distorted," "twisted," or "corrupt" (as in Philippians 2:15 and 2 Thessalonians 3:2). Men will say what others want to hear in order to gain confidence, support, and submission from those who will not hold them accountable to the truth.

❑ **"To draw away the disciples after them"**: This speaks not only of action, but more so of motive. The purpose for the "speaking perverse things" is to gain control of the weak and unsuspecting. Christians are supposed to "draw near to God" (James 4:8), but these men will seduce others to draw *away* from Him and *to* themselves. A person cannot draw near to God if he is being drawn away to (or by) something else.

❑ **"Therefore be on the alert"**: Safeguarding the flock requires an unrelenting attention to what exactly is happening; any relaxing of the elders' efforts, settling into complacency, or dereliction of duty may provide opportunity for the enemy (2 Corinthians 2:11, Ephesians 4:27, and 1 Peter 5:8). Elders must not be paranoid, but wise; they must not resort to dictatorial methods to prevent anyone from "stepping out of line," yet vigilant against danger. They must be watchful, attuned to the needs of their "sheep," and attentive to any threat against the flock. "Forewarned is to be forearmed."[514]

❑ **"Remembering that...I did not cease to admonish each one with tears"**: Paul uses himself as an example of what he is saying. To "admonish" means to both warn and encourage simultaneously; it implies reminding someone of their duty (to which they themselves had once committed). Paul did this regularly; he expects the Ephesian elders to do the same. That he did this "with tears" indicates the gentleness and care that he exercised while admonishing others (see 1 Thessalonians 2:1-9). That he did this "night and day for...three years" attests to his pattern of behavior. He did not do this just once or twice, or now and then, but regularly and deliberately. ("Three years" is likely a rounded-up number, not meant to exaggerate but simply to summarize quickly.)

"And now I commend you" (20:32)—lit., I commit (to you) this charge; I entrust this responsibility to you (see Acts 14:23, 1 Timothy 6:12-14, and 2 Timothy 4:1-2 for similar commendations). Elders are expected

---

514   Robertson, *Word Pictures*, 355.

to "build up" the church (cf. Ephesians 4:11-12); they themselves will be built up if they carry out their responsibilities rightly. In due time, they will receive the inheritance promised by God (Colossians 3:23-24, 1 Peter 5:4). Paul then reminds the elders of his integrity and conduct among them, how he has not taken advantage of them in any way (20:33-34).[515] "Working hard" (20:35) is not limited to physical labor; it includes mental, emotional, and spiritual exertion as well.[516] His intentions have been godly; his hands have been busy earning his own keep, not idle or engaged in any impropriety ("we toil, working with our own hands"—1 Corinthians 4:12). His attention to the (spiritually) "weak" and (economically) "poor" is clearly evident to these men (Romans 15:1, Galatians 2:10, et al); he is not one to show partiality to those who are wealthy or popular. "It is more blessed to give than to receive" (20:35) is a quote from Christ that is found nowhere in the gospels. (See Paul's further comments on this thought in 2 Corinthians 8:9 and Philippians 4:15-19.) This indicates that he has knowledge of Jesus' teachings that exceeds our own.

After this, the elders (and others?) become emotionally and visibly upset over Paul's departure (20:36-38). "He knelt down and prayed" gives us a glimpse into what may have been a common posture of prayer among the early saints (see also Acts 21:5 and Ephesians 3:14). Kneeling physically demonstrates the humility and submission of the heart; kneeling in prayer is an act of worship of God. "Whenever love has welded souls together, a time of parting is a time of open crying."[517] It is impressive to see how dear to these people Paul has become—and how passionately he worked and prayed for them. "And they accompanied him to the ship"—it is an ancient custom to escort family and friends on the early part of their journey abroad, or to the point of their actual departure (as in Genesis 18:16). Paul has his share of enemies, but he also has numerous fellow workers in the Lord who support him, care about him, and offer him encouragement.

---

515   One cannot help but note the similarities here to Samuel's address to the people near the end of his own ministry (1 Samuel 12:1-5).

516   Kistemaker, *Acts*, 738.

517   Reese, *Book of Acts*, 757.

∼ Chapters 21 – 23 ∼
Paul's Arrest and Defense before the Jews

The third missionary journey winds to a close (21:1-6)
The narrative concerning Paul's journey to Jerusalem by way of Antioch of Syria (beginning in 20:3) is more detailed than usual, and employs a number of nautical terms and geographical information (21:1-6). There are two main reasons for this. First, Luke is present on this journey, and his eyewitness account of these things is to be expected. Second, this account culminates in Paul's arrest in Jerusalem, an event (and its aftermath) which dominates the rest of the book. Those who maintain that Acts is largely a defense of Paul's legal innocence find their strongest support in the following chapters. So far, Luke has made great efforts to inform the reader that Paul has:

❑ Been exonerated in every civil case in which he has been accused (directly or indirectly) with violating Roman law.

❑ Been exonerated in every doctrinal matter (including the issue of circumcision—Acts 15) in which he has been accused of disregarding the Law of Moses.

❑ Shown consistent and virtuous character in all his dealings with men and women, which contradicts the false claims of his rivals and enemies that he preaches only for fame and/or money (as addressed in 2 Corinthians 10 – 12).

❑ Preached a unified and consistent gospel to all people, without being selective or partial to anyone in any place.

❑ Labored with his own hands when it was necessary to generate his own income (Acts 18:3, 20:34, and 1 Thessalonians 2:9). When it was expedient to do so, Paul relied on private donations from fellow Christians, but not necessarily from those whom he was teaching at the time (cf. 2 Corinthians 11:7-9).

❑ Suffered physically and personally—perhaps more or more often than any apostle, evangelist, or other Christian has ever suffered—for his ministry and in honor of his Lord (cf. 2 Corinthians 11:23-28 and 2 Timothy 1:12).

There is no need to limit Luke's narrative to a legal defense for Paul, however. It is more appropriate and practical to see Paul as a representative of *all* Christians as they stand trial before opposing religions or secular governing authorities. It is true that Paul's case is the one under scrutiny here; it is not true that his case serves as the overriding purpose for this account, or that this was ever Luke's or the Holy Spirit's purpose for preserving this record. It is one thing, in other words, to learn what happened to Paul when he went through his legal ordeals; it is another thing to know that *any* Christian going through his or her own legal ordeal will benefit from Paul's experiences.

The ship carrying Paul and his companions sails from Miletus and stops at two small islands just off the mainland, Cos and Rhodes.[518] From there, it puts in at the small port of Patara on the southern coastline of the small province of Lycia. At this point, the traveling party changes ships, having found one that is bound directly for Tyre on the Palestinian coastline. The ship sails south of the island of Cyprus ("leaving it on the left") and lands on the coast of Syria[519] at Tyre where it unloads its cargo. Tyre is an ancient Mediterranean seaport of great historical reputation, being once one of the most powerful trade centers in the world. In the present account, however, Tyre's status has been considerably reduced; it is no longer the proud, self-sufficient city that it once was (see comments on Acts 12:20ff). Paul probably visited the Christians in Tyre when he came through Phoenicia on his way to Jerusalem for the council with the other apostles (recall 15:3); now he has opportunity to rekindle his friendship with them. This church was likely established as a result of the scattering of Jewish Christians from Jerusalem, as noted in Acts 11:19—a scattering for which Paul himself was, ironically, largely responsible.

---

518   "Rhodes" means "roses"; this island received a great deal of sun throughout the year and this produced remarkable roses. At the entrance to the city of Rhodes (on the island of the same name) once stood a bronze statue of the god Helios. This statue, called the Colossus of Rhodes, stood just over one hundred feet tall and is considered one of the Seven Wonders of the ancient world. It was built in 300 BC, but destroyed by an earthquake in 244 BC; the remnants of it were still visible when Paul visited that island on this journey (McGarvey, *Acts of Apostles*, 2:196; Coffman, *Commentary on Acts*, 399). "'In 600 AD, its remains were sold to a Jew by the conquering Saracens. It took 900 camels to carry the brass away'" (quoted in Reese, *Book of Acts*, 778).

519   "'Syria' was the name given to the whole eastern coast of the Mediterranean Sea from Cilicia in the north to Egypt in the south. It included Phoenicia and Palestine" (Reese, *Book of Acts*, 779).

Paul and company stay with the brethren in Tyre for a week, during which time the prophets among them "kept telling Paul through the Spirit not to set foot in Jerusalem" (21:4). This statement must be taken in context: it cannot be that Paul is intentionally going to defy the Holy Spirit, especially since the Lord gives His blessing to this entire journey (see Acts 9:15-16, 23:11, and Romans 15:15-32). Rather, it must mean that this is these people's *interpretation* of the situation as they understand it. "Through the Spirit" here does not have the same context as an actual prophecy or divine revelation (where we would expect a "the Spirit *says*"-kind of statement), as what Agabus will shortly provide (in 21:10-11). "When our days were ended" (21:5) means literally, "When our time was up," referring to the fact that the ship's cargo has been unloaded and the captain is ready to continue the voyage down the coastline.[520] The traveling party is given a very personal and tender farewell, joined not only by the Christian men of Tyre but also their wives and children (21:5-6).

Paul in Caesarea (21:7-14)

About 30 miles south of Tyre is the coastal city of Ptolemais in what once was the tribal territory of Asher. It was originally known as Acco (Judges 1:31), and re-named after Ptolemais II of Egypt (ruled 285 – 246 BC).[521] Paul and his companions meet with another group of Christians that we have not known about until now (21:7). Another 35 miles southward—about a two days' journey—is Caesarea, the city of Herod's private residence (recall 12:19). This is Paul's third known visit to this city (recall 9:30 and 18:22). While in Caesarea, he stays at the home of "Philip the evangelist" (21:8)—the same Philip who was "one of the seven" chosen to serve tables in the early church (recall 6:1-6) and who brought the gospel to Samaria (recall chapter 8, especially verse 40). This may have been an awkward meeting for Paul and Philip—or perhaps it was intentional—since Philip and Stephen were fellow workers at the time of Stephen's martyrdom (an execution which Paul had supported at the time). Yet, we do not sense animosity

---

520   Kistemaker, *Acts of the Apostles*, 746.

521   Bruce, *The Book of the Acts*, 423.

or bitterness, but mutual friendship and respect, and especially Philip's generous hospitality. This is an excellent example of how two men refused to allow an ugly past to interfere with their far more important obligation to Christ and His church. Philip also has "four virgin daughters who were prophetesses" (21:9), indicating that the (miraculous) gift of prophecy has not been limited to men, but is also extended to women (recall Joel's prophecy, quoted in 2:18).[522]

During the travelers' stay in Caesarea, Agabus—probably the same prophet as mentioned in 11:27-28—finds Paul and prophesies concerning him (21:10-14). He does not just provide a verbal testimony, but demonstrates his prophecy in a manner similar to that of an Old Testament prophet (i.e., using an object lesson to symbolize what is to come). He binds his hands and feet as a premonition of Paul's being bound by the authorities in Jerusalem (recall 20:22-23). Paul will thus be delivered "into the hands of the Gentiles [i.e., the Romans]" (21:11), language similar to what Jesus spoke (Mark 10:33). Upon hearing this, the brethren try convincing Paul from even going to Jerusalem, but he will not hear them. "What are you doing, weeping and breaking my heart?" (21:13)—their tears and appeals certainly weigh heavy on him, but he is resolved to go nonetheless.[523] He is fully committed to his servitude to the Lord. Thus, "The will of the Lord be done!"—this is not a sigh of resignation, but instead defers to Paul's intimate knowledge that the Lord would not purposely lead him anywhere that He did not want him to go.[524]

---

522   "The designation 'virgin' probably indicates not merely the bare fact that they were not yet married, but may also indicate that they had devoted themselves to the single life in order that they could devote their whole time to the service of Christ" (Reese, *Book of Acts*, 785); see 1 Corinthians 7:32-34.

523   "The verb 'breaking' is a very picturesque word, being used of the pounding that a washerwoman would give clothes to get them to yield in her efforts to clean them. ... It was with no stoic hardness that he [Paul] resisted their pleadings. They almost talked him out of going on with the trip" (ibid., 788).

524   In Acts 16:6-7, the Holy Spirit (also referred to as "the Spirit of Jesus") *forbade* Paul and Silas from going into either Asia Minor or Bithynia. Thus, it would have been a sin on these men's part to have gone into these regions against the will of God's Spirit. In the present case, however, the Spirit is not *forbidding* Paul to go, but most certainly is predicting that severe difficulties await him when he *does*. Thus, Paul is not acting against the Holy Spirit by going to Jerusalem, but is simply being warned of what lies ahead.

Paul arrives in Jerusalem (21:15-26)

The route from Caesarea to Jerusalem follows well-traveled roads, but is still a difficult, 65-mile journey through the mountains of Judea (21:15). "Some of the disciples from Caesarea" indicates a church in that city that we did not know of until now; "Mnason of Cyprus" is mentioned only here; he may have a residence in Jerusalem (21:16). Paul's entourage now consists of perhaps a dozen or more men. Once they arrive in Jerusalem, the weary travelers are received "gladly" (21:17)—not only because they are special and important guests, but also because they bring a large sum of money that will be distributed to needy brethren in that area. Palestine has been hit very hard with drought and subsequent crop losses for years; people are starving, and the resources of the brethren have been severely strained. Since this monetary relief will allow them to purchase food from areas not devastated by drought, it is most certainly a welcome gift. The "pillars" of that church—James, Cephas [Peter], and John—entrusted Paul with the responsibility to "remember the poor" (Galatians 2:9-10), and this collected donation certainly fulfills that request. Incidentally, this officially ends (what we refer to as) Paul's third missionary journey.

"James" (21:18) is the same man who was mentioned in Acts 12:17 and 15:13. As mentioned earlier, he is the physical brother of Christ, probably an elder of the church in Jerusalem, and most certainly a very influential man among the brethren. Paul (and his companions) meet with James and the other elders, and relate their experiences—and successes—during their long ministry to the Gentiles (21:19). But it appears that James' real intent of this meeting is to involve Paul in a strategy designed to help address Jewish sensitivities toward bringing the gospel to uncircumcised heathens. James begins by stating the obvious (21:20-21): There are "many thousands...among the Jews of those who have believed, and they are all zealous for the Law"—i.e., there are many Jewish Christians in Jerusalem who still hold the Law of Moses in high regard, some continuing to teach it or even practice it in part. They believe that Jesus is the Christ, but they refuse (as yet) to release their tenacious grip on the Law. Accordingly, these Jews believe that Paul is dishonoring the Law by telling Gentile believers that they do not have to observe it. (Remember that this is the same James who earlier [15:19-21] agreed that the Law is not binding on Gentiles, so he is stating what *others* believe, not what he himself believes.)

"What, then, is to be done?" (21:22). James is in a predicament: he sympathizes with both sides, but cannot support them both equally. Nonetheless, he has a plan (21:23ff). He indicates that four Jewish Christians are "under a vow"—i.e., they have taken an oath according to the Law, possibly a temporary Nazirite vow (cf. Numbers 6:1-21)—and are near its completion. The final stage of this vow requires the shaving of their heads as well as an offering of certain animals. James asks Paul to enter into the Temple and participate in this process, which requires Paul also to undergo the process of ritual purification (21:26). The purpose here apparently is to show that "there is nothing to the things which they [i.e., the Jewish Christians] have been told about you, but that you yourself also walk orderly, keeping the Law" (21:24).

This last phrase appears problematic, since it seems to imply that Paul is still *under* the Law of Moses, and that he has not fully conceded that the gospel of Christ is the only "law" which Christians are to obey. If we compare this with other passages which Paul has written, however, this cannot be the case (recall 13:38-39, Galatians 2:15-21, Romans 8:1-4, et al).[525] Furthermore, Paul's intention is to become all things to all people, in order to win them to Christ (cf. 1 Corinthians 9:19-23). The fact that the people he is trying to win here are already Christians does not nullify this principle. He has said elsewhere that he is willing to forego his own will in order to avoid being a stumbling block for his fellow brother in Christ (Romans 14:13-19, 1 Corinthians 10:23-33).[526]

---

525   It was not a violation of the gospel for Paul to offer *ceremonial* blood sacrifices designed for the purpose of ritual cleansings and matters of personal conscience. Such are the offerings that Paul is asked to make for the sake of these men. However, it *would* be a violation of the gospel for him to offer blood sacrifices for the purpose of *atonement* (i.e., to re-establish fellowship with God through the blood of animals), since this contradicts and is offensive to the "once for all" offering of Jesus Christ for this purpose (see Hebrews 10:1-18).

526   While Paul has every right to become "all things to all men" (cf. 1 Corinthians 9:22) for the sake of winning them to the gospel, he does *not* have the right to: violate his own conscience (Romans 14:22-23); or violate any of the commandments of the gospel. Likewise, *no* Christian today has the right to violate these things, no matter how

He does not want it being said that he is trying to discredit the Law of Moses—especially not while in Jerusalem. The preaching of the gospel must not be at the *expense* of the Law, but a *fulfillment* of it (see Acts 24:14-15, for example).

Even so, this entire scenario raises all sorts of unanswerable questions and invites a variety of speculations. Some commentators accuse Paul of not yet fully understanding the break between the Law of Moses and the gospel of Christ.[527] Other commentators think that both James and Paul are doing what they *think* is right, but are swept up in circumstances beyond their control.[528] Robertson offers a sound assessment:

> The question arises whether Paul acted wisely or unwisely in agreeing to the suggestion of James. What he did was in perfect harmony with his principle of accommodation in 1 Cor. 9:20 when no principle was involved. It is charged that here on this occasion Paul was unduly influenced by considerations of expediency and was willing for the Jewish Christians to believe him [to be] more of a Jew than was true in order to placate the situation in Jerusalem. Furneaux calls it a compromise and a failure. I do not so see it. To say that is to obscure the whole complex situation. What Paul did was not for the purpose of conciliating his opponents, the Judaizers, who had diligently spread falsehoods about him in Jerusalem as in Corinth. [Rather] it was solely to break the power of these "false apostles" over the thousands in Jerusalem who have been deluded by Paul's accusers.[529]

At the same time, James maintains the same position that was decided upon during the so-called council in Jerusalem: the Law is not imposed upon the Gentiles, who have been given specific instructions concerning

---

noble, seemingly important, or urgent the matter is with which he is confronted.

527   McGarvey, *Acts of Apostles*, 2:208-209.

528   Coffman, *Commentary on Acts*, 408-410.

529   Robertson, *Word Pictures*, 374-375; bracketed words are mine.

their behavior (recall 15:19ff). This seems at first to be hypocritical, for it *does* appear that James and the others *do* believe that "God had two plans, one for Gentiles and another for Jews."[530] There may be a kernel of truth to this thought, since the Jews might still think of themselves as *more enlightened* Christians, and therefore still have a positional advantage over the Gentiles (given the attitude of "certain men from James" [i.e., Jewish Christians from Jerusalem] mentioned in Galatians 2:11-14). "He [Paul] might well have hoped, by thus complying with the legal ceremony, to conciliate those, at least, who were only hostile to him because they believed him hostile to their national worship. And, so far as the great body of the Church at Jerusalem was concerned, he probably succeeded."[531] But we will never know if even this is truly the case. Bruce says, "There is no evidence that his action produced any such reassuring effect on the zealots for the law as James and his fellow-elders had hoped; and it certainly brought Paul himself into trouble of the gravest kind. But he cannot fairly be charged with a compromise of his own gospel principles."[532]

The situation that Paul agrees to is hardly a simple one, but is complicated by deeply embedded traditions, preconceived ideas, racial tension, and religious zeal. "The issue between them [Paul and James]," Stott writes, "concerned culture, ceremony and tradition. The solution to which they came was not a compromise, in the sense of sacrificing a doctrinal or moral principle, but a concession in the area of practice."[533] Whether or not it is wise for Paul to have consented to James' plan is not easy to determine, likely because there is more to this scenario than we are told or would even appreciate (from our 21st century perspective). Adam Clarke has well summed up this scenario: "However we may consider this subject, it is exceedingly difficult to account for the conduct of James and the elders, and of Paul on this occasion. There seems to be something in this transaction which we do

---

530   Coffman, *Commentary on Acts*, 408.

531   Conybeare and Howson, *Life and Epistles*, 576; bracketed word is mine.

532   Bruce, *The Book of the Acts*, 432.

533   Stott, *The Spirit, the Church, and the World*, 342; bracketed words are mine.

not fully understand."[534] God allows Paul to make his own decisions,
unless it is necessary for Him to intervene otherwise. The rest of Acts
will indicate for certain that God's hand is in this matter (consider
23:11, for example), regardless of whether or not we personally
approve of it.

Paul's arrest in Jerusalem (21:27-40)

The "seven days" (21:27) refers to the period of "days of purification"
from 21:26. Paul must give notice to the priests as to when he and the
four other men will be ready (or, ritually purified) to enter the temple
area where the sacrificial altar is located. Jewish men who are not
priests may enter, however, into the so-called Court of Israel, which is
apparently where Paul is when the "Jews from Asia" happen upon him.
(These Jews are perhaps those who contended with Paul in Ephesus
[recall 19:9], and who are now in Jerusalem to observe Pentecost.) A
Gentile is not permitted to enter into the restricted area of the temple
(i.e., the Court of Israel); he is instead confined to the Court of the
Gentiles, which is an open court that surrounds the inner court.[535] In
fact, stone plaques on the wall of the courtyard warn trespassers that
this is a capital offense: "These stones are known as the Thanatos
Inscription Stones, and they state, 'No man of alien race is to enter
within the barricade which surrounds the temple. Anyone who is
caught doing so will have himself to blame for the penalty of death that
follows.'"[536]

These "Jews from Asia" inflame the suspicions of the Jewish
community in Jerusalem by accusing Paul of exactly what it most
feared—that is, that Paul opposes the Law of Moses and is thus
purposely desecrating the temple, "this holy place" (21:28). These Jews
have seen Trophimus, who is a Gentile from Ephesus, associating with
Paul in the city, and erroneously assume that Paul has brought this man
into the temple (21:29). Given the volatile, hypersensitive passions of

---

534   Adam Clarke, *Clarke's Commentary on the Whole Bible*, vol. 5 (New York:
Abingdon-Cokesbury Press [no date]), 860.

535   Bruce, *The Book of the Acts*, 433.

536   Mitchell, "Acts of the Apostles," 21.3-4; see also Bruce, *The Book of the Acts*,
434.

the Jews regarding Paul's ministry to the Gentiles—passions shared by both (Jewish) Christians and non-Christians alike on this particular matter—this is the only spark necessary to ignite a riot (21:30). Boles says: "They based their charges against Paul on a mere supposition, but their supposition was false; they did not care whether it was false or true, [since] it served them well to make charges against Paul."[537] Gaertner agrees: "The charges of the Asian Jews were ridiculous. Why would Paul risk violating the customs of the temple on the very day that he was participating in a ceremony to show his respect for Jewish religious customs?"[538]

Despite the lack of proof behind the accusations, Paul is literally dragged out of the temple, the inner court of which is immediately locked up by temple police (21:30).[539] The mob begins beating Paul, and may well kill him except that news of the tumult reaches the attention of Claudius Lysias (cf. 23:26), the commander of the Roman military battalion stationed in Jerusalem (21:31-32).[540] (Roman soldiers are on high alert anyway, since Jerusalem is swollen with visitors because of Pentecost.) The close proximity of the Fortress of Antonia,[541] where the Roman soldiers are stationed, allows these soldiers to intervene almost immediately. Their presence may well have saved Paul's life, since the Jews are pummeling him in a serious attempt to kill him. Upon seeing the soldiers coming, however, these Jews stop beating Paul for fear of themselves being beaten, arrested, or killed.

---

537   Boles, *A Commentary on Acts*, 345; bracketed word is mine.

538   Gaertner, *Acts*, 339.

539   This refers to the doors between the Court of the Gentiles and the Court of the Women. "The captain was in charge of maintaining order in and around the temple complex. By shutting the doors, he prevented the crowd from rioting within the courts. If the crowd should kill Paul on the sacred temple grounds, his blood would defile the temple (II Kings 11:15-16, II Chron. 24:21)" (Kistemaker, *Acts*, 769).

540   Lysias is referred to as a *chiliarch* (also known as a "tribune"), one who commanded a thousand men (760 infantrymen and 240 cavalrymen), or one-sixth of a legion. He had ten centurions under his command. Today, he would be commensurate with a major or colonel (Reese, *Book of Acts*, 803; Kistemaker, *Acts*, 769; and Gaertner, *Acts*, 340).

541   This is an ancient fortress rebuilt by Herod the Great and named after his friend, Mark Antony. It had four towers, and was directly connected to the Court of the Gentiles by two flights of stairs (Reese, *Book of Acts*, 803).

Paul's arrest in the midst of the capital of Judaism is an enormous blow to his credibility among the Jews in general. "Paul was put in chains to show the crowd he wasn't being rescued. However, this has damaged Paul and the gospel before the eyes of the Jews, some of whom are new Christians or investigators. It was seen as confirmation of his guilt in the ancient prejudice surrounding putting a person in chains."[542] But Lysias is still unable to make any sense of the reason for the commotion, so he decides to bring Paul up to the barracks (in the Fortress of Antonia) for questioning (21:33-34). On the stairs leading to the barracks, however, Paul addresses Lysias directly in Greek. Until this time, Lysias assumed Paul to be an Egyptian messiah-figure who, three years before, had led a large number of followers to the Mount of Olives to witness the alleged collapse of the walls of Jerusalem (21:37-38). Once the walls collapsed (so it was predicted), armed men would rush in, overthrow the Romans, and take full possession of the city. Once Felix the governor heard of this, however, he sought this leader (who conveniently disappeared) and killed 400 of his followers.[543] Lysias thus assumes that Paul is this Egyptian against whom the people want to vent their anger and have executed.

But Paul is not this Egyptian (21:39). He speaks in fluent *Koine* Greek, and identifies himself as a Jew *and* "a citizen of no insignificant city"—Tarsus in the Roman province of Cilicia—which is among the most influential cities in the Roman Empire.[544] Paul has not (yet) stated

---

542   Mitchell, "Acts of the Apostles," 21.5.

543   See Josephus, "Wars," 2.13.5; "Antiquities," 20.8.6. This crusade against the Romans was especially supported by Jewish zealots, who believed that Roman rule should be overthrown with violence; such zealotry later incited the Jewish Revolts (AD 66 – 70) and the destruction of Jerusalem. "Assassins" (or "dagger-men") is here translated from *sicarii*, which is an adaptation of the name for the short, curved daggers (*sica*) these men used. The assassins would secretly infiltrate the crowds in Jerusalem and quietly murder Roman sympathizers (especially Sadducees), then join those who crowded around the fallen victim as though they were innocent passersby (Reese, *Book of Acts*, 806; Bruce, *The Book of the Acts*, 437; et al).

544   "...Paul's assertion that he was both a Jew and a Tarsian was probably more than simply a legal self-description. It may also have amounted to an offended rebuttal. To be mistaken for an Egyptian was a social slur of no small degree. Jews who lived in Alexandria resented being identified as Egyptians. The offensiveness of the designation would have been compounded if, as in this case, a Jew who boasted his religious faithfulness was identified as an Egyptian false-prophet" (Rapske, "Paul in Roman

that he is a Roman *citizen*; he will play that card only when absolutely necessary. For now, Paul insists on speaking to the crowd in "the Hebrew dialect," or Jewish Aramaic, the vernacular used by the Jews since their return from Babylonian captivity. "Paul had faced many audiences and crowds, but never one quite like this."[545] Nonetheless, he seems to believe that, if given a chance to explain himself, he will dispel the fears and suspicions of this crowd. Also, by addressing the people in their own native tongue, he identifies with them and comes across as less threatening (21:40). Motioning or gesturing to the people with his (likely outstretched) hand indicates informs the audience that Paul is about to speak. Bruce provides a dramatic analogy:

> If an audience of Welsh or Irish nationalists, about to be addressed by someone whom they regarded as a traitor to the national cause, suddenly realized that he was speaking to them not in the despised Saxon tongue but in the Celtic vernacular, the gesture would no doubt call forth at least a temporary measure of good will. So it was with this Jerusalem mob as they realized that the man whom they execrated as a renegade was addressing them in Aramaic. The silence which they had reluctantly granted to Paul's beckoning hand became deeper still, and they allowed him to go on.[546]

Paul's Defense before the Jews (22:1 – 23:35)

Paul recounts his conversion story to the Jews (22:1-22)
Until his arrest, Paul has been a free man. From this point forward (in Acts), he will be held in Roman custody. Luke pays a great deal of attention to Paul's arrival at Jerusalem, then his arrest, and then his subsequent speeches. It is clear that he (Luke) seeks to exonerate Paul's character as well as his ministry through accurately detailing exactly what happened (versus what people *think* has happened through rumors or misinformation). We should not forget, however, that Christ

---

Custody," 137).

545   Robertson, *Word Pictures*, 383.

546   Bruce, *The Book of the Acts*, 439.

is still the main character of this work, not Paul. Paul would not have been arrested except for his devotion to Christ; he would have no gospel to preach—or defend—except for the apostleship entrusted to him by Christ (Romans 1:1). While much attention will be given to the political and legal factors surrounding Paul and his detainment, we can see the work of Christ still being accomplished. As Paul will write later, "Remember Jesus Christ, risen from the dead, descendant of David, according to my gospel, for which I suffer hardship even to imprisonment as a criminal; but the word of God is not imprisoned" (2 Timothy 2:8-9).

While no formal charge is yet brought against him, Paul is fully aware of the animosities toward him by his own countrymen. He is accused of being hostile to the Law of Moses and (thus) the temple. Ironically, these are the same accusations made against Stephen (recall 6:13), to whose martyrdom Paul had given his consent.

Paul begins his speech: "Brethren and fathers, hear my defense..." (22:1). In the Greek text, it reads, "Men, brethren, and fathers." "Men" [Greek, *aner*] is the general term for a male person, possibly to address the Gentile proselytes in the crowd. "Brethren" is the customary and familial manner in which the Jewish people regard each other. They are all "brethren" [Greek: *adelphos*, "brothers"]—thus, *family*—in the sense that they can all trace their lineage through the twelve patriarchs to a common ancestor (i.e., Jacob, but ultimately Abraham, who they regard as their most distinguished "father"—see Matthew 3:9, Luke 16:24, John 8:39, et al). "Fathers" [Greek, *pater*] likely is a term of respect that Paul uses to properly address the older Jewish men in the crowd who are heads of extended families, community leaders, and teachers of the Law.[547] Thus, Paul begins his address with an ascending recognition of respect. Upon hearing Paul speak in their own dialect, the crowd grows even quieter, no doubt because now they know that he is one of their own (i.e., a genuine Jew and not an Egyptian or some other foreigner).

---

547 Greek words and definitions taken from *The Complete Word Study: New Testament*, Spiros Zodhiates, ed. (© 1991, AMG International, Inc.; database © 2008 WORDsearch Corp.; electronic edition).

The substance of Paul's speech to the Jews is as follows (22:3-21):

- ❑ **22:3** Paul first authenticates his own integrity as a Jew, "educated under Gamaliel" (recall 5:34),[548] in strict observance of everything these Jews hold dear—and then some (see 2 Corinthians 11:22, Galatians 1:13-14, and Philippians 3:4-6). Thus, instead of desecrating God's Law *or* His Temple, he is certainly "zealous for God," just as these people claim to be. "Strictly" implies a mathematical precision or a minute exactness—i.e., there is nothing passive, cavalier, or half-hearted about his (former) adherence to the Law.[549]

- ❑ **22:4-5** The "Way" refers to Christianity, which Paul originally viewed as a threat to the Law. He had been determined to exterminate this so-called heretical sect "to the death" (recall 9:1-2), and had the priest's full cooperation for doing so, including "all the Council of the elders." In other words, there are a substantial number of significant witnesses who can attest to his sincerity and zeal in carrying out this persecution against the followers of Christ.

- ❑ **22:6-10** Only something as powerful as a divine revelation could have deterred a man so zealous and powerful—and fiercely stubborn—as Paul. The account of his on-the-road-to-Damascus experience, with minor (but not contradictory) differences, has already been covered in Acts 9:3-9. (A comparison of these accounts will be made in comments on 26:9ff.) Notice that Paul does not defend his campaign against "the Way" to the Lord, nor does he make any complaints to Him. Rather, he makes it clear to his listeners that Jesus was in full control of the situation; Paul was not in a position to do anything other than what he was told. ("Jesus of Nazareth" is how the Jews regarded the Lord. He did not on that occasion refer to Himself as "Jesus *Christ* the Nazarene," as Peter did when accusing the Jews of His death [recall 4:10]. Jesus' intent was only to identify Himself to Paul, not to indict him for his

---

548   Literally, "at the feet" of Gamaliel. "When Paul received his education, he and his fellow students would sit on the floor while their teacher sat on a platform. They literally sat at his feet" (Kistemaker, *Acts*, 781; bracketed words are mine). See more on Gamaliel in comments on 5:34.

549   Robertson, *Word Pictures*, 387.

actions, since this went without saying.)

❑ **22:11-16** This parallels Paul's account in 9:10-17, minus the discussion Ananias had with the Lord. However, we learn here more about Ananias' good reputation, which is Paul's way of saying, "It was not just *me* who became convinced of Jesus' authority, but virtuous men like Ananias did, too." We also learn more of what he said to Paul, which is significant. In fact, there was probably much discussion between Paul and Ananias that went unrecorded. It was necessary for Paul to "see the Righteous One" so that he could be "a witness for Him"—even though Jesus *blinded* him in order to get his attention. Furthermore, Paul's obedience to the gospel provides a critical link between baptism, forgiveness of one's sins, and "calling on His name" (recall 2:21). Ananias' expression, "the God of our fathers," and his reference to the "Righteous One" link Paul's experience to the Jews' anticipation of the Messiah (Isaiah 53:11, Jeremiah 23:5, et al). He also tells Paul what to do to identify with Christ (Messiah) and receive forgiveness in "His name" (22:16). "Here baptism is clearly set forth as one of the conditions of the remission of sins, and not merely as a symbol of what had already been done."[550] All modern allegations that Paul was not interested in baptism (which is almost entirely based upon a mishandling of 1 Corinthians 1:17) overlook the fact that he himself was baptized in

---

550   Boles, *A Commentary on Acts*, 355. Albert Barnes—despite his Calvinistic beliefs—writes: "There is nothing in baptism itself that can wash away sin. That can be done only by the pardoning mercy of God through the atonement of Christ. But baptism is expressive of a willingness to be pardoned in that way, and is a solemn declaration of our conviction that there is no other way of remission..." (*Barnes' Notes*, 53). While baptism *itself* does not remove sin, it is inseparable from the *process* of one's sins being removed, inasmuch as it is a required act of faith of the one who wishes to be forgiven. John MacArthur, on the other hand, speaks for the modern evangelical movement when he writes, "Ananias's words in verse 16, when properly understood, are in full agreement with the New Testament teaching that salvation is by faith alone" (*The MacArthur New Testament Commentary: Acts 13 – 28* [Chicago: Moody Press, 1996], 269). The word "alone" is the problem here, since nowhere in the NT is it stated that we are saved or justified by faith *alone*. Nonetheless, he goes on to say: "A literal translation of the verse says, 'Arise, get yourself baptized and your sins washed away, having called on his name.' Both imperatives reflect the reality that Paul had already called on the Lord's name, which is the act that saves" (269). Such creative interpretation is necessary in order to support a "faith only" dogma, but there is no logical way to evade the fact that *baptism* is the means by which Paul is told to *call* upon the Lord (or, make an appeal to Him) for salvation, which is consistent with what Peter instructed in Acts 2:21, 37-41, and 1 Peter 3:21.

order to become a Christian.[551]

❑ **22:17-20** This section is not found in Luke's earlier account, but
it is easily implied (see 9:29-30). Paul did not understand why
he had to leave Jerusalem, but Christ sent him away for his own
good *and* for the good of the church at that time. He protests
at first, however, claiming that his radical transformation from
a persecutor of "the Way" to a supporter of it will be especially
convincing to the Jews. Yet, this is not true; the reaction to Paul's
present speech will prove this. Furthermore, Christ has big plans
for Paul and knows what He is doing (recall 9:15-16). In any case,
it is important to Paul's audience that this vision took place while
he was "praying in the temple" (22:17). It is also at this point that
Paul identifies himself as a supporter of Stephen (whom he calls
Jesus' "martyr") rather than to identify any longer with those who
stoned him (recall 7:54-60). This is an indirect indictment against
those men, but also against himself for having supported Stephen's
martyrdom in the first place.

❑ **22:21** Jesus' plans for Paul are then clearly stated: "Go! For I will
send you far away to the Gentiles [Greek, *ethnos*, lit., non-Jewish
people or nations]."

The Jews listen intently to Paul until now, but as soon as he speaks of
being "sent" to the Gentiles, they tune him out (22:22). While the Jews
may tolerate Gentiles for their own reasons, they are certainly not going
to regard them as equals before God. In a very real sense, they are
not going to share *their* Messiah—assuming Jesus *is* Messiah—with a
bunch of uncircumcised foreigners. Not even a vision of God's Son, the
conversion of one of the most aggressive foes against the church, or the
testimony of a Jewish scholar could overcome the intense exclusivity
that the Jews claimed to have with God. Furthermore, what Christ said
to Paul underscores the Jews' guiltiness concerning Christ's crucifixion,
Stephen's stoning, and their persecution of "the Way." Inasmuch as
Paul was in error for persecuting Christ, then so are *all* Jews who do
the same thing.

---

551 "In light of these facts, what an incredible folly is the theological nonsense that
would make baptism into Christ either optional or unessential for them who would be
saved!" (Coffman, *Commentary on Acts*, 182).

Paul asserts his Roman citizenship (22:23-29)

The scene erupts again into a vicious, animalistic mob bent on nothing short of executing Paul—a scene somewhat reminiscent of the Jews' condemnation of Christ and, later, Stephen. The men throw off their cloaks (22:23), likely in preparation for stoning Paul, as we saw them do before (recall 7:58). The dust thrown into the air may be directed at Paul himself; "they would have pelted him with rocks if there had been any handy."[552] In any case, "These present participles give a lively picture of the uncontrolled excitement of the mob in their spasm of wild rage."[553]

The Romans believe that the best way to produce a genuine confession is through the application of much physical pain (22:24). To be "examined by scourging" is a barbaric and yet quite effective means of extracting information from someone—if indeed that person has anything to hide. This also is the scourging which Jesus Himself received prior to His crucifixion. Scourging refers to a whipping with leather straps (attached to a wooden handle), the ends of which have been weighted with bits of bone or metal so as to purposely lacerate the skin. Paul will later record that he had indeed endured "thirty nine lashes" five times at the hands of the Jews (2 Corinthians 11:24). Yet, Roman scourging can be more devastating than Jewish scourging, since the Romans have no limit to the number of lashes inflicted, whereas the Jews will give no more than 39 lashes (so as not to accidentally violate the Law; see Deuteronomy 25:3). Blows usually are applied to the back and thighs, though out of cruelty the scourger might strike the face or torso. Victims of scourging sometimes die during the bloody process or shortly thereafter, often from shock.[554]

As they tie Paul's hands to the whipping post with "thongs" (or, leather straps), Paul asks rhetorically, "Is it lawful for you to scourge a man who is a Roman and uncondemned?" (22:25). This is another way of saying, "This is *not* lawful, since I have not been convicted of any

---

552   Reese, *Book of Acts*, 810.

553   Robertson, *Word Pictures*, 393.

554   Henry E. Dosker, "Scourge; Scourging," *ISBE* (electronic edition).

crime!" When Paul addresses the Jews, he refers to his strong Jewish heritage; when he is before Roman officers, he refers to his privileged Roman citizenship. In neither case has Paul committed any injustice; he is simply using whatever resources he has at his disposal to promote his message (to the Jews) or protect his rights (as a Roman).

> The Tribune [Lysias] was the highest ranking officer in
> Jerusalem and an important man. [Yet he] is keenly aware that
> he stands in some peril for having mistreated a fellow Roman.
> …Long-standing prejudice would favour Paul above Lysias in
> the event of a formal complaint. Small wonder that the soldiers
> detailed to interrogate Paul withdrew immediately—perhaps
> even unbidden—and that the Tribune was seriously shaken by
> the disclosure…[555]

To claim Roman citizenship when it did not really exist is itself a crime punishable by execution[556]; therefore Lysias does not suspect that Paul is lying. But he does ask whether Paul's citizenship was natural (by birth) or acquired (by money); perhaps he does not think Paul is capable of such credentials because he does not seem capable of providing "a large sum of money" (22:26-27). (We must remember, too, that Paul's physical appearance at this point may contribute to Lysias' apparent skepticism: he has just been dragged and beaten, and is likely bruised, bloody, and disheveled.) Paul responds that "I was actually born a citizen" (22:28), making *his* citizenship more valuable and honorable than Lysias' own.[557] This not only impresses the

---

555   Rapske, "Paul in Roman Custody," 144-145; bracketed words are mine.

556   Conybeare and Howson, *Life and Epistles*, 589.

557   Gaertner writes: "Speculation abounds about how Paul became a Roman citizen. The fact that he was born a Roman citizen means that his father or grandfather before him was a Roman citizen. Often citizenship was awarded because of some notable deed performed for the state. Also slaves received citizenship when freed by their citizen-owners. Besides this, residents of cities were sometimes declared citizens if the city was made a Roman colony. Because nothing is known of Paul's family, his road to citizenship is unclear. It is also unclear how Paul would have proved his claim to Roman citizenship" (*Acts*, 351). Ramsay believes, "It is probable, but not certain, that the family [i.e., Paul's recent ancestors—CMS] had been planted in Tarsus with full rights as part of a colony settled there by one of the Seleucid kings in order to strengthen their hold on the city" (*St. Paul the Traveller*, 32). Regardless, Paul's claim

commander, but makes him all the more afraid of legal repercussions against him, since he has unwittingly violated Paul's legal rights. "Chains" here (in 22:29) is implied; literally, it reads "because he [Lysias] had bound him"; it refers to the bindings used to tie a prisoner to the scourging post, not mere shackles. (However, Paul will be bound with literal chains at least during some portions of his Roman imprisonment.)

Paul's defense before the Jewish Council (22:30 – 23:10)

The fact that Lysias is able to summon a special assembly of the Jewish Council (Sanhedrin) indicates his high command (22:30). This meeting has to be held in the Gentile Court of the Temple, if anywhere, since the Roman soldiers cannot enter the Jewish Court. The "chief priests" are actual members of the Council. Paul remains under Roman protection, but Lysias wants to resolve the matter, since he has been ordered to keep peace in Jerusalem—and he will be held accountable if he fails in this. Furthermore, because Paul is a Roman citizen, Lysias is legally bound to protect his rights.

Paul is set before the Council members, just as Peter, John, and Stephen had been set before them nearly 25 years prior. "Many times Paul had brought Christians before the Sanhedrin for trial. He was now to face this tribunal himself."[558] His first words—"I have lived my life with a perfectly good conscience before God up to this day" (23:1; see Acts 24:16)—incite immediate hostility. Literally, he says (in the Greek), "I have conducted myself as a good citizen...," which implies (since he is sitting trial for allegedly acting as an unlawful citizen) that his accusers are unjust.[559] Immediately, Ananias, the high priest, orders

---

has convinced the Philippian magistrates (16:37-39), a Roman commander (Lysias), and, later, Felix, Festus, and Agrippa II. While we do not have the details of how Paul acquired his citizenship, the *authenticity* of it is not under question. If he could convince those who lived in the Roman world (who have far better ability to ascertain these things than we do), then we also should be convinced by him. Their implicit testimony only buttresses Paul's own credentials.

558   Hester, *The Heart of the New Testament*, 313.

559   "Conscience" is from *suneidesis*, "joint-knowledge." It involves a perception of one's actions in the context of a guiding (moral) law (*Strong's* [electronic edition], #G4893). In the present case, Paul does *not* mean, "As far as I can tell, I have never sinned," since this cannot be true (Romans 3:23) and he admits elsewhere that he *has*

Paul to be struck on the mouth. It should be noted here that the text does not say that Paul *was* struck, but simply that the order was given for this.[560] Regardless, Paul counters this with a justifiable rebuke (23:3; see Matthew 23:27 and John 18:22-23). He had not spoken against the Law, nor did his conduct warrant the high priest's order. The identity of Ananias the high priest is not to be confused with Annas of Acts 4:6, Ananias of 5:1, or Ananias of 9:10. This is Ananias the son of Nedebaeus, who was appointed to this position by Herod of Chalcis (a brother of Herod Agrippa I) in AD 47, and who will serve as high priest until AD 58. A Roman-sympathizing Sadducee, he lives an extravagant lifestyle, and loves money (as do all the high priests of this time). He and his brother Hezekiah will later be killed mercilessly and disgracefully by Zealots during the beginning of the Jewish Revolts.[561] Paul apologizes for his comment (even though it is just), for even though he may not respect Ananias himself, he does respect his position (23:4-5). It is thought that Paul does not recognize Ananias *as* the high priest because: 1) Ananias is not adorned in his high-priestly attire (due to the haste in which the meeting was called); 2) Paul has been out of Jerusalem for some years, and may not recognize the high priest on sight; 3) there have been multiple changes in the priesthood due to politics, murders, and bribes, and it is difficult for anyone who is not a

---

sinned (Romans 7:7-13, 1 Timothy 1:13). He does mean, however, that he has lived faithfully as a Jew "up to this day," and thus has never apostatized from his Jewish beliefs and has never lived contrary to the Law (see 24:16). "He knew that he lived as a Jew who was faithful to his God and obeyed God's law to that very day" (Kistemaker, *Acts*, 808). Even so, the innocence of one's conscience is not sufficient to absolve a person of his moral crimes against God; it is God who has the final say, not one's conscience (see 1 Corinthians 4:3-4 and 2 Corinthians 10:18).

560   Lenski is probably correct in his assessment here: "Did someone strike Paul? We do not think so; some interpreters do. Of course, zealous police attendants would have leaped to execute the mighty one's order, but no such fellows were at hand. The chiliarch [Lysias] should have interfered at this point; a Roman could not be struck. Due to his usual brevity Luke does not report the chiliarch's reaction. If Paul had been struck, the chiliarch would probably have acted, and Luke would have had something to say about this" (*Acts of the Apostles*, 929; bracketed word is mine).

561   JFB *Commentary*, on 23:1; Bruce, *The Book of the Acts*, 449; Josephus, "Wars," 2.17.9. Mitchell rightly observes: "Why would Luke recount this incident, in which Paul made a serious breach of social law? It can only be to show that throughout the arrest and Sanhedrin hearings, the Jews want to use the laws of the land to silence Paul, but when the law doesn't work for them, they want to ignore it" ("Acts of the Apostles," 23.1).

priest or Council member to know for certain who the high priest is[562]; or 4) possibly all of the above.

It is already clear to Paul that he is not going to get a fair trial from this court. Thus, he resorts to an ingenious tactic: he pits the court members against themselves, effectively dividing them. First, he identifies himself as a Pharisee and the son of a Pharisee (23:6). This statement is true, since Paul's training and belief system *as a Jew* was according to the teaching and philosophy of the Pharisees. This is not misleading to the Council, since they know full well that he is on trial as a *Christian*, not as a Pharisee.[563] Nonetheless, in becoming a Christian, Paul did not have to sever all ties with his other beliefs, as long as they did not contradict his Christian beliefs. (This would be similar to a Christian today saying, "I am a Republican and the son of a Republican!" to a mixed audience of Republicans and Democrats.)

Second, he says, "I am on trial for... the resurrection of the dead," which refers to Paul's belief (as a Christian) in the future bodily resurrection of all believers.[564] Pharisees believe in spirits, angels, and the resurrection of the body; Sadducees believe in none of these things (see Matthew 22:23, Acts 4:1-2). The Pharisees, who shortly before were calling for Paul's execution, now—based upon this latter statement—side with him and "argue heatedly" in his defense (23:7-9). In any case, with a single declaration, Paul abruptly interferes with the official proceedings of the Council, such that it no longer is able

---

562   There were twenty-eight different high priests in Jerusalem between AD 37 and 70 (Reese, *Book of Acts*, 817).

563   F. F. Bruce says, "A Sadducee could not become a Christian without abandoning the distinctive theological position of his party"—namely, his beliefs about angels, the resurrection, and the afterlife—"[whereas] a Pharisee could become a Christian and remain a Pharisee—in the early decades of Christianity, at least" (*The Book of the Acts*, 453; bracketed word is mine).

564   See John 5:28-29, 11:23-26, Acts 24:14-15, Romans 8:11, 1 Corinthians 15:42-49, and 1 Thessalonians 4:13-17. While the *details* of this resurrection may be different between Pharisees and Christians, nonetheless both groups share the same fundamental belief *in* the resurrection of the righteous. "The chief point of difference between Pharisees and Sadducees was precisely this matter of the resurrection. And this was Paul's cardinal doctrine as a Christian minister....It was not a mere trick for Paul to proclaim this fact here and so divide the Sanhedrin" (Robertson, *Word Pictures*, 401).

to continue its prosecution of him (23:10). Paul is thus led away by Roman soldiers to their barracks for his own protection.

The conspiracy against Paul; his transfer to Caesarea (23:11-35)

After this debacle, the Lord appears in a vision to Paul to encourage him as well as provide a sense of purpose to what lies ahead (23:11). This serves to relieve the apostle of any personal doubts or wonderings he may have concerning what has happened to him in his arrest and imprisonment. He (the Lord) also makes it clear that Paul will indeed see Rome, as he had hoped (see Romans 15:22-25), but not in the manner in which he had originally intended. He will go to Rome as a prisoner of the state, not as a free man. Whenever the Lord provides visions to His servants, it is always during a time of great crisis (as in 18:9) or great change (as in 10:9-16). This present revelation indicates one or the other or both. This *is* a time of great crisis for Paul, but it also serves as a death-knell for the city of Jerusalem. Its religious leaders are uninterested in the truth; they claim to represent God but will not listen to His appointed spokesmen. They are unrepentant and relentless in their persecution of the many prophets sent to her (Matthew 23:34-38). There is nothing left for Jerusalem's future but a horrible and irrevocable curse (Luke 19:41-44). In about ten years from Paul's arrest (in AD 70), Jerusalem will be leveled to the ground, the temple will be burned, many Jews will be taken prisoner to Rome or condemned to hard labor, and many more will be killed.

Since the Jews' logic and reason have failed, and since they cannot overpower the Roman military's clamp on Jerusalem, they see only one final alternative: assassinate Paul through a surprise attack of their own device (23:12-14). The Greek wording in 23:14 is intentionally redundant: "We have anathematized ourselves with an anathema"—"anathema" means "devoted to a complete destruction" (as in 1 Corinthians 16:22 and Galatians 1:8). In other words, "We have willfully cursed *ourselves* to become a curse against *Paul's* life." "More than forty" men enter into this solemn oath. "The number 'forty' shows how many enemies Paul had; it also shows how difficult it will be to keep this secret from Paul's friends."[565] These men promise

---

565 Boles, *A Commentary on Acts*, 367.

to "neither eat nor drink until they had killed Paul," meaning (if not also taken literally) that they will think of nothing else until the deed is accomplished.[566] Feigning a second convening of the Council for "a more thorough investigation" of Paul, these men lay in wait to ambush the soldiers and kill their nemesis (23:15).

We have seen so far a consistent response from the unbelieving Jews—those who have resisted the preaching of the gospel of Christ. Their resistance defies all logic and reason, not to mention their own professed faith in the Old Testament Scriptures. Paul (among others) has presented factual, historical, biblical, theological, and even miraculous evidence to prove that Jesus (the Man) is the Christ (the Redeemer of prophecy). The Jews have brought forward no formal rebuttal to this teaching. Instead, they cling tenaciously to their ethnocentric view that they are the most important people on earth, and that their religion (the Law of Moses) cannot be superseded by any other religion. As part of this view, they also believe: the Jews are God's *only* chosen people, and this will never change; the promised Messiah will give the Jews worldwide prominence, domination, and glory; their deep-seated contempt for Gentiles is appropriate and just, since those who do not "know the Law" are accursed (cf. John 7:49); it is loathsome for Jews and Gentiles to be put on an equal plane in God's sight; those who in any way preach against the Law of Moses (and they alone know when this happens) are heretics and blasphemers, and thus deserve to be executed; Jesus is an impostor and a heretic, since He spoke against Moses (so they say) and violated their expectations of what the Messiah of prophecy should have done.

This characterizes the general mindset of a Jew who hears the gospel message of Christ (or, who hears what he *wants* to hear) and then rejects it. This rejection is not based upon a superior understanding of Scripture, but instead a profound ignorance of it (as Paul admitted of himself; see 1 Timothy 1:12-13). It is not based upon a rational

---

566   It should be noted, however, that the Jews were famous for wiggling out of their oaths through clever wording and technicalities; this is what Jesus referred to in Matthew 5:33-37 and 23:16-22. Furthermore, "the Mishnah [Jewish Law and commentary—CMS] makes provision for relief from such vows as could not be fulfilled 'by reason of constraint'" (Bruce, *The Book of the Acts*, 457).

disagreement with the facts and evidence provided, but is a passion-fueled intolerance for anything different than what a Jew has chosen to believe about himself, his people, and his heritage. Time and time again, the Jews violate their own Law (e.g., Deuteronomy 5:20, 18:15-22, and 19:15-20) in order to justify themselves; they violate their own Council proceedings in order to prosecute Christians; they travel over land and sea in order to poison the minds of Gentiles who are listening to the gospel of Christ (see Matthew 23:13, 15); they incite mobs and riots against Christians, revealing a failure to trust in God to fight for them (if indeed they are correct in their beliefs); they willingly hire the services of wicked men—men whom they otherwise view with great contempt—in order to oppose the preaching of Christ; they conspire, they plot, they make false accusations, they make unholy oaths, and they use their own biased court of law for the purpose of bullying, intimidating, and suppressing evidence. And all of this is being done *in the name of God*, thinking that they are actually "offering service to God" (cf. John 16:2-3). Satan has truly blinded the hearts of these men, as Paul revealed (in 2 Corinthians 4:3-4); no wonder Jesus calls these men children of Satan (John 8:44) and (collectively) a "synagogue of Satan" (Revelation 2:9).

But "the son of Paul's sister"—i.e., his nephew, probably a young boy under age 13 (?)—overhears this plot and informs Paul of it (23:16-22).[567] This indicates several things: Paul is not an only child; his family (or sister's family) may live in Jerusalem or have traveled there, possibly for Pentecost; and he is allowed to have certain visitors while being detained in the barracks. Upon hearing of this plot from his nephew, Paul immediately sends the young man to the commander, Claudius Lysias. The commander, after hearing of the news, takes it very seriously; the boy's knowledge of the Jews' plan is detailed and

---

567   "We receive the distinct impression that the boy is not even a teenager; no officer would take a teenager or an adult by the hand" (Kistemaker, *Acts*, 821)—a point with which I am in full agreement. Bruce says that this passage provides "one of the most tantalizing incidents in Acts, for all who are interested in Paul's private life and family relationships. Who was Paul's nephew, who received such prompt news of the plot— who perhaps was even present when it was hatched? We wish we knew more than we do about Paul's family; it would be illuminating to have a background against which we could appreciate better the action now taken by this nephew" (*The Book of the Acts*, 457).

specific. The commander has great respect for Paul (especially for his not having brought charges against him for violating his Roman rights), and he does not trust the Jewish leaders. He also does not want the responsibility of a Roman citizen being assassinated on his watch.

Paul's journey to Caesarea (23:23-35)

The commander, Lysias, wastes no time in getting Paul out of Jerusalem (23:23). The journey from Jerusalem to Caesarea is about 60 miles. The entourage that will accompany Paul is in fact a small army: two hundred foot soldiers, seventy horsemen, and two hundred spearmen—nearly five hundred men in all. This group leaves at 9:00 p.m. and travels under the cover of darkness. The letter Lysias writes to Felix the governor, as recorded by Luke, is likely only a form of what is written (23:25-30), even though it has all the characteristics of authenticity; it is also possible that Paul himself read the letter and conveyed its contents to Luke.[568] Regardless, it is necessary that Lysias has a good reason for sending Paul to the governor uninvited. (Lysias conveniently omits the fact that he was about to scourge Paul, a Roman citizen.)

About halfway to Caesarea, at a small city called Antipatris, the soldiers all turn back except for the horsemen (23:31-32). The entourage is now in predominantly Gentile country, making a Jewish ambush very unlikely. Both Paul and the accompanying letter are delivered over to Antonius Felix. Felix serves as the procurator (governor) of Judea from AD 52 to 59, and is one of the successors to the office of Pontius Pilate. He is believed to have been a slave who was later given his freedom, then ascended through the ranks in an uncommon way and with uncommon speed. Partly, this was due to the intercession of his brother Pallas, also a freedman, who became close friends with Emperor Claudius. Felix is not a brilliant man, and is certainly not a moralist, but he is shrewd and resourceful; the historian Tacitus said of him, "With savagery and lust, he exercised the power of

---

568 "If the letter of Claudius Lysias was not what it purported to be, then it was a forgery and therefore illegal in the light of Roman forensic conventions. Roman authorities severely punished those who tampered with documents or forged them" (Bruce W. Winter, "Official Proceedings and Forensic Speeches," *The Book of Acts in Its First Century Setting*, vol. 1, 335, fn. 118).

a king with the mind of a slave."[569] His (third) wife is Drusilla (24:24), the Jewish daughter of Herod Agrippa I, the Herod whose death is recorded in Acts 12.[570] Felix's home, during his tenure as governor, is in Caesarea Palestina, in the palace once inhabited by his father-in-law.

Felix asks Paul what province he is from (23:34), possibly because if that province is overseen by a territorial king, he is obliged to consult with its own ruler first (as Pilate did with regard to Herod Antipas; see Luke 23:6-7). He promises to give Paul "a hearing after your accusers arrive," which will take five days (24:1). Thus we see an escalation of the occasions of Paul's testimony: first, on the steps to the barracks in Jerusalem; then before the Jewish Council; soon, before two Roman governors; and ultimately before the Emperor (Caesar Nero) himself. Until then, he is kept comfortably in Herod's palace. "Vicious criminals would not have been kept in such a palace, and therefore it may be inferred that Paul was honorably treated and given the best accommodations available for a man under detention."[571]

Thus far, the Lord has allowed Paul to suffer for His name's sake, just as He promised (recall 9:16). At the same time, He has protected Paul from being overwhelmed by his enemies. While being imprisoned for his faith is perhaps the last thing that Paul wants for himself, nonetheless it has provided—and will continue to provide—opportunities for preaching the gospel to audiences that otherwise might never have heard it (see Matthew 10:18-20, regarding the apostles in general; and Philippians 1:12-14, regarding Paul himself). Not only has Paul been given opportunity to preach the gospel, but also to maintain his personal integrity under duress—something that God particularly favors. (We can only imagine the great damage Paul might have incurred against the gospel if he, as a representative of Christ, had refused to conduct himself honorably during his imprisonment.)

---

569 Bruce, *The Book of the Acts*, 462; Coffman, *Commentary on Acts*, 443.

570 Kistemaker, *Acts*, 851.

571 Coffman, *Commentary on Acts*, 445.

～ Chapter 24 ～
Paul's Defense before Felix

The Jews' accusations against Paul (24:1-9)
The word "attorney" [Greek, *rhetor*] can be translated "(forensic) orator" (in this case, a kind of advocate), which refers to one who, for a fee, will represent a person in a Roman hearing or trial.[572] Attorneys are skilled in their knowledge of Roman law and the proceedings of its courts, providing eloquent and professional representation for their clients. This man, Tertullus, may be a Roman citizen himself (see footnote on 24:6). He begins his client's prosecution by buttering up Felix (24:1-3). "By your providence" actually implies that Felix provides a certain divine-like oversight, as is applied to Caesar himself; the term will later appear on Roman coinage.[573] The truth is, "There was precious little about Felix's administration that one could praise because Felix was guilty of much corruption in his administration of affairs."[574] He is responsible for the murder of the high priest who preceded Ananias, and the corruption of his administration has many Jews believing that revolt against the Empire is the only just recourse possible.

"But, that I may not weary you any further" (24:4)—or, "In order that I might not detain you any longer [implied: so that you can continue bringing peace to your province]...." Such flattery is a typical part of the legal process; it is in the best interest of the counsel to show the governor utmost respect so as to win his favor immediately. This having been accomplished, "charges" are brought against Paul, who is now present to hear them (24:5-9):[575]

---

572   *Strong's* (electronic edition), #G4489; Robertson, *Word Pictures*, 412.

573   Mitchell, "Acts of the Apostles," 24.2.

574   Reese, *Book of Acts*, 837.

575   Many of the principal ancient manuscripts from which the New Testament is derived do not contain the latter part of verse 6 through the beginning of verse 8. Therefore, it is not certain whether these statements are genuine. Some translators leave them in the narrative with a margin note concerning their questionable origin. Even so, there is nothing in this material that is inconsistent with either the facts (that Luke has already presented) or the manipulative manner in which these Jews always portray themselves in the best light and everyone else (such as Lysias) in a bad one.

❑ "This man is a real pest and…stirs up dissension [lit., moves to sedition] among all the Jews throughout the whole world [lit., the inhabited earth, but refers to the Roman Empire by implication]"—this insinuates that Paul is an enemy of the state, since his conduct violates the *Pax Romana*, the "peace of Rome." This also implies that he (along with his organization of fellow believers) is an international problem, making this a type of class-action suit against him. Tertullus intentionally provokes Felix to *maintain* the "peace" that he has allegedly brought to the region by punishing Paul whom he portrays as a *threat* to that peace.

❑ "A ringleader of the sect of the Nazarenes"—a contemptuous designation of Paul's ties to Jesus Christ, the "Nazarene."[576] Tertullus wants to portray "the Way" as an entirely new religion, and therefore an illegal one—*religio illicita*. (Roman law banned the introduction of any "new" religion, except those assimilated by Rome through the conquest of foreign nations.) However, the use of the word "sect" actually sounds (to a man like Felix) like yet another Jewish splinter group.

❑ "He even tried to desecrate the temple"—earlier, the Jews claimed that Paul *did* desecrate the Temple; now this charge has been toned down (since there is no evidence to support it). This has no meaning to Felix, either, except that the Romans do defend Jewish law which forbids trespassing in the holy courts of the Temple (see comments on 21:28-30).

❑ "We wanted to judge him according to our own Law"—Tertullus speaks on behalf of his client, the high priest, portraying himself as a Jew[577]—"but Lysias … with much violence took him out of our

---

576 "This is the only place in the NT where the term 'Nazarene'—or 'Nazoraean,' as the particular Greek word here used may be more exactly rendered—is used of the followers of Jesus; elsewhere it is used only of Jesus Himself. …It was probably used of Jewish Christians from very early days, and remained their designation in Semitic speech; to this day Christians are known in Hebrew and Arabic as 'Nazarenes'" (Bruce, *The Book of the Acts*, 465).

577 Was Tertullus a Jew or a Gentile? "Although he bore a Roman name, he was not necessarily a Roman; Roman names were common both among Greeks and Jews, and most orators were at this time of eastern extraction. Nor is it definitely to be concluded from the manner of his speech (Acts 24:2-8) that he was a Jew; it has always been customary for lawyers to identify themselves in their pleading with their clients" (C. M. Kerr, "Tertullus," *ISBE* [electronic edition]).

hands." This is a sheer misrepresentation of the facts. Lysias may have used "much violence" against the Jews, but only because they were in the process of beating Paul to death for no apparent reason! This makes the Jews appear to be law-abiding, conscientious *victims* of (what we would call) "police brutality"—yet another ploy to win the favor of the governor. (This also ignores the fact of why Paul is before Felix in the first place: the Jews had formed a plot against Paul's life.)

❑ "And by examining him yourself…"—the "him" here (if 24:6b-8a is indeed genuine) points back to Lysias; otherwise, it must refer to Paul.[578] It appears to be "a protest against Lysias; Tertullus complains to the governor that the commander had exceeded his jurisdiction."[579] Regardless, Tertullus acts as if his client has an airtight, unassailable case. Whether or not he actually believes this to be true is irrelevant; this is all part of the lawyering process. (It is quite likely that Tertullus' speech is considerably lengthier than what Luke records.)

"And the Jews also joined in the attack" (24:9)—these are Jews who had come from Jerusalem to testify against Paul. They may have taken the stand as witnesses in defense of Tertullus' accusations. Yet, being a false witness is itself a crime against the Law of Moses (Exodus 20:16, Proverbs 6:16-19). Furthermore, "The first to plead his case seems right, until another comes and examines him" (Proverbs 18:17). In any case, there is no evidence supporting a single one of the charges brought against Paul. Tertullus may be an expert orator, but fails miserably as a prosecuting attorney. Even so, this entire experience is a very intimidating one for Paul, and would likely be overwhelming for him except that the Lord stands by him, just as He had promised (recall 23:11; see also Luke 12:11-12, regarding the apostles in general).

---

578   Verses 24:6b-28a are not found in the earliest manuscripts, which are considered the more accurate since they are closer in time to Luke's original text (JFB *Commentary*, on 24:7). Given these earlier manuscripts, the most natural identity of "him" is Paul, since this is the only antecedent or subject reference in Tertullus' statement. However, it does make Tertullus' words seem redundant, since Paul is already present to *be* examined by Felix; in this case, Lysias is the only other person to whom this can legitimately refer.

579   Kistemaker, *Acts*, 838.

Paul's testimony before Felix (24:10-23)

After these charges are filed against Paul—ambiguous and being wholly without evidence as they are—Felix motions for him to speak.[580] Notice that Paul does not provide empty praise for Felix, but does speak respectfully of his position. "I cheerfully make my defense"— i.e., because Felix is quite familiar with Jewish Law and religious philosophy, it is to Paul's advantage to speak before him rather than to one who is completely ignorant of these subjects. Felix has been governor for six or seven years and previously served in Galilee for an even longer period of time.[581] A summary of Paul's defense is as follows (24:11-21):

- ☐ **24:11a** "No more than twelve days ago"—i.e., a short enough time so as to reconstruct, if necessary, the events that have led to this point. Yet, *not* enough time to organize an insurrection against Rome.
- ☐ **24:11b** "I went up to Jerusalem to worship"—i.e., I did *not* go in order to instigate a riot; my intentions were peaceful and non-offensive.
- ☐ **24:12-13** Paul continues this line of reasoning: there is no proof of a riot or intent to riot; the Jews' accusations are based on presumptions and unfounded conclusions. The charges are all subjectively-chosen and arbitrarily-applied hearsay; they are fictitious allegations.
- ☐ **24:14-15** "But this I admit to you..."—Paul is not afraid or ashamed to admit his direct affiliation with "the Way" (a euphemism for Christianity). In a sense, he says, "I *am* guilty of *this*." But he explains that "the Way" is not in violation of the Jewish religion, but is in fact a natural *conclusion* to (or, fulfillment of) what has been anticipated in their Law and Prophets (Luke

---

580   "The matter of relative status between accusers and accused was equally important to Felix. The greater native social status of the accusers would have outweighed whatever he discerned concerning Paul. Paul's accusers were politically significant and by couching their charge in political terms thrust their status before Felix. Felix would have seen in Paul's leadership of a subgroup within Judaism a degree of influence, but he was more inclined to show regard for the representatives of the Jewish establishment" (Rapske, "Paul in Roman Custody," 151).

581   JFB *Commentary*, on 24:10.

24:44-47). Paul serves the Jews' God; he believes in the promises and prophecies of their Law. Therefore, this is not a "new" or illegal religion.[582] Paul's "hope in God" is not at odds with the mainline Jewish expectations (as expressed by Martha in John 11:23-24), but the *object* of that hope is different (Romans 10:2-4). The "resurrection of both the righteous and the wicked" reaffirms what Jesus Himself had said (John 5:25-29), and is shared by the majority of Jews everywhere. (Remember, however, that the Sadducees—the party to which many of the chief priests belong—do not believe in the resurrection.) Christ's resurrection remains at the heart of the preaching of the gospel, as seen throughout the New Testament (see Romans 1:4, Philippians 3:10-11, 2 Timothy 2:8, 1 Peter 1:3, and 3:21-22).

❑ **24:16** "In view of this…"—i.e., since these things are factual. Paul's reference to his "blameless conscience" must be understood here just as he meant it in 23:1. He is *not* saying that he has been absolutely sinless all of his life, but that he always strives to do what is right before God *and* men (Romans 14:18). Notice that this time Ananias the high priest dares not order Paul to be struck in the mouth (recall 23:2).

❑ **24:17-18a** "Alms to my own nation" refers to the collection of money he had brought to the church in Jerusalem which is comprised predominantly of Jews. Thus, instead of conspiring to harm the Jews, he has done much to help them—much more, in fact, than the Jewish leaders have done for their own countrymen. And instead of going into the temple to desecrate it, Paul had gone there as part of his own purification, and to offer the appropriate sacrifices for himself and others. The priests who attended to Paul would be able to corroborate this testimony, if necessary.

❑ **24:18b-19** "But there were certain Jews from Asia…"—this refers to Jews who were probably from Ephesus, since they recognized Trophimus the Ephesian (recall 21:29). But *those* Jews are not the same ones who are bringing charges against Paul, which smacks of falsifying evidence for a different cause than that of which he is being accused. The *real* evidence, if such even exists, lies with those who made the original charges, Paul says. And where are *those*

582   Conybeare and Howson, *Life and Epistles*, 608.

men? "The mention of the Asian Jews imposed upon the plaintiffs the necessity of either producing the witnesses or withdrawing the charges. The whole trumped-up affair was, by this time, appearing to the governor as fraudulent and irresponsible."[583]

❑ **24:20-21** Paul's only "misdeed"—and he says this a bit sarcastically[584]—is that he split the Council with his statement concerning the resurrection of the dead. In other words, this is not a crime at all—and certainly not a crime against the State—but it is the only thing which the present accusers can verify for certain; it is the only thing of which they are truly eyewitnesses. (Some think that Paul is here apologizing for his divisive statement before the Council, but the context will not allow for this. He has nothing for which to apologize; certainly Jesus [in 23:11] offered no rebuke for his comments, either.)

"But Felix, having a more exact knowledge about the Way, put them off…" (24:22). In other words, Felix knows more about "the Way" than he lets on—even more than do Paul's accusers, or so it is implied. Another interpretation of this statement is: Felix knows that the Jews are misrepresenting Paul as a troublemaker and a law-breaker for reasons of their own (just as Pilate did; see Mark 15:9-10). Indeed, Felix's long tenure as governor has provided him with numerous occasions in which he has heard of the gospel from Christians in Caesarea. He feigns the need for a deposition from Lysias before deciding Paul's case, but it is evident (from 24:27) that he has no such intention of pursuing this matter. It is politically expedient for him to sit on this and do nothing rather than take a stand one way or another. He does, at least, provide Paul with reasonable quarters, and allows his friends to have full access to him (24:23).

Paul's private conversations with Felix (24:24-27)
Obviously Felix left and then returned to Caesarea, bringing with him

---

583 Coffman, *Commentary on Acts*, 455.

584 Sarcasm, in this context (and as Paul used it extensively in the Second Corinthian letter), does not mean the same as what we think of it in a contemporary sense. Here, sarcasm is a rhetorical (persuasive speech) device meant to highlight the absurdity of something. It is not meant to be rude, malicious, or purposely offensive, as sarcasm may be used today.

Drusilla, his wife (24:24). Felix had persuaded this woman, who is the daughter of Herod Agrippa I, to leave her husband (Azizus, the king of Emesa, a petty state in Syria) to become his own wife.[585] She is young (barely twenty years old at this time) and strikingly beautiful, but her beauty is spoiled by her own self-serving agenda. The reference to her being "a Jewess" may be to show that she sympathized with the Jews rather than with Paul. (There is no proof that her mother [Cyprus II] was herself a Jewess.) Indeed, Drusilla's family has a long history of run-ins with men associated with the gospel: her father murdered the apostle James and imprisoned Peter (with the intent to murder him as well); her great-uncle (Antipas) murdered John the Baptist; and her great-grandfather (Herod the Great) murdered the children of Bethlehem—and many other innocents.[586]

Felix summons Paul often to speak further about this "faith in Christ Jesus," and no doubt Drusilla heard some of these talks.[587] (In the Greek, it reads, "the faith into Christ Jesus," that is, the means by which one becomes a Christian.) But such discussion requires Felix to be confronted with some very uncomfortable subjects—"righteousness, self-control, and the judgment to come"—so he dismisses Paul for the time being. (Remember, he is not a very noble or conscientious man, and has committed adultery with another man's wife.) "When I find time, I will summon you" (24:25)—these words will serve as the virtual epitaph of all those who hear the gospel message but refuse to commit to it. Hearing the gospel is not equal to obeying it; without faithful obedience, one's hearing of the gospel produces nothing (Hebrews 4:2). But Felix still wants to have an audience with Paul, thinking that he will give Felix money (in the form of a bribe) for his release. "Many of

---

585   Bruce, *The Book of the Acts*, 472. "The Roman historiographer Suetonius relates that Drusilla was the third wife of Felix. Drusilla likewise had her share of husbands....Yet she was sufficiently interested to come to Paul and listen to him preach the gospel of Jesus Christ" (Kistemaker, *Acts*, 851).

586   Robertson, *Word Pictures*, 422.

587   "To describe the prisoner Paul's interview with Felix and Drusilla and interviews thereafter as occasional and unfruitful...is to miss Luke's point; *viz.*, the prisoner's forthright, powerful and incorruptible proclamation of the gospel in the opportunities furnished" (Rapske, "Paul in Roman Custody," 356).

Paul's visitors were wealthy and could easily have bought Paul's release, but Paul would not allow it."[588]

Felix is succeeded as governor by Festus when he (Felix) is called to stand trial before Emperor Nero, ca. AD 59-60 (24:27).[589] "And wishing to do the Jews a favor"—not because Felix has any love for the Jews, but because the Jews are sending an embassy to Rome to make a case against him for his many crimes against them (including numerous murders), and he wants to be spared his life. He does escape execution only because of his very wealthy brother Pallas' influence on the emperor; however, he will be exiled in humiliation to Gaul (France) until his death. As for Drusilla, she and her son will die in the AD 79 eruption of Mount Vesuvius, which will bury the city of Pompeii in super-heated ash.[590]

It is difficult to imagine the frustration that Paul must be feeling at this time, now unnecessarily idle after being engaged in several missionary journeys in a row. Not only this, but while he is being unlawfully detained in prison, his false accusers are enjoying their freedom—a compounded injustice. No doubt these accusers also are busy assassinating Paul's character, being free to make all sorts of malicious and untrue statements about him. Even so, there is no indication that Paul's imprisonment has stifled the growth or led to the instability of the church in general. We have to believe that God is making good use of Paul's imprisonment because: 1) His heavenly will is not undermined by earthly situations; 2) Paul's imprisonment may be far more beneficial to Paul (and others) than we will ever know; and 3) if God wanted to get Paul out of prison, He would do so—He has already proven His ability to do this. Meanwhile, it is likely that Luke spends much time with Paul in Caesarea, and collects a great deal of information from him (and others?) that will contribute to the book of Acts itself.[591] His proximity to Jerusalem and Antioch of Syria—Caesarea being about

---

588   JFB *Commentary*, on 24:26.

589   Ibid., on 24:27.

590   C. M. Kerr, "Drusilla," *ISBE* (electronic edition).

591   Coffman, *Commentary on Acts*, 462.

halfway between the two cities—provides Luke with numerous contacts with intimate information about Jesus' life, eyewitness accounts to His crucifixion, the early church, Peter's ministries, etc. Thus, it may be that we are reading such an excellent historical account as a direct result of Paul's imprisonment—both the account *and* imprisonment being providentially arranged.

⁓ Chapter 25 ⁓
Paul's Defense before Festus

The Jews' second attack on Paul in a Roman court of law (25:1-12)
Porcius Festus (governor of Judea,, AD 60 - 62) is a better man than
Felix, but not a better ruler, "offering a startling proof that a strong evil
ruler is sometimes better than a good weak one."[592] His administration
does not have nearly the corruption and excesses of his predecessor, but
his ability to handle the volatile political—and religious—matters of
the province are seriously wanting. Josephus does record Festus' noble
(and largely successful) attempts to suppress the outright lawlessness
of the *sicarii* ("assassins") that had increased during Felix's tenure.[593]
Regardless, Festus will later die in office after serving for only two
years.

Festus arrives in Caesarea (probably from Rome) and then three days
later travels to Jerusalem (25:1). One might think that the Jews' furor
over Paul would have died down by now, but this is not the case. "Here
we see the implacable hatred of these Jews. Two years had passed,
a third high priest was in office, but their hate is as bloodthirsty as
ever."[594] Not only do these men attempt to have Paul returned to
Jerusalem, but they set yet another ambush for him when he comes
(25:2-3). Festus (perhaps through God's providence) does not submit
to this, but invites the Jews to bring their case again to Caesarea. He
invites the "influential men" of Jerusalem to bring their case against
Paul, but he appears to offer Paul himself no such advantage to Paul
(25:4-5). While the Jews accept this official gesture of courtesy, it still
lacks the substance of an honest trial. Paul's original accusers will
still not be present to produce their charges or their alleged evidence;
nothing has changed from the first trial before Felix. Instead, Festus
opens wide the door to "many and serious charges against him which
they could not prove" (25:7). Not only this, but:

---

592   Coffman, *Commentary on Acts*, 465.

593   Josephus, "Antiquities," 20.8.10.

594   Lenski, *Acts of the Apostles*, 989.

Luke may be accusing Festus of *ex parte*, one-sided communications with a party to the case. Festus spent 8-10 days among the Jewish leaders, and logic demands [that] this was inappropriate and highly unfair to Paul. Luke adds to this that no warning was given to Paul that the trial is starting *now*. Whatever witnesses or lawyer he might have summoned certainly had no time to appear.[595]

Nonetheless, Festus spends "eight or ten" more days in Jerusalem (25:6), then returns to Caesarea and takes his seat on his tribunal.[596] The team of Jewish "influential men" arrives, hurling all sorts of religious as well as political accusations against Paul, but providing no eyewitnesses or concrete evidence to support any of them (25:7). "Repetition and reiteration and vehemence took the place of proof."[597] Paul's defense is terse yet accurate to the three groups of charges: "I have committed no offense either against the Law of the Jews or against the temple or against Caesar" (25:8). But "wishing to do the Jews a favor," Festus still refuses to release Paul, and asks him if he is willing to go to Jerusalem to stand trial there (25:9). This begs an obvious question: if these men cannot defend their charges before the governor in Caesarea, then how will they do any better in Jerusalem? Or, if Paul cannot get a fair trial before a supposedly unbiased governor, then how will he get an even better one before those who hate him in Jerusalem (25:10)? In other words, the judicial process which is meant to protect Paul is nothing more than a political façade designed to placate the Jews and also spare Festus of making any unpopular decisions. (No doubt Festus regards Paul as expendable here in light of the terrible turmoil within his province. Palestine is a virtual powder keg waiting to explode; Festus is not in a position to strong-arm the Jews. Indeed, in

---

595 Mitchell, "Acts of the Apostles," 25.1; bracketed word is mine.

596 "The 'judgment-seat' [NASB, 'tribunal'] was an elevated throne or seat, reached probably by a step; sometimes it was fixed in some open place and was moveable; it was the symbol of authority of a Roman judge, and is frequently mentioned in the New Testament" (Boles, *A Commentary on Acts*, 389; bracketed words are mine).

597 Robertson, *Word Pictures*, 429.

just six short years, Jewish zealots will declare war on Rome and begin murdering Roman soldiers in Palestine.)

Festus leaves Paul with no choice but to appeal to a higher court of law (25:10-11). He first accuses Festus (and Felix) of having failed to provide the expected justice due a Roman citizen; he then asserts his Roman rights by declaring that "no one [i.e., not even Festus himself] can hand me over to them [the Jews]."[598] Thus, Paul "fearlessly confronted Festus with the fact that Festus knew that he was innocent of the charges brought against him."[599] That having been said, Paul then exercises his ultimate right as a Roman: "I appeal to Caesar." This appeal means that Paul requests his case to be transferred to the highest court of law in the Empire—the one over which Caesar Nero himself presides.[600] This is parallel to one appealing to the Supreme Court in our own country today. "Every Roman citizen had the right of appeal to the highest ruler. Paul used this power since the alternative was to be killed by an angry mob of Jews."[601] "Then when Festus had conferred with his council, he answered, 'You have appealed to Caesar, to Caesar you shall go'" (25:12).

Festus confers with his legal staff for advice and to verify procedure. Under Roman law, he had the ability to grant or

---

598   "Paul means to say that he is a Roman citizen before a Roman tribunal. Festus was the representative of Caesar and had no right to hand him over to a Jewish tribunal" (ibid., 430).

599   Boles, *A Commentary on Acts*, 391. This commentator says later, "There seems to be an undercurrent in Festus' conversation [to Agrippa; see 25:21] of his displeasure at the appeal to Caesar. He had to grant the appeal, but it was a [negative] reflection on Festus' fairness and justice that a Roman citizen should prefer the imperial tribunal at Rome to his own" (ibid., 396; bracketed words are mine).

600   "The right of appeal to Caesar had taken the place of the earlier right of appeal to the sovereign people of Rome, which Roman citizens had enjoyed since 509 BC. As the years went by, and power became more and more centralized in the emperor, the appeal to the people became an appeal to Caesar. Once a prisoner made an appeal to Caesar, the judge to whom the appeal was made was obliged to stop all proceedings in the case immediately, and to send the prisoner, together with his accusers, to Rome to be tried there with Caesar himself sitting as judge" (Reese, *Book of Acts*, 862).

601   JFB *Commentary*, on 25:10-11.

deny the appeal, but once he granted it, he could not resume jurisdiction. It then belonged to Caesar, and no man could take away a case from Caesar. Festus' answer hints that he feels Paul has made a foolish choice.[602]

While Festus may disagree with Paul's decision, it spares him from having to pursue this matter on his own. All that remains now is some kind of justifiable *explanation* why Paul felt compelled to appeal to Caesar, and why Festus himself could not render a decision. It is foolhardy and politically disastrous to send a prisoner to the Emperor without an excellent reason for doing so. Such a move would indicate a local ruler's incompetency to judge legal matters within his own jurisdiction.

Festus' discussion with Agrippa (25:13-27)

King Herod Agrippa II (25:13) is the son of Herod Agrippa I, whose death is recorded in Acts 12:20-23. Agrippa II rules over a small kingdom called Chalcis, northeast of Festus' own jurisdiction. Since he was only seventeen years old upon his father's death, the political complexities of Judea were thought by his advisors to be too much for him, and Judea was put under a Roman procurator's oversight. Soon afterward, Herod (younger brother of Herod Agrippa I), king of Chalcis, died, and his kingdom was given to the young Agrippa. With this appointment came the responsibility of appointing Jewish high priests and gaining custody of the ceremonial vestments which these men wear on the Day of Atonement. Agrippa will later give up this smaller kingdom for a larger one in Palestine; Nero will still later enlarge this jurisdiction for him.[603]

Bernice [pronounced ber-*nee*-kay] is Agrippa's sister, who was originally married to Herod of Chalcis (Agrippa's uncle) until that man died.[604]

---

602   Mitchell, "Acts of the Apostles," 25.3.

603   It is worth consulting Kistemaker's "Additional comments on Agrippa II and the Herodian dynasty" (*Acts*, 870) for further details of both Agrippa and Bernice, which are essentially handy summaries of the belabored information recorded in Josephus.

604   "Bernice" (or "Berenice") is "a Macedonian name meaning 'bringer of victory'.... In 1st-century Palestine, it was largely confined to the royal family"

She has since chosen to live with her brother in what many believe to be an incestuous relationship. (Intermarriage and similar indecent relationships are not new to the history of the Herodian family.) The two live in Caesarea Philippi at this time, but Agrippa will later rename this city Neronias in honor of Nero (because of the Caesar's benefactions to Agrippa). Agrippa's death in AD 100 will mark the end of the Herodian lineage, since he will die childless.[605]

The conversation between Festus and Agrippa reveals some of the candid and authentic behind-the-scenes struggles of governing officials (25:14ff). Festus cannot send Paul to Caesar without good reason; to waste the Emperor's time is not only politically disastrous, it can prove dangerous to one's own life. But Paul's case has left Festus bewildered and unable to reach a clear decision. In fact, he has yet to understand even the full scope of the controversy between the Jews and Paul. Festus candidly explains to Agrippa: "When the accusers stood up, they began bringing charges against him not of such crimes as I was expecting, but they simply had some points of disagreement with him about their own religion and about a dead man, Jesus, whom Paul asserted to be alive" (25:18-19). Ironically, Festus accurately states the truth of the matter—Jesus *was* dead, and now He *is* alive—but the impact of what he has heard is lost on him. Agrippa, however, has a much better comprehension of these matters (as Paul himself reveals; see Acts 26:2-3, 26). Therefore, he desires to hear Paul himself, to which Festus obliges: "Tomorrow ... you shall hear him" (25:22).

Festus' reception for Agrippa and Bernice (25:23-27)

Therefore, on the next day, Festus rolls out the red carpet for King Agrippa and Bernice with a lavish assembly. Included in this audience are "commanders" (*chiliarchos*, each one being the military leader of one thousand soldiers) and "prominent" or "principal" men of the city of Caesarea. In other words, this is an impressive gathering of men, which provides an ideal opportunity for Paul to lay out his defense and (at the same time) promote the central message of the

---

(Williams, "Palestinian Jewish Personal Names in Acts," 98).

605   Bruce, *The Book of the Acts*, 481-482; Page, *The Acts of the Apostles*, 243; Foakes-Jackson, *The Acts of the Apostles*, 221.

gospel. Festus' deference to Agrippa (25:24-27) seems sincere, since he genuinely entreats Agrippa's help in the matter of Paul and his arrest. The manner in which Festus lays out his situation before this gathering of men also seems genuine and surprisingly candid. Incidentally, Festus twice (in 25:21, 25) refers to the Emperor literally as *Augustus*, a Latin word meaning "revered" or "august," and here it specifically refers to Emperor Nero (reigned AD 54-68). "Festus makes it plain that this is not a 'trial,' but an examination for his convenience to help him out of a predicament."[606] An actual trial would be a violation of Paul's appeal to Caesar. In any case, "for the first time, and perhaps the last, an apostle stood face to face with a Herod [Agrippa], unless James had enjoyed that privilege just before he was beheaded."[607]

---

606   Robertson, *Word Pictures*, 441.

607   McGarvey, *Acts of Apostles*, 2:249.

∾ Chapter 26 ∾
Paul's Defense before Agrippa

Paul's opening address to Agrippa (26:1-11)

Once permitted to speak, Paul "stretched out his hand" to the crowd as a call for silence (26:1); his other arm likely remains chained to a guard (see 26:29). He then expresses gratitude for being able to give his defense before Agrippa, since he knows that he (Agrippa) is much more informed about Jewish law, customs, and sensitivities than either Felix or Festus (26:2-3). Indeed, Paul's entire address is made to Agrippa personally, as if he is speaking to him alone, despite the great company of other listeners that is present. Because of this, its style remains unique among all of Paul's speeches or addresses in Acts.

Paul begins his actual testimony by stating (as before) his zealous practice of the Jewish religion, and Pharisaism in particular, which is a matter of public knowledge among the Jews (26:4-5; see Galatians 1:13-14). "And now I am standing trial for the hope of the promise made by God to our fathers; the promise to which our twelve tribes hope to attain" (26:6-7)—in other words, the core of the controversy between Jews and Christians rests upon the Jews' own *misunderstanding* (or *subjective interpretation*) of God's promises to them from ancient times. If they had understood the promise correctly, Paul implies, then they would not have any contention with him (see Acts 3:17-18 and 1 Corinthians 2:6-8). The historical fact of Christ's resurrection ought to resolve the entire matter—as indeed it was intended to do (Acts 17:30-31)—but few people had investigated the matter objectively. Thus, Christ's resurrection seems "incredible" (26:8) when in fact it is both *real* and *believable*.[608]

---

608   "The Greek reads 'If God raises dead (people)'; there is no article in the Greek, and 'dead' is plural. A similar construction in Romans 1:4 certainly includes the resurrection of Jesus (and that as involving the resurrection of all men), and that would seem to be the point here. The great truth to which Paul has been building is that Jesus, although crucified, was at that moment living and seated at the right hand of God, proven by His resurrection to be the Messiah, the very one the Jews were looking for to fulfill their hope. Jews might believe in the idea of resurrection as part of their doctrine; then why could they not accept the well-authenticated resurrection of Jesus?" (Reese, *Book of Acts*, 876).

Nonetheless, Paul admits that he himself misunderstood all these things at first, which is why he so severely persecuted the "Way," tenaciously hunted down Christians, and was "furiously enraged at them" (26:11).[609] This testimony coupled with Luke's earlier description of Paul "breathing threats and murder against the disciples of the Lord" (cf. 9:1) presents the picture of a man obsessed with stamping out this heresy (as he perceived it to be) with a fanatical vengeance. Paul was not merely in disagreement with Christians; he believed them to be monstrous enemies of God. Thus, he wanted them to pay dearly for their beliefs—even with their own lives—and he pictured himself as the noble agent of God's divine justice.

Paul's account to Agrippa of his conversion (26:12-23)

Despite his self-righteous campaign against the church—which the Jewish priests had eagerly supported—Paul was not at all prepared for what he experienced while on the road to Damascus (26:12ff). It is helpful now to compare the three accounts of this experience:

---

609   "I cast my vote against them" (26:10) literally reads "I cast down my pebble"—a black one. "The ancient Greeks used white pebbles for acquittal (Rev. 2:17), black ones for condemnation as here (the only two uses of the word in the N.T.)....If Paul's language is taken literally here, he was a member of the Sanhedrin and so married when he led the persecution. That is quite possible, though he was not married when he wrote 1 Cor. 7:7f., but a widower. It is possible to take the language figuratively for approval, but not so natural" (Robertson, *Word Pictures*, 446). See also Boles' comments in his commentary (*A Commentary on Acts*, 402). Of course, there also remains the possibility for Paul to speaking figuratively and not literally, as when we say, "I had to put my foot down" or "I cast my hat into the ring." In my understanding, there is no reason to invent a wife for Paul just to satisfy an ambiguous phrase of his.

Acts 9:3-9	Acts 22:6-11	Acts 26:12-18
As he was traveling, it happened that he was approaching Damascus, and suddenly a light from heaven flashed around him; and he fell to the ground and heard a voice saying to him, "Saul, Saul, why are you persecuting Me?"	"But it happened that as I was on my way, approaching Damascus about noontime, a very bright light suddenly flashed from heaven all around me, and I fell to the ground and heard a voice saying to me, 'Saul, Saul, why are you persecuting Me?'"	"While so engaged as I was journeying to Damascus with the authority and commission of the chief priests, at midday, O King, I saw on the way a light from heaven, brighter than the sun, shining all around me and those who were journeying with me." "And when we had all fallen to the ground, I heard a voice saying to me in the Hebrew dialect, 'Saul, Saul, why are you persecuting Me? It is hard for you to kick against the goads.'"

Acts 9:3-9	Acts 22:6-11	Acts 26:12-18
And he said, "Who are You, Lord?" And He said, "I am Jesus whom you are persecuting, but get up and enter the city, and it will be told you what you must do." The men who traveled with him stood speechless, hearing the voice but seeing no one.	"And I answered, 'Who are You, Lord?' And He said to me, 'I am Jesus the Nazarene, whom you are persecuting.' And those who were with me saw the light, to be sure, but did not understand the voice of the One who was speaking to me. "And I said, 'What shall I do, Lord?' And the Lord said to me, 'Get up and go on into Damascus, and there you will be told of all that has been appointed for you to do.'"	"And I said, 'Who are You, Lord?' And the Lord said, 'I am Jesus whom you are persecuting. But get up and stand on your feet; for this purpose I have appeared to you, to appoint you a minister and a witness not only to the things which you have seen, but also to the things in which I will appear to you; rescuing you from the Jewish people and from the Gentiles, to whom I am sending you, to open their eyes so that they may turn from darkness to light and from the dominion of Satan to God, that they may receive forgiveness of sins and an inheritance among those who have been sanctified by faith in Me.'"
Saul got up from the ground, and though his eyes were open, he could see nothing; and leading him by the hand, they brought him into Damascus.	"But since I could not see because of the brightness of that light, I was led by the hand by those who were with me and came into Damascus."	"So, King Agrippa, I did not prove disobedient to the heavenly vision...."

This latter account of Paul's conversion experience has details that are not in the first two. This does not mean any of the accounts are in error; it simply indicates how certain details are emphasized (or not) based upon the present need. In fact, Boles rightly says, "The variations noted in the three records of his conversion impress us with the truthfulness of the narrative, because they are so natural as to be

a certain accompaniment of the same story told at different times."[610]
Stott adds:

> They [i.e., the three accounts] certainly indicate that Luke
> was no slavish literalist; he saw no need to ensure that each
> account was a precise, word-perfect replica of the others. On
> the contrary, since each time the story is told, the audience and
> therefore the purpose of telling it are different, this is naturally
> reflected in the detailed presentation. Our study of how a single
> author (Luke) tells the same story differently will help us to
> understand how the three synoptic evangelists (Matthew, Mark
> and Luke) could also tell their same stories differently.[611]

This present account is in Paul's own words, and therefore has, for
example, more detail concerning Jesus' personal commission to him
(26:16-18). This fact is also important since Paul's audience in Caesarea
is predominantly Gentile rather than Jewish (as opposed to the account
given in chapter 22). It is important that he underscores the *universal
application* of the gospel: it is a message from God for both Jews *and*
Gentiles alike. To "kick against the goads"—a "goad" being a sharp
stick used for directing cattle—means that resistance to the message of
God only brings harm to the one who resists it, not to the message itself
(26:14). "This illustration, borrowed from an agricultural setting, was
well known as a proverb throughout the Mediterranean world. King
Agrippa was no stranger to it."[612] The question arises: what "goad"
was Paul (Saul) kicking against? It is reasonable to assume, under the
circumstances, that Paul had been "kicking" against the obviousness
of Jesus' actual identity, given His teaching, His miracles, the large
number of Jewish converts to "the Way," and Stephen's own defense
and martyrdom. Blinded by his own pride, Jewish zeal, and training, he
later admits that he "acted ignorantly in unbelief" of these unavoidable
facts (1 Timothy 1:13).[613] (See also comments on 9:8.)

---

610   Boles, *A Commentary on Acts*, 403.

611   Stott, *The Spirit, the Church, and the World*, 380; bracketed words are mine.

612   Kistemaker, *Acts*, 895.

613   Gaertner disagrees: "Though this reference has been considered a reflection of
Paul's troubled conscience when he was on the road to Damascus..., the goads had

Paul's divinely-appointed mission is to open the eyes of unbelievers "so that they may turn from darkness to light and from the dominion of Satan to God, that they may receive forgiveness of sins and an inheritance among those who have been sanctified by faith in Me" (26:18). It is Satan's wicked influence that blinds men's hearts to the truth (2 Corinthians 4:3-4) and holds them in his "snare" (2 Timothy 2:26). He is the ruler of darkness (Ephesians 6:12) while Christ is the "Light of the world" (John 8:12). "Forgiveness of sins" is commensurate with fellowship with God and (also) the salvation of one's soul. These things—forgiveness, fellowship, and salvation—are mutually dependent: it is impossible to have any one of them without the other two. "Inheritance" refers to actual and permanent entrance into the kingdom of God, which is promised to believers but is also conditioned upon continued faithfulness to Him (2 Peter 1:10-11). "Sanctified by faith" refers to God's having set apart for His service those who put their faith in Him for salvation. This necessitates the atoning blood of Christ as well as the sanctifying work of the Holy Spirit (1 Corinthians 6:11, 1 Peter 1:2).[614]

---

nothing to do with the pangs of Paul's conscience, but rather with the will of Christ who was calling him to proclaim the truth of the gospel. Paul was fighting against what the Lord was goading him to do with his life." He adds in a footnote: "...Our tendency to interpret Paul as afflicted with a guilty conscience is more a product of the western habit of internalizing guilt than of any pangs of conscience Paul actually felt himself" (*Acts*, 394, including fn. 9). I respond: we are not here to psychoanalyze Paul's conscience. I, for one, am not accusing him of having had a *guilty* conscience; he himself admits (in 23:1) that he has always had a *clear* conscience, not a guilty one. The essential point hinges upon the acceptance or rejection of *evidence* for Jesus' true identity, not Paul's conscience about his actions until his conversion. Simply put: Paul "kicked" against every good reason to believe in Jesus, just as so many people continue to do today—even while claiming that their "conscience is clear."

614   On this verse, MacArthur writes: "The clear teaching of Scripture is that this salvation comes to a person only by faith in Jesus Christ apart from any human works" (*Acts: 13 – 28*, 336); he then cites Ephesians 2:8-9, but conspicuously does not cite verse 10 of that passage. As before (in dealing with MacArthur's assessment of 22:16), the word "only" is the problem here. "Faith without works is dead" (James 2:26), which means that human works *are* necessary in order to define "faith" in the process of salvation. These works do not equal or replace God's work of grace in one's salvation, but they are required to prove that the one who claims to believe in God's work is sincere and willing to demonstrate that belief in visible action. A believer does come to Christ in faith, but he proves that faith in his obedience to Christ's commands—an obedience that requires visible human effort, not just a heart-felt decision. *This* is the clear teaching of Scripture.

Paul argues his case similarly to how Peter argued his own case before the Jews in chapter 11 (in defense of going to Cornelius' house). In so many words, Paul says, "Since I received this heavenly vision, how was I supposed to ignore it?" Or even more pointedly, "What would *you* have done, King Agrippa, if you had been in my shoes—if indeed *you* had received such a revelation?" The answer being self-evident, Paul then relates how he complied with Christ's words and began preaching in Damascus, then in Jerusalem, then in the region of Judea, then throughout the regions of the Gentiles (26:20a). "That they should repent and turn to God, performing deeds appropriate to repentance" (26:20b)—i.e., repenting *of* one's sins means leaving those sins behind and at the same time turning *to* God. The declaration of the gospel of Christ requires also the declaration of the need for repentance, as Christ Himself said (Luke 24:46-47). This repentance cannot remain a professed statement or verbal promise, but must be demonstrated with (or, verified by) actual "deeds" that are consistent with that promise. A repentance without such deeds is no genuine repentance at all; "therefore bear fruit in keeping with repentance" (Matthew 3:8).[615]

"For this reason..." (26:21)—i.e., for a reason that is in *contradiction* to the heavenly vision that Paul received. Thus, while he was on a divine mission, the Jews—who claim to be God's people, though they continually resist Him (cf. John 8:42-47, Acts 7:51-53)—once again acted in defiance of God. Paul then restates his mission in light of the Law and the Prophets: "I stand to this day...stating nothing but what the Prophets and Moses *said was going to take place*" (26:22, emphasis added; see John 5:39-47, Luke 24:44-47, and Acts 24:14-15). Furthermore, the Jewish prophets spoke of a wrongfully executed and then resurrected Christ (Messiah), which is why Paul *preaches* about the resurrection (recall 26:8; consider Isaiah 53, Psalm 16:9-10, et

---

615 If "deeds"—works of human effort—are necessary for repentance, and repentance is necessary for salvation, then human effort is *necessary* for salvation. This does not mean that one is saved based on the power or performance of those works, but that they are a necessary component of one's salvation. God alone has the power to save, but God has given those who turn to Him the power to perform deeds of repentance. This biblical teaching completely refutes the popular "faith only" doctrine and the "just ask Jesus into your heart"-mantra of modern evangelicalism. Faith in Christ is nothing without repentance, and repentance is nothing without works to substantiate that repentance.

al). What Paul implies is: *he* is not against the Law (or a desecrator of the temple), but it is the *Jews* who are the enemies of God and whose resistance of His Messiah make them desecrators of His temple—the exact same conclusion Stephen drew in his defense before the Jews (recall 7:39-53).[616] The final words of his testimony are meant to serve as an invitation for both Jews and Gentiles alike to *respond* to the call of the gospel (26:23).

Festus, who is neither a Jew nor a man of great faith, cannot suppress his incredulousness toward this seemingly fantastic tale any longer, and especially to Paul's reference to Christ's bodily resurrection from the dead: "Paul, you are out of your mind! Your great learning is driving you mad" (26:24). This is both exasperation and a backward compliment: Festus is frustrated because he still cannot grasp the importance of what is being said, yet at the same time he acknowledges Paul's scholarly learning and his professional demeanor.[617] "With arrogance typical of ignorance, he concluded that if it made no sense to him, it simply made no sense!"[618] Yet, Paul is not deterred by Festus' outburst but continues to treat him with respect, even as he disagrees with him (26:25). "[Paul] had not spoken words of fancy, but solid facts; not [a] wild flight of the imagination, but literal and exact truth."[619] We should not forget, either, that Jesus Himself was accused of being insane and demon-possessed (John 8:48, 10:20).

---

616   Paul later refers to disbelieving Jews as "dogs," "evil workers," and those of "false circumcision" (Philippians 3:2; see also 2 Corinthians 11:13). Jesus also referred to them as being in league with Satan (John 8:44) and collectively as a "synagogue of Satan" (Revelation 2:9). In other words, the Jews who resisted the gospel of Christ are the true heretics, not Paul and his fellow Christians.

617   Lenski says that Festus' outburst is one of self-defense. "If Paul is just raving [mad], if his mind is unbalanced, that excuses Festus—he may brush aside all that Paul says. It is a helpless, pitiful, foolish self-defense, the only thing this Roman can think of in order to thrust Paul's words aside. Moreover, Festus' word is not sincere. If he really thought Paul unbalanced mentally he would not shout at him, he would smile in pity and try to catch Agrippa's eye with a significant look, gesture, or whisper. If Paul were crazy, the case would automatically end despite Paul's appeal to Caesar. No governor would send a lunatic to the emperor's court" (*Acts of the Apostles*, 1050; bracketed word is mine).

618   Reese, *Book of Acts*, 882.

619   Boles, *A Commentary on Acts*, 408; bracketed words are mine.

But Agrippa is a much different sort of man than Festus. He *does* understand the Law; he *does* "know about these matters." None of what the Christians have done has been hidden; there is nothing secret about their teachings; there is no substance to the charges of sedition, treason, or disloyalty to the Emperor. Furthermore, Paul's testimony is lucid and logical, and is void of the radical zealotry that is so typical of Jewish rhetoric or apocalypticism. Finally, Paul tightens the screws on Agrippa himself, who probably realizes—too late!—that really it is *he* who is on trial, not Paul (26:27): "King Agrippa, do you believe the Prophets? I know that you do."

> This is not a solicitous question, but rather Paul is calling upon Agrippa to choose. Paul has stated [that] Agrippa is well aware of the Nazarene history, from Jesus to now, the doctrinal positions and the well-documented miraculous proof it has given for decades. Paul is calling on Agrippa to choose the truth over the intransigence [i.e., inflexibility] of the established religious authorities, having reached the end of a much longer, more detailed speech than what Luke has recorded. Paul waits for his answer, hoping it would be as Sergius Paulus appears to have responded with [Acts 13:12]. However, Agrippa's power depended on Jewish acceptance, and Roman toleration. It is unlikely he would give a serious public answer to Paul that would undermine this.[620]

Indeed, Agrippa's answer—"In a short time you will persuade me to become a Christian" (26:28)—is as elusive and politically-correct as one could ever hope to offer.[621] It is difficult to determine if he was serious, ironical, or sarcastic. As Festus' guest, he certainly did not

---

620 Mitchell, "Acts of the Apostles," 26.3-4; bracketed words are mine.

621 "The Greek is 'in a little' [NASB, 'in a short'], and might mean 'in a few (more) words,' 'with a little (more) effort,' or 'in a little (more) time.' The word supplied after 'little' depends upon the context" (Reese, *Book of Acts*, 885; bracketed words are mine). Paul asks, "Do you believe the Prophets?" but Agrippa sees exactly where he is leading him, all the way to the end of the matter—i.e., in becoming a *Christian*. It is impossible to believe in all the prophecies concerning Messiah in the Old Testament yet refuse to believe that Jesus Christ is the fulfillment *of* those prophecies, given all the evidence He has provided (see John 8:24).

want to be accused of Paul's alleged madness; yet he cannot deny the sobering truth of what he has heard. "Paul had interpreted the prophets about the Messiah in a way that fell in with his claim that Jesus was the Messiah risen from the dead. To say, 'Yes' would place himself in Paul's hands. To say 'No' would mean that he did not believe in the prophets."[622] In any case, it is interesting that Agrippa responds only to where he realizes Paul is *leading* him rather than to the *facts* that he (Paul) has presented to him. Paul's testimony *is* meant to persuade Agrippa—and anyone else listening—to become a Christian, but Agrippa dismisses the potency of the argument itself because he does not want to commit to its conclusion. Such is the manner in which many people reject the gospel of Christ even today.

Paul's response is both classic and authentic: "I would wish to God, that whether in a short or long time, not only you, but also all who hear me this day, might become such as I am, except for these chains" (26:29).[623] This *does* seem to acknowledge at least the appearance of sincerity in Agrippa's tone, but we will never know for certain. Paul's reference to his "chains"—the literal shackle with which he is bound[624]—is mentioned elsewhere as the paradoxical hallmark of his successful ministry:

---

622   Robertson, *Word Pictures*, 453.

623   Rapske's lengthier quote is insightful here: "The first century Mediterranean culture was dominated by honour and shame; it is thus easy to underestimate the stigma attached to incarceration and bonds. Ancient literary sources link prison with dishonor. The process of being publicly conducted there, particularly while bound, was perceived (as was intended) to be degrading. Public exposure, irrespective of innocence or guilt, resulted in a shame that could be life-long. Because prisoners no longer possessed their former dignity there was great social pressure to withdraw from or abandon the prisoner. The pressure was felt most keenly by close friends, associates and family members. Christians too felt it despite calls for solidarity and loving care [see Matthew 25:36, 2 Timothy 1:8, 16, 2:9, and Hebrews 13:3]. All this naturally harmed a prisoner's sense of self-worth. The higher a prisoner's status and the more severe the form of custody (which could include public displays), the greater the sense of shame. The record of Paul's imprisonments reveals that he recognises the shame and fears the negative effects. The reader is left by the last verse of Acts, however, with the conviction that, far from being overcome by the shame of his circumstances, Paul overcame them" ("Paul in Roman Custody," 283; bracketed citations are mine).

624   It is not absolutely clear if Paul was bound with a chain at the time he made this statement, since he seems to use the "chain" reference both metaphorically and literally. Lenski, for one, writes that "Roman law forbade the use of chains on Roman citizens when they became prisoners" (*Acts of the Apostles*, 1059), yet in 28:20 it is clear that Paul is most certainly and literally chained.

- ❑ Acts 28:20, "...for I am wearing this chain for the sake of the hope of Israel."
- ❑ Ephesians 6:20, "...for which I am an ambassador in chains; that in proclaiming it I may speak boldly, as I ought to speak."
- ❑ 2 Timothy 1:16, "The Lord grant mercy to the house of Onesiphorus, for he often refreshed me and was not ashamed of my chains..."
- ❑ 2 Timothy 2:8-9, "...according to my gospel, for which I suffer hardship even to imprisonment as a criminal; but the word of God is not imprisoned."

The other men who hear Paul's testimony seem genuinely impressed by the apostle and his message (26:30-31). At the very least, they cannot find anything criminal or seditious in his actions. Even Agrippa appears (again?) sincere when he tells Festus, "This man might have been set free if he had not appealed to Caesar" (26:32). Indeed, neither Lysias, Felix, Festus, Agrippa, Bernice, nor the principal men of Caesarea have found any basis for Paul's imprisonment. Agrippa's words, however, seem to place the responsibility for Paul's appeal to Caesar upon Paul's own error of judgment, when in fact it was Festus' failure to provide him with a fair hearing that forced the appeal. Festus could write to Caesar, "Even though I found no guilt in this man, he nonetheless exercised his Roman right to an appeal before you, and so this is why I sent him to you—I'm just obeying the law." It would not be beyond a heathen Roman governor to seriously twist the facts in order to save his own neck.

Festus and Agrippa are abruptly left behind in the narrative at this point. Festus will die in office within two years (in AD 62), only to be succeeded by two of the worst procurators in Judean history: Albinus, and then Gessius Florus. These men's administrations will so inflame Jewish-Roman hostilities that the Jews will openly revolt against the Empire within a few years (from AD 66 – 70). Before Albinus receives his office, however, Ananus the high priest has James, the brother of Christ, put to death by stoning.[625] Agrippa and Bernice both will make

---

625   Josephus, "Antiquities," 20.9.1; see also John Foxe, *Foxe's Book of Martyrs* (Fincastle, VA: Scripture Truth Book Co., ca. 1995; originally published in 1554 as *The*

insistent appeals to the Jews not to go to war with Rome, but after the Jews burn their Jerusalem palace down in protest, the king and his sister join sides with the Romans and ultimately move to Rome.[626] Bernice will later become the mistress of Vespasian and then Titus (his son), both generals in the war against the Jews, and would have married Titus except that she was a Jewess.[627]

Actes and Monuments), 9-11.

626   Josephus, "Antiquities," 19.5.1; "Wars," 2.15.1, 2.17.6.

627   Coffman, *Commentary on Acts*, 471.

∼ Chapters 27 – 28 ∼
Paul's Journey to Rome

The journey to Rome begins without incident (27:1-8)
Chapter 27 is often ignored because of its extensive nautical and geographical detail and its seeming irrelevance to the rest of Acts. Yet, such details are necessary in establishing the credibility of the entire book. There is no hint here that Luke is making anything up, or just embellishing his "story" with a little bit of seafaring drama. Instead, this chapter bears the unmistakable stamp of authenticity: the events described herein really *did* happen, and they happened in exactly the way Luke has recorded them. Luke is not only writing *about* Paul's journey to Rome, he is also a first-person eyewitness of the entire ordeal. This means that whatever Paul endured, he endured, which deserves our praise of his character. Paul told Timothy, "...do not be ashamed of the testimony of our Lord or of me His prisoner, but join with me in suffering for the gospel according to the power of God..." (2 Timothy 1:8). Luke apparently accepted this as his own instruction, for he indeed suffered greatly alongside Paul.

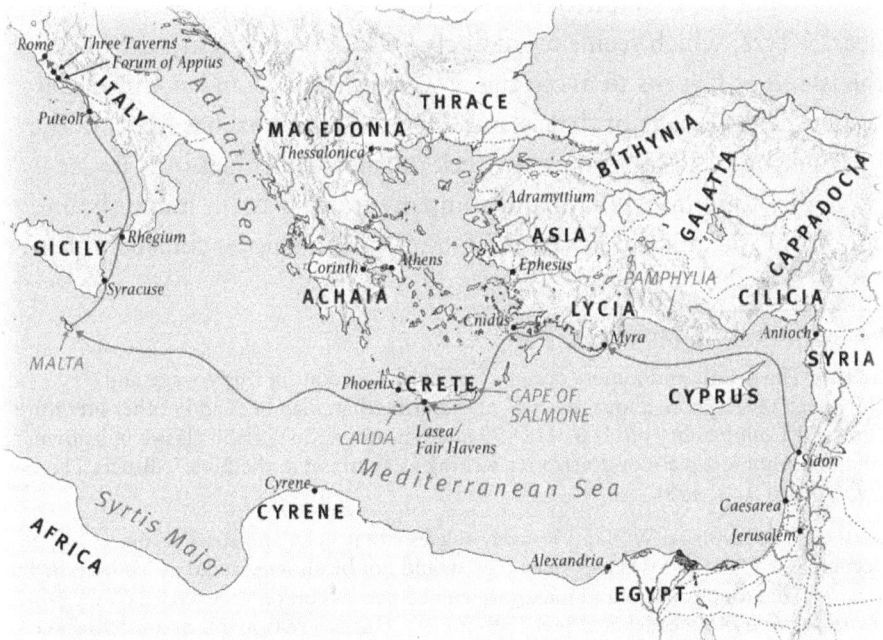

The voyage to Rome begins in Caesarea. It will not be a short one, even under ideal conditions. The shortest time which courier ships can make between Palestine and Rome is about forty-six days.[628] Paul is put into the custody of Julius, a centurion of the "Augustan cohort" (or battalion), the elite military attaché which works directly with the Emperor (27:1). Paul is accompanied by Luke, who chronicles this event, but also Aristarchus of Thessalonica, to whom we were introduced in 20:4.[629] Paul refers to Aristarchus as a "fellow prisoner" in Colossians 4:10; whether he means this literally (and refers to this actual scenario) or metaphorically will probably never be known for certain.[630] The particular ship with which these men begin their voyage is bound for Adramyttium, a seaport on the Aegean Sea near Troas. They will not remain on this ship for its entire voyage, but purposely intend to transfer to another ship later.

From Caesarea, the ship follows the Palestinian coast northward to Sidon (70 miles), then will head westward toward the southern shoreline of Cilicia (27:3-4). (Julius allows Paul to see his "friends" in Sidon, which may be a new group of Christians in that city to whom we have not yet been introduced, or these people are Christians from nearby Tyre, which seems more likely.) This route stays to the north of the island of Cyprus to avoid the powerful Mediterranean winds that buffet the other side of that island. Once the ship reaches Myra in the province of Lycia (about a two-week journey from Caesarea, under favorable conditions), Paul and company transfer to an Italian-bound ship from Alexandria, Egypt (27:5-6). This is a ship of considerable size

---

628 Mitchell, "Acts of the Apostles," 27.1.

629 "The details and minute accuracy of Luke's account of this voyage and shipwreck reveal more about the ancient seafaring than may be read in other literature" (Boles, *A Commentary on Acts*, 412); "Luke's narrative...is a small classic in its own right, as graphic a piece of descriptive writing as anything in the Bible" (Bruce, *The Book of the Acts*, 498).

630 "[The historian William] Ramsay suggests that Luke and Aristarchus accompanied Paul as his slaves since they would not be allowed to go as his friends. But Luke was Paul's physician and may have gained permission on that score" (Robertson, *Word Pictures*, 457; bracketed words are mine). This is a reasonable assumption, yet it remains an assumption. The truth is, we simply do not know all the details surrounding either Luke's or Aristarchus's presence on this ship—nor is such information critical to the present account.

and cargo; we find later (in 27:37) that there are 276 men on board. Boles and then Kistemaker offer some helpful information on this ship:

> The Alexandrian ships were very large; the vessel was steered, not by a rudder, but by two broad oars, one on each side of the stern. The rig consisted of one, or more than one, large square sail; flags floated from the top of the mast, as in modern vessels. The ancients had no compass, and all charts and instruments were very imperfect. This rig was specially favorable for running with the wind, but they could sail within seven points of the wind; they could make about seven knots an hour. A 'knot' is a nautical mile, or 6,085 feet; hence, it would sail about 8.5 miles [an hour]. These merchant ships were very large and could carry ten or eleven hundred tons...[631]

> By the standards of the day, the grain freighters were immense, measuring 180 feet in length, 45 in width, and 43 in depth. Some of the passengers on these vessels were given small cabins, but most of them had to stay on the open deck, where they made their own shelters. Conditions on board were excessively crowded...[632]

The journey then continues "with difficulty" to Cnidus, a seaport where the Mediterranean Sea meets with the Aegean Sea. The island of Crete is not too far from Cnidus (130 miles), but the ship is traveling slow because the winds are uncooperative, so it is estimated that it takes perhaps three weeks to cover this distance. The ship sails to the south side of the island of Crete, then anchors in a southern harbor of that island called Fair Havens (27:7-8).

The decision to sail (against Paul's advice) (27:9-13)

It is now late in the year for sailing (circa mid-October), since the Day of Atonement fast (late September or early October, depending on the exact year this voyage occurred) is already over (27:9). "The

---

631 Boles, *A Commentary on Acts*, 414-415; bracketed words are mine.

632 Kistemaker, *Acts*, 919.

ancients considered navigation on the Mediterranean unsafe from early October till the middle of March."[633] The Mediterranean winds are unforgiving, and yet sea captains are sometimes pressed to make their destinations because of financial benefits—and because they do not want to spend months in idleness waiting for the weather to clear.[634] Thus, the decision is often between saving the ship and losing its cargo (usually wheat) due to spoilage. Paul's advice here seems to be his own (uninspired) perception. Nonetheless, the ship pilot's and captain's word carries more weight with the centurion, who apparently outranks even the captain's own in making this decision (27:11).[635] In the end, it may be that these men reached a compromise: the ship will sail to a better port on Crete, a small town called Phoenix (40 miles away), and will winter there. A favorable wind provides what some perceive as a sign of good fortune (27:12-13).

A fierce storm overtakes the ship and crew (27:14-26)

"But..." (27:14-15) indicates that things quickly took a turn for the worse. "Euraquilo" refers to a northeastern wind which comes off the mainland (of Asia Minor) with violent, typhoon-like force.[636] The

---

633   Robertson, *Word Pictures*, 460. To be more specific: "Ancient sources speaking to this matter furnish the following indications: the period from 27 May to 14 September was considered the safe season for sea travel; the periods from 10 March to 26 May and from 14 September to 11 November, when weather and sea conditions were quite changeable, was considered risky; the period from 11 November to 10 March was extremely dangerous" (Rapske, "Acts, Travel and Shipwreck," 22).

634   Grain shortages in the Roman Empire due to drought and the loss of grain farmers in Egypt (due to excessive taxation) may have been the reason why this Alexandrian ship is sailing so late in the year in the first place (Bruce W. Winter, "Acts and Food Shortages," 60).

635   Ramsay explains why this is probably so: "To our modern ideas the captain is supreme on the deck of his ship; and, even if he held a meeting to decide on such a point as the best harbour to lay up in, or consulted the wishes of a distinguished officer in the military service, yet the ultimate decision would lie with himself. Here the ultimate decision lies with the centurion, and he takes the advice of the captain. The centurion, therefore, is represented as the commanding officer, which implies that the ship was a Government ship [carrying grain from Egypt to Rome—cms], and the centurion ranked as the highest officer on board. That, doubtless, is true to the facts of the Roman service" (*St. Paul the Traveller*, 323).

636   This is literally how Luke describes this wind in the Greek, "referring to the whirling motion of the clouds and sea caused by the meeting of contrary currents of air" (Bruce, *The Book of the Acts*, 509). It appears to have come upon the ship with all the ferocity of a hurricane.

ship's direction cannot be controlled against this powerful blast. The crew cannot point the ship to face the wind; "It was so violent the ship was being blown sideways."[637] "The ship's boat" (27:16) is a small craft used for transportation to shore and other uses. It is being thrashed about wildly in the winds and waves, and it is only with great effort that the crew manages to save it by hoisting it up to the main deck of the ship. The crew does find brief shelter near the small island of Clauda, where they—with the help of passengers, including Luke—only have time to tie everything down and wrap cables (ropes) around the ship's wooden hull for reinforcement. After this, the ship is driven out into the open sea (27:17-19). The "shallows of Syrtis" refers to a large sandbank ("quicksand" in the KJV) into which the ship could easily run aground; the crew is doing everything in its power to avoid this. The next day, fearing that it will be swamped, the crew begins lightening the ship by throwing its cargo overboard (as in Jonah 1:5).[638] The shifting of wheat can suddenly imbalance the ship, making it a "dangerous cargo" to transport through stormy weather.[639] Yet, the implication is that the ship is taking on water. On the following day, they throw anything else that can be spared overboard as well. "With these few words, Luke depicts the panic that gripped the crew."[640]

---

637   Reese, *Book of Acts*, 901.

638   "Luke was an intricate observer. James Smith, a seaman and yachtsman, in his *Voyage and Shipwreck of St. Paul* (1866) shows that Luke is accurate even in the storm and wreck. They cast goods out of the hold, threw off the rigging, bound the ship around—and precisely the proper term in Greek is used for each activity" (Reese, *Book of Acts*, xxxi). Smith's book was originally published in 1848, after he spent the winter of 1844-45 in Malta investigating Paul's voyage. A lifelong soldier and expert sailor, he concluded that Acts 27 was the testimony of a genuine eyewitness, but one who was a landlubber and not a sailor. "No sailor," he wrote, "would have written in a style so little like that of a sailor; no man not a sailor could have written a narrative of sea voyage so consistent in all its parts, unless from actual observation" (quoted from Smith's 4th edition [1880] in Stott, *The Spirit, the Church, and the World*, 386).

639   Coffman, *Commentary on Acts*, 498.

640   Kistemaker, *Acts*, 928. Conybeare and Howson provide a more graphic picture: "No one who has never been in a leaking ship in a continued gale can know what is suffered under such circumstances. The strain both of mind and body—the incessant demand for the labour of all the crew—the terror of the passengers—the hopeless working at the pumps—the labouring of the ship's frame and cordage—the driving of the storm—the benumbing effect of the cold and wet—make up a scene of no ordinary confusion, anxiety, and fatigue. But in the present case these evils were much aggravated by the continued overclouding of the sky…, which prevented the navigators

"And since neither sun nor stars appeared for many days" (27:20)—a perilous situation, since ancient sea navigation depends almost entirely upon fixed stellar points. The men do not eat (and many are probably nauseous with seasickness), and there is nothing else to do but wait out the storm. Ramsay notes: "One of the miserable accompaniments of a storm at sea is the difficulty of obtaining food; and, if that is so in a modern vessel, it must have been much worse in an ancient merchant ship, inconveniently crowded with sailors and passengers. Moreover, the sacrifice of the ship's furniture must have greatly increased the difficulty of preparing food."[641]

After about eleven days, Paul respectfully admonishes the captain, the centurion, and the crew: "You ought to have followed my advice" (27:21), which was likely based upon his own personal seafaring experience (see 2 Corinthians 11:25).[642] (This account is analogous to what we may face in life: when we see "light winds," we may assume that we are in for smooth sailing—and then a violent "storm" comes out of nowhere. While we cannot always avoid such storms, it is possible that we put ourselves in harm's way by not listening to the "good advice" of the gospel and/or wise Christians' counsel, just as the seamen did not listen to Paul's advice.) Nonetheless, Paul also provides some good news: God has revealed to him in a vision that everyone's lives will be spared, even though the ship itself will be lost (27:22-26).[643] Paul is on a divine mission to be presented before the Emperor, and all those who are with him will be delivered because of this mission.[644] (Recall the Lord's words to Paul earlier in 23:11.)

---

from taking the necessary observations of the heavenly bodies. ...[Thus] it was impossible to know how near they might be to the most dangerous coast" (*Life and Epistles*, 650; bracketed word is mine).

641   Ramsay, *St. Paul the Traveller*, 332.

642   "It was not the 'I told you so' of a small nature, 'but a reference to the wisdom of his former counsel in order to induce acceptance of his present advice' (Furneaux)" (Robertson, *Word Pictures*, 467).

643   Analogously, in coming to Christ, one must "jettison" everything else or regard it as lost; see Matthew 5:29-30, Romans 8:12-13, and Philippians 3:7-8. Likewise, one's *soul* can be saved even though his physical *life* is lost; see Matthew 16:24-26.

644   We have a number of biblical examples of the salvation of one's life by association with someone who stood in God's favor: Shem, Ham, and Japheth were

But Paul has also been told that "we must run aground on a certain island"—rather than upon the dangerous shoals of North Africa, as the sailors feared.

The voyage ends in shipwreck (27:27-44)

After two weeks of drifting at sea, the experienced sailors perceive that land is near (27:27). (The "Adriatic Sea" is the modern-day name for that body of water between ancient Greece and Italy. Yet, "'Adria' was a name given to the wide sweep of the Mediterranean lying between Greece, Italy, and Africa; this is not the Adriatic Sea as we now know it."[645]) Perhaps they hear the breakers from a distance, but since it is midnight, they cannot confirm this visually. But, having taken soundings[646] as they moved along, it is apparent that they are heading toward shallower water; to avoid running aground, or being thrust upon the rocks of an island, they anchor the ship from the stern in order to keep its bow pointed toward land.[647] At this point, some sailors try to escape from the ship (on the small skiff mentioned earlier) under a false pretense, but Paul is aware of their ruse (27:30-32). "Unless these men..." means that there are specific conditions to God's salvation of the crew. His words now carry a great deal of influence with the centurion, since his advice has proved to be more credible than

---

saved because of Noah; Lot was saved because of Abraham; Pharaoh was saved (from a crippling drought) because of Joseph; Israel was saved because of Moses; etc. In the present text, the entire ship's passengers and crew are saved because of Paul (27:24). "Saved" here has no reference to spiritual salvation, but only to the protection of one's earthly life or position. The only one whose association can save us *eternally* is Jesus Christ; without His advocacy, it does not matter who else associates with us, stands with us, or intercedes for us (consider Ezekiel 14:12-20, in parallel).

645 Boles, *A Commentary on Acts*, 422.

646 "To take a 'sounding' they made use of a line with a lead weight on the end of it. They would have heaved the leaded end of the rope into the depths to learn how much water was underneath them. Usually, there were knots on the rope, each a fathom apart. They learned there was 120 feet of water where they were [at the first sounding; 90 feet of water at the second—CMS]" (Reese, *Book of Acts*, 909-910).

647 "Anchoring by the stern was unusual; but in their situation it had great advantages. Had they anchored by the bow, the ship would have swung round from the wind; and, when afterwards they wished to run her ashore, it would have been far harder to manager her when lying with her prow pointing to the wind and away from the shore. But, as they were, they had merely to cut the cables, unlash the rudders, and put up a little foresail (v. 40); and they had the ship at once under command to beach her at any spot they might select" (Ramsay, *St. Paul the Traveller*, 335).

that of the ship's captain; therefore, the soldiers are ordered to cut away the ship's smaller boat.

Paul's "Unless…" statement is a binding, under-no-exceptions instruction. It is not one that can be broadly interpreted. Only *if* it is obeyed will these men be saved; God will not save the passengers and crew *anyway* if the instruction is not honored. This simple but very important observation illuminates the seriousness of other "unless" statements in the New Testament:

- ❑ "…Unless your righteousness surpasses that of the scribes and Pharisees, you will not enter the kingdom of heaven" (Matthew 5:20).
- ❑ "Truly I say to you, unless you are converted and become like children, you will not enter the kingdom of heaven" (Matthew 18:3).
- ❑ "He went away again a second time and prayed, saying, 'My Father, if this cannot pass away unless I drink it, Your will be done'" (Matthew 26:42).
- ❑ "I tell you, no, but unless you repent, you will all likewise perish" (Luke 13:3, 5).
- ❑ "Rabbi, we know that You have come from God as a teacher; for no one can do these signs that You do unless God is with him" (John 3:2).
- ❑ "Jesus answered and said to him, 'Truly, truly, I say to you, unless one is born again he cannot see the kingdom of God'" (John 3:3).
- ❑ "Jesus answered, 'Truly, truly, I say to you, unless one is born of water and the Spirit he cannot enter into the kingdom of God'" (John 3:5).
- ❑ "No one can come to Me unless the Father who sent Me draws him; and I will raise him up on the last day" (John 6:44).
- ❑ "…Unless you believe that I am He, you will die in your sins" (John 8:24).
- ❑ "Truly, truly, I say to you, unless a grain of wheat falls into the earth and dies, it remains alone; but if it dies, it bears much fruit" (John 12:24).

❑ "Test yourselves to see if you are in the faith; examine yourselves! Or do you not recognize this about yourselves, that Jesus Christ is in you—unless indeed you fail the test?" (2 Corinthians 13:5).

Paul now provides more hope to the ship's crew and passengers (27:33-34): "…not a hair from the head of any of you shall perish"—if indeed they follow what he says to do. He then requires them to eat food for strength, and gives thanks to God for this food "in the presence of all" (27:35). In other words, Paul demonstrates to these men that the God who preserves their lives also deserves their gratitude for even the simplest of provisions (such as bread). After this, even the remaining wheat (which had been kept for food and probably ballast) is thrown overboard.[648] This also means that all other options are abandoned: the passengers and crew must do what Paul says in order to be preserved by his God. (Their own patron saints or pagan gods have not helped them—or even offered to help—in the least.) Even though God has promised (through Paul) that no one's life will be lost, this does not mean that there is nothing expected of these men. The sailors still have to struggle with the ship; they still have to eat and drink to sustain their strength; Paul still has to provide instruction and rebuke, as needed; the centurion still has to give commands; etc. This scenario provides an excellent illustration of the balance between God's grace (divine promise and performance) and human faith (personal responsibility and effort). It is *God* who will save these men, yet this salvation does not nullify the need for human effort, but works in association with it.[649]

By daybreak, it is obvious that the ship is near land, but the crew is not certain *what* land. The sailors are skilled seamen; they do their very

---

648   "We suspect that the grain was transported loose in the hold of the ship. It had been carried aboard in sacks that were emptied in the hold; now the grain was put back in sacks to be dumped overboard. The task of scooping the grain into sacks and carrying them to the deck was laborious; the men undoubtedly formed a brigade to facilitate the work. …All this happens while it is still night" (Kistemaker, *Acts*, 937).

649   So it is with the divine grace and human effort that are both required—not equal in power or scope, but *required*—for salvation in Christ. Mark Buchanan says it well: "…Grace and faith are not opposites. Grace and *earning* are opposites. *Working for* your salvation is a heresy. *Working out* your salvation is basic Bible [cf. Philippians 2:12]. Grace and effort are allies" (*Your God Is Too Safe*, Sisters, OR: Multnomah Publishers, 2001; bracketed citation is mine).

best to drive the ship in the best direction possible using a combination of two rear-quarter steering paddles ("rudders") and a sail. However, their efforts are hampered by an invisible reef, and the ship's bow is grounded some distance from land. ("Where two seas met" [27:41] creates a large deposit of mud or silt, resulting in an irregular sea bottom.) Meanwhile, the waves pound against the stern of the ship, causing irreparable damage. At this point, the soldiers determine to kill their prisoners rather than let them escape. (The penalty for a soldier or jailer who allows his prisoner to escape is his own execution; recall comments on 12:19.) "At this critical juncture the soldiers proved themselves as unfeeling as the sailors had [who tried to escape in the smaller boat] in the night. They could now see plainly that they owed their lives to Paul, yet they had no sense of gratitude for it."[650] This plan is deterred by the centurion's desire to spare Paul (and by divine providence), so that every man is allowed to abandon ship and head for shore by whatever means he is able.[651] "The supernatural promise made to Paul in their darkest hour had been fulfilled to the letter: the ship and cargo were lost, but every life on board was saved."[652]

Taking refuge on the island of Malta (28:1-10)

Malta is a small island, with a surface area of only about 240 square miles; it is about 60 miles into the sea from Sicily.[653] The natives—

---

650   McGarvey, *Acts of Apostles*, 2:273-274; bracketed words are mine.

651   In 2 Corinthians 11:25, Paul says, "…Three times I was shipwrecked, a night and a day I have spent in the deep." We should remember that this was written several years *before* our present account, which gives us some insight into the very difficult and dangerous ordeal that all travelers faced in the ancient world.

652   Bruce, *The Book of the Acts*, 519. Today, the site of this shipwreck is known as St. Paul's Bay. Someone may ask, "Why did God allow Paul to go through all this?" An appropriate response might be: "Which is more convincing of God's providence: a ship making safe harbor without incident (for which sailors would credit their own skill and their pagan gods' oversight) or promising the saved lives of every person on board despite the most dire of circumstances? "To this end, Luke furnishes his readers in the record of a divine assurance at Acts 27:23ff the hermeneutical tool by which known pauline [*sic*] difficulties—storm, the threat of summary execution, the shipwreck, and the snakebite [that occurs on Malta]—may be carefully deciphered. These actual experiences, when properly interpreted by this key, indicate that neither the messenger nor his message is disqualified" (Rapske, "Acts, Travel and Shipwreck," 46; bracketed words are mine).

653   The older name of this island is Melita, as it reads in the KJV. It is known to us

called "barbarians" in older texts because they did not speak Greek[654] and thus did not embrace the Hellenistic culture which dominated much of the Roman Empire—showed "extraordinary kindness." "'Barbarian' does not indicate, as the word sometimes does with us, that the people are savage, uncultured, and of cruel habits. The Maltese and the people who just suffered shipwreck may have had difficulty communicating with each other, but the natives receive the shipwrecked people with warm hospitality."[655] They build a fire for their unannounced guests and provide general hospitality (28:1-2)—and Paul and other shipwrecked men offer their personal assistance in maintaining this fire.

> Paul was not a preacher after the style of a modern clergyman, who is particular not to soil his hands with menial labor, and who expects everybody to be ready to serve him, while he preserves his dignity and looks on. He did not stand by the fire which others had kindled, and allow others without his help to keep it burning; but he took a hand in the disagreeable job with the barbarians and the sailors.[656]

As Paul collects wood for the fire, however, a venomous snake latches itself onto his hand.[657] The superstitious islanders perceive this to be a sign of Justice[658]: they infer that Paul has done something worthy of death and, even though he has eluded his punishment so far, he

---

today as Malta, so modern translations have used this name over the ancient one.

654   It is believed that the ancient Maltese are of Phoenician descent, and spoke a variation of that people's language (Bruce, *The Book of the Acts*, 521).

655   Reese, *Book of Acts*, 920.

656   McGarvey, *Acts of Apostles*, 2:275.

657   "The objections which have been advanced, that there are now no vipers in the island, and only one place where any wood grows, are too trivial to deserve notice. Such changes are natural and probable in a small island, populous and long civilised [*sic*]" (Ramsay, *St. Paul the Traveller*, 343).

658   "Justice" here should be capitalized, since (by implication) it refers to a goddess of theirs that they believe metes out justice, "an abstraction personified" (Page, *The Acts of the Apostles*, 265). Reese adds: "In heathen mythology, 'Justice' was a goddess, the daughter of Jupiter; and it was her duty to take vengeance and to inflict punishment for crimes" (*Book of Acts*, 924).

cannot escape it forever (28:3-4). Yet Paul shakes the viper off of his hand and "suffered no harm" (see Mark 16:18 and Luke 10:19). After this, the islanders regard Paul as a god (28:5-6), reminiscent of his original reception in Lystra. "At Lystra Paul was first received as a god (Mercury) and then they stoned him to kill him (Acts 14:11, 19). So fickle is popular favour."[659]

Publius, the legate or "leading man" of the island, shows exceptional hospitality to the ship's company and crew (28:7). Three days is a long time to feed and entertain 276 men, not to mention the expense that this incurs. However, it is entirely possible that the "us" Luke refers to is a smaller group of guests—perhaps the centurion, some other soldiers, and Paul and his companions. Meanwhile, Publius' father suffers from "recurrent fever and dysentery" (KJV, "a bloody flux"); likely, this refers to some sort of infection and/or severe infliction of the bowels—a miserable condition, for which there is no cure (in Paul's day).[660] But Paul lays his hands on the sick man and heals him—a priceless gesture of appreciation for Publius' kindness, as well as an open door for preaching the gospel (28:8). The news of this healing attracts many other islanders who are also suffering with sickness or disease (28:9; see Matthew 4:23-24, Acts 5:14-16, and 19:11-12). Publius (and other islanders) respond in kind, providing Paul's company with everything they need to make the rest of their journey to Rome (28:10). Incidentally, the "we" references from this point forward do not necessarily imply anyone except for Paul and his companions (including Luke) and those soldiers who are required to escort him. The narrative leaves the ship's crew and the rest of the passengers behind.

Paul's arrival in Rome (28:11-16)

Paul and company must wait three months for another opportunity to sail, even though the mainland of Italy is not far from Malta. It is winter now, and the weather simply does not permit sea travel. When it is time to leave (around late February), they board another Alexandrian

---

659   Robertson, *Word Pictures*, 480.

660   "The ailment, now known as Malta fever, is caused by the [infected] milk of Maltese goats. Medical authorities have [since] been able to prescribe proper treatment and preventive measures" (Kistemaker, *Acts*, 951; bracketed words are mine).

ship (recall 27:6) with the "Twin Brothers" on its bow (28:11).[661] It seems that Luke records this ship's feature for no other reason than that of its sheer irony: God had preserved Paul and 275 other men through a terrible ordeal, yet sailors put their trust in false gods that can neither speak nor deliver them!

Syracuse (28:12) is a port on the eastern side of the island of Sicily; Rhegium (28:13) is on the southernmost extension of Italy (the "toe" of the "boot"). Puteoli is due north of Rhegium, and the speed in which they reach this city indicates a very favorable "south wind." It is not uncommon for most of the inhabitants of this small city to come out to greet the wheat ships, since they depend so much upon their cargoes.[662] Paul and company find—probably to everyone's surprise—a group of Christians here. He is able to spend time with them even though he remains in custody of Julius the commander. After seven days, the party finally leaves Puteoli and follows the land route on the west coast of Italy known as the Appian Way (*Via Appii*) for 125 miles.[663]

"And thus we came to Rome" (28:14) is a profound and loaded statement, considering all of the events, trials, fears, emotions, and prophecies concerning their arrival in this city. Paul is there greeted by brethren from the Market of Appius (*Appii Forum*), which is about 43 miles from Rome, and those from the Three Inns (or Three Taverns), which is ten miles closer (28:15).[664] (A "tavern" in the ancient world

---

661   In Greek, this is *Diskouroi*, the mythical twin brothers of Jupiter [Greek: Zeus], Rome's principal god. These twins serve as kind of patron saints to the ancient sailors of the Mediterranean. They are better known to us today as Castor and Pollux, the Gemini Twins of astrology. "After their death, so the fable goes, because of their brotherly love, they [Castor and Pollux] were translated by Zeus into the heavens where they became the constellation we call Gemini. Neptune also wanted to honor them, and so gave them power over the winds and the waves so that they might assist shipwrecked sailors. Castor and Pollux thus came to be known as the tutelary gods of sailors" (Reese, *Book of Acts*, 929; bracketed words are mine).

662   Coffman, *Commentary on Acts*, 516.

663   "The Appian Way was 'the oldest, straightest, and most perfectly made of all the Roman roads, named after the censor Appius Claudius who started its construction in 312 B.C.' [Longenecker]" (JFB *Commentary*, on 28:15).

664   "Paul probably struck the Appian Way at Capua. Portions of this great stone highway are still in use. If one wishes to tread where Paul trod, he can do it here. Appii Forum had a bad reputation, the haunt of thieves, thugs, and swindlers. What would

refers to any kind of shop or station offering services and/or provisions on the highway.) Paul had written an epistle to the Romans a few years before, and it is with great joy that these brethren are finally able to meet the man about whom they had heard so much. It appears that in "three days" he has been able to acquire lodging, possibly in the home of another Christian (see 28:23). He is allowed to remain by himself, except that he is continually guarded by (and possibly chained at the wrist to) a soldier (28:16). "This privilege was given to many of the better-class prisoners who were not charged with any serious crime. Festus's letter and Julius's high recommendation probably helped Paul to secure this arrangement. His guards were changed often, which gave him a good chance to spread the gospel among the Praetorian Guard (see Phil. 1:7, 13; 4:22)."[665]

Paul's meeting with the Jews in Rome (28:17-29)

Paul's intent, as has been his custom, is to meet with the Jews of the city to present the gospel to them.[666] Upon having called these men together, he briefly outlines the reason why he has been brought to Rome (28:17-20).[667] It is natural for Paul to assume that the Roman Jews have received bad press concerning him, since he has made many enemies among the Jews during his missionary journeys. Yet, Paul's

---

this motley crowd think of Paul chained to a soldier?" (Robertson, *Word Pictures*, 484).

665 JFB *Commentary*, on 28:16.

666 "The number of Jews in Rome during the apostolic age is estimated at twenty or thirty thousand souls. They all spoke Hellenistic Greek with a strong Hebrew accent. They had, as far as we know, seven synagogues and three cemeteries... The Jews were twice expelled from Rome under Tiberius and Claudius, but soon returned to their transtiberine [lit., across the Tiber River] quarter, and continued to enjoy the privileges of a *religio licita* [lit., a legal religion] which were granted to them by heathen emperors, but were afterwards denied them by [so-called] Christian popes" (Schaff, "St. Paul and the Conversion of the Gentiles: The Jews in Rome," *History*, vol. 1 [electronic edition]; bracketed words are mine).

667 "'I was *forced* to appeal to Caesar,' says Paul. To appeal to Caesar was something distasteful to the Jews, for they were turning away from their own 'religious' court and asking a heathen judge to decide their case. It was a surrender of Jewish independence in religious matters. So Paul emphasizes that he was *forced* to appeal to Caesar; it was something quite unavoidable, but the only way to avoid being handed over to a prejudiced tribunal (the Sanhedrin), or to the plots of assassination (like Acts 25:3)" (Reese, *Book of Acts*, 938).

intent is not merely to clear his own name. His primary concern is to rightly represent the gospel message: "for I am wearing this chain for the sake of the hope of Israel" (28:20). This manifests Paul's understanding that the hope of Israel—her restoration, regeneration, and the message of her prophets—is consummated in the gospel of Christ (recall 24:14-15).

But the Jews in Rome have not heard any negative reports concerning Paul (28:21). In fact, they have not heard anything about him at all from among "the brethren" (i.e., fellow Jews, not Christians).[668] However, they *are* familiar with "this sect" [lit., heresy, though used here in a neutral sense], a reference to the Way, and that "it is spoken against everywhere." Paul and the Jews settle upon a certain day in order to discuss this "sect," and an impressive number of men come to hear him at his own place of lodging. The scene here is reminiscent of 17:2-3: Paul argues from the Hebrew Bible (our Old Testament) that the man *Jesus* must of necessity also be the divine *Christ* (Messiah of prophecy), and therefore Jews everywhere must give their allegiance to Him (recall Peter's sermon in 3:18-26). It is unlikely that Paul is the only speaker during this meeting; this is far more likely an active and passionate dialogue, possibly even characterized as an informal debate (28:23).

"Some were being persuaded by the things spoken, but others would not believe" (28:24)—so it has been in any case in Acts when the gospel has been preached, and so it is today. Some listen, some reject; some turn to the Lord, others turn away from Him. If people rejected the gospel preaching of Paul, Peter, and Jesus Himself, they will certainly reject our own gospel preaching today (see John 15:18-20). Yet, the power and success of the gospel message is not measured by who believes or how many believe, but in its divine truth. God has not given

---

668   "'Letters' is from the Greek 'grammata,' which means an official document from the Sanhedrin containing charges against Paul. They do not mean to say that they have never heard of Paul, but that no official charges had been preferred against him in any way, either written or oral" (Boles, *A Commentary on Acts*, 439). This is in part because the news of Paul's transfer to Rome could not have gotten to Rome any faster than did Paul himself, since those who accused him were constrained by the same weather and travel restrictions as he was.

us a message that everyone will believe; He has given us a message that is *believable* because it is *true*—and thus He has given us every reason *to* believe it. Even so, the gospel divides families, marriages, business partnerships, communities, societies, nations, and all men: some believe, some do not believe (Matthew 10:34-36, John 6:63-64). Those who *do* believe are united in Him and by Him in whom they believe, leading to salvation. Those who do not believe are united with all other unbelievers, but nothing good will come of this union, regardless of how large or strong it appears to be up front.

This discussion continues "from morning until evening," but Paul enjoys only moderate success. Sensing that nothing else will be accomplished if he is to continue, Paul finally cuts to the heart of the issue: the unbelieving Jews are *blind* to the message of the Holy Spirit (28:25-27). "So skillful a preacher as Paul would not have closed his discourse with a warning like this, had he not seen or heard something in his audience to call forth these burning words from the sixth chapter of Isaiah."[669] (Jesus had laid this same charge—and used the same passage [Isaiah 6:9-10]—against the Jews of His day [Matthew 13:14-15].) Since these men reject the message of God, Paul has no choice but to offer it to the Gentiles instead (recall 13:46-47). "They [the Gentiles] will also listen" (28:28)—i.e., not only will the gospel be *presented* to the Gentiles, but they will obey it and thus be welcomed into the kingdom of God instead of those who were originally invited into it (see Matthew 8:11-12). "The gospel has a universal message for all people. Accordingly, the Book of Acts ends not on a negative note of unbelieving Jews refusing to accept the gospel. To the contrary, the last word of Paul is positive. He states that the Gentiles will listen to the gospel of salvation and by believing in Jesus will be saved."[670] Many ancient manuscripts do not contain 28:29, although it does seem a natural conclusion to the meeting.

---

669   McGarvey, *Acts of Apostles*, 2:285.

670   Kistemaker, *Acts*, 964.

Conclusion

This sums up the book of Acts: the gospel message, while being made available "to the Jew first" (cf. Romans 1:16), nonetheless is largely rejected by the Jewish nation. Instead, the gospel's far greater success is among the Gentiles, who welcome an opportunity for salvation from their own spiritual darkness and hopelessness (as described in Ephesians 2:11-16). "If the Jews will not hear him, he must turn to those who would hear him. The Jews could destroy themselves, but they could not destroy the kingdom of God or prevent the Messiah from reigning over his kingdom. The Gentiles would hear."[671] At the same time, we would do well to recognize that the first Christians were Jews, and the first missionaries were also Jews—men and women who devoted their lives to the cause of Christ. Thus, while most of the Jewish nation did reject the gospel of Christ, its propagation and success was in part based upon the faithful remnant of Israel that diligently obeyed it.

Paul remains in Rome for "two full years" (28:30-31) awaiting a formal hearing before the Emperor (Caesar Nero, ruled AD 54 – 68). Despite various speculations, we simply do not know for certain why Paul must wait so long for this event.[672] It is almost certain that during this time he pens the so-called "prison epistles" (Ephesians, Philippians, Colossians, and probably Philemon). In any case, he is able to preach the gospel from his rented quarters "with all openness, unhindered," which may provide the most comfortable season Paul has enjoyed since the beginning of his ministry. This preaching also has a profound influence upon certain members of the Roman government and the Praetorian Guard as well (see Philippians 1:12-14). F. F. Bruce says: "We need not go so far as to suppose that Luke compiled his narrative to supply the information required for Paul's defence before the imperial tribunal… But we may indeed believe that Luke wrote in order to win sympathy for Christianity among the intelligent reading-

---

671   Boles, *A Commentary on Acts*, 443.

672   "We conclude that the whole two years Paul spent in Rome were due to the heavily congested Roman court calendar and that the name Jewish accusers were as much at the mercy of the grindingly slow process [and travel time to get there] as the prisoner" (Rapske, "Paul in Roman Custody," 323; bracketed words are mine).

public of Rome at a time when the government had not yet finally committed itself by taking up a hostile attitude to it."[673]

"The kingdom of God" (28:31) refers in essence to the gospel age—the time and circumstances in which men can call upon the name of the Lord for salvation. As discussed earlier, "kingdom of God" is a descriptor of the reign of Christ (our Redeemer) for the very purpose of this salvation. "The Lord Jesus Christ" is a loaded title: He is *Lord*, the King over God's kingdom; He is *Jesus*, the historical Man whose unique earthly ministry culminated in His death, burial, resurrection, and ascension into heaven; He is *Christ*, the Messiah of Old Testament prophecy, the One who has fulfilled everything that had been predicted of Him from centuries past.

There is no concrete history concerning the outcome of this imprisonment or the end of Paul's life. Strong tradition claims that Paul is exonerated by Nero and released from Roman custody.[674] Whether or not he ever made it to Spain (as he intended—see Romans 15:22-24) is unknown to us for certain. After Nero begins his downward spiral into madness and burns a disheveled district of Rome (AD 64), he blames this fire on the Christians. This begins a brief but intense persecution of Christians in Rome that also provides a template for a much larger imperial persecution against the church beginning in the late first century AD.[675] Most likely, as a result of this persecution, Paul is arrested as a ringleader of the Christian "sect" and brought to trial. It is widely believed that Paul is found guilty of conspiracy and/or treason against the Empire, and is beheaded just outside of Rome, on the Ostian Way. The year of his execution is unknown for certain, but must be between the burning of Rome (AD 64) and Nero's own death (AD 68).[676]

---

673   Bruce, *The Book of the Acts*, 536.

674   Conybeare and Howson, *Life and Epistles*, 781; Foxe, *Book of Martyrs*, 13; Schaff, "St. Paul and the Conversion of the Gentiles: Paul's Missionary Labors," *History*, vol. 1 (electronic edition).

675   Lane Fox, *Pagans and Christians*, 432.

676   A. T. Robertson, "Paul, the Apostle," *ISBE* (electronic edition).

Concerning Paul, the final words of J. W. McGarvey's commentary on Acts are fitting here: "We bid him adieu till the resurrection morning, well pleased that the course of the narrative on which we have commented has kept us for so long a time in his company."[677] But really, Acts has not been about Paul as much as it has been about Christ: His ascension to the right hand of God; His having sent the Holy Spirit to those to whom He (the Spirit) was promised; the growth and success of His church; the propagation of His gospel to the Jews first and then the Gentiles; the providential oversight of His ambassadors; etc. Thus, while Paul's life ends due to the selfish ambition of ungodly men, the church continues to grow and flourish through the selfless and undefeatable intercession of Christ and the work of the Holy Spirit under His kingship. Christ cannot and will not be defeated, and His bride (the church) awaits the time when she will enter into glory forever with her Bridegroom, the Son of God.

～ END ～

---

677 McGarvey, *Acts of Apostles*, 2:292.

Sources Used for This Study

Barnes, Albert. *Barnes' Notes*, vol 10. Robert Frew, ed. Grand Rapids: Baker Book House, 1987 (originally published 1884).

Barnett, Paul. *Jesus and the Rise of Early Christianity.* Downers Grove, IL: InterVarsity Press, 1999.

Beasley-Murray, G. R. *Baptism in the New Testament.* Grand Rapids: Eerdman's Publishing Co., 1962.

Boles, H. Leo. *A Commentary on Acts of the Apostles.* Nashville: Gospel Advocate Co., 1976.

Bruce, F. F. *The Book of the Acts.* Grand Rapids: Wm. B. Eerdmans Publishing Co., 1964.

Buchanan, Mark. *Your God Is Too Safe.* Sisters, OR: Multnomah Publishers, 2001.

Calvin, John. *Acts.* Wheaton, IL: Crossway Books, 1995.

Clarke, Adam. *Clarke's Commentary on the Whole Bible*, vol. 5. New York: Abingdon-Cokesbury Press, no date (originally published 1831).

Coffman, James Burton. *Commentary on Acts.* Austin, TX: Firm Foundation, 1976.

Cogdill, Roy E. *The New Testament: Book by Book.* Marion, IN: Cogdill Foundation Publications, 1975.

The Complete Word Study: New Testament (electronic edition). Spiro Zodhiates, ed. © 1991 AMG International, Inc. Database © 2008 WORDsearch Corp.

Conybeare, W. J. and J. S. Howson. *The Life and Epistles of St. Paul.* Grand Rapids: Eerdmans Publishing Co., 1964.

Edersheim, Alfred. *The Life and Times of Jesus the Messiah.* Peabody, MA: Hendrickson Publishers, 1993.

Foakes-Jackson, F. J. *The Acts of the Apostles*. New York: Harper and Bros., 1931.

Fox, Robin Lane. *Pagans and Christians*. New York: HarperCollins Publishers, 1986.

Foxe, John. *Foxe's Book of Martyrs*. W. Grinton Berry, ed. Fincastle, VA: Scripture Truth Book Co., ca. 1995 (originally published 1563 by John Day).

Gaertner, Dennis. *The College Press NIV Commentary: Acts*. Joplin, MO: College Press Publishing Co., 1993.

Gloag, P. J. *The Pulpit Commentary*, vol. XXI. J. S. Exell and H. D. Spence-Jones, gen. eds. Peabody, MA: Hendrickson Publishers, no date (originally published late 19th century).

Hester, H. I. *The Heart of the New Testament*. Liberty, MO: The Quality Press, Inc., 1963.

International Standard Bible Encyclopedia (electronic edition). Database © 2004, WORDsearch Corp.

Jamieson, Robert, Andrew R. Fausset, and David Brown. *New Commentary on the Whole Bible: New Testament Volume* (electronic edition). J. D. Douglas, gen. ed. © 1990 Tyndale House Publishers; © 2012 WORDsearch Corp.

Josephus: Complete Works. William Whiston, trans. Grand Rapids: Kregel Publications, 1978.

King, Sr., Daniel H. *At the Feet of the Master: Studies in the Background, Content and Methods of Jesus' Teaching*. Bowling Green, KY: Guardian of Truth Foundation, 1997.

Kistemaker, Simon J. *New Testament Commentary: Acts*. Grand Rapids: Baker Book House, 1990.

Le Bon, Gustave. *The Crowd: A Study of the Popular Mind*. Atlanta, GA: Cherokee Publishing Co., 1982.

Lenski, R. C. H. *Commentary on the New Testament: The Interpretation of the Acts of the Apostles.* Peabody, MA: Hendrickson Publishers, 1998.

MacArthur, John. *The MacArthur New Testament Commentary: Acts 1 – 12.* Chicago: Moody Press, 1994.

_____. *The MacArthur New Testament Commentary: Acts 13 – 28.* Chicago: Moody Press, 1996.

McGarvey, J. W. *New Commentary on Acts of Apostles.* Delight, AR: Gospel Light Publishing Co., no date (originally published 1892).

McGuiggan, Jim. *The Reign of God.* Fort Worth, TX: Star Bible Publications, 1992.

Merriam-Webster's 11th Collegiate Dictionary (electronic edition). © 2003 by Merriam-Webster, Inc., ver. 3.0.

Mitchell, Paul. "Acts of the Apostles and New Testament History." Unpublished; cited 2001.

Page, Thomas Ethelbert. *The Acts of the Apostles, Being the Greek Text.* London: MacMillan and Co. Ltd., 1911.

Philo. *The Works of Philo.* C. D. Yonge, trans. Peabody, MA: Hendrickson Publ.'s, 1993.

Ramsey, William. *The Cities of St. Paul: Their Influence on His Life and Thought, The Cities of Eastern Asia Minor.* Whitefish, MT: Kessinger Publishing, 2004 (originally published 1907).

_____. *The Letters to the Seven Churches* (update edition). Mark W. Wilson, ed. Peabody, MA: Hendrickson Publishers, 1994.

_____. *St. Paul the Traveller and the Roman Citizen.* Grand Rapids: Baker Book House, 1965 (originally published 1895).

Reese, Gareth L. *A Critical and Exegetical Commentary on the Book of Acts.* Joplin, MO: College Press, 1976.

Robertson, A. T. *Word Pictures in the New Testament*, vol 3. Grand Rapids: Baker Book House, no date (originally published ca. 1927).

Schaff, Philip. *History of the Christian Church* (electronic edition). © 1910 Chas. Scribner's Sons; database © 2004 WORDsearch Corp (originally published in 1882).

Stott, John. *The Spirit, the Church, and the World*. Downers Grove, IL: InterVarsity Press, 1990.

Strong, James. *Strong's Hebrew and Greek Dictionary* (electronic edition). © 2012 by QuickVerse 10 (originally published 1890).

Sychtysz, Chad. *1 & 2 Thessalonians Study Workbook*. Summitville, IN: Spiritbuilding Publishing, 2014.

_____. *Being Born of God: The Role and Significance of Baptism in Becoming a Christian*. Summitville, IN: Spiritbuilding Publishing, 2014.

_____. *The Holy Spirit of God: A Biblical Perspective*. Summitville, IN: Spiritbuilding Publishing, 2010.

Turner, Mark. *Paul of Tarsus: Apostle to the World*. Self-published, no date.

Winter, Bruce W. (series editor). *The Book of Acts in Its First Century Setting*, 6 vols. Grand Rapids: Eerdmans Publishing Co., 1993 – 1996.

Winter, Bruce W. and Andrew D. Clarke, eds. *Ancient Literary Setting* (vol. 1), 1993.

Gill, David W. J. and Conrad Gempf, eds. *Graeco-Roman Setting* (vol. 2), 1994.

Rapske, Brian. *Paul in Roman Custody* (vol. 3), 1994.

Bauckman, Richard (ed.). *Palestinian Setting* (vol. 4), 1995.

The Zondervan Pictorial Encyclopedia of the Bible, 5 vols. Merrill C. Tenney, gen. ed. Grand Rapids: Regency Reference Library, 1976.

More Bible Study workbooks that you can order from Spiritbuilding.com or your favorite Christian bookstore.

Inside Out (Carl McMurray)
Studying spiritual growth in bite-sized pieces
Night and Day (Andrew Roberts)
Comparing New Testament Christianity and Islam
Church Discipline (Royce DeBerry)
A study on an important responsibility for the Lord's church
Exercising Authority (John Baughn)
How we use and understand authority on a daily basis
Compass Points (Carl McMurray)
22 foundation lessons for home studies, prospects, or new Christians
We're Different Because... (Carl McMurray)
A workbook on authority and recent church history
Communing with the Lord (Matthew Allen)
A study of the Lord's Supper & issues surrounding it
Parenting Through the Ages (Royce & Cindy DeBerry)
Bible principles tested & explained by successful parents
Marriage Through the Ages (Royce & Cindy DeBerry)
A quarter's study of God's design for this part of our life
What Should I Do? (Dennis Tucker)
A study that seeks Bible answers to life's important questions
How To Study the Bible (Jeff Archer)
25 lessons on how to study & understand the Bible
From Fear to Faith (Matthew Allen)
Coming to grips with the doctrine of grace
The Messiah's Misfits (Bryan Nash)
A study of the apostles of Jesus Christ
Living a Spirit Filled Life (Matthew Allen)
A study of Galatians & Ephesians with practical applications
The Lion Is the Lamb (Andrew Roberts)
A study of the King of Kings, His glorious kingdom, & His promised return
When Opportunity Knocks (Matthew Allen)
Lessons on how to meet the J.W./Mormon who knocks on your door
The Last Mile of the Way (Kipp Campbell)
A workbook study of the last week of the Messiah's life
Ancient Choices for Modern Dilemmas (John Baughn)
Biblical view of the modern family, current culture, and American politics
In Search of Christian Confidence (John Baughn)
A study to help one find the confidence God intended for His people

Textual Studies

The Parables, Taking a Deeper Look (Kipp Campbell)
A detailed look at our Lord's teaching stories
That I May Know Him (Aaron Kemple) Vol. 1 & 2
A chronological study of the life of Christ in a harmony of the gospels
1st Corinthians study guide (Chad Sychtysz)
Studies to take the student through this important letter
2nd Corinthians study guide (Chad Sychtysz)
Studies to take the student through this important letter
Hebrews study guide (Chad Sychtysz)
Studies to take the student through this important letter
Romans study guide (Chad Sychtysz)
Studies to take the student through this important letter
Galatians study guide (Chad Sychtysz)
Studies to take the student through this important letter
Ephesian study guide (Chad Sychtysz)
Studies to take the student through this important letter
Philippian, Colossians, Philemon study guide (Chad Sychtysz)
Studies to take the student through these important letters
1 & 2 Timothy and Titus (Matthew Allen)
A commentary workbook on these letters from Paul
Faith in Action: Studies in James (Mike Wilson)
Bible class workbook and commentary on James
From Beneath the Altar (Carl McMurray)
A workbook commentary on the Book of Revelation
1 Samuel (Matthew Allen)
Studying the life and times of this prophet, priest, & judge
Proverbs, Wisdom for Dummies (Carl McMurray)
A workbook study including every verse in Proverbs, divided into topics
An Overview of Isaiah (Chad Sychtysz)
A workbook study of this messianic prophet
An Overview of Jeremiah (Chad Sychtysz)
A workbook study of this prophet
Esteemed of God, Studying the Book of Daniel (Carl McMurray)
Covering the man as well as the time between the testaments
The Minor Prophets, Vol. 1 & 2 (Matthew Allen)
Old lessons that speak directly to us today

Special Interest

The AD 70 Doctrine (Morris Bowers)
The truth about Realized Eschatology
The Holy Spirit of God (Chad Sychtysz)
A diligent, thorough study of this important subject
The Gospel of Forgiveness (Chad Sychtysz)
A presentation of this subject from different biblical angles
Letters to Young Preachers (Warren Berkley)
Letters from older preachers to younger on what they face
Behind the Preacher's Door (Warren Berkley and Mark Roberts)
Issues that preachers will have to deal with
Seeking the Sacred (Chad Sychtysz)
How to know God the way that HE wants us to know Him
Will You Wipe My Tears? (Joyce Jamerson)
Wisdom & resources to teach us how to help others through sorrow
Do Things Well (Warren Berkley and Mark Roberts)
Encouraging and teaching churches to worship with passion

Studies for Women

I Will NOT Be Lukewarm (Dana Burk)
A ladies study on defeating mediocrity
Reveal in Me... (Jeanne Sullivan)
A study to assist ladies in discovering and developing their talents
Will You Wipe My Tears? (Joyce Jamerson)
Wisdom & resources to teach us how to help others through sorrow
Bridges or Barriers (Cindy DeBerry & Angie Kmitta)
Study encouraging harmony with younger/older sisters-in-Christ
Learning to Sing at Midnight (Joanne Beckley)
A study book about spiritual growth benefiting women of all ages
Re-charging Your Prayer Life (Lonnie Cruse)
Workbook for any woman wanting a richer prayer life
Does This Armor Make Me Look Fat? (Lonnie Cruse)
A study of the Christian armor and how it fits women
Heading for Harvest (Joyce Jamerson)
A study of the fruit of the Spirit
Behind Every Good Man (Joyce Jamerson)
Studying the women that stand behind faithful men of today
Forgotten Womanhood (Joanne Beckley)
Studying the traits of godly womanhood
Look Into Your Heart (Joyce Jamerson)
Studying how to calm one's heart, to develop one that is God approved